The Canadian Modernists Meet

29

REAPPRAISALS:
CANADIAN
WRITERS

The Canadian Modernists Meet

Edited by
Dean Irvine

University of
Ottawa Press

REAPPRAISALS: Canadian Writers
Gerald Lynch, General Editor

Library and Archives Canada Cataloguing in Publication

The Canadian modernists meet / edited by Dean Irvine.

(Reappraisals, Canadian writers)
ISBN 0-7766-0599-2

1. Canadian literature—20th century—History and criticism. 2.
Modernism (Literature)—Canada. I. Irvine, Dean, 1971- II. Series.

PS8077.1.C353 2005   C810.9'112   C2005-902260-4

University of Ottawa Press gratefully acknowledges the support extended to its publishing program by
the Canada Council and the University of Ottawa. We also acknowledge the support of the Faculty of
Arts of the Univrsity of Ottawa for the publication of this book.

We acknowledge the financial support of the Government of Canada through the Book Publishing
Industry Development Program (BPIDP) for our publishing activities.

 University of
Ottawa Press

Cover illustration: Adaptation (Sharon Katz) from Marion Dale Scott's pen-and-ink drawing, *F.R. Scott
Reading in Bed* (National Archives of Canada, Acc. 1995-115-24). Reproduced by permission of the
Estate of Marion Dale Scott.
Cover design: Sharon Katz

ISBN 0-7766-0599-2

Printed and bound in Canada

Contents

Native, Cosmopolitan, Post-Cosmopolitan

Eclectic Travellers: From Peterborough to Paris

Political Bodies: Stages and Stations, Casts and Broadcasts

Modernism's Archives and Ledgers

Beyond Impersonality

Contributors

D.M.R. BENTLEY is a professor of English at the University of Western Ontario. He is the editor of *Canadian Poetry: Studies, Documents, Reviews* as well as numerous scholarly editions of early Canadian literary texts and documents, and is the publisher of Canadian Poetry Press. He has published widely in the fields of Canadian and Victorian literature, including *The Gay]Grey Moose: Essays on the Ecologies and Mythologies of Canadian Poetry, 1690–1990* (1992), *Mimic Fires: Accounts of Early Long Poems on Canada* (1994), *Mnemographia Canadensis: Essays on Memory, Community, and Environment in Canada, with Particular Reference to London, Ontario* (1995), and *The Confederation Group of Canadian Poets, 1880–1897* (2004).

STEPHEN CAIN is an assistant professor at Atkinson's School of Arts and Letters, York University. At York, he completed a doctoral thesis on Coach House Press and House of Anansi Press. His publications include essays in *Studies in Canadian Literature* and *Open Letter*, editing a special issue of *Open Letter* on Canadian little magazines, and two forthcoming collaborative projects: with Tim Conley, *Encyclopedia of Fictional and Fantastic Languages* and, with Steve McCaffery, *Zebras Progress: The Dick Higgins/ Steve McCaffery Correspondence (1976–1998)*.

WANDA CAMPBELL is Associate Professor of Women's Literature and Creative Writing at Acadia University. Her books include *Hidden Rooms: Early Canadian Women Poets* (2000) and *The Poetry of John Strachan* (1996). She has published essays in *Dominant Impressions* (1999) and *Bolder Flights* (1998) and her articles on Canadian writers have appeared in *Contemporary Literary Criticism, Mosaic, Canadian Poetry, Essays on Canadian Writing, SCL/ÉLC, Canadian Literature,* and *Wascana Review.*

TIM CONLEY is an assistant professor in the Department of English at Brock University. His essays have appeared in *James Joyce Quarterly, Papers on Language and Literature, The Midwest Quarterly, Comparative Literature, Ariel,* and *Open Letter.* He is the author of *Joyces Mistakes: Problems of Intention, Irony, and Interpretation* (2003), and co-author (with Stephen Cain) of *Encyclopedia of Fictional and Fantastic Languages* (2006).

COLIN HILL is an assistant professor in the Department of English at the University of Toronto. He is currently revising his dissertation "The Modern-Realist Movement in English-Canadian Fiction, 1919–1950"—for publication as a book, and editing scholarly editions of Irene Baird's *Waste Heritage* and some of Raymond Knister's and Hugh MacLennan's previously unpublished novels. He is a co-editor of *English-Canadian Literary Anthologies: An Enumerative Bibliography* (1997), and the author of articles on the beginnings of modernist fiction in Canada and representations of technology in early twentieth-century Canadian literature.

SHELLEY HULAN is an assistant professor of Canadian literature at the University of Waterloo. She specializes in late nineteenth-century and early twentieth-century Canadian writing. At the University of Western Ontario, she completed a dissertation on the idea of nostalgia in Canadian literature and philosophy between 1880 and 1920. Her work has appeared in *Canadian Poetry: Studies, Documents, Reviews* and *Journal of Canadian Studies.*

DEAN IRVINE is an assistant professor in the Department of English at Dalhousie University. He is the editor of *Archive for Our Times: Previously Uncollected and Unpublished Poems of Dorothy Livesay* (1998) and *Heresies: The Complete Poems of Anne Wilkinson, 1924–1961* (2003). He is the English-language General Editor of the University of Ottawa Press's Canadian Literature Collection, and is currently working on a book about Canadian women modernist poets and little-magazine editors, a scholarly edition of the complete poems and translations of F.R. Scott, and a study of scholarly editing and editions in Canada.

MEDRIE PURDHAM is a doctoral candidate in Canadian literature at McGill University, where she is writing a dissertation entitled "The Encyclopedic Imagination and the Canadian Artist-Figure." Her publications include reviews in *Canadian Literature* and *Books in Canada* as well as contributions to *The Literary Encyclopedia*.

ANNE QUÉMA teaches at Acadia University. A specialist in theory and twentieth-century British literature, she has published *The Agon of Modernism: Wyndham Lewis's Allegories, Aesthetics, and Politics* (1999). She has written articles for *Studies in Canadian Literature, Philosophy and Literature, West Coast Line,* and *Gothic Studies.*

CANDIDA RIFKIND is an assistant professor in the Department of English, University of Winnipeg. At York University, she completed a dissertation entitled "Labours of Modernity: The Literary Left in English Canada, 1929–1939." She has published articles in *Essays on Canadian Writing, Studies in Canadian Literature, Journal of Canadian Studies,* and *TOPIA: Canadian Journal of Cultural Studies.*

MARILYN ROSE is a professor of English, Director of the Humanities Research Institute, and Dean of Graduate Studies at Brock University. Her scholarly work includes publications and presentations on such poets as Pauline Johnson, Florence Randall Livesay, Dorothy Livesay, Elizabeth Brewster, and P.K. Page, as well as on the auto/biographical dimensions of contemporary Canadian poetry. She is currently constructing a web site on Canadian Poetry and Poetics, with a special emphasis on twentieth-century Canadian women poets and their work.

PAUL TIESSEN is a professor of English and Film Studies at Wilfrid Laurier University. He is the co-editor (with Frederick Asals) of *A Darkness That Murmured: Essays on Malcolm Lowry and the Twentieth Century* (2000) and (with Patrick McCarthy) *Joyce/Lowry: Critical Perspectives* (1997), as well as several other books on literature, film, radio drama, art, and photography. He has published widely in the fields of modernism, cultural theory, and film theory, and recently co-edited (with Hildi Froese Tiessen) the forthcoming annotated edition of L.M. Montgomery's letters to Ephraim Weber. He is the former editor of the *Malcolm Lowry Newsletter* (1977–84) and *The Malcolm Lowry Review* (1984–2002), and the publisher of MLR Editions Canada.

BRIAN TREHEARNE teaches Canadian literature, modernism, and creative writing at McGill University. He is the author of *Aestheticism and the Canadian Modernists: Aspects of a Poetic Influence* (1989) and *The Montreal Forties: Modernist Poetry in Transition* (1999). He is the General Editor of the Canadian Modern Poetry: Texts and Contexts series for Canadian Poetry Press and is currently editing scholarly editions of the complete poems of A.J.M. Smith and John Glassco.

TONY TREMBLAY is an associate professor of Canadian and Cultural Studies at St. Thomas University. He has published several essays on Louis Dudek, Marshall McLuhan, and Ezra Pound, edited *David Adams Richards: Essays on His Works* (2005), and is working on a critical biography of Richards.

GLENN WILLMOTT is a professor of English at Queen's University, where he teaches courses on modernism and Canadian literature. His publications include the books *McLuhan, or Modernism in Reverse* (1996), *Unreal Country: Modernity in the Canadian Novel in English* (2002), and a scholarly edition of Bertram Brooker's *Think of the Earth* (2000), as well as articles on national and aboriginal identities in literature.

Acknowledgments

FOR THREE DAYS in May 2003, a group of literary critics, historians and theorists, textual editors, biographers, librarians, art historians, and filmmakers from cities across Canada convened at the University of Ottawa and took part in "The Canadian Modernists Meet: A Symposium." The symposium's events included a guided tour of the modern Canadian holdings at the National Gallery of Canada, an exhibition of manuscript and print materials at the Library and Archives of Canada, a premiere screening of the director's cut of Donald Winkler's *A Red Carpet for the Sun: The Life of Irving Layton*, multimedia plenary presentations by Zailig Pollock and Donald Winkler, and eleven panels of papers. My symposium co-chair Seymour Mayne proved both wise and generous in helping to orchestrate these events and in sharing his thirty years of symposia experience. *Toda raba*, Seymour.

Many others helped to organize and stage symposium events at venues around Ottawa: Daniel Amadei and Louise Filiatrault of the National Gallery of Canada; Michel Brisebois, Allison Bullock, Kevin Joynt, Linda Sigouin, Pierre Ostiguy, Jocelyne Potyka, and Pauline Marie Portelance of the National Library of Canada; Lynne Armstrong, Ami Arsenault, Louisa Coates, Cathy Craig-Bullen, John Cullen, Robert Ferris, Robert Lamoureux, Denise McCulloch, and Denise Rioux of the National Archives of Canada. Catherine Hobbs of the National Library and Anne Goddard of the

National Archives deserve special recognition for their expert assistance with my curatorial work on the exhibition. Randall Ware of the National Library of Canada kindly arranged for the reception sponsored by the Library and Archives of Canada. Laurie Jones of the National Film Board generously offered the NFB's support for Donald Winkler's presentation, and Ari Cohen of Diversus helped to sponsor the reception prior to the screening of *A Red Carpet for the Sun*.

In addition to the student volunteers from the University of Ottawa, my assistants Tobi Kozakewich and Amanda Mullen contributed invaluable hours to the symposium's coordination. My thanks for advice and encouragement extend to members of the Department of English at the University of Ottawa, especially the Canadian Literature Symposium Series Committee; David Rampton, Chair; and Marie Tremblay-Chénier, Administrative Assistant. Following the symposium, I joined a new group of colleagues in the Department of English at Dalhousie University, where I have benefited from the collegiality of graduate students and faculty whose interests in both Canadian and international modernist literatures continue to stimulate my research.

Gerald Lynch, general editor of the Reappraisals: Canadian Writers series, and Ruth Bradley-St-Cyr, editor-in-chief of the University of Ottawa Press, deserve special thanks for their editorial guidance as I compiled and edited the manuscript. Thanks also to Stephanie VanderMeulen for her patient copyediting of the final manuscript. My beloved wife, Ava Kwinter, read, edited, and listened to drafts of my introduction, and her parents, Alf and Gayle Kwinter, thoughtfully offered me the green world of the family cottage, where I finished working on the manuscript. As always, my parents, Ray and Helen Irvine, have continued to support my work on Canadian modernists that started in my hometown of Victoria.

Marian Dale Scott's pen-and-ink drawing, *F.R. Scott Reading in Bed* (National Archives of Canada, Acc. 1995-115-24), has been reproduced on the cover by permission of her estate. I am grateful to Sharon Katz for her adaptation of the drawing and elegant design of the symposium poster and book cover.

Neither the symposium nor the present collection of essays could have happened without grants received from the Social Sciences and Humanities Research Council; the Faculty of Arts Research and Publications Committee, University of Ottawa; and the University Research Fund,

University of Ottawa. I would also like to acknowledge the support of a SSHRC Postdoctoral Fellowship, which afforded me the time and resources to organize the symposium. For this financial support, and for the opportunity to gather these scholars together at the symposium and assemble their essays in this collection, I am deeply grateful. Finally, thank you to the contributors to this volume, for their commitment to what promises to be a renaissance in the study of modernisms in Canada.

Introduction

DEAN IRVINE

Far in a corner sits (though none would know it)
The very picture of disconsolation,
A rather lewd and most ungodly poet
Writing these verses, for his soul's salvation.
—F.R. Scott, "The Canadian Authors Meet"

F.R. SCOTT's portrait of modernist disconsolation calls attention to the contingencies of literary history, the variant lines of an emergent cultural movement. When "The Canadian Authors Meet" first appeared in the *McGill Fortnightly Review* in April 1927, Scott's "very picture of disconsolation" situated the Canadian modernist poet in a far corner of postwar literary culture. At once distant from the metropolitan centres of international modernisms and detached from the antimodernism of the Canadian authors he satirizes, Scott locates the Canadian modernist of the 1920s at the peripheries of the contemporary scene. This may seem incongruous with the poem's later canonical centrality to early twentieth-century Canadian poetry and, more recently, its repeated citation as representative of a dominant, elitist, masculinist, reactionary, and exclusionary Canadian modernism (see Gerson 54; Harrington 70–71; Kelly 62–63). Scott's allegations against the Canadian Authors Association (CAA; 1921)—its sentimental colonialism, its lingering Victorianism, its nationalist boosterism, its feminization of literary culture, among others—have been challenged in recent years by critics of Canadian modernism. These critics have sought to displace Scott's modernist persona from his position as satirist and cultural critic, to decentre the canonicity of his modernist cultural values, and to redirect critical attention to the marginalized figures he satirizes; their critiques, however, have not targeted the image of the marginal, transitional, disconsolate modernist of the late 1920s but rather the canonical persona represented in the poem's revised version. Consequently, Scott's "very picture of disconsolation" has become as relevant to the critical reception of Canadian modernism in the early twentieth century as to its reassessment in the early twenty-first century.

Scott's decision to excise the poem's original final stanza during the interval between its publication in 1927 and its reappearance in the mid-1930s, when it was printed in the *Canadian Forum* (1935) and *New Provinces: Poems by Several Authors* (1936), coincided with a series of transformations in the field of Canadian modernism. While the cancelled stanza presents the poet as a liminal figure metonymically linked to an incipient modernist movement, this figure in the midst of cultural transition is lost in revision. Rather than the original version's concluding portrait of an "ungodly poet" who writes verses "for his soul's salvation," the revised version closes with parodies of "O Canada" and "new authors springing / To paint the native maple" that target the country's unreflective postwar cultural nationalism. Without the self-reflexive invitation to consider the contradictions between the poet's emergent modernism and his residual "Victorian saintliness," Scott's revision elides the poem's terminal uncertainties and ends instead with the voice of a confident, aloof, tongue-in-cheek satirist. The complex and ambivalent portraiture of the poet as "transitional modern" (Djwa 55) thus cedes to the undifferentiated caricature of the CAA's "new authors" writing in archaic idioms.

By the mid-1930s when "The Canadian Authors Meet" reappeared in the *Canadian Forum* and *New Provinces,* Scott and the rest of the *McGill Fortnightly* alumni could fairly assume that "the very picture of disconsolation" no longer captured the Canadian modernist's self-image. Still, the Montreal modernists' various polemics against the CAA continued into the 1930s: Leo Kennedy's article "The Future of Canadian Literature" (1928) pronounced the CAA a "pillar of flim-flam" and advocated its continued "ridicule" (35); A.J.M. Smith's article "Wanted: Canadian Criticism" (1928) suggested that the CAA admit its commercial profit motives and rename itself "the Journalists' Branch of the Canadian Manufacturers' Association" (32); and his "Rejected Preface" (1934) to *New Provinces* insisted that Scott's satire still provided a "much needed counterblast" (41) against the CAA. Perhaps the most trenchant critique of the CAA came from within its own organization, when in response to E.J. Pratt's request for submissions to the CAA's *Canadian Poetry Magazine* (1936–63), Scott replied that "[t]he only poem I feel like submitting to you is my satire 'The Canadian Authors Meet'" (Letter to E.J. Pratt, 15 Oct. 1935). Whether Pratt ever formally accepted the poem is uncertain, since Scott subsequently wrote to inform Pratt that the *Canadian Forum* planned to print it in an upcoming issue and that he would send others instead (Letter to E.J. Pratt, 28 Nov. 1935). Among the poems Pratt accepted and published in the first issue of *Canadian Poetry Magazine* is "O Tempora!" Scott's double parody of both the traditionalist versification favoured by the majority of CAA authors who appeared in the magazine and the *vers libre* experimentations adopted by his fellow modernists. Although Scott never saw fit to include the poem in any of the collections he published during his lifetime, "O Tempora!" marks a definite shift in Canadian modernist self-fashioning. With its ludic, self-mocking caricature of the modernist poet, Scott's poem at once plays into the hands of its CAA audience and deploys modernist self-parody to critique that same audience's tendency to ridicule his technique:

> He rhymes as little as he can
> Without admitting rhyme has gone.
> More often he discards such frills
> And writes damn plain words nude.
> The same economy prevails
> In metre.
> While as for logical sequences of ideas,
> All punctuation is another word,
> And the size of letters is musical!
> Don't you SEE
> How as-TON-ish
> i
> n
> g
> ?
> theprogressis

Although directed to an audience highly sceptical of progressive poetics, one likely to concur with the speaker's self-reflexive critique of the superficial features of the so-called "new poetry" (Scott, "Preface"), the actual progress marked by the poem may be measured by the modernist's confidence in his ability to judge the excesses of his own poetics, to render it the object of satire, to risk its ridicule. This is a transformative moment in Canadian modernism, as the modernist's autosatiric critique no longer seeks to distance himself from his traditionalist, antimodernist contemporaries but rather places himself alongside them. Scott's inclusive gesture is appropriate to the context of the poem's publication, for Pratt's mandate as editor of *Canadian Poetry Magazine* was to bridge tradition and modernity, to provide a public meeting ground for Canadian modernism and antimodernism alike (see Pratt).

The spirit of inclusiveness that shapes Scott's bifocal critique of Canadian modernism and antimodernism also informs the collection of essays in the present volume. If, as those critical of "The Canadian Authors Meet" have suggested, canonical narratives of modernism in Canada have been exclusionary, the essays collected here call these narratives into question and participate in the decentring of national and international modernisms' canonicity by attending to what Chana Kronfeld calls "marginal modernisms" (4). Modernism in Canada is, in itself, among the marginal modernisms outside the Anglo-American canons, but even within Canadian modernism there are numerous figures who have been relegated to the margins of literary history and canonicity. Essays in this collection on Canadian women modernists such as Louise Morey Bowman and Katherine Hale (Campbell), Anne Marriott (Rose), and Elizabeth Smart and Cecil Buller (Quéma) foreground their marginality in relation to canonical masculinist modernisms. Another, on the theatrical left in Canada, documents the "convergence of avant-garde theatres and militant working-class movements" in the 1930s and thus resituates historically marginalized cultural groups among the aesthetic practices of canonical modernisms (Rifkind). More than reclaiming marginalized figures and groups in the interests of more comprehensive literary-historical representation of the period, the study of marginal modernisms not only performs a critique of canonical modernism's exclusionary practices but also provides insight into the historical marginality of its avant-garde aesthetics. "Theories of modernism that are modeled on belated, decentered, or linguistically minor practices," writes Kronfeld, "may provide some insight into the processes that have become automatized or rendered imperceptible in the canonical center" (5). For instance, the revision and canonization of Scott's "The

Canadian Authors Meet" provides one example of canonical modernism's blindness to its own exclusivity: just as the marginality that Scott inscribes in the excised final stanza has been cancelled by canonical narratives of Canadian modernism, so its canonicity has instead enabled the marginalization of other co-emergent modernisms in Canada. By adopting theories of modernism that acknowledge the historical marginality of its canonical centre, then, we may begin to reassess the historicity of modernist canonization that led to the construction of its centres and peripheries.

In pursuit of decentring canonical narratives of Canadian modernism, the essays collected here engage in the repositioning of its major and minor figures, groups, and movements. The event from which this collection emerges—"The Canadian Modernists Meet: A Symposium," held at the University of Ottawa on 9–11 May 2003—was the first of its kind: a meeting of literary critics, historians and theorists, textual editors, biographers, librarians, art historians, and filmmakers whose collective research probes Canadian men's and women's participation in the formation of cultural modernisms. Although for various reasons it has not been possible to publish papers by every presenter at the symposium, the essays gathered here nevertheless attest to the current expansion of Canadian modernist studies. The collection stages a major reassessment of the origins and development of multiple modernisms in English-Canadian literature and theatre, their relationship to international modernist literatures and theatres, their regional variations, their gender and class inflections, and their connections to visual art, architecture, and radio.

Not since the appearance of Louis Dudek and Michael Gnarowski's *The Making of Modern Poetry in Canada* (1967; rev. ed. 1968), Peter Stevens's *The McGill Movement* (1969), and John Moss's *Modern Times* (1982) has a collection of essays by multiple authors addressed the subject of literary and theatrical modernism in Canada. There have been, however, several single-author volumes on Canadian modernist poetry and fiction published in the interim, including Ken Norris's *The Little Magazine in Canada, 1925–80: Its Role in the Development of Modernism and Post-modernism in Canadian Poetry* (1984), Brian Trehearne's *Aestheticism and the Canadian Modernists* (1989) and *The Montreal Forties: Modernist Poetry in Transition* (1999), T. Nageswara Rao's *Inviolable Air: Canadian Poetic Modernism in Perspective* (1994), Clarence Karr's *Authors and Audiences: Popular Canadian Fiction in the Early Twentieth Century* (2000), and Glenn Willmott's *Unreal Country:*

Modernity in the Canadian Novel in English (2002). The influence of these monographs filters through the essays in the present volume, most notably that of the studies by Trehearne and Willmott, which have initiated the most significant transformation of the critical field since its mid-twentieth-century beginnings. With new essays by Trehearne and Willmott included here, their presence is indicative of the collective and continued efforts among scholars to enact the restructuring of the field. Attention to canonical modernists such as A.J.M. Smith (Trehearne) and Sheila Watson (Willmott) demonstrates the ways in which the critical repositioning of Canadian modernism is underway not only at its peripheries but also at its centre. Trehearne's sequel to his chapter on Smith in *Aestheticism and the Canadian Modernists* presents "[a] less familiar and more exuberant Smith, and a more various Canadian modernism" that acknowledges its central poet's practice of surrealist poetics, and Willmott's follow-up to *Unreal Country* addresses the confluence of cosmopolitan modernism and aboriginal discourse in Watson's *The Double Hook*. If for Smith his better-known aestheticism and imagism of the 1920s is complemented by his surrealist phase in the 1930s, and if for Watson her adaptation of a cosmopolitan-modernist "mythical method" is reinterpreted in relation to aboriginal discourse, then our new narratives about these canonical modernists must admit that their respective interests extend to modernity's peripheries—that is, avant-garde aesthetics and marginalized cultures.

Other essays collected here on major modernists such as A.M. Klein and F.R. Scott (Bentley), Raymond Souster (Cain), Klein, Elizabeth Smart, and James Joyce (Conley), Louis Dudek, Marshall McLuhan, and Ezra Pound (Tremblay), Dorothy Livesay, Malcolm Lowry, and Wyndham Lewis (Tiessen), P.K. Page (Hulan), Sinclair Ross (Hill), and Ernest Buckler (Purdham) address key figures from both Canadian and international modernist canons, but not without decentring canonical narratives. To read international modernism in relation to Canadian modernism typically produces critical narratives about Canada's belated modernists—their imitation of American and European modernist aesthetics, their delayed development of non-commercial "little" presses, magazines, and theatres, and so on. Instead, to read Canadian modernism as Tim Conley does, we may consider the possibility that "Canada's modernism is not tertiary or 'after' European and then American modernisms, but 'between' them." This is not to deny the fact that the formation of American and European "high" modernisms antedates and influences the emergence of Canada's modernisms but rather to ascertain the latter's medial position between dominant modernisms. To speak of Canada's canonical modernism is to misidentify its formative mediations—that is, its emergence in the interstices between European and American modernisms. Canada's modernists are always enmeshed by and, at the same time, peripheral to these canonical modernisms. Modernisms in Canada therefore represent transnational cultural formations among the matrices of European and American modernisms—and, simultaneously, marginal modernisms on the edges of principal cultural modernities. These are the medial and peripheral relations among modernist cultural formations, the structures of affiliation through which Canadian modernisms meet with canonical modernisms.

This structural relationship between Canadian and international modernisms assumes multiple configurations in *The Canadian Modernists Meet*. While all of the contributors to the collection acknowledge the Canadian response to international modernism, this collage of Canada's modernists demarcates contiguities with and discontinguities from their American, British, Irish, and continental European counterparts. The internationalism of Canada's modernists is not merely a record of influence on a national arts community but instead a register of modernism's localized formations and deformations. Essays in the present volume frequently juxtapose Canadian modernists with their international predecessors and contemporaries: D.M.R. Bentley's analysis of the "architexts" of Canadian modernism, which correlates Le Corbusier's architectural theories with the representation of architectural structures in Klein's poetry and unfinished novel "Stranger and Afraid" and Scott's poem sequence "Letters from the Mackenzie River"; Stephen Cain's semiology of the modernist city, which relates Souster's Toronto poems to international modernist representations of urban space; Wanda Campbell's recovery of Canadian women's modernism since 1922, which points to its emergence at the apex of international modernism; Glenn Willmott's investigation of Watson's Paris diaries of the 1950s, which documents her readings of Samuel Beckett while writing *The Double Hook*; Tim Conley's examination of the prolonged censorship of *Ulysses* in Canada, which tracks Joyce's surreptitious influence on Smart's *By Grand Central Station I Sat Down and Wept* and Klein's *The Second Scroll*; Brian Trehearne's inquiry into the sources of Smith's surrealism of the 1930s, which posits connections between the Montreal modernists and continental European modernism; Tony Tremblay's exposition on the importation of Pound's "dialectical modernism" to Canada, which elaborates theories of culture expounded by Dudek and McLuhan; Candida Rifkind's findings on leftist theatre in the 1930s, which probe the intersections between agitprop theatre in Canada and avant-garde theatre in Europe; Paul Tiessen's identification of the "housewife" as an audience of Canadian modernism, which locates Livesay's writings on and for radio in relation to that of British and expatriate Anglo-modernists; Anne Quéma's critique of Eliot's theories of modernist impersonality, which finds in the intertextuality of Smart's writing and Cecil Buller's visual art "a gendered subjectivity that has no truck with impersonality but that has much to do with individual talent"; Medrie Purdham's reassessment of the damaging effects of impersonalist aesthetics, which offers Buckler's *The Mountain and the Valley* as a case study of its artist figure's "modernist new eyes"; and Shelley Hulan's reading of Page's enigmatic poem "Arras," which contests modernist theorizations of emotion in the writings of Eliot and of Canadian critics such as A.J.M. Smith and Northrop Frye. This collocation of Canadian, British, Irish, and continental European modernisms presents a reconfigured internationalism in contemporary modernist studies, a critical field that has largely failed to acknowledge the concurrent development of Canadian and other marginal modernisms.

If the recognition of Canada's modernists aims to decentre certain canonical constructions of international modernisms, the present volume's critical reassessment of Canadian modernism's centres and peripheries moves toward similar objectives. Colin Hill's essay, for instance, which focuses on the most critically studied modernist novel in Canada, Sinclair Ross's *As For Me and My House*, unsettles its canonical position by arguing that Arthur Stringer's popular trilogy of prairie novels from the 1910s and 1920s provides the "blueprint" for Ross's 1941 novel. The implications of Hill's thesis are not unrelated to the matter of canonical modernisms' indebtedness to marginal modernisms, for both raise questions about the historical predications of modernist canonicity. Ross's debt to Stringer exhibits the ways in which early twentieth-century popular fiction, once culturally prominent but since relegated to the margins of literary history, plays a formative role in the making of Canadian modernism and modernist canonicity. Marilyn Rose's essay on the Anne Marriott archives shifts our critical gaze to the analysis of archival institutions, the writing of literary biography, and the revaluation of women modernists' marginality. Contrary to Scott's portrait of the marginal modernist's disconsolation, Rose concludes that Marriott's discovery of a "poetics of the margin" toward the end of her writing life signifies the transformation of her early modernism's marginality into a poetry of affirmation. As a counternarrative to that of modernists like Scott whose historical marginality verges into canonicity, Rose's practice of reading archives and "telling lives" offers an alternative biocritical model for further research on other marginal modernists and modernisms.

To read the marginality of Canada's modernisms is to generate counternarratives that contest the canonical narratives of both national and international modernisms. Rather than seeking to recentre a nationally defined canon according to modernist literary values, the critical project of reading Canada's marginal modernisms in both national and international contexts necessitates the devaluation of modernist canonicity and the revaluation of its marginality. This call for counternarratives to canonical modernisms is certainly not without precedent. For Raymond Williams, the canonization of early twentieth-century modernisms embodies a cultural logic that sees "marginal or rejected artists become classics of organized teaching," and that in turn provokes his proposition to "search out and counterpoise an alternative tradition taken from the neglected works left in the wide margin of the century" (34, 35). As an alternative tradition, Canadian modernism emerges in the margins of international modernisms; its formation in counterpoint to canonical modernisms is constitutive of its alterity. If Canada's modernists are characterized by their "eclectic detachment," in A.J.M. Smith's durable phrase ("Eclectic" 23), namely, their capacity to draw selectively from the cultural traditions of European and American modernisms without becoming assimilated by them, we may find that this alternative tradition is marked by its resistance to incorporation into the narratives of dominant literatures and its facility to develop its own marginal counternarratives. By positing Canadian modernists' "detachment," Smith evokes Eliot's notion of tradition and the individual talent as well as his poetics of impersonality, but not without caution and discrimination: "Detachment surely does not imply in this context detachment from the self or from personality.... The term *detachment* in this context has nothing to do with objectivity or impersonality. It is actually an affirmation of personality" ("Eclectic" 24). Whether Smith's

theory is more or less an acknowledgment of the personalist *and* impersonalist poetics that coexist in both Canadian and international modernisms is less crucial than the implications of his method: his conception
of Canadian modernists' "affirmation of personality" at once alludes to
Eliot's canonical statement of modernist poetics and, at the same time,
rejects its central premise. In doing so, Smith places Canadian modernists in an alternative tradition, one that borders European and American
modernisms. The alterity of Canadian modernisms, however, is not only
determined by its external relations to an international arts community
but also by its internal relations among major and minor figures, movements, and groups. The "marginal and rejected" modernists in Canadian
literature are as relevant to an alternative tradition as its already recognized
figures; rather than a preliminary stage in the reformation of modernist
canonicity, the recovery of neglected modernists is a constituent element
in the formulation of Canadian modernism's marginality. Their detachment from canonical formations of Canadian literature confirms—as in
the cases of Bowman, Hale, and Marriott, among others—the emergence
and eclecticism of Canada's marginal modernisms and cultural counternarratives.

While there is little question of Canadian modernism's marginality on an international scale, the notion of its current marginality in
Canadian literary criticism may seem incommensurate with its widely
perceived canonicity. For certain contributors to Robert Lecker's collection
Canadian Canons: Essays in Literary Value (1991), Canadian modernism's
canonicity is a given (Gerson 54–56; Lecker 11; Scobie 57–58)—though
others acknowledge that the opposite is true of English Canada's avant-
garde theatre (Knowles 106; Salter 90). Insofar as Canadian literary critics
reproduce the typical perception of modernism—principally its masculinist formations—as the canonical centre of twentieth-century national
literatures, they take for granted the equivalence between the canonicity
of international and Canadian modernisms. Their definitions of Canadian
modernism's canonicity not only inscribe it as the imagined centre of a
national literature; they conflate modernist and nationalist literary values
(see also Berland 22, 28; Boire 3). It would be an overstatement, in any case,
to claim that modernism occupies the same canonical position in Canadian
literature as it does in other national literatures. As Trehearne argues in his
analysis of the modernist literary-critical archive, "Writers who dominated

criticism of Canadian literature through to the late 1970s—Grove, Livesay, Smith, Scott, Layton, Purdy, Buckler—have effectively gone marginal in the current recentring (not decentring) of the discipline" (6; see also 322 n6). If the recent marginalization of Canadian modernism's canonical writers proves more than a periodic interruption in the literary-critical record, we may review Robert Kroetsch's infamous pronouncement in 1974 about Canadian modernism's absence—"Canadian literature evolved directly from Victorian into Postmodern" (1)—as something other than the self-interested proclamation of a postmodernist and, instead, as the premonition of a modernist literary-critical decline. For those anti-, counter-, and postmodernist critics who disagree with Kroetsch but retain the faded image of Canadian modernism's mid-twentieth-century canonicity, the modernist of Scott's "The Canadian Authors Meet" is no longer shunned to a far corner but instead occupies the head table of Canadian literature's "most delightful party." The reality, however, is that Scott's image of a marginal, disconsolate modernist not only preserves the historical portrait of an emergent Canadian modernism in the 1920s but also presages the contemporary literary-critical picture of one—among many—of its residually canonical figures. This decentring of Canada's modernist canon has nevertheless opened the way for the production of multiple counternarratives to contest the more restricted narratives promulgated during the period of Canadian modernism's canonicity; these current literary-critical and -historical projects hold the promise of recovering alternative traditions. To this end, the essays collected in *The Canadian Modernists Meet* seek to redress recent lapses in critical attention to Canada's early-to-mid-century modernists and offer a broad range of new perspectives on the period's marginal and canonical modernisms.

WORKS CITED

Berland, Jody. "Nationalism and the Modernist Legacy: Dialogues with Innis." *Capital Culture: A Reader on Modernist Legacies, State Institutions, and the Value(s) of Art.* Ed. Berland and Shelley Hornstein. Montreal: McGill-Queen's UP, 2000. 114–38.

Boire, Gary. "Canadian (Tw)ink: Surviving the Whiteouts." *Essays on Canadian Writing* 35 (winter 1987): 1–16.

Djwa, Sandra. "The 1920s: E.J. Pratt, Transitional Modern." *The E.J. Pratt Symposium.* Ed. Glenn Clever. Ottawa: U of Ottawa P, 1977. 55–68.

Dudek, Louis, and Michael Gnarowski, eds. *The Making of Modern Poetry in Canada: Essential Articles on Contemporary Canadian Poetry in English.* Toronto: Ryerson, 1967.

Gerson, Carole. "The Canon Between the Wars: Field-notes of a Feminist Literary Archaeologist." Lecker, ed. 46–56.

Harrington, Lyn. *Syllables of Recorded Time: The Story of the Canadian Authors Association 1921–1981.* Toronto: Simon and Pierre, 1981.

Kelly, Peggy. "Politics, Gender, and *New Provinces*: Dorothy Livesay and F.R. Scott." *Canadian Poetry: Studies, Documents, Reviews* 53 (fall/winter 2003): 54–70.

Kennedy, Leo. "The Future of Canadian Literature." *Canadian Mercury* 5–6 (Dec. 1928): 99–100; rpt. in Dudek and Gnarowski 34–37.

Knowles, Richard Paul. "Voices (off): Deconstructing the Modern English-Canadian Dramatic Canon." Lecker, ed. 91–111.

Kroetsch, Robert. "A Canadian Issue." *Boundary 2* 3.1 (autumn 1974): 1–2.

Kronfeld, Chana. *On the Margins of Modernism: Decentering Literary Dynamics.* Berkeley, Los Angeles, and London: U of California P, 1996.

Lecker, Robert. Introduction. Lecker, ed. 3–16.

———, ed. *Canadian Canons: Essays in Literary Value.* Toronto: UTP, 1991.

Pratt, E.J. "Pratt as Editor: The *Canadian Poetry Magazine* Editorials." *Pursuits Amateur and Academic: The Selected Prose of E.J. Pratt.* Ed. Susan Gingell. Toronto: UTP, 1995. 111–17.

Salter, Denis. "The Idea of a National Theatre." Lecker, ed. 71–90.

Scobie, Stephen. "Leonard Cohen, Phyllis Webb, and the End(s) of Modernism." Lecker, ed. 57–70.

Scott, F.R. "The Canadian Authors Meet." *McGill Fortnightly Review* 27 Apr. 1927: 73; rpt. in *Canadian Forum* Dec. 1935: 388; rpt. in *New Provinces: Poems of Several Authors.* Toronto: Macmillan, 1936. 55.

———. Letter to E.J. Pratt. 15 Oct. 1935. F.R. Scott Fonds. MG 30 D211, box 1, file 8. National Archives of Canada, Ottawa.

———. Letter to E.J. Pratt. 28 Nov. 1935. F.R. Scott Fonds. MG 30 D211, box 1, file 8. National Archives of Canada, Ottawa.

———. Preface. *New Provinces: Poems of Several Authors.* Toronto: Macmillan, 1936. v.

———. "O Tempora!" *Canadian Poetry Magazine* 1.1 (Jan. 1936): 17.

Smith, A.J.M. "Eclectic Detachment: Aspects of Identity in Canadian Poetry." *Towards a View of Canadian Letters: Selected Critical Essays 1928–1971.* Vancouver: UBC P, 1973. 22–30.

———. "A Rejected Preface." *Canadian Literature* 24 (spring 1965): 6–9; rpt. in Dudek and Gnarowski 38–41.

————. "Wanted: Canadian Criticism." *Canadian Forum* 8 (Apr. 1928): 600–01; rpt. in Dudek and Gnarowski 31–33.

Trehearne, Brian. *The Montreal Forties: Modernist Poetry in Transition.* Toronto: UTP, 1999.

Williams, Raymond. "When Was Modernism?" *The Politics of Modernism: Against the New Conformists.* Ed. Tony Pinkney. London and New York: Verso, 1989. 31–35.

NORTH OF MODERNISM: MONTREAL   TORONTO   UNREAL

"New Styles of Architecture, a Change of Heart"? The Architexts of A.M. Klein and F.R. Scott

D.M.R. BENTLEY

I

In "Like an Old Proud King in a Parable," the *symboliste* lyric that A.J.M. Smith first published as "Proud Parable" in December 1928 and subsequently used as a prefatory piece in all his collections of poems, the creation of a modern Canadian poetic persona and stance is closely allied to the creation of a new imaginative place and habitation. In "anger to be gone / From fawning courtier and doting queen," the "bitter king" of the poem's opening verse paragraph "break[s] bound of all his counties green" and "ma[kes] a meadow in the northern stone" where he "breathe[s] a palace of inviolable air" (12). Very much an offspring of the early Yeats (see MacLaren), Smith's "old proud king" is an expression of the modern poet's desire to create in and for Canada a poetry remote from the gushiness that F.R. Scott so wittily satirizes in "The Canadian Authors Meet."[1] To juxtapose "Like an Old Proud King in a Parable" with Scott's poem is to be reminded that the rage for newness that came to Canada with the McGill Group and other modernists had both a transcendent and a satirical component, a visionary mode directed towards the future and an attack mode aimed at the present. In view of the central *rôle* that architecture has always played as an embodiment and signal of change in Western culture, it is scarcely, if at all, surprising that Canada's modern poets frequently turned to architectural structures and semiotics in their meditations on the present condition and potential future of Canadian society. For the obvious reason that Smith remained committed to the ideal of pure poetry expressed in "Like an Old Proud King in a Parable" and, moreover, spent most of his creative life in the United States, actual Canadian architectural structures rarely figure in his work. But this is decidedly not the case with Scott and A.M. Klein, both of whom lived in Montreal and wrote extensively about Canada and, especially during the 1940s and 1950s, produced numerous Canadian architexts—works that treat of Canada's architectural structures and built environments. Among these are some of the most engaged and engaging poems by both writers, including the extraordinary and largely unappreciated novel entitled "Stranger and Afraid" that Klein left unfinished at his death in 1972.

Partly because of the prominence accorded to the *Report of the Royal Commission on National Development in the Arts, Letters and Sciences 1949–1951* (Massey Commission) (1951) in most discussions of postwar Canadian culture, it has been easy for students and scholars of Canadian literature to overlook the work of the Federal Advisory Committee on Reconstruction that was created in April 1942 to make recommendations in six areas: agricultural policy, conservation and development of natural resources, publicly financed construction projects, postwar employment opportunities, postwar problems of women, and, most important for the present discussion, housing and community planning. Chaired by C.A. Curtis, a professor of economics at Queen's University, the subcommittee on Housing and Community Planning issued its Report in March 1944 to a Canadian public already primed for government action by the League for Social Reconstruction (1932) and the Co-operative Commonwealth Federation (1933), both of which, of course, counted Scott among their founding members. Citing a "desire ... deeply rooted in the minds of people in all walks of life" for "better housing and better living standards," the Curtis Commission recommended the implementation of a "housing program of large dimensions" that would utilize "pre-fabrication and mass assembly" (9, 22) as advocated by Le Corbusier in his enormously influential *Vers une architecture* (1923; trans. 1931) and given practical form in such texts as C. Sjonstrom's *Prefabrication in Timber: A Survey of Existing Methods* (1943).[2] Unlike "construction" in today's critical usage, the term "re-construction" in the years surrounding the Second World War was an expression of the wedding of progressive social and aesthetic ideas that lies at the heart of most strains of modernist architecture and literature.

In W.H. Auden's words, "a change of heart" was to find expression in "New Styles" of building and writing (7).

II

As good a place as any to begin an examination of the relationship between Klein's poetry and Canadian architecture is with one of the most striking and intriguing instances of that relationship: "Grain Elevator." First published in 1948 in *The Rocking Chair and Other Poems* and probably written a year or two earlier,[3] Klein's poem stands in a tradition of poetic meditations on the form and significance of a particular artefact that stretches back to and beyond Keats's "Ode on a Grecian Urn," but it is also a work that is unmistakably modern in its inspiration and message. This is not just because of the particular architectural structure chosen by Klein—namely, one of the enormous grain elevators on the Montreal waterfront that were built earlier in the century—but also because these very elevators had been made locally and internationally famous before the Second World War by Le Corbusier's enthusiastic endorsement of their mass and form in *Vers une architecture* (see fig.1).[4] To make his point that the productions of engineers are aligned with "good art" by virtue of their employment of "simple ... geometrical forms" that "satisfy our eyes by their geometry and our understanding by their mathematics," Le Corbusier includes photographs of Montreal's grain elevators in *Vers une architecture* and implies by his surrounding commentary that their effect on the viewer can be spiritual as well as physical:

> Architecture ... impresses the most brutal instincts by its objectivity [and] it calls into play the highest faculties by its very abstraction. Architectural abstraction is rooted in hard fact [but] it spiritualizes it, because the naked fact is nothing more than materialization of a possible idea....
>
> •   •   •
>
> Architecture is the masterly, correct and magnificent play of masses brought together in light. Our eyes are made to see forms in light; light and shade reveal these forms; cubes, cones, spheres, cylinders or pyramids are the great primary forms which light reveals to advantage.... It is for this reason that these are beautiful forms, the most beautiful forms. Everyone is agreed as to that, the child, the savage and the metaphysician. (25–26, 29)

These and other passages in *Vers une architecture* resonate loudly enough with the final stanza of "Grain Elevator" to support the conjecture that they provided at least part of the inspiration for Klein's poem:

> A box: cement, hugeness, and rectangles—
> merely the sight of it leaning in my eyes
> mixes up continents and makes a montage
> of inconsequent time and uncontiguous space.
> It's because it's bread. It's because
> bread is its theme, an absolute. Because
> always this great box flowers over us
> with all the coloured faces of mankind....
> (*Complete Poems* 2: 650–51)

Of course, the dialectical relationship between diversity and universality that is figured here in the conception of bread as an "absolute" that sustains people of all races is central to *The Rocking Chair* volume as a whole,⁵ but the stanza's celebration of the grain elevator as a structure whose formal characteristics transcend its particular "time" and "space" smacks strongly of Le Corbusier's insistence in *Vers une architecture* and elsewhere that architecture must free itself from history and the local if it is to serve the needs of twentieth-century humanity. For Scott in "Social Notes II, 1935" "grain elevators / Stored with superfluous wheat" and capable of "unload[ing] a grain-boat in two hours" are manifestations of the excessive "efficiency of the capitalist system" (*Collected Poems* 71). For Klein and Le Corbusier they are manifestations of fundamental and universal human traits and needs.

Vers une architecture also raises resonances in earlier stanzas of "Grain Elevator." Immediately after the second of the two passages quoted above, Le Corbusier observes that "Egyptian, Greek or Roman architecture is an architecture of prisms, cubes and cylinders, pyramids or spheres" and proceeds to list several examples: "the Pyramids, the Temple of Luxor, the Parthenon, the Coliseum, Hadrian's Villa ... the Towers of Babylon, the Gates of Samarkand ... the Pont du Gard, Santa Sophia, the Mosques of Stamboul ...," and so on (29–31). In the opening stanzas of "Grain Elevator," Klein also embarks on a wide-ranging search for similar architectural forms: after observing that the grain elevator rises above its surroundings "blind and babylonian / like something out of legend," he relates it to "some eastern tomb," to "the … bastille," and to a variety of near and far eastern locales and cultures: "here, as in a Josephdream, bow down / the sheaves.… Sometimes it makes me think Arabian … Caucasian … Mongolian" (*Complete Poems* 2: 650). So striking are the conceptual parallels between *Vers une architecture* and "Grain Elevator" that it is tempting to see something of Le Corbusier's thinking even in the form of Klein's poem, a series of four rhymed, eight-line stanzas whose rectangular appearance on the page mimics as well as a traditional poem can the "box … and rectangles" of the architectural structure that they describe. (Anyone who doubts that Klein was intent on such mimetic effects should ponder his remark that in the statement "Saskatchewan / is rolled like a rug of a thick and golden thread" in the poem's second stanza "[t]he longest-syllabled flat province [is] in monosyllables unfolded" [*Complete Poems* 2: 1008].)[6]

"Grain Elevator" is an especially complex and layered instance of the relationship between and among architecture and architexts that is also evident in other poems in *The Rocking Chair* volume. In "Lookout: Mount Royal," for example, Klein recalls "boyhood" excursions to Mount Royal Park but describes the view from the "parapet" there in decidedly adult terms that may also reflect a knowledge of Le Corbusier and other writers on architecture, urban design, and the buildings and layout of Montreal:

> … from the parapet make out
> beneath the green marine
> the discovered road, the hospital's romantic
> gables and roofs, and all the civic Euclid
> running through sunken parallels and lolling
> in diamond and square, then proud-pedantical
> with spire and dome
> making its way to the sought point, his home.
>
> home recognized: there: to be returned to—
>
> lets the full birdseye circle to the river,
> its singsong bridges, its mapmaker curves, its
> island with the two shades of green, meadow and wood;
> and circles round that water-tower'd coast.…
> (*Complete Poems* 2: 686–87)

These lines are reminiscent of countless eighteenth- and nineteenth-century prospect pieces and, intriguingly, they also recall Pierre de Charlevoix's description of early eighteenth-century Montreal as "a long rectangle,"[7] but their most insistent intertext is Wordsworth's "Sonnet Composed upon Westminster Bridge, September 3, 1802." However, where Wordsworth describes London in very general terms ("Ships, towers, domes, theatres, and temples ... All bright and glittering in the smokeless air" [3:38]), Klein provides enough details to enable buildings to be identified—"the ... romantic / gables and roofs" of the Hôtel-Dieu (1860) and the "proud-pedantical / ... spire and dome" of McGill's Palladian Arts Building (1839, 1862). The fact that Klein was once "nursed ... by the sisters of the Hôtel-Dieu" (*Complete Poems* 2: 1006)[8] and, of course, had close ties with McGill University merely confirms that "Lookout: Mount Royal" is the product of a man who felt profoundly at home in the public spaces as well as in his own personal place in Montreal.

The impression that Klein was able to construe Montreal in quite other than the orthodox modern sense of an Eliotic "Unreal City"[9] of Durkheimian *anomie* is confirmed and reinforced in *The Rocking Chair* volume by poems such as "Pastoral of the City Streets," "The Snowshoers," and "Parade of St. Jean Baptiste" in which public spaces become vibrant places where the poet-speaker feels comfortably at home. In "Pastoral of the City Streets" a "friend's father" pelting neighbourhood children with water from a garden hose temporarily transforms the "geometry" of the street and sidewalk into a "crystal stream ... cavelike and cool" (*Collected Poems* 2: 695). In "The Snowshoers," "the street moves with colours" as the snowshoers "snowball their banter below the angular eaves," and in "The Parade of St. Jean Baptiste" the floats "move as through a garden ... / of flowers, populous / of all the wards and counties" of the city and province (2: 652, 691). As will be seen in a few moments, some of Montreal's architectural structures provoke expressions of disgust and condemnation in *The Rocking Chair and Other Poems*, but far more common in Klein's responses to the city are feelings of delight, gratitude, and tenderness. This is not only true of poems in *The Rocking Chair* volume or, indeed, of Klein's poems about Montreal: in "Greeting on This Day," a poem written in 1929 but not published until 1940, the "white roofs" of Safed in Galilee transform "prose" into poetry, and in "Autobiographical," a poem written circa 1942 and first published in *The Book of Canadian Poetry* (1943), the "fabled city" that the speaker seeks in "memory" is the source of a "joy" that is tinged with "sadness" only because it is past (*Complete Poems* 1: 143; 2: 566).

Nowhere in Klein's oeuvre does Montreal figure more as the ideal city of memory and imagination than in the poem in *The Rocking Chair* for which it provides a title. A linguistic tour-de-force designed to be accessible to both French and English readers, "Montreal" envisages the city as a living museum of its own history that exists as a "Mental" as well as an actual entity, "Travers[ing] [his] spirit's conjured avenues" and "populat[ing] the pupils of [his] eyes" with its "scenes and sounds" (*Complete Poems* 2: 621–23). Unlike Le Corbusier, who had famously argued in *Urbanisme* (1925; trans. 1929) for the complete demolition of existing cities and their replacement by cities based on a single design and suitable to any locale, the Klein of "Montreal" revels in his city's characteristic trees, distinctive architecture, and allusive cultural semiotics and continuities: "Splendor erablic of your promenades / Foliates there," he exclaims in the opening stanza, "and there your maisonry / Of pendant balcon and escalier'd march, / Unique midst English habitat, / Is vivid Normandy." With the aid of Gothic fantasy, Montreal's streets, monuments, and buildings become catalysts to historical memory:

> Thus, does the Indian, plumèd, furtivate
> Still through your painted autumns, Ville-Marie!
> Though palisades have passed, though calumet
> With tabac of your peace enfumes the air,
> Still do I spy the phantom, aquiline,
> Genuflect, mocassin'd, behind
> His statue in the square![10]

> Thus, costumed images before me pass,
> Haunting your archives architectural:
> *Coureur de bois*, in posts where pelts were portaged;
> Seigneur with his candled manoir; Scot
> Ambulent through his bank, pillar'd and vast.[11]
> Within your chapels, voyaged mariners
> Still pray, and personage departed,
> All present from your past!

In addition to being rich with "permanences"—buildings, artefacts, monuments, and streets that constitute a historical past that can still be experienced (see Rossi 57–58)—Montreal is for Klein a cosmopolitan and industrial city whose distinctiveness partly derives from its hybrid "music": the "multiple / ... Lexicons" on its "quays," the "double-melodied vocabulaire" of its English- and French-speaking inhabitants, the daily and weekly rhythms of its "manufactory" and "argent belfries." A site of both modern commerce and collective or cultural memory, Klein's Montreal is at once a living museum and a living city.

It is not until the final stanzas of "Montreal" that the city is fully recognized by Klein as the locus of his cognitive as well as his physical existence and, thus, as the place that more than any other engenders feelings of loyalty, homesickness, and nostalgia. "You are part of me ... You are locale of infancy," intones the poet as he moves towards his concluding paean to Montreal as the home of his heart and, as such, a place *in* his heart:

> Never do I sojourn in alien place
> But I do languish for your scenes and sounds,
> City of reverie, nostalgic isle,
> Pendant most brilliant on Laurentian cord!
> The coigns of your boulevards—my signory—
> Your suburbs are my exile's verdure fresh,
> Your parks, your fountain'd parks—
> Pasture of memory!
>
> City, O city, you are vision'd as
> A parchemin roll of saecular exploit
> Inked with the script of eterne souvenir!
> You are in sound, chanson and instrument!
> Mental, you rest forever edified
> With tower and dome; and in these beating valves,
> Here in these beating valves, you will
> For all my mortal time reside!

Appropriating Eliot's "O city, city," Klein reworks the phrase into an expression of affection rather than dismay that is entirely consistent in emotion and attitude with the echo of Wordsworth's "Westminster Bridge" sonnet (and Klein's own "Lookout: Mount Royal") that sounds in "tower and dome." Here as elsewhere in *The Rocking Chair and Other Poems* the Montreal that "reside[s]" in Klein's heart is partly "vision'd" and "script[ed]" by modernism, but its deeper affinities lie with the "beauteous forms" of the "sylvan Wye" that Wordsworth "fe[els] along the heart" in "Tintern Abbey" (2: 260).[12]

This is not to say that Klein (or, indeed, Wordsworth) was blind to the negative aspects of life in the post-industrial cities of Europe, North America, and elsewhere that gave birth to the urban realism of Hogarth, Engels, Dickens, and countless other artists and writers. Surrounding "Lookout: Mount Royal" and "Montreal" in *The Rocking Chair* volume are numerous poems such as "Commercial Bank," "Indian Reservation: Caughnawaga," and "Quebec Liquor Commission Store" in which the social institutions and architectural structures of contemporary Canadian culture occasion dismay and satirical commentary rather than affection and emotive reverie. The marbled and hushed interior of the bank in "Commercial Bank" is in reality a "jungle" in which the "beasts" of capitalism are no less deadly for being "toothless, with drawn nails" (*Complete Poems* 2: 618–19). The Mohawk reserve in "Indian Reservation: Caughnawaga" is not a "home" but a "museum," a "crypt," and a "grassy ghetto" in which specimens of an exotic and supposedly vanishing species can do little other than cater to the demands of gawping tourists (*Complete Poems* 2: 242). The nondescript sales area of "Quebec Liquor Commission Store" is "Nonetheless" an Ali Baba's "cave" whose contents rival Aladdin's lamp in their power to create illusions and thus perpetuate social inequalities (*Complete Poems* 2: 659). In these and similar poems, Montreal is "vision'd" and "script[ed]" by Klein's socialism and, hence, seen and written not as a site of "permanences" in Aldo Rossi's sense of "urban artifacts" that provide a meaningful and valued connection with the city's past (see Rossi 57–58) but as a site of institutions that are so destructive and dehumanizing that they demand radical change.

The earliest and one of the most scathingly critical architexts in *The Rocking Chair and Other Poems* is "Pawnshop," which was written in about 1942 (that is, at approximately the same time as "Autobiographical" and "The Hitleriad") and bears a deeper imprint than most poems in the volume of the leftist sensibility that had produced such poems as "Barricade Smith:

His Speeches" (c. 1938) and "Of Castles in Spain" (c. 1937). The final but first-written stanza of "Pawnshop" provides an almost Foucauldian analysis of the power embodied in the "grim house" "Near [the] waterfront, a stone's throw from the slums" and, thus, from its most vulnerable clients:

> This is our era's state-fair parthenon,
> the pyramid of a pharaonic time,
> our little cathedral, our platonic cave,
> our childhood's house that Jack built. Synonym
> of all building, our house, it owns us; even
> when free from it, our dialectic grave.
> Shall one not curse it, therefore, as the cause,
> type, and exemplar of our social guilt?
> Our own gomorrah house,
> the sodom that merely to look at makes one salt?
> (*Complete Poems* 2: 576–77)

This remarkable verse paragraph effectively figures the pawnshop as the paradigm of space arranged on the capitalist principles enunciated by Adam Smith, whose name is in fact mooted earlier in the poem as its "architect" (*Complete Poems* 2: 576). A site of exploitation and incarceration that should have been "razed ... to the salted ground / antitheses ago" (as, of course, was Carthage, another centre of rapacious commerce), the pawnshop is a visible testament to the power of "kapital" to make masters of some, slaves of many, and inmates of all (*Complete Poems* 2: 576–77), for, even if they delusively imagine themselves "free," all members of a capitalist society are metaphorically housed in its structures. The final lines of the poem might seem to suggest that no escape is possible from capitalism's all-encompassing pawnshop, but, of course, it was only Lot's wife who was turned to a pillar of salt by the sight of Sodom and Gomorrah in Genesis 19: Klein's namesake, Abraham, was able to look "toward all the land of the plain" where the cursed cities lay burning and go on to found a new religion and a new people. In the dialectic of *The Rocking Chair and Other Poems*, to look unflinchingly at architectural structures that exemplify the negative aspects of human nature is as important as it is to take to heart those that bespeak humanity's capacity to build a good and better world.

III

For much of the century that was supposed to belong to Canada, the locus of Canadian hopes for social renovation was less likely to be a city steeped in history and tradition such as Montreal than the West or the North, two regions scarcely mentioned by Klein but central to the thinking and writing of F.R. Scott from the 1920s to the 1950s. Before the Second World War, Scott, like Smith, saw the North partly through the works of the Group of Seven and their associates as a pristine and all but uninhabited repository of a fresh, vivid, and manifestly Canadian natural beauty. "Child of the North," Scott urges in "New Paths" (1926),[13]

> Yearn no more after old playthings,
> Temples and towers and gates
> Memory-haunted thoroughfares and rich palaces
> And all the burdensome inheritance, the binding legacies,
> Of the Old World and the East.
>
> Here is a new soil and a sharp sun.
> (*Collected Poems* 37)

After the Second World War, however, the focus of Scott's northern poems shifted from the icy waters and granite river courses that he had celebrated in such poems as "Laurentian" (1927), "Old Song" (1928), and "North Stream" (1930) to the social and economic consequences of the development of the Canadian North that was to become the basis of "a 'new National Policy'" (Abele 314) in the "Northern Vision" articulated by John Diefenbaker's Conservatives in the federal elections of 1957 and 1958. In Scott's pre-war poems, "winds that have swept [the] lone cityless plains" of the North tell principally of "fresh beauty." In his postwar poems, they herald and document economic growth and new cities.

An early indication of this shift appears in "Laurentian Shield" (1946) where the silence and emptiness of the North are read by an unapologetically masculinist observer as evidence of a desire to be made productive. Envisioning the North as it was, is, and could be from a socialist perspective[14] and with a linguistic metaphor as an ordinal, Scott sees "Cabin syllables, / Nouns of settlement," and "steel syntax" where once there were "the cry of the hunter" and the "bold command of monopolies" and where now there is "the drone of the plane scouting the ice, / Fill[ing] the emptiness with neighbourhood / And link[ing] our future over the vanished pole" (*Collected Poems* 58). The concluding vision of "Laurentian Shield" is of a Canadian North that has been humanized rather than merely exploited:

> ... a deeper note is sounding, heard in the mines,
> The scattered camps and the mills, a language of life,
> And what will be written in the full culture of occupation
> Will come, presently, tomorrow
> From millions whose hands can turn this rock into children.
> (*Collected Poems* 58)

It is a vision curiously tainted by the military resonances of the world "occupation" and strongly reminiscent of the perception of the Canadian West that drove "Manitoba fever" in the closing decades of the nineteenth century and provided Isabella Valancy Crawford with part of the inspiration for *Malcolm's Katie,* one difference between the two being that, regrettably, Scott seems to have been less apprehensive in 1946 than Crawford was in 1884 about the environmental impact of "mines ... camps and ... mills."[15]

That Scott perceived homologies between and among poetry, architecture, town planning, and statecraft is nowhere more evident than in the paper entitled "The State as a Work of Art" that he delivered in 1950 in "The Search for Beauty" series of the McGill Department of Architecture.[16] After tracing part of the inspiration of "Laurentian Shield" to a "description of the English Black Country" (that is, the industrial Midlands) by Stephen Spender and then reading the poem itself, Scott explains that the "potential social evolution in Canada's northland is not just a question of economics, but also of aesthetics in the sense that we really can choose the language which shall be the mode of living in this new world":

> Geology has given us the mineral wealth, history has given us the legal title, to this gigantic workshop; our own creative energy, our social imagination, or lack of it, will determine what use we make of this opportunity. Let us hope it does not become another Black Country. If everything man makes and builds is a language, I fear that we Canadians have so far spoken more in prose than poetry. Yet

we can create a beautiful social language through our daily work of making and building a society, and in this sense the social order is a work of art and we ourselves are the artists. (9)

Later in the paper, Scott refers admiringly to the American jurist and educator Roscoe Pound, whose concept of "the law [as] 'social engineering'" provided impetus to the creation of the Tennessee Valley Authority (TVA), and hails the TVA itself as a shining example of what can be achieved by "direct[ing] the dynamic forces of society into socially desirable channels": "it took a region [that was] depopulated and economically depressed … and by … building … dams, producing cheaper power under public ownership … and above all by teaching people how to live co-operatively, subordinating selfish interest to public welfare, restored the faith of whole communities…" (14). "[I]f [the law-maker] is a social engineer, may he not also be called a social architect?" Scott asks; "[i]s [the work of the TVA] not something more than good government and good economics? Is it not more than social justice? Is it not also beautiful in the aesthetic sense of the word? … And if it can be done in a single community or region, cannot it be done in the state as a whole?" (14). It is but one of many intimations of the Romantic and Victorian underpinnings of Scott's modernism that his conception of the lawyer, the politician, the engineer, and the architect as the poets of a progressive society recalls both the Shelleyan notion of the poet as the unacknowledged legislator of the world and the Arnoldian notion of the poet as the physician of the age of iron.

Six years after he wrote "The State as a Work of Art," an opportunity for Scott to see for himself whether or not the Canadian North was being developed in a manner that could be described as "beautiful" came by way of an invitation from Michigan State University to deliver a series of lectures on "Canada and Canadian-American relations" (Djwa 318). When Scott and his travelling companion, Pierre Trudeau, flew north from Edmonton in August 1956, Diefenbaker's "Northern Vision" was still a year in the future, but the pace of northern development had already been accelerating for several years as a result of the Second World War (which, among other things, had led to the construction of the Canol Pipeline from Norman Wells to Whitehorse), the Cold War (which had resulted in the continuation of American military activity in the North), and a number of initiatives by the federal government, including the creation in 1943 of a Department of Mines and Resources (DMR), the publication in 1947 of *Canada's New Northwest* (a DMR report that "treated the region as an economic unit of potential importance to the national economy" [Abele 314]), and the consequent establishment of an Advisory Committee on Northern Development (1948) and a Department of Northern Affairs and National Resources (1953).[17] Scott had good reason to visit the North as preparation for a series of lectures on "Canada and Canadian-American relations."

As he flew courtesy of Eldorado Mining and Refining Limited towards Fort Smith, the one-time Hudson's Bay Company (HBC) trading post on the Slave River north of Alberta, Scott saw "A huge nowhere / Underlined by a shy railway" and apparently cast his mind back to "Laurentian Shield" for appropriate metaphors: here was an "arena" as "Large as Europe ... Waiting the contest" in "Silence"; here, "Underground," were "cities sleep[ing] like seeds" with the rocks as their "coins" (that is, their economic wealth and/as their cornerstones) (*Collected Poems* 223). In the Company's camp near Fort Smith at Bell Rock, where Scott and Trudeau had to wait for a Northern Transportation Company tugboat to take them downriver to Fort Providence, Scott continued to experience the romance of the Northwest, "dipp[ing] his hand in water / That muddies the Beaufort Sea"; remarking that "The Slave river rolled past / Downhill to the North, / Running away from America / Yet bringing America with it"; chanting the exotic names of the places visited by riverboats ("Radium Dew, Radium Yellowknife, Radium King," and so on); and proclaiming the human and material cargoes of the boats fluent in "the language" (*Collected Poems* 224–25). The poem from which all these affirmations are taken, "The Camp at Bellrock," concludes with a figure for Canadian hybridity that anticipates in its bathetic lack of subtlety the child with one "deep brown" and one "blue" eye that results from the relationship of an English explorer and a Native woman in Rudy Wiebe's *A Discovery of Strangers* (314):

> Walking behind the bunk-house
> We saw a great white dog,
> Long-haired for cold, feet broad for snow,
> Standing firm and friendly,
> No husky, but mixed with the breed.
> Behind him his ugly mother

Slept, a short-haired bitch
Brown and patchy, an import,
Half his size, but source of his power.
So it is in the North
Where opposites meet and mate.
(*Collected Poems* 225)

In this lamentable passage and elsewhere in the two poems that begin the "Letters from the Mackenzie River" sequence, the architectural structures of northern development—here, the "bunk-house"—are merely imagined or mentioned in passing, but in "Fort Smith" and ensuing pieces they become of central importance as Scott seeks to understand the economic, social, and cultural ramifications of northern development.

Beginning, significantly, with the sound of the "town siren," a signal of disaster that causes curious children to "Bound ... like little wolves" to the scene of a supposed fire (it turns out to be a false alarm), "Fort Smith" narrates Scott's recovery of moral perspective through a recognition of the resemblance between the "gentle Anglican face" of his father, Frederick George Scott, and a local Anglican clergyman, the Reverend Burt Evans (*Collected Poems* 226). At this point, Scott's concerted attempt to sound a real alarm at the ramifications of northern development for the region and its peoples plunges the poem into another paroxysm of bathetic over-determination from which, however, it quickly recovers to provide an increasingly disturbing catalogue of the architectural structures that embody the process of economic, religious, bureaucratic, social, and cultural colonization that is underway:

The Rev. Burt Evans
Picked us out as strangers
And offered to show us around
In his new Volkswagen.
So we shoved aside a baby-crib
And filled up the Nazi car
To explore Canada's colony.
There was the Bank of Commerce
In a new tar-paper bunk-house
Opened six days ago,

> The Hudson's Bay Store and Hotel,
> Government Offices, Liquor Store,
> RCMP Headquarters, Catholic Hospital,
> Anglican and Catholic Churches,
> The Imperial Oil Compound,
> The Barber Shop and Pool Room,
> A weedy golf course, the Curling Club,
> And the Uranium Restaurant, full of young people
> Playing song-hits on the juke-box.
> (*Collected Poems* 226)

Once identified by the signage of capitalism, a "tar-paper bunk-house" reveals itself for what it is: an architectural structure whose external material—"tar-paper"—embodies the logic of the economic imperialism of which it is a part—the logic, that is, of extractable resources and cheap labour in exchange for expertise, capital investment, manufactured goods, and the various institutions necessary for the process to function in an efficient and "enlightened" fashion: law, health care, religious education, metropolitan culture. Whether serving as a bank, a "guest-house" ("The Camp at Bell Rock"), or a workman's home ("Steve, the Carpenter" [*Collected Poems* 224, 228]), a "bunk-house" is a manifestation of an alliance between development and consumerism that is powerful enough to determine not only where and how people earn and spend their money but also where they live, how they relax and conduct themselves, and what they eat, hear, and think. As Scott must already have been becoming painfully aware, the development of the Canadian North was not following the blueprint of the Tennessee Valley Authority.

In the ensuing verse paragraph of "Fort Smith" Scott turns his attention to the racial assumptions and social hierarchies that are manifest in the town's built environment:

> We drove on sandy streets.
> No names yet, except "Axe-handle Road."
> There was the "native quarter,"
> Shacks at every angle
> For Slave Indians and half-breeds,
> And overlooking the river

> The trim houses of the civil servants
> With little lawns and gardens
> And tents for children to play Indian in.
> (*Collected Poems* 227)

"[T]ents for children to play Indian in" insists too much, but denotation and connotation fuse quite effectively in "Slave Indians," and Scott's perception that the local people are treated as inferiors—literally looked down upon—by southern bureaucrats gains in stature through corroboration by Native commentators. "We [saw] how … the housing provided to us was very inferior," the one-time president of the Inuit Tapirisat Michael Amarook would observe many years later, "[a]nd … at the same time we saw government employees in ever increasing numbers arriving in our communities and being provided with high quality housing, with running water, furniture and lots of space, often at lower rents…" (qtd. in Robson 18).[18] That it was a southern perception of the cultures and therefore needs of northern Natives that determined the levels of housing observable in Fort Smith is an obvious enough point that Scott brings home later in the poem by having the Reverend Evans explain, not without regret, that a shrine to the Virgin Mary near the Roman Catholic church "'has an appeal … / To the superstitious element in the population'" (*Collected Poems* 227).[19] No more than the bureaucrats and the corporations is the Catholic Church exempted from Scott's charges of racist imperialism and condescension. "Fort Smith" ends with the well-known vignette of Trudeau stripping himself naked, walking into a rapid, and

> Standing white, in whiter water,
> Leaning south up the current
> To stem the downward rush,
> A man testing his strength
> Against the strength of his country.
> (*Collected Poems* 227)

Djwa is right in hearing an echo of "the romantic nationalism of the twenties" in these lines (324), but surely the lines also imply that Trudeau has the ability to resist the potentially devastating power of the south–north (black gold) "rush" whose negative effects are chronicled earlier in the poem.

To a greater or lesser extent, the poems that follow "Fort Smith" in "Letters from the Mackenzie River" display the same combination of insight and lugubriousness as they further chronicle the manifestations and ramifications of the flow of people and materials into and out of the North. Surrounded by "pin-ups" and family photograph albums in "Steve, the Carpenter," Steve Bard laments his loneliness in terms tellingly reminiscent of the juke-box ("'Sometimes I get so lonely I could cry'") while outside his bunkhouse the Slave River, now a correlative for his status as well as his loneliness, "roll[s] on, / Farther and farther from home" (*Collected Poems* 228–29). On a "tug … dedicated / To a single purpose— / Pushing freight in the Territories," in "The Radium Yellowknife," "George Bouvier the Pilot" is a Métis whose "father came from the Red River by canoe / And married into the Lafferty's [*sic*] at Providence" (*Collected Poems* 232). In the galley on the same tug in the same poem, Grace Fischer, the "sole woman aboard," "utters her soul in pastry" and "reads long letters from daughters / Who are peopling the world 'outside'" (*Collected Poems* 233). Like Edwin Arlington Robinson's Town down the River, the communities on the Slave in "Letters from the Mackenzie River" contain characters who are of interest because they exhibit certain psychological traits or cultural qualities, in Scott's case those that dispose individuals to live and work in the North and thus to participate in one way or another and more or less harmfully in its colonization and development.

In sharp contrast to Scott's relatively sympathetic portraits of Steve Bard, George Bouvier, Grace Fischer, and the Reverend Burt Evans is his depiction of Father Denis, "an Oblate from Rennes, Brittany," in "Fort Providence," the poem named for the small community on the Mackenzie River that came into existence in the nineteenth century because of the presence of an HBC trading post and a Roman Catholic mission (*Collected Poems* 230). "Young, cheerful," and informal, Father Denis seems benign enough until he shows his visitors over the Catholic mission school, a building "four storeys high, / Grey, square, isolate, / More fortlike than anything in Fort Providence" (*Collected Poems* 230), and at least as implicated as any other corporate or bureaucratic entity in the business of colonization. Writing about the 1950s in *The Government of Canada and the Inuit, 1900–1967*, Richard Diubaldo observes that, despite the fact that "[i]n 1955 the federal government announced a new educational programme for the Northwest Territories after reaching certain understandings and agreements with the

Roman Catholic and Anglican [C]hurches," the missionaries continued to provide "the bulk of educational services" in the North, a situation that was distressing to people in the Department of Indian Affairs "who may have been suspicious of missionaries or held a low view of their teaching abilities" (150–51). That Scott shared this distress is abundantly evident in the remainder of "Fort Providence," where the priests and nuns of Father Denis's school are roundly condemned, first for the promulgation of American corporate propaganda, then for their abominable teaching, and finally for their aggressive proselytizing: "In the entrance hall / Walt Disney illustrations for the Kleenex Company[20].... Priests from France, nuns from Quebec, / [Teaching] Slavies (who still speak Indian) / Grades I to VIII, in broken English.... Everywhere religious scenes, / Christ and Saints, Stations of the Cross, / Beads hanging from nails, crucifixes..." (*Collected Poems* 230–31).

As repellant to Scott was the almost complete neglect of Canadian and Native cultures in the educational programme of the Oblate mission school: "Silk-screen prints of the Group of Seven" provide images of the Canadian landscape that mechanical reproduction has robbed of freshness, but "No map of Canada or the Territories" is anywhere to be seen, and "crayon drawings and masks / Made by the younger children" are "The single visible expression / Of the soul of these broken people" (*Collected Poems* 231). In the final lines of the poem, the mission school is recognized as less "fortlike" than prison-like:

> Upstairs on the second storey
> Seventy little cots
> Touching end to end
> In a room 30' by 40'
> Housed the resident boys
> In this firetrap mental gaol.
> (*Collected Poems* 231)

By the end of "Fort Providence," the architectural structure in which the mission school is housed has become the outward and visible sign of an educational programme whose primary goal—the purgation of one culture and the inculcation of another—is eerily similar to the processes of extraction and imposition at work in the Imperial Oil Compound and the Uranium Restaurant in "Fort Smith."

Despite the fact that the Northern Transportation Company tug that transported Scott and Trudeau downriver from Fort Smith was engaged in the same business (and, indeed, "burn[ed] diesel oil / Pumped at Norman Wells / And so live[d] off the land" [*Collected Poems* 232]), it is largely exempt from the ideological criticism directed at other targets, the reason apparently being that, more than any other entity encountered in the North, it resembles a socialist society. On its "upper-deck" strolls a representative of the era's most celebrated welfare state, "A wise old Swede"[21] named Captain Svierson who wears "No braid" and below him is George Rush, a "talkative man" who "Jollies the crew along." In short, "Nobody seems to give orders, / Yet everyone knows what to do" (*Collected Poems* 232). Even the external appearances of George Bouvier, the Métis pilot, and Grace Fischer, the soulful pastry cook, seem to reflect a sense of near-utopian well-being: Bouvier's face is "As wild and gentle as riverlands seen from a plane" and Fischer, although a "Mother of nine," "look[s] thirty-five" (*Collected Poems* 232–33). Certainly, the microcosm of society aboard "The Radium Yellowknife" appears to draw from each of its crew members according to his or her abilities and, in return, to reward each with a sense of respect and dignity that is denied to the majority of northerners by the hierarchies of the federal bureaucracy, the mission schools, and the extractive industries.

As "The Radium Yellowknife" nears Norman Wells (which has the distinction of being "the first settlement in the N[orth] W[est] T[erritories] to be established entirely as a result of non-reversible resource development" [Pool]), the ideological ideal and satirical norm represented by the community on the tug is brought to bear with clumsy stridency on the extractive activities and proprietorial attitudes of such companies as Imperial Oil (a subsidiary since 1898 of Standard Oil):

> Now we see tanks of oil
> Standing white on the rocks
> Amid stacks of cans and drums.
> The first industrial wealth
> Marked by Mackenzie himself—
> Power and light and heat
> For whatever the uses of man.
> Bringing out Yellowknife gold

And the burning ore from Port Radium,
Driving the tugs and planes
And keeping the bureaucrat snug.

        •   •   •

Curving in toward shore
We read on a kind of gallows
In the utterly public land
The words PRIVATE PROPERTY.
Behind is its counterpart:
TRESPASSERS WILL BE PROSECUTED
BY ORDER, IMPERIAL OIL.
Trespassers! In the North!
Man is the absent fact
Man is the aim and need
Man is the source of wealth
But Property keeps him out.
And the Indians wonder, who first
Lived off this soil
And now are outcast and dying
As their substance is drained away.
(*Collected Poems* 233–34)

As Djwa has observed, this passage is "full of politics" (330), not least but certainly most subtly in its deployment of metaphors of hanging ("a kind of gallows") and bloodletting ("their substance … drained away") to figure the deadly and vampiric effects on the Native peoples of the (American) extractive industries. "Norman Wells" ends, somewhat lamely, by naming a white man, Jimmy O'Brien, who was also a victim of Imperial Oil (this time in collusion with Canadian Pacific Airways [CPA]) and by suggesting that if the "bomb on Hiroshima" had not hastened the end of the Second World War the depletion of the Norman Wells oil fields through the Canol pipeline would have completely exhausted "this Canadian wealth" (*Collected Poems* 234). In "Norman Wells to Aklavik," the last poem that Scott wrote during or immediately after his tour of the North in 1956, the onslaught against American and Canadian corporations continues with a jibe at CPA for "Exact[ing] a first-class fare / Plus an extra charge / To prove its monopoly power" (*Collected Poems* 235).

Scott's conviction that corporate and bureaucratic insensitivity were killing the Canadian North and its peoples re-emerges architecturally in the penultimate poem in the "Letters from the Mackenzie River" sequence, "A New City: E3," which was begun in 1956 but not completed until 1970.[22] Here "Indian and Eskimo watch / The slow, inescapable death / Of this land which has waited so long / For the sentence already pronounced" as "America's overspill / Invades the tundra and lakes / Extracting, draining away, / Leaving a slum behind ... Like brown water on snow" (*Collected Poems* 236). Neither entirely accurate nor merely figurative, the word "slum" in these lines provides an imagistic transition to Scott's heavily ironical assessment of Inuvik or, as it was initially known, E-3, the settlement on the Mackenzie Delta that was constructed in the late 1950s to replace Aklavik, which had come under threat from erosion:

> But wait! A new city is planned.
> Across from Aklavik's mud,
> Free from the perma-frost,
> Set upon solid rock,
> Blue-printed, pre-fab, precise,
> A model, a bureaucrat's dream.
> (*Collected Poems* 236)

Following this round condemnation of a bureaucratically driven scheme that owed more than a little to Le Corbusier's championship of planned cities and mass-produced houses in *Vers une architecture* and elsewhere, Scott turns his irony on "The first Council meeting / North of the Arctic Circle," an event that he and Trudeau witnessed in E-3/Inuvik in September 1956. Disdainfully and "'mischievous[ly]'"[23] observing that "No Indian or Eskimo face" was visible at the ceremony, he dismisses the laws ratified by the Council as "Pre-cast in Ottawa" and, as such, homologous with the "pre-fab" buildings of E-3 and imbricated with the other imported structures represented by the two other witnesses at their ratification: "a priest in a black soutane, / And the RCMP in its braid" (*Collected Poems* 236). The remainder of the poem draws an incautious parallel between the continuation of the ceremony without a mace because the boat carrying it had run "aground / Crossing the Delta" and the continuation of the British Parliament without the Great Seal because it had been "dropped in the

Thames / By a fleeing Jacobite King" to make two plonkingly sophomoric points: "Symbols are magic, and work / As well in idea as in fact" and a gap "in … ritual" can be "Covered by common sense" (*Collected Poems* 237). Fortunately, the sequence does not end on that note but instead with "Mackenzie River" (1963),[24] the final lines of which succeed brilliantly in investing the river and the North with poignant cultural significance:

> A river so Canadian
>   it turns its back
>   on America
>
> The Arctic shore
>   receives the vast flow
>   a maze of ponds and dikes
>
> In land so bleak and bare
>   a single plume of smoke
>   is the scroll of history.
> (*Collected Poems* 239)

That the "plume" of Scott's penultimate line evokes the "feathers … in the helmet of an adventurous knight" as well as "Indian smoke signals" and the French word for "pen" (Djwa 331) is almost to be expected, for in "Mackenzie River" distance has restored enchantment and romance to the North by rendering invisible the architectural evidences of alien exploration that had occasioned so much of the satire and irony of the preceding "Letters."[25] Those evidences had been registered and understood for what they were, however, and, despite the regressive conclusion of "Mackenzie River," the North would never again be seen by Scott as a "scroll" upon which a brighter future would be inscribed.

Of course, "Letters from the Mackenzie River" are not the last poems in which Scott combines architectural observation and social or political commentary. Less than a year after returning from his northern tour in September 1956, he revisited his long-standing hostility to William Lyon Mackenzie King (who died in 1950) in "W.L.M.K.," a mordant satire whose fragmentary form serves as a fitting reflection not only of King's deformation of Canada ("We had no shape / Because he never took sides / And no

sides / Because he never allowed them to take shape") but also of the collection of "ruins" (*Collected Poems* 78) that he assembled on his estate near
Ottawa (and which are themselves surely a manifestation of his fixation
on "longevity" and on lost objects of desire, particularly his mother).[26] In
the ensuing years, Scott continued to find material for thought and poetry
in architectural structures and built environments. "What is it makes a
church so like a poem?" he asks in "Unison" (1963): "The inner silence—
spaces between words? … The ancient pews set out in rhyming rows…?"
His full answer—that it is the "unfolding of the heart / That lifts us upward
in a blaze of light / And turns a nave of stone or page of words / To Holy,
Holy, Holy without end" (*Collected Poems* 138)—is a message repeated
many times over in increasingly ecumenical and humanistic terms in his
works of the 1960s and 1970s—in his perception of the "great temples
and tombs" of Asia, Europe, North Africa, and South America as empty
"shells" that reverberate with "the old far sound / Of tides in this human
sea" in "Journey" (1962), in his affirmation of the power of human love to
"bridge" divisions and create unity in "Place de la Concorde" (1969), and
in his unflagging conviction, first fully articulated in "The State as a Work
of Art" in 1950, that "beauty" is a term that can and should be applied to
society as well as art (*Collected Poems* 128, 158–59).

In *Vers une architecture*, Le Corbusier confronts his "epoch" with a stark
choice: "*Architecture or Revolution*"; either address society's problems
through "building" or allow the "alarming symptoms" of social discontent
to erupt into violence (265, 288–89). Neither Scott nor Klein had such faith
in the power of architecture per se to remedy society's ills, but clearly both
poets perceived architectural structures and built environments as, in some
instances, manifestations of deep-seated social problems and, in others,
contributions to their inhabitants' sense of connectedness with one another
and with the external world. Whether repressive or comforting, dismaying
or heartening, the Canadian buildings, towns, and cities that figure in the
architexts of Scott, Klein, and other modern Canadian poets are products
of the "epoch" that has come to be known as the short twentieth century.
Inspired by actual entities that, in most cases, are still available for refer-
encing, they are also—to quote Klein's "Montreal" again—"Mental" as well
as textual reminders of those fraught and terrible years between the First
World War and the demolition of the Berlin Wall when horror and anxiety
about human beings' newly manifest capacity for inhumanity and destruc-

tiveness generated perhaps unprecedented levels of dismay at the current state of things, nostalgia for a better past, and hope for a better future. At the close of the final prose poem in Italo Calvino's *La Cita invisibli* (1972), Marco Polo counters the Great Khan's contention that civilization is drawing ever closer to "*the infernal city*" by urging him to recognize that the "*inferno of the living…, if there is one, … is what is already here…where we live today*" and to adopt an attitude of "constant vigilance and apprehension" that will enable him to "recognize who and what … are not inferno" and "then [to] make them endure, give them space" (165). It is advice that A.M. Klein and F.R. Scott had already followed, nowhere more darkly than in the unfinished Dostoevskyan, Joycean, and Kafkaesque novel of alienation to which Klein gave the title "Stranger and Afraid."

IV

Klein began work on "Stranger and Afraid" during the period between the publication of *The Hitleriad* (1944) and *The Rocking Chair and Other Poems* (1948) when he was writing and revising the poems about Montreal that were collected in the latter volume. Narrated by its partly autobiographical protagonist, a convict named Drizen ("Thirteen") who has been imprisoned in Montreal's Bordeaux Jail for a "mysterious, unknown crime," the unfinished novel contains "vivid recollections" and observations of Montreal that, as Zailig Pollock suggests in his introduction to *The Notebooks: Selections from the A.M. Klein Papers* (1994), "constitute the most elaborate description of the city in Klein's work" and the "counterpart of the Montreal poems in *The Rocking Chair*" (xi–xii). Of special interest here for their extraordinarily perceptive and imaginative responses to Montreal's architectural structures and built environment are three portions of Drizen's narrative: his account of travelling in a van from the Montreal Court House (Palais de Justice) "a few blocks" from the eastern shore of Montreal Island to Bordeaux Jail near the opposite shore, his description of the jail itself, and his imaginary "superimposition … [of] the cartographic outlines of the Island" on the floor of his cell as an exercise in mnemonics (*Notebooks* 63, 87).

As he is transported from east to west "across the whole length of [Montreal] Island" in "a large coffin-like vehicle" with no windows, Klein's Underground Man experiences the heightening of intellectual and imaginative awareness that can sometimes accompany sensory deprivation.

Unable to "make out the route" that the van is following or to see the passing cityscape, he ponders the "ingenious paradox" of being "bound" and yet in motion and attempts "at least to catch [Montreal's] vagrant sounds" and from them deduce his location in "the impersonal city which he love[s]" (*Notebooks* 63). As well as being a variation on the imaginative return to scenes of alienation that is characteristic of Underground Men, the result is akin to an urban psychogeography in its evocation of the physical and psychological ambiance of the city in the mid-1940s. As Drizen recounts his enforced and sightless journey across Montreal, the streets of its various zones are figured as an animal that sounds by turns aggressive ("growling") and peaceable ("purring"), friendly and alienating:

> Now … we are travelling over one of the older streets, the cobbles gabble with antiquity. Now we have approached an intersection— the brakes have screeched, and the van has hunched and slowed down.… We are on a tram-route now, and the round rumble of steel growling announces a streetcar travelling by. Now we are travelling upon asphalt, the sound is the sound of the purring intimacy of rubber and macadam. The voices of children: *Les Prisonniers, Les Prisonniers*. This must be the East End, and our passing a daily interruption of the children's play. They must wait for it, as for the iceman's waggon, the baker's horse. And then a quiet street, and the voices of women as across a clothesline. An intersection again; the honk of a horn, and a truckdriver's curse. A long stretch, and not smooth riding; I can hear the crunch of clods of ice, thrown on the road to melt. (*Notebooks* 63)

To exploit the capacity of sounds to provoke memories and feelings in this sequence of sharply realized observations, Klein draws on his knowledge and experience of Montreal to give Underground Man a distinctively Canadian location and identity and to convey a vivid sense of Montreal as an "impersonal" metropolis that is nevertheless intimately known because it has been lived in by Drizen and now lives within him. As the journey towards Bordeaux Jail continues, the number of turns made by the van destroys Drizen's ability to "name … streets" and "surmise direction" so he "give[s] up eavesdropping on the outer world" and reconciles himself to the "riddlesome and labyrinthine" "darkness and bewilderment" of modernity for which his imprisonment is clearly a metaphor. It is part of the brilliance and power of "Stranger and Afraid" that it presents Drizen as a man in the process of becoming an outsider (*étranger*) and thus renders the situation of the alienated modern self as a loss rather than a fact, a cause for regret as well as documentation.

In the ensuing paragraphs, the "native city" (*Notebooks* 68) that emerges from Drizen's recollections after his incarceration in the Bordeaux Jail is both a home place and the place of his home, a Montreal of ethnic zones and racist texts, physical boundaries and psychological assaults, to which, as Jews, he, his family, and his friends are continually exposed. Notice especially the way in which, near the end of Drizen's recollections, racism causes him to postpone his reading of poetry and to see the ethnic group of which he is a member as grotesque, threatening, and vulnerable to obliteration:

> On our way home, we have to pass the streets where the Frenchies live. At the corner a group of boys, somewhat older than ourselves, stands scrutinizing us. Suddenly ... they burst out in song: Meestah with da wheeskas! Meestah with the wheeskas! We hurry on, afraid.... Safely away from them, on the other side of the ghetto boundary, we turn back, and yell: Pea-soup! French pea-soup!
>
> •   •   •
>
> At the corner of St. Denis and Ste. Catherine, I have just bought, at the French bookstore, *Les Fleurs du Mal*. I am waiting for the streetcar home, and in the meantime I read the large type on the newspapers suspended outside the corner kiosk.... On [the] cover [of *Le Chameau*] there is displayed an ugly cartoon—a frightened female, scrolled Quebec, and a leering Jew hovering over her, all nose and lechery. *La verité,* ... says [the newspaper vendor], *pour cinq sous.* I give him his nickel for the truth. I will read this before the poetry.
>
> I am walking with my father to the synagogue.... We arrive and find that the door of the synagogue is scribbled over with all kinds of symbols and graffiti. In the centre is a double triangle, a swastika superimposed upon it, as if to cancel it out. (*Notebooks* 68–69)

Looking back on these and other manifestations of racism, Drizen at first attempts to dismiss them as "anomalies" but then recognizes that he has so internalized them that they have become a major component of his identity as a fearful stranger:

> [A]s I pause to consider my Self, myself, the focus taken from off my
> environment, I am amazed to discover that these things have never
> passed through my consciousness, as through a sieve, at all, at all.
> They cling to my mind, and at the most unwelcome moments reveal
> themselves in the strangest forms. I meet a casual acquaintance on
> the street, engage in conversation, and am soon embarrassingly aware
> that he is talking too loud, his thoughtways, his inflections are objec-
> tionably Jewish. Objectionable to whom? I shudder at the revelation:
> objectionable to me.... I walk into a room, and unintentionally and
> unknowing gravitate towards my own—it is I who make the ghetto
> bench. A horrible dialectics has taken place. The hater has converted
> the hated. (*Notebooks* 70–71)

In recognizing that the "Self" is not separate from its "environment" but to
a significant extent a product of it, Drizen uses a terminology of emana-
tion, reflection, and convergence—"the focus taken from off"—that indicates the complexity of the process of transference that he finally labels
"[a] horrible dialectics." The "Self" that Drizen "pause[s]" to consider" is
as immaterial as an effect of light—but an effect of light whose trajectory
and intensity have been determined by its situation within the physical and
psychic space of a city demarcated both spatially and textually by modern
racism.

The description of Bordeaux Jail[27] that constitutes the architectural epicentre of "Stranger and Afraid" has as its historical and textual
context not only the racism of mid-1940s Montreal but also the black
hole in human nature that led to the Holocaust. In "Portrait of the Poet
as Landscape," the archetypal modern poet imagines himself "Set apart,
/ ... with special haircut and dress, / as on a reservation," and in "Indian
Reservation: Caughnawaga" the Iroquois reserve near Montreal is figured
as "a grassy ghetto, and no home" in which the inmates and their culture
are all but extinct (*Complete Poems* 2: 637, 642). In "Stranger and Afraid,"
Drizen describes Bordeaux Jail as seen from the outside as an enormous
and utterly opaque site of nullity and seeks metaphors in the realm of the
inhuman to render its "ugly geometry": it is "like some huge and cara-
paced monster, motionless in the sun"; its "ponderous dome" is "like a
heavy leaden weight" that is "held down" by "the cupped hand of a giant";

its "solidity and weight" invite the thought that "some eccentric architect had thought to design the model dwelling-place for the force of gravity" (*Notebooks* 79), that force whose "gape" human aspiration continually attempts to "defy," whether physically, poetically, or spiritually (*Complete Poems* 2: 638). No less than the Pritzker Prize-winning Austrian architect Hans Hollein (1934–), Klein was apparently struck by the "enigmatic and sinister metaphoric power of large structures set in a rural or a wild landscape" (Rykwert [x]), a combination that prompted Thomas Moore in 1804 to liken Quebec City to "a hog in armour upon a bed of roses" (*Letters* 1: 79).[28] The jail's "walls, pierced only by ... regularly placed slits, seem black as if of some metal, all else implacable blankness," continues Drizen, and

> the dome, the dome again, it suffocated thought; and then the outer walls, thick, impenetrable, not to be climbed, a cement negation. The intrusion upon our view [when driving towards the Laurentian Mountains], sudden, and in ... bucolic surroundings so unexpected, of this bastille oppressed us; its stone, its steel, its cement dungeoned our spirits; we felt as if in the midst of density itself, encased in the heart of some irrefragable tremendous solidarity. We sped on, across the bridge ... onto the highway; in a few moments we ... gave ourselves over to a full enjoyment of the more splendid and less terrifying dome which extended all above us. (*Notebooks* 79)

A structure intended to communicate feelings of fear and security[29]—fear of crime and punishment and security from knowing that its inmates cannot escape—the Bordeaux Jail does more in this passage than temporarily curtail the freedom and expansiveness of Drizen and his companion as they head for the open road and the Laurentian Mountains. Like a vast, man-made gravitational device, it draws matter and thought down and into itself in a nullification so monstrous, so nearly complete, and so seemingly inhuman as to beggar description and defy explanation, except as a simulacrum of the "impenetrable" "negation" that Drizen never names: the concentration camps, the gas chambers, and the ovens of the Holocaust.

In the second of two paragraphs on Bordeaux Jail whose suggestive density matches the density attributed to the structure itself, Drizen contrasts his response to the prison from the outside to his experience of it as a prisoner. Besides indicating a full understanding on Klein's part of the "central-inspection principle" from which Jeremy Bentham developed the notion of the panopticon (4: 40),[30] the penal structure brought to prominence in postmodern thought by Michel Foucault's *Surveiller et Punir : naissance de la prison* (1975; trans. 1977), the description of the interior of Bordeaux Jail takes the reader further into the consciousness of an individual who, like his ancestors in Dostoyevsky and Kafka, has been forced to exist in and yet without both community and solitude:

> … now that I am … within this solid brick interred, it is not all its heaviness which is my burden. On the contrary, it is the systematic and designed transparency of this place—yes, transparency—which afflicts me. I realize now that the dome was no dome, but a bell-jar under which might be viewed, as by a passionless scientist, the insects that lie beneath it, and vainly crawl up its walls. Indeed, in the very hub from which the six spokes of the prison extend, there sits a turnkey; there he is placed so that he may at will have look-out upon all the sides of his hexagonal domain. This point of advantage is called a panoptikon, an all-seeing Eye; like God's. No one can pass along or across any of these extending corridors without being spied by the watchful overseer. He sees everything. His agents and subordinates, moreover, stroll along these self-same corridors, and peer, as the inclination prompts them, into our cells. They are made of stone and steel, for exit; for entrance, for inspection, they are all lucidity. One is isolated, but one is never alone; always a pair of eyes is on its way to catch you in seclusion's occupations, shameful or innocent. If that is not enough, your very thoughts are subjected to close censorious scrutiny, and, when they think necessary, deleted. So they look at you from on top, and they look at you from the side—this is not a mortared tomb, but a glass case.
>
> I am a smear on a slide of a microscope. (*Notebooks* 79–80)

The effect of what Bentham calls "the *apparent omnipresence* of the inspector" (4: 45) is thus a "systematic" and progressive dehumanization that leaves the "I" intact but emptied, minified, and almost as two-dimensional as the caricatures in *Le Chameau*. Taken together, Drizen's responses to Bordeaux Jail from the outside and from the inside reflect Klein's recognition in the wake of the Holocaust that "transparency" *within* opacity—

total control and "lucidity" within an utterly dark and "impenetrable" structure—furnishes authority with the means and the opportunity to view people as "insects," to scrutinize and erase "thoughts," to reduce the "Self" to a "smear." The Bordeaux Jail of "Stranger and Afraid" is tied referentially to a prison complex on Montreal Island, but its dark psychic energies also flow from other "model dwelling-places for the force of gravity" such as those in the woods near Auschwitz and Treblinka and Buchenwald.

A few paragraphs before Drizen's narrative descends into Joycean word-play and then breaks off, he renders Montreal and the past present in his cell by engaging in what he calls "the game of superimposition":

> Given the area of the cell as the size of … [a] map I superimpose thereon the cartographic outlines of the Island of Montreal. It fits— nine miles wide, twenty-seven miles long. Here is the Back River, as indeed, there it is; here the city of Westmount—self-contained houses, flower-beds, cellar-garages; and here Sherbrooke Street full of nursemaids wheeling perambulators and gentlemen walking canes. A quiltwork, patched and parallelogrammed, with the city's wards: Laurier, Ste. Cunegonde, Ahuntsic, Mercier, Montcalm, Villeray, St. Jean Baptiste, Notre Dame de Grace, Papineau, Cremazie. My world, my cosmos. The quadrature of the globe. All time and space within my cubits four. (*Notebooks* 87)

Having laid out this *aide-de-mémoire* and conjured up his city through the romance of its place names, Drizen returns in imagination to three psychologically charged and potentially cathartic settings in his mappemounde: "the cemetery of the Chevra Thillim Linath Hatzedek" where "four feet underground [his] father lies," "Fletcher's field" on Mount Royal where he and a friend "sat down, and hung [their] coats upon a crabapple tree,… and snoozed …, and dreamed," and the Montreal "Art Gallery" where "in Maia's month" the "barbaroi" did "chatter and lalagate … enchiridion in hand" (*Notebooks* 88). Entered by way of a psychogeographical map, Drizen's Montreal is here a place haunted not only by memories of people but also by texts that in some cases—*The Waste Land*, the *Oxford English Dictionary*, and, of course, *Ulysses* and *Finnegans Wake*—are in turn haunted by other texts. (For example, "four feet underground my father lies" may be a direct echo of *The Tempest* or an echo of *The Waste Land*, as is "we sat down, and hung our coats upon a crabapple tree.") The sense that both narrator and author are slipping into an insanity characterized by detachment from reality and verbal obsession becomes inescapable when an allusion to Samuel Butler's "Psalm of Montreal" provides the pretext[31] first for the contemptuous (and Eliotic) attack on chattering gallery-goers that was quoted a moment ago and then for the logorrhoeac (and Joycean) diatribe with which "Stranger and Afraid" moves towards silence:

> O georgic, bucolic, architectonic, this patria is no country for art. Pragma & Gasteropragma—this the bride Kalla, that the sister Agatha. Numismatic is the true hedonic. Along galactic marble they walk—the patrons—through hyaline corridors, accomplishing a rite. Gemmadactylate towards glucosity; to callipyginous marmour [   ]. Their rhetoric is of the morphology Kanadian: hyperborean landscape with dryads anemonate; zeugmic hippos at hespertime; halcyon biograph; the oneiratic West; Lake Superior brontapopulect; portrait of the archon of the Kappa Pi Rho.
>
> They admire; but anaesthetes, psilaformal is their panegyric. Not this their sarcocarp; unpragmatic. The dolytrichose—for them these ikons and chormes. For them the hoi phalloi, the proctoscopists— these gluteal petrifactions, alpha and omega, genesis and eschatology. But not for heroes and athletes [   ]. (*Notebooks* 88–89)

Anything like a complete unpacking of this pastiche with variations from *Ulysses, Finnegans Wake,* and in one instance ("portrait of the archon of the Kappa Pi Rho") *Portrait of the Artist as a Young Man* would take several paragraphs and would probably be more trouble than warranted or necessary, for surely its gist is clear enough: the people of Kanada (spelt with a K like Marx's "Kapital" and Kafka's "Amerika") are too rural, provincial, rigid, practical, hedonistic, materialistic, and backward to appreciate art and beauty, specifically the modern art and sophisticated classicism that are valorized both in the passage's Joycean wordplay and in its esoteric allusions.[32] The passage as a whole is the cry of a modernist, a socialist, and an aesthete in the wilderness of the Canadian Goths and Philistines, and, of course, it gains poignancy from the slide into silence and suicide that it seems to prefigure. Here in the madness of proliferating meanings lies a marker on the road of Canadian modernism that led some writers from the "difficult, lonely music" (12) of A.J.M Smith's "Like Old Proud King in a Parable" to the dark hole at the centre of the short twentieth century that claimed first Klein's voice and then his life.

Figure 1. Grain Elevator No. 2, from Le Corbusier, *Towards a New Architecture* (28).

Figure 2. Bordeaux Jail, from William Henry Atherton, *Montreal* (2: facing 418).

[1] For a discussion of "Like an Old Proud King in a Parable" in the context of other Canadian manifestations of what David Trotter has called "paranoid modernism," see Bentley, "Psychoanalytical Notes." The notion that poetry should be pure in the sense of above morality and social relevance would have reached Smith by various channels in the 1920s, including George Moore's *Pure Poetry: An Anthology* (1924) and Henri Brémond's *La Poésie pure* (1926).

[2] See the chapter entitled "Mass-production Houses" in *Vers une architecture/ Towards a New Architecture*, particularly (in the translation) 234–36:

> One thing leads to another, and as many cannons, airplanes, lorries and wagons had been made in factories, someone asks the question: 'Why not make houses?' There you have a state of mind really belonging to our epoch. Nothing is ready, but everything can be done…. In the next twenty years …[d]wellings, urban and suburban will be enormous and square-built and no longer a dismal congeries; they will incorporate the principle of mass production and of large-scale industrialization.

Sjostrom's *Prefabrication in Timber* is one of the architectural works mentioned in the appendix on "Prefabrication and Building Techniques" (see 297n) in the Report of the Curtis Commission, the others being Arthur C. Holden's "Prefabrication" in the *Review of the Society of Residential Appraisers* and A. Bruce and H. Sandbank's *A History of Prefabrication*.

[3] The compositional dates of Klein's poems are based on those provided or conjectured by Zailig Pollock in his edition of the *Complete Poems*.

[4] As Joshua Wolfe observes in "Architectural Heritage: More than Preserving Old Buildings," "Grain Elevator No. 2, at the foot of Place Jacques Cartier [in Montreal], acquired international fame when the Swiss architect Le Corbusier included a photograph of it in his seminal work *Vers une Architecture*" (146). Both Grain Elevator No. 1 and Grain Elevator No. 2 were demolished in the 1980s, the latter, as Wolfe observes, "not only because some considered it ugly, but also because it was out of scale with Place Jacques Cartier and blocked the view of the St. Lawrence River" (149).

[5] For discussions of Klein's dialectics, see Pollock, *A.M. Klein* 151–58, 160–63, 175–79, 243–49, and elsewhere, and Bentley, "Klein, Montreal, and Mankind."

[6] Klein's mimetic use of form is further discussed in Bentley, *The Gay]Grey Moose*

31–32, 201–09, and 214–15. In "The Poetry of A.M. Klein" 62–63, Noreen Golfman quotes Klein's comparison of Petrarchan sonnets to the "self-contained cottages" of "suburbia" in an early notebook as an anticipation of "his preoccupation with spatial arrangement in [his] later work, especially in *The Rocking Chair* poems."

[7] After quoting Charlevoix's observation in *Building a House in New France*, Peter N. Moogk comments that "[a]fter the irregularity of Quebec and Trois-Rivières, Montreal appeared orderly and regular, even if the streets within the town were not really regular" (14). See Harold Kalman's *A History of Canadian Architecture* 1: 247 for a reproduction of the 1704 plan for Montreal and 1: 250 for the British superimposition of a "regular gridiron" on the French plan in the early nineteenth century.

[8] See *Collected Poems* 2: 648–49 for Klein's grateful tribute to the hospital's nursing sisters, "For the Sisters of the Hotel Dieu."

[9] This and other phrases from T.S. Eliot's *The Waste Land*, particularly "O city, city" (*Collected Poems* 73), are repeatedly echoed by Klein in his poems about Montreal, a prominent instance being in the opening lines of the first and final stanzas of "Montreal": "O city metropole" and "City, O city" (*Complete Poems* 2: 621, 623).

[10] Pollock notes that "[t]he statue of Maisonneuve in Place d'Armes has four figures at its base, including an Iroquois" (Klein, *Complete Poems* 2: 998).

[11] The reference here is probably to the Bank of Montreal building that was designed by John Wells and built beside the bank's original home in 1845–48. A product of "the Palladian-Gibbsian tradition of England and Scotland," it "features a large freestanding classical portico" (Kalman 1: 249) that is indeed "pillar'd and vast."

[12] See also Pollock, *A.M. Klein* 120 for the last two stanzas of "Montreal" as "meditations on the passage of time, centring on the relationship of the body and the city" in such a way as to fuse "the ideal and the real, the city and the body," so completely that "the poet's body has been transformed into a place of residence for a living community."

[13] The compositional dates of Scott's poems are based on those provided in the index to his *Collected Poems*.

[14] As Sandra Djwa points out, these last lines are a poetic expression of the CCF programme of "northern social and economic development" (227). They may also be a reflection of Lester B. Pearson's call for more scientific co-operation among arctic nations in "Canada Looks 'Down North'" (1945–46). "Canada desires to work not only with the United States, but with all the Arctic countries—Denmark (for Greenland), Norway and the Soviet Union—in exploiting to the full the peaceful possibilities of the Northern Hemisphere," Pearson wrote; "[p]articularly is this true of the U.S.S.R., which is well ahead of the rest of the world in the development of its polar areas and which, Canadians are beginning to realize, is their neighbour across the North Pole" (643–44). Pearson's essay also contains some

astute observations on the importance of the aeroplane for the perception and development of the North:

> The war and the aeroplane have driven home to Canadians the impor-
> tance of this Northland, in strategy, in resources and in communica-
> tions. We should no longer be deceived by the flat maps and 'frigid
> wasteland' tales of our public school geographies. The earth remains
> round, and the shortest routes between many important spots on it
> lie across Arctic ice and over the North Pole…. There was little use
> discovering gold or oil or radium in the Canadian Arctic thirty years
> ago. You could not get the mining machinery in or the ore product
> out. Aviation has changed all that…. The northern skies are humming
> with activity; smoke is coming from northern chimneys; adventurous
> settlers are moving in. (638, 645)

The striking resemblances between Pearson's essay and "Laurentian Shield" raise the possibility that it provided some of the inspiration for Scott's poem. That the poem also carries the unfortunate implication that in the future Canada should be "link[ed]" with Stalinist Russia raises the further issue, which is too complex to address here, of Scott's attitude to Stalin and Stalinism as expressed, for example, in "Impressions of a Tour of the u.s.s.r." and in "The State as a Work of Art" 15–17 (and see Ware 830–31 for a valuable point of entry to the issue and Campbell for a pertinent discussion of Scott's social vision).

[15] See *Malcolm's Katie* 2: 230–39. Scott's lack of apparent concern is all the more surprising in view of his manifest sensitivity to environmental issues in earlier and later poems and in light of the fact that other writers, most notably Malcolm MacDonald in *Down North* (1943), had written eloquently of the devastating effects of northern development on the natural environment (see MacDonald 176ff. and Grant, "Northern Nationalists" 50–51).

[16] The date of Scott's paper is given on an anonymous typescript in the F.R. Scott Fonds, MG30 D211, box 80, file 12. The Scott Fonds (MG 30 D 211, box 82, file 24) contain two undated typescripts of the paper, the first of which bears the title "Beauty in Society," which has been changed to "The State as a Work of Art," which is the title of the second. All quotations are from the latter. I am grateful to Dean Irvine for procuring me a copy of Scott's paper and furnishing me with a transcript of the anonymous note.

[17] In addition to Abele, see Coates and Morrison; Asch; Grant, "Northern" and *Sovereignty*; Judd; Rees; Diubaldo; and Dacks. In "Social Notes I, 1932" and "Dew Lines 1956" Scott brings his irony to bear on the American exploitation of Canada's natural resources and on the American military presence in the Canadian North (*Collected Poems* 65, 295).

[18] Abele observes that "nomadic and scattered native societies were induced and persuaded" to locate in "[l]ow-rent housing ... in settlements" in order "to facilitate the delivery of educational, medical, and social services" (315), Dacks remarks that one of the results of "northern urbanization" was "welfare dependence" (35), and Judd cites a 1964 survey showing that "of some 817 one-room houses in the Arctic ... the majority ... contained from five to eight people" (348).

[19] See Abele for a balanced assessment of southern attitudes to northern Native peoples (they were "'disadvantaged'" but with assistance could become "full and equal ... Canadian citizens" both economically and politically) and the reasons for the lack of consultation with the Native peoples themselves ("in this period, only a handful of people in Canada had any level of knowledge about northern native societies, communication with and among these societies was inhibited by linguistic, technological, and geographical barriers, and there were powerful economic and social welfare incentives to proceed quickly" [315]).

[20] See also Scott, *Collected Poems* 271 for the irony of Coca-Cola's sponsorship of a Canadian Centenary Council document.

[21] The fact that Sweden had been an increasingly socialistic state since the introduction of workmen's compensation legislation had, of course, made it a darling of left and left-liberal intellectuals.

[22] There are prelusive references to Aklavik/E-3 in "The Camp at Bell Rock" and "Steve, the Carpenter" (*Collected Poems* 224, 228).

[23] This judgment came from one of the participants in the ceremony, who observed that "the whites included four representatives from Northwest Territories constituencies, elected in most cases by native majorities; and the site [E-3] ... was [then] merely a construction camp in the wilderness; there was no resident native community to come to the meeting" (Djwa 332).

[24] The poem is so dated in the index to Scott's *Collected Poems*, but it may well have been partly or even wholly composed in 1956 or shortly thereafter.

[25] See also Scott's "Trans Canada" (1943) and "Landing" (1967) in *Collected Poems* 56–57.

[26] For a discussion of the fitness of the fragmentary form of the subject matter of "W.L.M.K." see Bentley, *The Gay]Grey Moose* 34–35 and 99.

[27] Bordeaux Jail was built in 1907–12 as a result of the Quebec government's recognition in 1890 that the number of male prisoners in the Montreal area had grown beyond the capacity of the existing Pied de Courant Jail. Built on land in the Bordeaux district of the city near Rivière-des-Prairies and intended to house 1200 prisoners, it was modelled on prisons in the Belgian system in which different types of criminals are separated so that they cannot influence each other (Di Lenardo n. pag.). Its architects were Marchand and Brossard, whose senior partner, J.-Omer Marchand (1872–1936), had recently designed the Maison Mère des Soeurs de la

Congrégation de Notre-Dame (1905–08) and the cathedral (1907) in St. Boniface, Manitoba and would subsequently work with John A. Pearson (1867–1940) on the Centre Block of the Parliament Buildings (1916–27) in Ottawa (see Kalman 2: 589–91 and 712). (The St. Boniface Cathedral was destroyed by fire in 1969, the Maison Mère is now the CÉGEP Dawson, and, of course, the Centre Block remains a stamping ground for buffoons.) As can be seen from the illustration above (fig. 2), the Bordeaux Jail is topped by a cupola in the Romanesque Beaux-Arts style that makes it squatly reminiscent of a late nineteenth-century American state capitol (or, indeed, a western Canadian provincial parliament building). In addition to housing the surveillance tower, the cupola contains the prison's Roman Catholic chapel, which, together with the Protestant chapel above the guard house, reflected current beliefs in the importance of religion in the penitential process. The Jail's six wings, one of which is truncated to make provision for the guard house, are surrounded by two sets of walls, the inner 16 feet (4.88 metres) and the outer 25 feet (7.62 metres) high (Di Lenardo n. pag.). Both walls are constructed of reinforced concrete with pillars every 30 feet (9.14 metres). The motif on the two-storey entrance building was described by the prison governor who helped to design the Jail as a "triumphal arch" (Di Lenardo n. pag.).

[28] See Thomsen 122 for an illustration of Hollein's *Railroad Car Monument* (1963), one of several works that reflect his exploration of the impact of large man-made forms in open landscapes (another is his *Flugzeugträger in der Landschaft* [*Aircraft Carrier in a Landscape*] [1964]). In "One More Utopia," a short story of 1945, Klein's narrator describes a "skyscraper" in "rolling grounds," observing how "[i]ncongrous [is] ... this metropolitan architecture midst country scenery" (217). See also Lee Calkins's "Dorchester Prison" (1991), where the New Brunswick jail's "towers stand / tall against the fields ... —an ancient castle structure / brooding on the pastures / of the nearby farms" (12).

[29] See Tuan 187–201 for a perceptive discussion of this aspect of prisons.

[30] In elaborating the principle, Bentham explains that the purpose of having an "inspector" who is able to "*see ... without being seen*"—is to give the prison inmates the sense that they are "always ... under inspection, at least as standing a great chance of being so" (4: 44–45).

[31] Pollock notes that the lines surrounding the word "Discoboloi" in Klein's text refer to Butler's denigration of Montreal and Montrealers after discovering that in the Montreal Museum of Natural History a plaster cast of the "Discobolus" (Discus-Thrower) was "banished from public view to a room where were all manner of skins, plants, snakes, etc., and ... an old man stuffing an owl," who explained that antiques were not placed on display because they were considered "'rather vulgar'" (Butler, *Works* 20: 392; and see Klein, *Notebooks* 222).

[32] A request for Joycean assistance with the passage that my colleague Michael

Groden very kindly sent to two chat groups yielded a wealth of responses: Robert Janusko (who shares Klein's fascination with the Oxen of the Sun episode of *Ulysses*) detected echoes of Joyce's De Quincey pastiche, Ruth Bauerle detected a resemblance to the passage in which Bloom thinks of the naked goddesses in the Kildare Street Museum in Circe, Jack Kelb heard "rhythmic, rather than verbal echoes … of Stephen's more impersonal rememberings and imaginings, e.g., the Jews at the Paris Stock Exchange in Nestor," and Matthew Creasy wondered whether "the 'patria' reference" might echo Bloom's misquoting of Cicero in Eumaeus, where there is "also a reference to the 'hoi polloi,'" and drew attention to "the comic list of 'rites' observed by Bloom during the day in Ithaca." In Klein's "gammadactyl" and "Along galactic marble … callipyginous marmor" Ronald Ewart also heard echoes of Bloom "thinking of the statues of naked goddesses" in Circe, and also of his thoughts about blind people ("Things they learn to do. Read with their fingers. Tune pianos") in Lestrygonians. John Gordon and Clarence Sterling together suggested more than thirty verbal echoes of *Ulysses* and *Finnegans Wake*. I am indebted to all these scholars for their generous help and valuable suggestions.

WORKS CITED

Abele, Frances. "Canadian Contradictions: Forty Years of Northern Political Development." *Interpreting Canada's North: Selected Readings*. Ed. Kenneth S. Coates and William R. Morrison. Toronto: Copp Clark, 1989. 309–32.

Asch, Michael I. "Capital and Economic Development: A Critical Appraisal of the Recommendations of the Mackenzie Valley Pipeline Commission." *Interpreting Canada's North: Selected Readings*. Ed. Kenneth S. Coates and William R. Morrison. Toronto: Copp Clark, 1989. 299–308.

Atherton, William Henry. *Montreal, 1535–1914*. 3 vols. Montreal: S.J. Clarke, 1914.

Auden, W.H. *Selected Poems*. Ed. Edward Mendelson. London: Faber and Faber, 1976.

Bentham, Jeremy. *Works*. Ed. John Bowring. 11 vols. 1838–43. New York: Russell and Russell, 1962.

Bentley, D.M.R. *The Gay]Grey Moose: Essays on the Ecologies and Mythologies of Canadian Poetry, 1690–1990*. Ottawa: U of Ottawa P, 1992.

———. "Klein, Montreal and Mankind." *Journal of Canadian Studies*. Spec. issue. *A.M. Klein's Montreal* 19.2 (summer 1984): 34–57.

———. "Psychoanalytical Notes upon an Autobiographical Account of a Case of Paranoia (*Dementia Paranoides*): Mrs Bentley in Sinclair Ross's *As for Me and My House*." *University of Toronto Quarterly* 73.3 (2004): 262–85.

Butler, Samuel. *Works*. Ed. Henry Festing Jones and A.T. Bartholomew. 22 vols. 1926. New York: AMS, 1968.

Campbell, Wanda. "The Ambiguous Social Vision of F.R. Scott." *Canadian Poetry: Studies, Documents, Reviews* 27 (fall/winter 1990): 1–14.

Canada. *Advisory Committee on Reconstruction. IV: Housing and Community Planning. Final Report of the Subcommittee*. Ottawa: Edmond Cloutier, Printer to the King, 1944.

Calkins, Lee. *Equinox*. Fredericton: Fiddlehead, 1991.

Calvino, Italo. *Invisible Cities*. Trans. William Weaver. London: Vintage, 1997.

Coates, Kenneth S., and William R. Morrison. Introduction. *Interpreting Canada's North: Selected Readings*. Ed. Coates and Morrison. Toronto: Copp Clark, 1989. 1–5.

Crawford, Isabella Valancy. *Malcolm's Katie: A Love Story*. Ed. D.M.R. Bentley. London, ON: Canadian Poetry P, 1987.

Dacks, Gurston. *A Choice of Futures: Politics in the Canadian North*. Toronto: Methuen, 1981.

Di Lenardo, Guido. "Prison." Unpub. essay. Architecture U2. McGill University, 1973.

Diubaldo, Richard. *The Government of Canada and the Inuit, 1900–1967*. Ottawa: Indian and Northern Affairs Canada, 1985.

Djwa, Sandra. *The Politics of the Imagination: A Life of F.R. Scott*. Toronto: McClelland and Stewart, 1987.

Eliot, T.S. *Collected Poems, 1909–1962*. London: Faber and Faber, 1963.

Foucault, Michel. *Discipline and Punish: The Birth of the Prison*. Trans. Alan Sheridan. London: Allen Lane, 1977.

Golfman, Noreen. "The Poetry of A.M. Klein." 2 vols. Diss. University of Western Ontario, 1986.

Grant, Shelagh D. "Northern Nationalists: Visions of 'A New North,' 1940–1950." *For Purposes of Dominion: Essays in Honour of Morris Zaslow*. Ed. Kenneth S. Coates and William R. Morrison. North York: Captus University Publications, 1989. 47–67.

———. *Sovereignty or Security? Government Policy in the Canadian North, 1936–1950*. Vancouver: UBC P, 1988.

Judd, David. "Canada's Northern Policy: Retrospect and Prospect." *Canada's Changing North*. Ed. William C. Wonders. Carleton Library 35. Toronto: McClelland and Stewart, 1971. 338–50.

Kalman, Harold. *A History of Canadian Architecture*. 2 vols. Toronto: Oxford UP, 1994.

Klein, A.M. *Complete Poems*. Ed. Zailig Pollock. 2 vols. Toronto: UTP, 1990.

————. *Notebooks: Selections from the A.M. Klein Papers.* Ed. Zailig Pollock and Usher Caplan. Toronto: UTP, 1994.

————. *Short Stories.* Ed. M.W. Steinberg. Toronto: UTP, 1983.

Le Corbusier. *The City of Tomorrow and Its Planning.* Trans. Frederick Etchells. London: John Rodker, 1929.

————. *Towards a New Architecture.* Trans. from the 13th French ed. by Frederick Etchells, 1931. New York: Dover, 1986.

MacDonald, Malcolm. *Canadian North.* London: Humphrey Milford; Oxford UP, 1945.

————. *Down North.* London: Oxford UP, 1943.

MacLaren, Ian. "The Yeatsian Presence in A.J.M. Smith's 'Like an Old Proud King in a Parable.'" *Canadian Poetry: Studies, Documents, Reviews* 4 (spring/summer 1979): 59–64.

Moogk, Peter N. *Building a House in New France: An Account of the Perplexities of Client and Craftsmen in Early Canada.* Toronto: McClelland and Stewart, 1977.

Moore, Thomas. *Letters.* Ed Wilfred S. Dowden. 2 vols. Oxford: Clarendon, 1964.

Pearson, Lester. "Canada Looks 'Down North.'" *Foreign Affairs* 24 (Oct. 1945–July 1946): 638–47.

Pollock, Zailig. *A.M. Klein: The Story of the Poet.* Toronto: UTP, 1994.

————. Introduction. *Notebooks: Selections from the A.M. Klein Papers.* By A.M. Klein. Ed. Zailig Pollock and Usher Caplan. Toronto: UTP, 1994. ix–xix.

Pool, Annalies. "Norman Wells." *The Canadian Encyclopedia.* 3 vols. Edmonton: Hurtig, 1985. 2: 1266.

Rees, William E. "Development and Planning North of 60E: Past and Future." *Northern Transitions.* Vol. 2. Ed. Robert F. Keith and Janet B. Wright. Ottawa: Canadian Arctic Resources Committee, [1978]. 42–62.

Robson, Robert. "Housing in the Northwest Territories: the Postwar Vision." *Urban History Review* 24 (Oct. 1995): 3–20.

Rossi, Aldo. *The Architecture of the City.* Trans. Diane Ghirardo and John Ockman. Cambridge, Mass: MIT P, 1982.

Rykwert, Joseph. *The Idea of a Town; the Anthropology of Urban Form in Rome, Italy and the Ancient World.* 1988. Cambridge, MS: MIT P, 1999.

Scott, F.R. *Collected Poems.* Toronto: McClelland and Stewart, 1981.

————. "Impressions of a Tour of the U.S.S.R." *Canadian Forum* 15 (1935): 382–85.

————. "The State as a Work of Art." F.R. Scott Fonds. MG30 D211, box 82, file 24. National Archives of Canada, Ottawa.

Smith, A.J.M. *Poems New and Collected.* Toronto: Oxford UP, 1967.

Thomsen, Christian W. *Visionary Architecture from Babylon to Virtual Reality.* Munich and New York: Prestel-Verlag, 1994.

Trotter, David. *Paranoid Modernism: Literary Experiment, Psychosis, and the Professionalization of English Society.* Oxford: Oxford UP, 2001.

Tuan, Yi-Fu. *Landscapes of Fear.* Minneapolis: U of Minnesota P, 1979.

Ware, Tracy. "The Shifting Sand of a Son's Radical Faith in Peter Dale Scott's *Coming to Jakarta: A Poem about Terror.*" *University of Toronto Quarterly* 71.4 (fall 2002): 827–42.

Wiebe, Rudy. *A Discovery of Strangers.* Toronto: Knopf, 1994.

Wolfe, Joshua. "Architectural Heritage: More than Preserving Old Buildings." *Grassroots, Greystones, and Glass Towers.* Ed. Bryan Demchinsky. Montréal: Véhicule, 1989. 145–53.

Wordsworth, William. *Poetical Works.* Ed. E. de Selincourt. 1940. 5 vols. Oxford: Clarendon, 1963.

Yeats, W.B. *Collected Poems.* 2nd ed. 1950. London: Macmillan, 1969.

Mapping Raymond Souster's Toronto

STEPHEN CAIN

That the city is an essential component of literary modernism—as image, as site, as trope—has long been accepted in modernist studies. As Michel de Certeau most succinctly notes, the city "is simultaneously the machinery and the hero of modernity" (155).[1] In Europe, this would include the London of *Mrs. Dalloway*, the Dublin of *Ulysses*, and the Paris of the expatriates—while in the United States there are the examples of Carl Sandburg's Chicago, John Dos Passos's New York, William Carlos Williams's Patterson, and Charles Olson's Gloucester, among others. Yet, in the Canadian context of modernism, clearly represented urban spaces are something of a rarity. With regard to fiction Glenn Willmott, in *Unreal Country: Modernity in the Canadian Novel in English*, argues (following William Arthur Deacon) that the setting of Canadian modernist writing, "despite the unprecedented growth of cities after the turn of the century and the urban experience and culture of authors, is not the city" (61). In terms of poetry, this is also somewhat the case: while the Canadian city is present, it is certainly not predominant. While some metropolitan settings are aestheticized, others are strangely absent and, moreover, some modernist writers in Canada appear to reject the city as subject altogether. For example, Earle Birney writes of his Vancouver but there are few other modernist British Columbian authors who have followed his example. Similarly, many of Canada's major modernist poets, including E.J. Pratt,

Margaret Avison, Anne Wilkinson, and W.W.E. Ross, frequently appear to eschew direct or mimetic representations of specific cities in their writing.

One exception to this absence would be Montreal which, as D.M.R. Bentley observes, has been well-represented by such modernist poets as Leonard Cohen, Irving Layton, Louis Dudek, F.R. Scott, "and, above all," A.M. Klein (34).[2] Surprisingly, however, Montreal's primary urban rival Toronto does not, for the most part, fare as well in terms of poetic documentation. For much of the modernist period, this city appears absent from Canadian poetry, and it is not until the rise of postmodernism, post-colonialism, and feminism that sustained and concrete examinations of Toronto and its districts begin to appear: Joe Rosenblatt's Kensington Market, the Annex environs of bpNichol's *The Martyrology Book 5*, the punk bars and Queen Street watering holes of Lynn Crosbie's "Alphabet City," and the city centre of Dennis Lee's *Civil Elegies*.

Yet, long before Lee was officially made the poet laureate of Toronto, Raymond Souster was the acknowledged poetic chronicler of Toronto. Indeed, Souster has been represented, in both the popular media and in academic criticism, as *the* poet of Toronto for much of the twentieth century.[3] While certain other modernist writers have occasionally used Toronto as a subject for their poetry—such as Miriam Waddington, and Dorothy Livesay in her "Queen City" suite—it is only Souster who has consistently returned to Toronto as subject and inspiration for his verse over a lengthy poetic career of nearly half a century.[4] In doing so, Souster has created a significant body of work that explores the site of urban modernism, and an investigation of his work raises questions about aesthetic representations of the city and its functions in the context of Canadian literary modernism.

Although Malcom Bradbury has noted the importance of cities in both Europe and North America for the development of modernism (96), if Souster has any non-Canadian models for his vision of Toronto as a modernist city they appear to descend less from the Baudelarian lineage that influenced writers such as Eliot and more from the work of USAmerican poets, particularly Williams and Olson. As Souster comments in a 1977 interview: "From Williams, I think of learning, together with Charles Olson, the idea of place, the city" ("Interview" 8). Souster would be more specific in 1983, noting that "[t]he Olson influence isn't the Black Mountain connection. I like the way he wrote about his city, Gloucester, and it made me think I could do the same in terms of Toronto" ("Raymond" 6).

But what has Souster "done" with Toronto? Following Roland Barthes's essay "Semiology and Urbanism," I approach Souster's representation of Toronto by engaging in the semiological act of reading the city. As Barthes suggests, "the most important thing is not so much to multiply investigations or functional studies of the city as to multiply the readings of the city, of which [...] only the writers have given us some examples" (201). My readings of Souster's Toronto follow the first four volumes of his *Collected Poems*, which include poems from 1940 to 1977. These four volumes contain approximately 1400 poems and, as many critics have noted, since Souster's writing does not shift radically over several decades, they can be viewed as representative of his modernism.[5] While reading these four volumes I prepared a concordance of his references to Toronto and its specific landmarks. Rather than seeking a general impression of Toronto as a monolithic entity, this concordance uncovers a textual map of Souster's Toronto and thus identifies specific sites of aesthetic representation. As Barthes comments, "a city is a fabric formed not of equal elements whose functions can be inventoried, but of strong elements and neutral elements, or else, as linguistics tells us, of marked elements and non-marked elements" ("Semiology" 194). What then, are these marked and unmarked places of Souster's Toronto? Which regions of the city are represented poetically and which are excluded?

It should be noted, however, that Souster himself has often rejected the notion that he is solely a Toronto poet: "I've been labelled as a poet of Toronto which may be true, but I've written hundreds of poems about other things" ("Raymond" 12). This is certainly correct; only around 300 or twenty percent of the approximately 1400 poems in the first four volumes of his *Collected Poems* specifically mention Toronto and its sites. In his monograph *Raymond Souster and His Works*, Bruce Whiteman observes that "Humberside, Sunnyside, and High Park in west-central Toronto are to [Souster] what Gloucester was to Charles Olson: extensions of his skin and the objects of his local pride" (1). This is accurate in the sense that specific areas of Toronto are privileged in Souster's work, rather than Toronto as a whole, but unlike Olson (or Williams), Souster does not anthropomorphize the city, nor is the city an extension of his "skin" or his psyche in any proprioceptive way. Instead, places in Toronto serve as loci for poetic expression or observation, and the poet is more often disconnected from his environment than immersed in it.

When generalized, Toronto is often depicted as "a very sleepy Anglo-Saxon city" (Souster, "Raymond" 9), particularly when contrasted with Montreal, to which Souster occasionally travelled. In the early volumes, poems such as "Leaving Montreal" (1: 185), "Toronto O" (2: 169), and "One Face of Toronto" (2: 171) compare the two cities, with the ongoing question of city superiority always falling in favour of Montreal. In the first, the "gleaming" Sherbrooke and "colour[ful]" St. Catherine Streets are contrasted to "Toronto and [its] drabness [...] its slow death [...] wait[ing] to smother" the poet, while in "Toronto O" two unnamed Montreal poets (perhaps Irving Layton and Louis Dudek) "have noted with feeling / the coldness, frustrations / of you, my Toronto" and "cursed your name fondly / all the long drive back / to Montreal." Souster's broad critique of Toronto as "a very sleepy Anglo-Saxon city" is not, however, limited to unfavourable comparisons to Montreal. In "Sleep Toronto" (1: 159), for instance, the poet surveys and assesses his city in an extremely negative light, totalizing Toronto and expressing his ideological objection to the materialism it represents:

> [...] sleep from the putrid Don to the puny Humber,
> sleep from Hog's Hollow all the way to the lake cold and dark,
> sleep down in Cabbagetown, sleep up in Forest Hill,
> sleep soundly on the beds of gold, the bunks of hunger.
>
> Sleep on, knowing well you're both spendthrift and miser,
> bigoted, hypocrite, little wise, much foolish,
> sleep with the dreams of profits, mergers, margins,
> sleep with the dreams of garbage-dump and dole.
>
> Sleep city sleep
> your Yonge Street narrow as the hearts that own you.

Although this poem includes references to locales as far apart as Cabbagetown and Forest Hill and to watercourses as distant from one another as the Humber and the Don Rivers, this is an exception in his oeuvre, and Souster's poetic speaker rarely aestheticizes places so disparate.

If one were to visualize a map of metro Toronto—not including, for example, Scarborough, Etobicoke, or North York—it would cover an area of approximately 400 square kilometres, which incorporates an immense number of parks, businesses, communities, and institutions. Yet if one were to represent Souster's poetic geography of Toronto—the sites that ninety percent of his Toronto poems mark—it would depict a region no larger than sixteen square kilometres. In his work there are few poems describing locales north of Bloor, none concerning areas west of the Humber, and only a handful of sites east of Yonge. This is the extent of Souster's Toronto, a fact of which Souster is aware and that he concedes in a 1983 interview:

> I was born in the west end and have lived all my life in the west-end and I'm still there but I don't know the rest of the city very well. The only part I can say I really know is my own little district—the Runnymede area. I'm not a very adventuresome person. I've just tried to zero in on what I do know—tried to make that my little world, I suppose. ("Raymond" 9)

Although Souster mentions approximately eighty different streets, parks, and buildings within this space—ranging from St. Joseph's Hospital to City Hall, and from Jane Street to University Avenue—these sites can be clustered into three distinct kinds of poetic places: (1) pastoral or peaceful points (Toronto Island [particularly Hanlan's Point], Sunnyside, High Park, Old Mill, and the Humber); (2) points of poverty (streets east of Yonge such as Jarvis, Church, and the Danforth); and (3) problematic points, or sites of "otherness," where the poet encounters the homeless, prostitutes, and other dispossessed individuals. Most often this last site is Yonge Street, but it also extends to the corner of Bay and King. In all of these places it is rare that the locale is actually vividly described, mimetically represented, or articulated as places in and of themselves—rather, they are *sites* for poems: launching pads for pastorals, observational lyrics, and encounters with alterity.

In considering the examples of positive, pastoral places, one might begin with Souster's aestheticization of the Toronto Islands. When invoking Hanlan's Point, the most common representation is that of a dream, as in "Airman Coming Out of a Dream" (1:176) or "A Dream of Hanlan's" (1: 124). Alongside its oneiric status, Hanlan's Point also often serves as a metaphor for the poet's emotional state, as in "The Lagoon" (1: 58) where

"My heart is that Hanlan's lagoon, / quiet, very still in its depths, / cool as the morning wind that rocks / the pads of the water-lily." Rarer is the poem in which a clear image of the site appears—such as "Lagoons, Hanlan's Point" (1: 136) in which the flora and fauna are described. Yet, again, this poem is not an objective description but a dreamlike recollection of a scene where "A small boy / in a flat-bottomed punt [...] mov[es] with wonder / through the antechamber / of a slowly waking world."

Sunnyside Amusement Park and boardwalk are treated in a similar manner, its idyllic nature either invoked in contrast to World War II, as in "False Spring" (1: 36), or as a metaphor for joy, as in "You Are" (1: 170). Even in one of his most anthologized poems, "The Flight of the Roller Coaster" (1: 316)—subtitled "Old Sunnyside Beach, Toronto"—where details are given of amusement rides, ice-cream booths, and crowds, the representation is not one of veracity; it is, rather, a site for a poetic flight of imagination, where the roller-coaster leaves the rails, flies above the witnesses, and "disappear[s] all too soon behind a low-flying flight of clouds."

Considering these idyllic and almost pastoral depictions of the Toronto Islands and Sunnyside alerts one to the fact that to encounter both pastoral and counter-pastoral elements in a modernist author's writing is not an uncommon occurrence. In *All That is Solid Melts into Air*, Marshall Berman illustrates how Charles Baudelaire, who "[i]f we had to nominate a first modernist [...] would surely be the man" (133), begins his writing career in a pastoral mode, praising the success of bourgeois culture, yet due to increasing revulsion at military action and growing mob mentality, moves to a counter-pastoral position "in which modern people and life are endlessly abused, while modern artists and their works are exalted to the skies" (141). In the Canadian context, Bentley has observed a similar structure at work in Klein's *The Rocking Chair*, where poems that appear critical of French-Canadian characters (53) follow paradisal scenes and a "transformation of the city streets into a pastoral landscape" (52). Likewise, in his reading of Morley Callaghan's Toronto novel *Strange Fugitive*, Justin D. Edwards illustrates the consistently expressed dichotomy between the urbanism of downtown Toronto and pastoralism of its parks: "the narrative [...] works to contain [...] the city as a threat by assimilating the social conventions that establish the park as a retreat from urban stresses and steering [the protagonist] to a pastoral space where he is able to think about his future" (218).

Yet Souster has a somewhat different view of the pastoral than Baudelaire, Klein, or Callaghan. Whereas the pastoral vision of Baudelaire is displaced by the counter-pastoral and Klein's and Callaghan's pastorals exist simultaneously with negative impressions of the city, Souster's pastoralism is consistently linked to the past. It is a retrospective pastoralism that more resembles the Romantic conception of this mode than any of his modernist forerunners or peers. That is, many of Souster's poems of positive places appear to follow the pattern of the greater Romantic lyric in which, according to M.H. Abrams, a poetic speaker revisits a scene and the remembered landscape is superimposed on the picture before the viewer; the two landscapes fail to match and this causes a problem for the speaker, which compels a meditation—usually upon time and mortality (76–77). This pattern is clear in several of Souster's poems set at the Humber River and the Old Mill. In "Humber Valley Revisited" (2: 45) the poet observes, "This must be near where we stole / the young, not-yet-ripened carrots / from [...] the farmhouse we knew so well // But the farm's gone now, the field's gone, [...] a nothingness now, a desolation." Similarly, in "Old Mill Bridge" (1: 242), Souster writes: "Under the arch of this bridge twenty years ago / I froze both feet playing hockey [....] Now that bridge is still there, only older, but I don't play hockey any more." Although these poems are modernist in their diction, lineation, and prosody, they follow a Romantic lyric structure.

Souster's shift from pastoralism to urbanism is often paralleled by his movement through Toronto itself. For the most part, Souster's trajectory is not one of a wandering *flâneur*, but more often one of traversing back and forth by subway between two locales—from the west end of the city (where Souster has resided within six blocks of his birthplace for his entire life) to the corner of Bay and King (where he worked at the Canadian Imperial Bank of Commerce for forty-five years until his retirement in 1984). This city core of Bay and King is cited in a significant number of Souster's Toronto poems and, once images and tropes are established, the poems of this district tend to fall into similar patterns. As Barthes reminds us, "[t]he city, essentially and semantically, is the site of our encounter with the other" ("Semiology" 199); this is certainly the case with Souster's poems set in the city's core, which sharply contrast with his portraits of the pastoral west end. East of Yonge is particularly notable as a poverty point: on Jarvis Street the poet encounters sexual otherness through figures such as the prostitute in "Jeanette" (1: 247) or the streetwalkers of "On a Cool November Night" (1: 238), who "hop[e] to catch someone's eye, / anyone with a couple of dollars." The alterity of madness and poverty is also found on Church Street where the speaker tries to avoid "the heavy woman with the limp, / the woman with the crazy look [...] talking mostly to herself" ("Bad Luck" 3: 93). And class difference is examined in "Gerrard Street East" (1: 192) where a lone walker passes "peeling store-fronts, settling houses, smelly alleys, / the unswept sidewalks raising a little dust or a piece of old newspaper."

Yet one need not move past Yonge to encounter the Other in Souster's Toronto. Otherness resides in problematic points, most often on Yonge Street—itself the most frequently aestheticized site of his city, mentioned in over forty of Souster's 300 Toronto poems. Here the most common representation is that of a place of transient encounters with the Other—alcoholics, the homeless, beggars, the mad, religious fanatics, and orphans. While the poet is often sympathetic to these figures, there is also a sense of abjection in his reactions, as in the opening lines of "Nightmare at Noon" (4: 53):

> Suddenly he was there
> on noon-hour Yonge Street,
> in the full glare of winter sunshine.
>
> I had to turn away,
> I couldn't take any more,
> I couldn't watch any longer
> his body wracked with shaking,
> his head snapping down to his knees,
> trunk crazily out of control,
> and all the time his hands
> clutching at the nearest store-front
> with the grip of a drowning man.
>
> I turned away,
> my eyes had had more than enough,
> I wanted to be through with him,
> I wanted no more of his misery,

no more of his twisted life,
I wanted to forget I'd ever seen him.

This scene of abjection and alterity depicts the way in which otherness is often necessitated to construct selfhood—that is, what is projected onto the Other is what one fears in oneself. This is often the case in those encounters in which being poor and alcoholic are potential fates for the speaker, or could have been his fate had he not chosen his middle-class conformity. Thus we find such guilty poems as "It's Time" (2: 272) in which, considering a man asking for a meal, the poet notes:

I've never known
what it is to go hungry
not one single time.
[…]
As for me,
it's time I learned hunger,
it's time I learned to beg my first meal,
it's time I knew
this man's shame.[6]

Despite this "danger," Yonge is also frequently a place of joy and companionship where the speaker visits jazz bars—in such poems as "Yonge Street Saturday Night" (1: 110) or "Jazz Concert, Massey Hall" (1: 156)—or else a site for carnivalesque events, as in "Yonge Street Reopening" (1: 286) or "Ten Elephants on Yonge Street" (3: 70).

Carnival and disruption is, in fact, also inherent Barthes's view of downtown city life, for, as he observes, "the center-city is always experienced as the space in which certain subversive forces act and are encountered, forces of rupture, ludic forces" ("Semiology" 200). Toronto's city centre, New City Hall, is seldom the site for Souster's poetry, but in one case it is certainly subversive and ludic, as expressed in the poem "The Hippies at Nathan Phillips Square" (3: 288) in which, under the eyes of city hall employees

The young, bearded, unkempt boy
camped out below on the Square,
waved a greeting from his sleeping-bag

to the long-haired blonde
with bare toes showing in her sloppy joes,

and helped her
as she wiggled in beside him,
was then last seen as his hand reached out
and zippered up the bag....

In the bright morning sunlight
that sleeping-bag was seen
first to shake, then to roll,
indeed was the most moving thing
in all of Nathan Phillips Square.

Despite this exception, the city centre is more often the site of lone figures such as the early-morning ice athlete in "Skater" (3: 341) or the carefree animal of "Dog in the Fountain" (4: 48).

Yet the city centre need not only be the place of government buildings. To Souster, Bay and King is far more central as it is the intersection to which the poet travelled five days a week for forty-five years, and is thus often the centre of his poetic gaze. This, however, might also be characterized as a problem point: it is at once problematic in that, like Yonge Street, this intersection is often the site for poetic encounters with the Other and causes the poet to consider the problem of poverty or class, and in that this intersection is seldom fully rendered in his poems. As in his depictions of Hanlan's Point or Sunnyside there is no *there* there. Souster rarely invokes the skyscrapers, office buildings, or traffic of this busy intersection. Perhaps then, as Barthes writes of Tokyo in *Empire of Signs*, while there is a clear city centre, it is an empty centre—forbidden and ignored (30). As a sign of the centre's absence, even more strangely, among Souster's 300 Toronto poems in the first four volumes of his *Collected Poems*, only one actually refers to his occupation at the bank or the bank itself. For a poet who has been characterized as a social realist—and in Marxist terms, by Frank Davey, as a poet who has resisted commodification in his desire to remain small in the face of expansive and hegemonic capitalism—the absence of his own labour is a strange lacuna.[7]

But if we are to consider Souster through Marxist theory, he does have one laudable quality compared to his modernist peers when dealing with the city and its inhabitants. In *The Image of the City in Modern Literature*, Burton Pike notes that the typical modernist expression of urban life is one in which an isolated character (often an artist figure) encounters alienating cityscapes and indifferent masses:

> Joyce, Kafka, and Musil, for instance, present isolated individuals moving within cities which for most of the other characters are communities. The protagonists are excluded from these communities and feel their exclusion, although at the same time they may reject the communities as inferior or ignorant. (101)

Yet, in contrast, in Souster's poetry individuals are always emphasized and the masses are rarely present. The conception of the masses is in fact, as Raymond Williams argues, an illusion of bourgeois capitalism and relies on sociological exclusion: "there are in fact no masses; there are only ways of seeing people as masses […] we mass them, and interpret them according to some convenient formula" (qtd. in Pike 111). To Souster's credit, as a social realist he makes his Torontonians individuals first and they are represented as such. While some masses do exist in his work (as the gawkers witnessing a subway suicide or as Christmas shoppers blindly rushing about) these are often capitalist figures (bankers, businessmen) rather than downtrodden proletarians.

Alongside the emptiness of Bay and King we can place the rest of Toronto as part of Souster's exclusions. If, as James Joyce once claimed, were Dublin destroyed, it could be rebuilt from a reading of *Ulysses*,[8] rebuilding Souster's Toronto after the cataclysm would give us, at most, three pockets—the west end of Humber Valley and High Park; the waterfront of Toronto Island and Sunnyside; and the downtown core of Bay, Yonge, and King. This remains consistent throughout fifty years of his work despite the city's transformation. In his architectural study *Accidental City*, Robert Fulford describes the extraordinary developments Toronto has undergone in the last fifty years, beginning with the building of the New City Hall, which caused radical changes in both the character of the city and its inhabitants. Similarly, in "Immigrant City: The Making of Modern Toronto," Harold Troper recounts the amazing changes of the city's demographic since 1950, and the ways in which this diversity has fundamentally altered Toronto's streets and communities. Yet to read Souster's poetry from the 1940s to the 1980s one would never get this impression. While the city changes, Souster's poetry does not; hence, his poetic expression of the city remains static. While more recent events such as the Vietnam War or the emergence of the 1960s countercultures are mentioned in his later work, the representation of these phenomena remains the same and these images merely replace older constructions. That is, the Vietnam War as in "Spring Offensive '72" (4: 63) is opposed and critiqued in the same fashion and tone that World War II was in his earlier work; and, rather than describing pitiful alcoholics wandering Yonge in the 1950s, in the early 1970s Souster now, in poems like "High Noon" (4: 99), depicts stoned hippies but in exactly the same manner:

> Two kids wandering the Yonge Street Mall
> at high noon are also so high
> on grass, speed or whatever,
> they yell out WHEE together [...]
> and are only saved
> by an updraft
> from the cooling system
> of ALWAYS SIX GIRLS COMPLETELY NUDE.

The signifiers in Souster's poetry shift, yet what they signify remains static. This stability has been mentioned by several critics, perhaps most astutely by Douglas Fetherling who warns as early as 1973: "do not be misled by the statement that [Souster] is a great chronicler of the physical city, an archivist. A friend once told me that having read most of Souster's books, he moved to Toronto expecting it to be filled with 1940s taxis, soldiers on leave and crippled newsies, cloth caps sideways on their heads, hawking the *Mail and Empire*" (38).

Many of the changes that Toronto has undergone, as indicated above, are qualities of what might be considered the postmodern city—a city of flux, of multiple architectural and urban spaces, and with a diverse and constantly changing racial and ethnic demographic. Yet what Souster describes in his poetry, even up until the present (his most recent collection from Oberon Press, *Twenty-Three New Poems*, appeared in 2003) is a modernist city: static, mostly corrupt, and a place where a sensitive consciousness is frequently barraged by negative images, situations, and personages. Small moments of happiness can also be found, but mostly in remembrance or in a fleeting encounter with a fellow urban survivor. This refusal to engage with Toronto as a postmodern or even contemporary space might be compared to Souster's own poetics which, despite spanning a period of over half a century, have also remained fairly static. While poetic movements ranging from Projective Verse to Deep Image, to concrete and sound, and to language-centred poetries have emerged in the last fifty years, Souster has largely remained as he began—utilizing imagistic techniques within a conversational, confessional, and observational structure. He continues to be a modernist poet and his Toronto remains a modernist urban space: a limited, static, and imagined city. Not that this representation is an act of mendacity, for Souster represents the city with the personal sense of honesty and accuracy that he carries within himself. It just so happens to be a place where the present is always corrupt, the future foreboding, and the only way it can be seen positively is in retrospect.

NOTES

[1] For other commentaries on modernism and the city see Bradbury's essay, as well as the book-length studies of Spears, Timms, Kelley, and Pike.

[2] While Bentley's article is excellent, it does not provide a model for the type of investigation I wish to conduct in this paper. Bentley uses Klein's poems of Montreal to demonstrate the unified nature of his collection *The Rocking Chair*, and links them to an overall theme of humanism. Other essays from the special issue of the *Journal of Canadian Studies* on "A.M. Klein's Montreal," edited by Zailig Pollock, explore social history and are primarily demographic; see, for example, Tulchinsky. Of these essays, only David Kaufman's approaches my methodology in linking historical and family photos to quotations from Klein's poetry, although his approach is primarily visual rather than textual.

For a more recent foray into the exploration of literary Montreal, which does map various contemporary poetic locales in Montreal and has served as an inspiration for this investigation, see McGimpsey.

[3] Popular views of Toronto's centrality to Souster's work include Greg Gatenby's comment that "Raymond Souster [is] ... for many the ultimate Toronto poet" (355) and Robert Fulford's claim that "Raymond Souster is the poet laureate of the Toronto streets" ("Poet" 63). Similar observations from academic critics include

Munro Beattie's assessment of Souster being "much more the poet of Toronto than Dudek or Layton is the poet of Montreal" (290) and Tom Marshall's assertion that Souster's poetic "universe is, for the most part, the city of Toronto as it is known to a particular sensibility" (79).

[4] Livesay's poem presents the impressions of a speaker who travels to Toronto by train in order to be interviewed "by *The Star* / In an intimate, ingratiating way" (85) at the Royal York Hotel. Livesay's text shares many of the concerns of Souster's poetics—anger at industrialism and class disparity, descriptions of distinct districts in Toronto, and an ear for urban slang and dialect—yet it appears to be a singular moment in her *Collected Poems* (1972). While Livesay has written poems concerning Victoria, Vancouver, Winnipeg, and Montreal, no other piece in her oeuvre appears to so forcefully foreground Toronto as a site of her poetic expression, nor can Livesay be honestly considered a "poet of Toronto." Nevertheless, "Queen City" is a fascinating poem and a comparison between this work and Souster's Toronto writings would require a substantial interrogation, well beyond the scope of this paper. My thanks to Dean Irvine for alerting me to the presence of this sequence.

Similarly, while there are a number of Waddington poems that use Toronto as a site for poetic exploration—notably "The Bond" (1945), "Toronto the Golden Vaulted City" (1966), "Song of North York between Sheppard and Finch" (1966), and "Folkways" (1955) (which is comparable to Souster's "Sleep Toronto" in its pessimism)—she is equally prone to aestheticize Montreal, Winnipeg, or New York throughout her career. Moreover, a great number of Waddington's poems concern an unnamed, perhaps "unreal," metropolis and the general tendency of her verse is to use the city as a trope for alienation and degeneration rather than to mimetically represent specific cities. An analogous case can be made for P.K. Page who, although she has written a number of poems concerning urban malaise, rarely mentions the exact locale or concretely represents the geographic spaces in which these poems are set.

[5] See, for example, Marshall's observation that "the obsessive way in which [Souster] returns to winos, strippers, prostitutes, cripples and wounded animals in poems representing thirty years of work can give the impression of limited range" (80).

[6] Souster's sympathy for the downtrodden, his curiosity about their history, and the thin margin that separates his lifestyle from theirs has remained a constant throughout his career. In a recently published interview with Tony Tremblay, Souster comments:

"people who are having a hard time, sleeping in bus shelters or outdoors in packing cases through the winter [...] these are the more interesting people to me. I want to know what brought them to where they are, who injured them or broke their spirits [...] Some of these people are being let out of institutions and shouldn't be on the street, but the greater number, I believe, are independent people, gamblers and alcoholics and wanderers who are lonely or loveless or living out the consequences of a series of bad breaks" ("Heart" 196).

[7] In *Louis Dudek and Raymond Souster*, Davey argues: "Souster seems to have been influenced by minimalism through his close friend W.W.E. Ross and Ross's fascination with haiku and imagism through William Carlos Williams. Minimalism resists directly the quantitative emphases of commodity fetishism" (127).

[8] In *James Joyce and the Making of Ulysses* (1972), Frank Budgen reports the following Joycean quip: "'I want,' said Joyce, as we were walking down the Universitätstrasse, 'to give a picture of Dublin so complete that if the city one day suddenly disappeared from the earth it could be reconstructed out of my book'" (69). Thanks to Tim Conley for locating this reference.

WORKS CITED

Abrams, M.H. "Structure and Style in the Greater Romantic Lyric." *The Correspondent Breeze.* New York: Norton, 1984. 76–108.

Barthes, Roland. *Empire of Signs.* Trans. Richard Howard. New York: Hill and Wang, 1982.

———. "Semiology and Urbanism." *The Semiotic Challenge.* Trans. Richard Howard. New York: Hill and Wang, 1988. 191–201.

Beattie, Munroe. "Poetry (1935–1950)." *Literary History of Canada: Canadian Literature in English.* 2nd ed. Vol. 2. Ed. Carl F. Klinck. Toronto: UTP, 1977. 254–96.

Bentley, D.M.R. "Klein, Montreal, and Mankind." *Journal of Canadian Studies* 19.2 (1984): 34–57.

Berman, Marshall. *All That is Solid Melts into Air: The Experience of Modernity.* New York: Simon and Schuster, 1982.

Bradbury, Malcom. "The Cities of Modernism." *Modernism: A Guide to European Literature 1890–1930.* Ed. Malcom Bradbury and James McFarlane. London: Penguin, 1991. 96–104.

Budgen, Frank. *James Joyce and the Making of Ulysses.* London: Oxford UP, 1972.

Davey, Frank. *Louis Dudek & Raymond Souster.* Vancouver: Douglas and McIntyre, 1980.

de Certeau, Michel. "Walking in the City." Trans. Steven Rendall. *The Cultural Studies Reader.* Ed. Simon During. London: Routledge, 1993. 151–60.

Edwards, Justin D. "*Strange Fugitive*, Strange City: Reading Urban Space in Morley Callaghan's Toronto." *Studies in Canadian Literature* 23.1 (1998): 213–27.

Fetherling, Doug. "The Cities Within." *Saturday Night* Jan. 1973: 36–38.

Fulford, Robert. *Accidental City: The Transformation of Toronto.* Toronto: Macfarlane, Walter, and Ross, 1995.

————. "On Raymond Souster." *Maclean's* 18 Apr. 1964. Rpt. in *The Making of Modern Poetry in Canada: Essential Articles on Contemporary Canadian Poetry in English.* Ed. Louis Dudek and Michael Gnarowski. 2nd ed. Toronto: Ryerson, 1970. 245–46.

————. "The poet laureate of the Toronto streets looks sadly backward." *Toronto Star* 7 Oct. 1973: 63.

Gatenby, Greg. *Toronto: A Literary Guide.* Toronto: McArthur, 1999.

Kaufman, David. "A.M. Klein and His Montreal: A Photographic Essay." *Journal of Canadian Studies* 19.2 (1984): 82–95.

Livesay, Dorothy. "Queen City." *Collected Poems: The Two Seasons.* Toronto: McGraw-Hill, 1972. 80–85.

Marshall, Tom. *Harsh and Lovely Land: The Major Canadian Poets and the Making of a Canadian Tradition.* Vancouver: UBC P, 1979.

McGimpsey, David. "A Walk in Montreal: Wayward Steps through the Literary Politics of Contemporary English Quebec." *Essays on Canadian Writing* 71 (2000): 150–68.

Pike, Burton. *The Image of the City in Modern Literature.* Princeton: Princeton UP, 1981.

Souster, Raymond. *The Collected Poems of Raymond Souster Volume One: 1940–55.* Ottawa: Oberon, 1980.

————. *The Collected Poems of Raymond Souster Volume Two: 1955–62.* Ottawa: Oberon, 1981.

————. *The Collected Poems of Raymond Souster Volume Three: 1962–74.* Ottawa: Oberon, 1982.

————. *The Collected Poems of Raymond Souster Volume Four: 1974–77.* Ottawa: Oberon, 1983.

————. "The Heart Still Singing: Raymond Souster at 82." Interview with Tony Tremblay. *Studies in Canadian Literature* 27.2 (2002): 183–201.

————. "Interview." Interview with John Nause and J. Michael Heenan. *CV/2* 3.2 (1977): 8–11.

————. "Raymond Souster: The Quiet Chronicler." Interview with Bruce Meyer and Brian O'Riordan. *Waves* 11.4 (1983): 5–12.

Spears, Monroe. *Dionysus and the City: Modernism in Twentieth-Century Poetry.* New York: Oxford UP, 1970.

Timms, Edward, and David Kelley. *Unreal City: Urban Experience in Modern European Literature and Art.* Manchester: Manchester UP, 1985.

Troper, Harold. "Immigrant City: The Making of Modern Toronto." *A Passion for Identity.* Ed. David Taras and Beverly Rasporich. Scarborough: Nelson, 2001. 335–54.

Tulchinsky, Gerald. "The Third Solitude: A.M. Klein's Jewish Montreal, 1910–1950." *Journal of Canadian Studies* 19.2 (1984): 96–112.

Waddington, Miriam. *Collected Poems*. Toronto: Oxford UP, 1986.

Whiteman, Bruce. *Raymond Souster and His Works*. Toronto: ECW, [1984].

Willmott, Glenn. *Unreal Country: Modernity in the Canadian Novel in English*. Montreal and Kingston: McGill-Queen's UP, 2002.

NATIVE, COSMOPOLITAN, POST-COSMOPOLITAN

Moonlight and Morning: Women's Early Contribution to Canadian Modernism

WANDA CAMPBELL

I. MASCULINIST MODERNISM

WHEN ARTHUR STRINGER described the rhyming poet in his preface to *Open Water* (1914) as "pathetically resplendent in that rigid steel which is an anachronism and no longer an armour" (5), he used a masculinist and military discourse. To read the table of contents in Louis Dudek and Michael Gnarowski's book *The Making of Modern Poetry in Canada*, described by the editors as "a collection of essential source material" (vi), one would assume that there were no female contributors at all to the modernist movement in Canada (only P.K. Page has a minor three-sentence entry). Scholars have come to question what one critic has called "Canadian modernism's insistence on its own immaculate conception, at McGill University in Montreal in the late 1920s" (Strong-Boag 125), suggested by Dudek and Gnarowski's phrase "It all began in 1925..." (24). In his evocative study of the influence of aestheticism on Canadian modernism, Brian Trehearne expands this narrow perspective: "Properly speaking, Canadian Modernism begins somewhere in the [*McGill*] *Fortnightly* [*Review*], yes; as well as in the *Newfoundland Verse* of Pratt and the early volumes of [Dorothy] Livesay, the manuscripts of [Raymond] Knister and ledger books of [W.W.E.] Ross..." (252). Dorothy Livesay's important contribution with the publication of *Green Pitcher* (1928) and subsequent volumes has been explored by scholars such as David Arnason and Dean Irvine, but just as the work of Stringer in 1914 with *Open Water* and Frank Oliver Call in 1920 with

Acanthus and Wild Grape prepared the way for those who followed, women were also publishing collections that served as important precursors.

In *No Man's Land: The Place of the Woman Writer in the Twentieth Century*, Sandra Gilbert and Susan Gubar outline the male-modernist attempt to construct a literary history based on "an implicitly masculine aesthetic of hard, abstract, learned verse that is opposed to the aesthetic of soft, effusive, personal verse supposedly written by women and Romantics" (153). As Carole Gerson points out in "The Canon between the Wars: Field-Notes of a Feminist Literary Archaeologist," this exclusionary process was further exacerbated in Canada by the "retrogressive cultural agenda" of the canonizers:

> During the 1920s and 1930s, when Louise Morey Bowman, Constance Lindsay Skinner and Dorothy Livesay were the major female figures among the poets interested in introducing imagist and modernist practice to Canadian poetry, the darlings of the country's conservative establishment were Marjorie Pickthall and, after the latter's untimely death, Audrey Alexandra Brown. (50–51)

During the early years of the century, Canadian women poets, including Sophia Hensley, Susan Frances Harrison, and Annie Charlotte Dalton, were expanding their thematic horizons but still writing primarily in rhyme. If we argue, as Glenn Willmott does in *Unreal Country: Modernity in the Canadian Novel in English,* that "modernism applies to the intersection of certain innovative aesthetic characteristics with a certain period of social and technological development" (40), then two of the earliest Canadian female poets to write as modernists were Louise Morey Bowman (1882–1944) of Quebec and Katherine Hale (1878–1956) of Ontario. In 1922, the year that saw the publication of *Ulysses* by James Joyce, *Jacob's Room* by Virginia Woolf, *The Enormous Room* by e.e. cummings, and *The Waste Land* by T. S. Eliot, Bowman published her first collection of poetry, *Moonlight and Common Day*, to be followed two years later by *Dream Tapestries*, a collection that would show even more formal variation. In 1923, the year in which Pratt's *Newfoundland Verse* was published, Amelia Beers Warnock Garvin, using the pen name Katherine Hale, published *Morning in the West,* her first mature collection written largely in free verse. These collections, almost entirely ignored by critics, deserve a second look for what they reveal about women's early contribution to Canadian modernism.

In *Reading 1922: A Return to the Scene of the Modern*, Michael North argues that the significance of that year rested not only in a literary upheaval but "rather a new social and cultural world of which the new works were merely a part" (4). Exploring specific events of 1922, North identifies several significant modernist trends, including four that are pertinent to the present discussion: a new mobility (across social, geographic, and gender lines), a postwar reassessment, a rise in nationalism that marked the beginning of the post-colonial era, and a resurgence of interest in the ancient. These four themes are implicitly explored in various poems included in Bowman's *Moonlight and Common Day* (1922) and *Dream Tapestries* (1924) and also, from a more distinctly Canadian perspective, in Hale's *Morning in the West* (1923), especially in the four sections of "Going North," the longest poem in the collection. The poetry of these two women reminds us that the early masculinist version of the advent of modernism in Canada is incomplete.

II. MOONLIGHT

Written in free verse, the title poem of Bowman's *Moonlight and Common Day* appears to argue for an alternative voice to expand the Canadian poetic scene then ruled by the all-male group of Confederation poets, including Charles G.D. Roberts who had published *Songs of the Common Day* in 1893. However, conscious of the "limitations of her power in a patriarchal literary structure" (Cimon 28), Bowman suggests that the story of the moonlight and the "sweet, wet earth" lies "written / Between the lines" (14). Even before the publication of *Moonlight and Common Day*, Bowman's poems had appeared in prestigious American magazines including *Poetry* (Chicago). The founding editor Harriet Monroe, whose words A.J.M. Smith would quote in his 1926 article "Contemporary Poetry" in the *McGill Fortnightly Review*, wrote a positive review of Bowman's first book, drawing attention to her "modern and individual imagination" (43). James Doyle argues that Monroe's editorial standards must be acknowledged "as among the most important factors in the evolution of literary modernism" but dismisses her support of Bowman's work as an indicator of "how unpredictable her standards were" (47–48). Amy Lowell, another leader in American imagist circles, was a judge for a 1922 competition in which Bowman's poem "Oranges" was awarded an honourable mention. This poem appeared in Bowman's 1924 collection *Dream Tapestries*, tellingly misnamed *Dress Tapestries* in Deborah Blenkhorn's brief entry on Bowman in the *Encyclopedia of Literature in Canada* (2002).

Despite the critical neglect of Bowman's work that prompted Rosemary Sullivan to ask in her introduction to *Poetry by Canadian Women*, "Where, for instance, is the name of Louise Morey Bowman in the history of Canadian Modernism?"(xi), Bowman can be considered one of the initiators of the modernist movement in Canada both directly through her published collections and indirectly through her bid to bring Amy Lowell to Canada, her friendship with Dorothy Livesay's mother, Florence Randall Livesay, and her strong alliance with fellow Eastern Townships poet, Frank Oliver Call. As Avrum Malus, Diane Allard, and Maria van Sundert point out, "contemporary reviewers take account of the way in which Call and Bowman are in the avant-garde of significant change in poetry" (60). Part of this "significant change" is in relation to form and part is in relation to content, particularly in response to the modernist trends that, according to Michael North, characterized the year 1922.

The new mobility that North explores is certainly apparent in "Oranges," the free-verse poem that received an honourable mention from Amy Lowell in 1922. The New England setting of the poem can be explained by the fact that it was entered in an American contest and may also reflect Bowman's time studying at Dana Hall in Wellsley, Massachusetts as well as her memories of her Puritan grandmother. Even so, there is much about the "Austere, repressed / Severe" setting that resembles turn-of-the-century Canada and the "dead white and black" of the worst of the period's verse: "How it all lies, before our modern eyes, / So grim" (*Dream* 25). Bowman goes on to paint a vivid picture of a Puritan village with its "Ruthlessly neat" main street, "Quite bare of all the withered, dead, brown leaves" except for those "Caught / In the corners of the neat, white, picket fences" (26). She describes the "stiff white houses built by rigid rule" and the stern hymns "Sung in proud, solemn majesty of menace and woe" (25). She then proceeds to herald the arrival of "Some wild, rich wind from wild rich worlds beyond, / That folk cannot entirely withhold" (26). In the village store, next to the "sad-toned materials for matrons' robes, / And piles of iron-gray wool for their men's winter stockings," one finds ripe pyramids of "voluptuous" oranges that "glow like balls moulded of molten gold" (29). These unexpected oranges are symbolic of a new mobility out of habitual geographies and modes of perception. Bowman contrasts the oranges and the "joyous tones they hold / Of vivid, bold, / Hot colour!" with "Innumerable strings of dull, dried apples!" (29). The traditional, "thin" northern harvest dulled, especially for women, by the implications of exile and the fall, can never compete with this "rare / Drifted salvage" (26) from other, more sensual, worlds. Bowman concludes the poem with the burning question posed by modernism: "Who now is sure what shall endure?" (30).

The exotic and organic sensuality represented by the oranges in this poem is echoed in the moon-drenched world of "Moonlight and Common Day." Here the poet-persona admits to loving "well-ordered, punctual living / Behind tall, well-clipped hedges" (13), but yearns to open her casement window. Unlike the "magic casements" of Keats's "Ode to a Nightingale," to which Bowman alludes in her poem "The Mountain that Watched," this window opens on a world where "dark leaves stir in the silence / And the sweet, wet earth breathes softly / And murmurs an exquisite word"(*Moonlight* 13). In the 1924 poem "Green Apples," in which the apple shows "black dents where strong white teeth / Have bitten it" and "the green wine of moonlight is drenching / The perilous garden" (*Dream* 21), moonlight is explicitly associated with female power. It should be remembered that it was only in 1922 that the first woman was called to the English bar (North 184), and Canada's Famous Five would be working throughout the decade for Canadian women to be seen as persons under the law. The world was changing, especially for women, in part because of the new roles they were called upon to play during World War I.

Part of the postwar reassessment was a new ambivalence toward technology, which had once seemed the answer to the world's woes but was now revealed to be a destructive as well as a creative force. Bowman, like many of her contemporaries, was at once fascinated and overwhelmed by the machine, a complex relationship almost certainly influenced by her husband's profession. In 1909, she married an electrical engineer, Archibald Abercromby Bowman, and moved to the city of Toronto. In her poem "A Sketch," which appears in *Dream Tapestries*, she describes her husband and "the crowded city streets, / Through which he presses" among the "Factories and shipyards where his vast machines / Whirr steadfastly, obedient to his brain—" (57). In the end she reveals that it is "the small and golden hours" (57) away from all this that she truly cherishes. In the poem "Timepieces" from *Moonlight and Common Day*, Bowman writes of the old sundial in the garden and the old clocks in the house, but she does so while "waiting in the power-house of a great factory" (58). Initially, the "monstrous whirring engines" (58) are reminiscent of the nightmare vision of Archibald Lampman's "The City of the End of Things" in the fear they inspire: "At first their rush and their crashing roar / Terrified me. / I wanted to scream and run....gasping..." (58). Eventually, however, "the noise has become rhythmical" (58) and the poet-persona becomes accustomed to the "hurrying, rhythmical beat of these mighty engines, / Timed to the fraction of a second" (59). In fact, by comparison, the old clocks seem "slow...slow...slow..." (58). Bowman implies a disjuncture between old forms and rhythms and the speed and intensity of the modern world:

> The sundial is very, very old
> To be counting the hours in my modern garden
> Where flowers bloom in wild riot of colour
> And modern poets read *vers libre*
> Under the shade of a jolly young maple tree. (57)

As a poet in a time of transition, she recognizes that there is likely to be some confusion in the beginning. Surrounded by "the roar and the rhythm," the poet-persona "understand[s] nothing" (59), but comes "laboriously" and "reverently" to realize that engines, like sundials and clocks before them, can be a means to contemplate "TIME AND ETERNITY" (59).

Despite the passing mention of the maple tree in "Timepieces," there is nothing explicitly Canadian about Bowman's early poems. However, all that changes in her long poem, "The Mountain That Watched," about the city of Montreal that would eventually become her home. In *Reading 1922*, North suggests that a rise in nationalism is an important trend in modernism, and in Bowman's detailed descriptions of this "new-world city" and its people, she adopts a distinctly post-colonial attitude. The Romantic language of Wordsworth and Keats is inadequate, she argues, to render the contemporary reality of dirty docks, crowded slums, "shops, hovels, factories" (*Dream* 36), and orthodox Jews shaking their sins into "the dirty oily water" of the St. Lawrence (35). "We've dropped our classic daffodils and trod / upon them! But we've really seen—something" (36). Appropriately, in this poem, Bowman abandons the traditional practice of capitalizing the opening word of each line for one that follows the conventions of prose. Once a blizzard overtakes the mountain and the poem—"while through the streets / the snow-ploughs move like huge primeval beasts / glutted with power" (36–37)—the flurry of voices that follows ranges from the colloquial slang of casual conversation and advertising to quotations from the Bible, interspersed with haiku-like images indented and italicized: "*Stark twisted branches black against the snow / Snapping and cracking of frost-tortured trees—*" (38). Through all the revolutions in seasons, fashions, and patterns of speech, the mountain watches and endures.

Another key tenet of modernism identified by North in *Reading 1922* is a return to the past reflected in the Egyptomania ignited by Howard Carter's discovery of King Tutankhamun's tomb in "the very month *The Waste Land* reached the bookstores" (19) and in an interest in literary forms such as the haiku that were at once ancient and new. In "Twelve Hokku on a Canadian Theme" and "Life Sequence" Bowman adopts the haiku form, beginning this section of *Dream Tapestries* with a definition from Yone Noguchi's *The Pilgrimage* (1908): "'Hokku' (seventeen-syllable poem) in Japanese mind might be compared with a tiny star, I dare say, carrying the whole sky at its back.[…] It is simply a guiding lamp. Its value depends on how much it suggests" (63). The first Japanese national to publish poetry in English, Noguchi was an influence on Ezra Pound and others in his imagist combinations of the contemporary and the ancient. In his book *Waking Giants: The Presence of the Past in Modernism*, Herbert N. Shneidau explores the "legacy of atavism" that is characteristic of modernism. In the work of Joyce, Pound, and Eliot he finds this admission: "We must admit the power of the past within us, and turn it into a source of life rather than try continually to exorcise it" (61). In the poem "Darkness," which appeared in *Moonlight and Common Day*, Bowman speaks of her allegiance to both ancient and modern, and the confusion that can result:

> It seems to be a foregone conclusion;
> That if I worship the new gods
> Sincerely, in the sunshine—
> I must not pray in the moonlight,
> By the shrines of the old gods
> Where the cherry blossoms still shine.
> But sometimes in the darkness
> I mistake the shrines. (20)

She ultimately concludes that it does not matter, since she receives answers at both shrines and finds the intersection between past and present to be a fruitful one. In "The Creators," the penultimate poem in her 1922 collection, Bowman argues that the "new-born things" of the world are capable of "illumining / Dim, darkened Beauty, / With new, blinding light" (63). As a transitional figure, Bowman does not often achieve the success of those who followed her, but her work casts sufficient moonlight—associated not with romance but with "new-born" female power—to illuminate her previously overshadowed contribution to Canadian modernism.

III. MORNING

The poetry of Katherine Hale, another important early but neglected contributor to Canadian modernism, reflects trends similar to those found in Bowman, though her work is characterized by more Canadian subject matter and less formal innovation. While working to build a reputation for Isabella Valancy Crawford, Hale published several of her own books, including *Morning in the West* in 1923. Despite the fact that this book and *The Island, and Other Poems* (1934) contain her strongest and most significant work, they are not even mentioned in the Hale entry in the *Encyclopedia of Literature in Canada*. With the exception of Susan Atkinson's paper published in the *Proceedings of the 6th International Literature of Region and Nation Conference* (1998), her poetry has received no critical attention.

Hale's contribution has been obscured for reasons similar to those affecting Bowman but, in her case, there were several additional factors, among them her conservative entry onto the poetic scene during World War I with three rhyming collections of sentimental and patriotic poetry of the home front: *Grey Knitting* (1914), *The White Comrade* (1916), and *The New Joan* (1917). These collections were immensely popular but already in the title poem of *The New Joan* about women "warriors"—like those pictured in Manly MacDonald's *Land Girls Hoeing* (1919) who worked the land while husbands and brothers fought overseas—Hale recognizes that nothing will ever be quite the same. In a poem entitled "I Who Cut Patterns," which first appeared in the *Canadian Magazine* in August of 1921, she exposes the deficiencies of familiar themes and old fashions while expressing a longing for "themes that are new" (*Morning* 42).

By the time Hale published *Morning in the West* in 1923, she had found not only new themes but new forms in which to express them. Ironically, it was this book that garnered positive feedback from the old guard in Canada. Charles G.D. Roberts wrote to her saying, "Verily, Lady Dear, I had not realized before how great your gift. These lyrics grip & delight me. They are fresh & spontaneous & haunting" (324). A newspaper article entitled "Canadian Poetess Warmly Acclaimed by Local Audience" in the *Globe* (13 January 1926) describes the "unstinted praise of such literary experts as Charles G.D. Roberts and Lorne Pierce" (12). After Hale's poetry reading, Roberts read from a letter by Bliss Carman describing Hale as a "kind, sincere lyrist with dramatic power added" (12). Such support was clearly a mixed blessing for a poet seeking recognition as a new voice. In her poem entitled "Poetesses" (a term she found objectionable), addressing both her foremothers and her own early writings, she writes:

> You were a thing so feminine
> That even of war you sang in tender notes.
> But now another one has come,
> Who is herself at war. (44)

One is struck by this attempt to express the transition from passive to active, songstress to warrior, Penelope to Odysseus, but also by the syntactical ambiguity of the phrase "herself at war," which describes both a figure who is learning to fight and one who is experiencing internal conflict. Hale completes the stanza with the figure of women's songs as swords with which they "mean to cut tradition" (44). Hale's choice of verb is significant since the many meanings of "cut" fill several pages of the dictionary: to wound, to excise, to pass through, to reduce, to rebuke, to re-tailor, to castrate, to dilute, to surpass, and so on. Just how would female writers "cut" tradition, and make the transition to a new, modernist poetic?

In the long free-verse poem "Going North," which appeared in the 1923 collection *Morning in the West*, Hale explores four central themes of international modernism—movement across social, geographic, and gender lines; postwar reflection; rising nationalism; and a renewed interest in the past—all within a Canadian setting. Hale chooses to go north, rather than south or east for her inspiration but, ironically, the journey north turns out to be a journey into modernity. The first section of "Going North," entitled "White Porches," describes the beginning of the journey north from the urban grey asphalt of the city past the white porches of villages, but it can also be interpreted as a discussion of women's changing roles in the early decades of the twentieth century. In this case, the poet-persona is observing the women on the "narrow but shining porches"(48), not entirely free but no longer trapped within the static domestic life as the angel of the house, a figure that Virginia Woolf felt she must kill if she was to survive. The women are caught in the liminal space of the porch, which signifies both liberation and confinement in its cage-like setting that is at once transparent and enclosed. Similarly, in Harriet Monroe's 1915 poem "On the Porch," the woman is kept "roofed in, screened in" (82) and separate from the earth-shattering experience of war, but change eventually intrudes even here. In contrast to the women on the porches, the poet-persona of Hale's poem is on a journey northward into more wild and liberated conditions, a new mobility made possible by the technological change represented by the automobile and the ideological change represented by the freedom enjoyed by the New Woman. The poet wonders about the women who find contentment in domestic tasks when the wide world awaits:

> "Just what is life," we wondered,
> "For those who sit contented
> Throughout the magic summer
> On those pale country porches,
> Patching—knitting—talking—
> Serenely shelling peas?" (48)

War-time images of women making shells in munitions factories like those represented in the paintings of Montreal artist Mabel May provoke us to think primarily of the changes affecting urban women, but women's roles had changed in rural settings as well, as demonstrated in Hale's poem "The New Joan." As Eric Brown, Director of the National Gallery of Canada, said in 1918, "I think there should be some fine landscape subjects in connection with girls' work on the land, farming of various kinds, fruit picking, etc.; the clothes are picturesque and this side of the war should certainly be pictured." The sunshine sketches of little towns that dominate the first section of Hale's poem will soon be left behind. The concluding punctuation mark of this first section confirms that the world as it had been known would be forever called into question.

Significantly, the poem's sudden turn to the north is signalled in the second section ("Grey Willows") by an encounter with a symbol of technology, a railway train. Hale makes specific references to the speed, "the stifling cab," and the "careless hand" of the engineer (49). The speeding train heralds the entry into a world that is less gentle and less humane:

> And in a moment we had lost
> All thought of shining porches
> And sleepy village streets.
> This was a thinner world
> Of smaller, leaner orchards;
> Taller, barer houses;
> Drier, keener air.
> […] Stark tree trunks
> Showed where bush fires had run,
> Charred columns of lost forests
> Dried by the sun into fantastic shapes. (49)

By the time this poem was published, Hale and her contemporaries had had time to reflect upon just how the postwar world was a "leaner" world. According to North, though the armistice was signed years earlier, 1922 was the "first real postwar year" (5) in which reassessment and reaction began in earnest. World War I changed not only gender roles but what captured the artist's imagination. To find art in the waste land, the aesthetic sense had to be retrained. Part of shoring the fragments against the ruins involved a new appreciation not just for the flesh but for the bones. In Canada, this aesthetic transition to "a thinner world" was facilitated by the Group of Seven. As Maria Tippett and others explain, the art of the Group of Seven was profoundly affected by the experience of World War I in which several of the artists participated: "After the war [A.Y.] Jackson and his fellow artists deliberately sought to paint 'swampy, rocky, wolf-ridden, burnt and scuttled country...'" (109). For Hale, the poet experiences this stark new world as the vivid "preface of the North" (50):

> But now at every jagged, ugly turn
> Only a brush heap where the woods had been.
> The very soil is scorched—

Scorched the brown ferns
Descended from the ones that long ago
Were licked into a burning wind of flame. (50)

In one of the poem's rare rhyming couplets, Hale describes the "Poor, narrow little stream, / Bereft of that green dream" (50). Her use of the adjective "narrow" to describe the stream, and "green dream" to describe the wild garden lost to fire, echoes the description of the lost porches of section one, but this stark new landscape leaves no room for nostalgia.

In the third section of "Going North," entitled "Bush Road," the land is given a voice to recollect those who have explored and exploited its territory throughout history, from voyageurs to woodmen. Though the "soft green forest" lived "an ardent, powerful, various sort of life" (51), it was raped by various intruders. The bush, which was once to cause such hardship and consternation for Susanna Moodie and other pioneers, is now an avenue for pleasure: "A trail up to the playground of the North, / A bracken-haunted, snaky road, / A soft surprise to strangers, a delight" (51). For those who come not for pillage but for play, the journey to the north is a sensual and creative experience, as it was for the male artists of the Group of Seven. As Lawren Harris writes:

> One can almost guarantee that two months in our North country of direct experience in creative living in art will bring about a very marked change in the attitude of any creative individual. It will bring *him* an inner release and freedom to adventure on *his* own that is well-nigh impossible amid the insistences and superficialities of Europe. (48; emphasis added)

Going north to one's own wilderness yields rich rewards, and Hale claims this previously gender-exclusive freedom for women.

According to Milton A. Cohen, modernism survived World War I, but "profoundly changed" (165). Its international character, elitism, and abstract experimentation seemed less relevant now that so many had been killed and the dark side of technological progress had been revealed. One result of the war was a new nationalism that on the one hand resulted in the rise of fascism, and on the other in the dawn of the post-colonial era with "imperial unity" being challenged on many fronts (North 111). In recognizing the exploitation of the colonial past and the excitement of a post-colonial future in which national resources can be enjoyed without being destroyed, Hale hints at the rise of nationalism that reshaped modernism in the postwar era. In Hale's poem, "the axe and spike" (51) of voyageur and lumberman have been replaced by the surprise and delight of artists and pilgrims discovering the wonders of their own nation. For Hale, the movement toward a post-colonial vision of the Canadian north takes place as the granite beneath the "softly yielding earth" (51) is revealed and the ability of the land to endure as an independent entity is celebrated.

If the "Bush Road" section of "Going North" implies some kind of subtle aesthetic foreplay with its inverted Edenic imagery and frequent reference to tactile sensation, the language that opens the final section, "Painted Rock," is frankly sexual. However, there is a curious gender shift in the conventional representation of the land as a passive female to be penetrated. The north emerges here as the more aggressive, powerful partner:

> Then the North took us,
> Forced us through rocky walls,
> Tore at our tires,
> Gave us no inch of earth
> Upon our steady climb. (51)

The journey to the north is almost complete, and the quest culminates in a place made sacred by a Holy Grail like none other the poet has ever imagined: "And suddenly, like a blue cup held high, / The lake Mazinawa…" (52). In contrast to Bowman who uses ellipses with alarming frequency (35 times in the 102-line poem "Timepieces"), Hale uses them very sparingly— as on this occasion when she seeks to express the sublime silence of the lake that is at once ancient and new. Lake Mazinaw in Bon Echo Provincial Park was a draw for many well-known Canadian artists and writers. In 1910, the Toronto feminist Flora MacDonald Denison purchased the Bon Echo Inn to create a wilderness retreat for the avant-garde, and many artists including members of the Group of Seven came to vacation and work there before it was closed in 1928. Dominating this section of Hale's poem is the great rock "sacred to Indian tribes how long ago?" (52).

The impact of the "primitive" on modern art has been well documented, beginning with Paul Gauguin and others and continuing with Pablo

Picasso's groundbreaking painting *Desmoiselles D'Avignon* (1917). Just as African and Eastern art had an influence on European modernism, Native art had an influence on North American modernism. As Veronica Strong-Boag and Carole Gerson point out, "the connection between imagism, one of the first phases of literary modernism, and the recording of Native songs at the beginning of this century, has been noted by several critics" (129) including Helen Carr, author of *Inventing the American Primitive* (1996). Constance Lindsay Skinner, a contemporary of Bowman and Hale, is often mentioned in this regard, but although some of her free-verse poems based on Squamish legends were published in *Poetry* (Chicago) before 1922, her collection *Songs of the Coast Dwellers* was not published until 1930, seven years after Hale's *Morning in the West*.

The power of the aboriginal past is evoked in one of the strongest passages in "Going North," Hale's description of the painted rock:

> It looms up larger than I dreamed;
> Roadways of rock
> And canyons full of light;
> Niched balconies for pines bent all one way;
> Small birds in flight,
> Dashing against the dark
> Of that vast rocky flank,
> Whose sides of iron seams,
> Laid under golden lichen
> Have a been a place of dreams
> And of brute sacrifice. (52)

The lean, vivid language and phallic imagery of this passage exempt Hale from the company of virginal poetesses denigrated by F.R. Scott in "The Canadian Authors Meet" (248). Significantly, the quintessentially Canadian vessel that transports the poet toward the painted rock is a canoe, a craft that since the days of Crawford signals a strain of intense sexual imagery in Canadian poetry, a theme carried forward in Pauline Johnson's love poems such as "The Idlers" and "The Song My Paddle Sings." Johnson, who often travelled solo in her canoe called the *Wild Cat*, spoke early on of the virtues of a woman paddling her own canoe:

> We all have a scrap of the savage, a dash of the primitive man concealed about us somewhere—give it play girls, at least once a year. Be the roving nature-loving, simple-living being that the soul of your ancestors burning yet within you clamors out so loudly at times; just try the old heathen etiquetteless life in a canoe for one summer week, you will be a more womanly woman for the quaffing of nature's wines in the wilderness. (qtd. in Strong-Boag and Gerson 74)

The lone male adventurer in search of "the muskeg snatch / of the old north," as Robert Kroetsch puts it in his "Meditation on Tom Thomson" (50), is now joined by a female partner actively participating in the search for a passionate new syntax fuelled by the energy of the ancient:

> What are we floating towards
> In this small, low canoe?
> A naked, ceremonial singing past
> Seems to reach out and whisper. (53)

This is not merely a dead past, but one possessed of power and voice. The modernist poetic Hale finds in going north is "naked," stripped of all fashion and frippery, and yet still ceremonial and still singing as fine poetry should be.

In an address entitled "The Future of Our Poetry" written for the Canadian Authors Association convention in Toronto in 1931, Vancouver poet Annie Charlotte Dalton stated that the virtues she found in Lawren Harris's painting *Mountain Forms* (1928) would soon be the strongest characteristics of Canada's poetry: "its restraint and freedom, its gifts of spiritual illumination and expression; the extraordinary depth and quality of its feeling; its symbolism, and its wonderful suggestion of light"(1). This startling painting would unsettle many who saw it because of its effort to cut tradition and go north, a process that would eventually lead to complete abstraction both in Harris's own work and in the paintings of those he influenced, such as Bertram Brooker, who sought a kind of synaesthesia between music and art. The highly problematic willingness of the Group of Seven and others to remove the First Nations presence from their artistic representations of the land is, to some degree, avoided by Hale who acknowledges the immense power and beauty of the indigenous art she encounters.

Hale sought a new vocabulary and a new syntax to express a new world order. In "Going North" four phases of a conspicuously national journey echo trends in international modernism, bringing together concerns for and about the increase in mobility across social, gender, and geographic boundaries, the rise in postwar nationalism, the events of contemporary history, and the influence of legend and myth on modern art. To look north was to look forward and to look back. The Canadian north, inspiring to her male contemporaries, became a kind of spiritual home for Hale, and the subject of some of her finest poems. "My own country," Hale once said in an interview, "has never become to me just a place I'm used to, but one full of hidden surprises that I'm always wanting to explore" (qtd. in Dempsey 80). Her preference for hinterland over baseland and marginalized over centralized may have contributed to critical neglect from those who sought a more cosmopolitan poetry. According to Susan Atkinson, who has written the only critical article on Hale's writing since 1948, Hale was seeking to develop a distinctly feminist poetic that would challenge prevailing notions of the exotic Other. Hale's most frequently anthologized poem, the ekphrastic "Cun-ne-wa-bum," written in response to viewing Paul Kane's 1847 portrait of a Cree woman, "openly enacts a synchronous collusion with and resistance of the dominant, partriarchally and Eurocentrically informed, discourse" (Atkinson 158). In many of the poems about marginalized figures that appear in *Morning in the West*, Hale explores how extreme historical conditions actually served to strengthen women by allowing them a courageous and active role. In "Buffalo Meat," a woman once satisfied with lilac chintz and London theatre writes from the frontier, "I am as much a hunter as a wife" (20) and in "She Who Paddles," the dynamic central figure "softly walks in the forest / in no great need of men" (30). Atkinson argues that "Hale's poetry is an example of discourse which combines an existing sociolect with a refusal to accept the prescribed limitations of that dominant culture" (165). That Hale repeatedly envisioned the woman poet as a warrior, independent, active, and sensual, was a direct challenge to those who preferred to limit their female counterparts to "dear / Victorian saintliness" (Scott 248).

It may well have been an ambivalent reception that moved Hale away from poetry and toward the lecture circuit and the writing of several popular prose works of cultural history, including *Canadian Cities of Romance* (1933) and *Historic Houses of Canada* (1952). A new collection of poetry, *The Island, and Other Poems,* did not appear until eleven years after *Morning in the West,* though several of the poems were written as early as 1926. Hale's one other collection, *The Flute,* containing only three new poems, did not appear until 1950. In an obituary entitled "Katherine Hale Knew Triumph and Tragedy," Lotta Dempsey quotes from a letter Hale had once written to her:

> I believe that one just has to take every experience fearlessly and satu-rate it with life, expurgate ruthlessly the un-essentials and then, as best one can, re-think it into poetry…. But everyone has his own method; and after all, so far as the boundless world of art is concerned, we are all like pigmies, lost in its tremendous ramifications. (14)

This "boundless world of art" was ultimately to engender not one but many modernisms.

IV. MANY MODERNISMS

In his 1983 article "'Back to the Woods Ye Muse of Canada': Conservative Response to the Beginnings of Modernism," Donald Precosky argues that "the two questions of modernism and a national tradition were closely related" (44). He describes a battle between the traditionalists with their "rhyme schemes and their nature description" and the modernists who introduced "something new and disturbing" from foreign models on the "grounds that traditional Canadian writing was worthless" (44). In the two decades since this was written, the portrait of modernism, both inter-nationally and in Canada, has become far more layered and complex. As Paula Rabinowitz points out, "Where once there was a certain consensus about the tenets of modernism—formal innovation, surface over depth, self-referentiality—now there are one, two, many modernisms, spanning various continents, unevenly developed among multiple populations" (194). Trehearne and others have shown how this complexity applies to the Canadian context, resulting in at least two modernisms that "never really reconciled themselves into a single compelling movement" (313). The early poems of Bowman and Hale are a part of this intricate amalgam of "many modernisms."

Bowman's poetry appears to fulfill Glenn Willmott's definition of modernism as "the intersection of certain innovative aesthetic charac-

teristics with a certain period of social and technological development"
(40). Her work is marked by formal innovation that draws upon such
diverse international sources as imagism, haiku, slang, and the rhythms
of jazz (Arnason 8), and she was drawn to modern themes including
the changing role of women, the impact of the factory on the imagination, and portraits of urban Montreal, and yet mention of her in the
literary history of Canada "is brief and limited" (Malus et al. 60). When
Bowman is at her best, her work intrigues and enlightens. Some readers
may be disconcerted, as was one contemporary reviewer, by her frequent
use of ellipses, but these appear to result from a sincere if awkward effort
to find a formal equivalent for that which lies between the lines. Indeed,
subsequent poets would find more sophisticated strategies to cope with
the challenges posed by free-verse lineation, and their exploration of
modern life would be more sustained and profound, but still Bowman's
contribution to early modernism should not be ignored. As Monroe said
of *Moonlight and Common Day*, "such faults as she might be accused of
are not Victorian reminders" (43). In a 1978 article on Bowman, Precosky
concludes that her "struggle to break free of techniques which she inherited from the nineteenth century proved ultimately futile" (108), and yet
there is in her work "a foreshadowing" (Malus et al. 67) of what is to come.
Hale's work is also intriguing because it reflects what Malcolm Bradbury
calls "an oscillation between modernism and a changing native tradition"
(73). Perhaps by discovering "something new and disturbing" within one's
own borders, as did the Group of Seven in visual art and A.J.M. Smith in
his poem "The Lonely Land" (originally subtitled "Group of Seven"), one
could contribute to the development of a distinctly Canadian modernism.
As Lawren Harris, who published a collection of free-verse poems entitled
Contrasts in 1922, wrote: "Our aim is to paint the Canadian scene in its
own terms. This land is different in its air, moods, and spirit from Europe
and the Old Country. It invokes a response which throws aside all precon-
ceived ideas and rule-of-thumb reactions" (48). Hale seems particularly
attuned to this difference. In contrast to Bowman, who wrote of factories,
cities, and high art, Hale often wrote of Canadian history and landscape,
beloved themes of the traditionalists, but her approach to the Canadian
scene was less conventional and more multi-faceted than it first appears.
Admittedly, like her contemporaries who were also struggling to express
the story that "lies written / Between the lines" (*Moonlight* 14), Hale was a

transitional figure whose poetry is sometimes uneven. Bowman and Hale may be minor poets but, as Trehearne points out, "to be a minor poet is to make a significant contribution to a literature," and we would benefit, especially in the Canadian context, from an effort to "reduce or eliminate if possible the opprobrium that has clung" to the term in the past (71). Both Bowman and Hale sought a passionate new poetic, "less vague, less verbose, and less eloquent" (29) (to quote A.J.M. Smith quoting Harriet Monroe) than that of their predecessors to describe the profound changes within and around them. That they did so several years before the emergence of the Montreal group in the mid-1920s secures for them a place among the early contributors to Canadian modernism.

WORKS CITED

Arnason, David. "Dorothy Livesay and the Rise of Modernism in Canada." *A Public and Private Voice: Essays on the Life and Work of Dorothy Livesay.* Waterloo: U of Waterloo P, 1986. 5–18.

Atkinson, Susan. "Challenging Exoticism: Race, Gender and Nation in the Poetry of Katherine Hale." *Proceedings of the 6th International Literature of Region and Nation Conference.* Ed. Win Bogaards. Saint John: SSHRC, 1998. 2: 157–67.

Blenkhorn, Deborah. "Bowman, Louise Morey." *Encyclopedia of Literature in Canada.* 148. Toronto: UTP, 2002. 469.

———. "Hale, Katherine." *Encyclopedia of Literature in Canada.* Toronto: UTP, 2002. 469.

Bowman, Louise Morey. *Dream Tapestries.* Toronto: Macmillan, 1924.

———. *Moonlight and Common Day.* Toronto: Macmillan, 1922.

Bradbury, Malcolm. *The Social Context of Modern English Literature.* New York: Schocken, 1971.

Brown, Eric. "Canvas of War: Masterpieces from the Canadian War Museum." <http://www.civilization.ca/cwm/canvas/1/cwd330e.html> 18 Jan. 2004.

"Canadian Poetess Warmly Acclaimed by Local Audience." *Globe* 13 Jan. 1926: 12.

Cimon, Anne. "Louise Morey Bowman." *Dictionary of Literary Biography* 68 (1988): 27–29.

Cohen, Milton A. "Fatal Symbiosis: Modernism and the First World War." *The Literature of the Great War Reconsidered.* Ed. Patrick J. Quinn and Steven Trout. New York: Palgrave, 2001. 159–71.

Dalton, Annie Charlotte. *The Future of Our Poetry.* Vancouver: Privately printed, 1931.

Dempsey, Lotta. "Katherine Hale." *Leading Canadian Poets.* Ed. W.P. Percival. Toronto: Ryerson, 1948. 79–87.

————. "Katherine Hale Knew Triumph and Tragedy." *Globe and Mail* 11 Sept. 1956: 14.

Doyle, James. "Harriet Monroe's *Poetry* and Canadian Poetry." *Canadian Poetry* 25 (1989): 38–48.

Dudek, Louis, and Michael Gnarowski, eds. *The Making of Modern Poetry in Canada: Essential Articles on Contemporary Canadian Poetry in English.* Toronto: Ryerson, 1967.

Gerson, Carole. "The Canon between the Wars: Field-notes of a Feminist Literary Archaeologist." *Canadian Canons: Essays in Literary Value.* Ed. Robert Lecker. Toronto: UTP, 1991. 46–56.

Gilbert, Sandra M., and Susan Gubar. *No Man's Land: The Place of the Woman Writer in the Twentieth Century.* New Haven: Yale UP, 1988.

Hale, Katherine. *Morning in the West.* Toronto: Ryerson, 1923.

Harris, Lawren. *Lawren Harris.* Ed. Bess Harris and R.G.P. Colgrove. Toronto: Macmillan, 1969.

Irvine, Dean. "Editorial Postscript." *Archive for Our Times: Previously Uncollected and Unpublished Poems of Dorothy Livesay.* Ed. Irvine. Vancouver: Arsenal Pulp, 1998. 250–72.

Kroetsch, Robert. *The Stone Hammer Poems.* Lantzville, BC: Oolichan, 1976.

Malus, Avrum, Diane Allard, and Maria van Sundert. "Frank Oliver Call, Eastern Townships Poetry, and the Modernist Movement." *Canadian Literature* 107 (1985): 60–69.

Monroe, Harriet. "On the Porch." *The Difference and Other Poems.* New York: Macmillan, 1925. 81–82.

————. Rev. of *Moonlight and Common Day,* by Louise Morey Bowman. *Poetry: A Magazine of Verse* 21 (1922–23): 43–45.

North, Michael. *Reading 1922: A Return to the Scene of the Modern.* New York: Oxford UP, 1999.

Precosky, Donald. "'Back to the Woods Ye Muse of Canada': Conservative Response to the Beginnings of Modernism." *Canadian Poetry* 12 (1983): 40–45.

————. "Louise Morey Bowman." *Canadian Literature* 79 (1978): 108–11.

Rabinowitz, Paula. "Great Lady Painters, Inc.: Icons of Feminism, Modernism, and the Nation." *Modernism Inc.: Body, Memory, Capital.* Ed. Jani Scandura and Michael Thurston. New York: New York UP, 2001. 193–218.

Roberts, Charles G.D. *Collected Letters of Sir Charles G.D. Roberts.* Ed. Laurel Boone. Fredericton: Goose Lane, 1989.

Schneidau, Herbert N. *Waking Giants: The Presence of the Past in Modernism.* New York: Oxford UP, 1991.

Scott, F. R. *Collected Poems of F.R. Scott.* Toronto: McClelland and Stewart, 1981.

Smith, A.J.M. "Contemporary Poetry." *McGill Fortnightly Review* 15 Dec. 1926. Rpt. in Dudek and Gnarowski 27–30.

Stringer, Arthur. Preface. *Open Water*. Toronto: Bell and Cockburn, 1914. Rpt. in Dudek and Gnarowski 5–9.

Strong-Boag, Veronica and Carole Gerson. *Paddling Her Own Canoe: The Times and Texts of E. Pauline Johnson / Tekahionwake*. Toronto: UTP, 2000.

Sullivan, Rosemary. Introduction. *Poetry by Canadian Women*. Ed. Sullivan. Toronto: Oxford UP, 1989. x–xiv.

Tippett, Maria. *Art at the Service of War: Canada, Art and the Great War*. Toronto: UTP, 1984.

Trehearne, Brian. *Aestheticism and the Canadian Modernists: Aspects of a Poetic Influence*. Montreal and Kingston: McGill-Queen's UP, 1989.

Willmott, Glenn. *Unreal Country: Modernity in the Canadian Novel in English*. Montreal and Kingston: McGill-Queen's UP, 2002.

Sheila Watson, Aboriginal Discourse, and Cosmopolitan Modernism

GLENN WILLMOTT

I

SHEILA WATSON'S WORK has been insightfully discussed in both modernist and postmodernist terms. This essay will aim to enhance our understanding of the influence of cosmopolitan modernism in the writing of *The Double Hook*. No doubt there is an irreducibly diverse range of modernisms, and what cosmopolitan modernism will signify in this context demands initial clarification. By modernism I refer conventionally, if not unambiguously, to a self-reflexively experimental aesthetic practice that produces its meaning in dialogue with a social field characterized by historical modernization, specifically in that phase which sees the global reach of the economic and power structures of patriarchal monopoly capitalism, its class conditions and struggles, its web of technological media (for the communication of force or knowledge), and its tendency to material and migratory urbanization. With the notion of a cosmopolitan modernism I wish to emphasize in part the historical welter of exiled, expatriate, and otherwise mobile artists out of whose networks grew the fertile array of markedly transnational or even postnational (as opposed to national, regional, or even linguistically-based) movements all with the aim, as Ezra Pound announced, to "make it new."[1] These are artists whose work and whose conception of the work of art responded to the virtually ineluctable perception of the globalization of institutional and social systems and conflicts (for example, in the persistence of patriarchy under advanced capitalism, in the technics and technologies of global warfare, or in international communist organizations) irrespective of languages and national borders. On this field of modernism, broadly conceived, artists were able to respond to historical specificities of a "modern" world—to "what the age demanded," as Pound's Hugh Selwyn Mauberley puts it—yet from the rather unspecific location of a "modern" artist. The term "cosmopolitan" will suggest this paradoxically located but dislocated position. But the term will also suggest this modernism's prevalent mode of discourse, which in a variety of ways is itself dizzily mobile or dislocated (as per T.S. Eliot's famous injunction)[2] rather than anchored in a marked region or situation.

The position Watson's novel takes with respect to this cosmopolitan field, variegated and volatile as it is, allows unique insight into the primitivist elements of her work, including those regionally specific, indigenous figures—people and gods (Coyote, for example) of First Nations heritage—which have seemed integral to its meaning, and which may seem enigmatic or even politically troublesome to contemporary readers. The cosmopolitan-modernist influence is most inescapable when we turn to Watson's journals during the mid-1950s, the period during which she resided in Paris and her final and quite substantial revisions to *The Double Hook* manuscript were undertaken. The journals are fragmentary and juxtapositional in structure rather than linear and narrative. Their fabric comprises countless imagist articulations of the city and her room (not a "room of her own," since her husband's work there took priority), woven with literary and historical intertexts and personal reflections. What is oftentimes a dense fabric of resonating elements can suddenly depend upon a merest spider's thread of word or image. Such a text may be grasped by any one of these threads, which then becomes a warp string around which other threads appear woven and knotted.

Such a thread is Watson's encounter with Samuel Beckett—not in the flesh, although Beckett of course resided in Paris; I mean her voracious reading of his work at this time. When Watson lived in Paris, from 1955 to 1956, what are now Beckett's best-known works, *Waiting for Godot* and the novel trilogy, *Molloy*, *Malone Dies*, and *The Unnamable*, as well as *Stories and Texts for Nothing*, were also his most recently performed and published works. (The radio play *All That Fall* was broadcast and the play *Endgame* staged and published in the months after she left.) This too is the year that Beckett found himself suddenly transformed from obscurity to celebrity: *Godot* was first staged in English to actively hostile audiences in England and America, and both the enigmatic play and author became notorious and widely discussed. "How can a man, who has charmed the youth of America as the lion in *The Wizard of Oz*," actor Bert Lahr was hotly accused, "appear in a play which is communistic, atheistic, and existential?" (qtd. in Cronin 455). Simultaneously, English translations of his fiction were published. Watson read *Godot* (in English) immediately in the wake of these theatrical and intellectual-political scandals, beginning in March 1956, and by the end of July had read all his works listed above (in French). The journals show her to be a sensitive and wide-ranging, indeed tireless, reader; but rarely if ever do they reveal her reading the same author thus consistently, with separate volumes in close succession. The extent to which Beckett spoke intimately to Watson may be gauged by the way that his texts become part of her everyday life and even of her perceptions. She heard resonances of *Godot* on the streets (17 June 1956), and even began to assimilate, so to speak, Beckett's world. After remarking that the hobo had "taken possession of Beckett—the infinite misery of unaccommodated man," and quoting and commenting upon a long passage from the Trilogy, she adds: "Today I saw the blind man with his dog at the corner of the rue Roche—The dog sits alert and elegant—vigilant and selfpossessed [*sic*]. After the spring clipping her coat grows into soft black curl—Her winter coat was dull and thick matted as a bear's. Now I go particularly to see them; they are part of my life—though we do not speak" (11 June 1956).[3] Her assimilation of Beckett at this time was thus profound. Two observations may also be made regarding this journal entry, which will be pertinent to the argument that follows. First we must note a chain of sympathetic if ambivalent identifications: (a) the writer with the blind man: the gaze, mute and asymmetrical to his blindness, as if in a mirror, so that he is "part of" her life, yet without speech, hence without symmetrical recognition of her for him; (b) the blind man with his "alert and elegant" dog: a synecdoche that turns inside-out the perceptual disability and poverty of the man; and (c) the dog with a bear: crossing the borderline between the tame and the wild, or the urban and the undeveloped landscape. I do not mean that Watson identifies in some one-to-one, personal way with these figures. With a transcendental freedom, combined with a sort of abjection or humility, she gives herself *as a writer* to these objective correlatives of the "infinite misery of unaccomodated man"—a misery she not only lives herself, in a special sense to be discussed below, but which she believes to be universal. The other point to note is the chain of signs of property, exchange, and appropriation. Beckett is "possessed" by the hobo. The hobo is, both by definition and implicitly as described here, a figure of dispossessions. And the dog is "selfpossessed." The hobo and dog are themselves possessed, in a sense appropriated: they are made "part of [her] life." Considerable anxiety surrounds this navigation of signs of possession of material wealth (property), possession of self by self (propriety), possession of self by another (assimilation or appropriation), and the possibility of exchange between self and others. The strangely seductive pleasure of dispossession, which belongs to the register I called abject, is expressed in the crushing phrase that ends Watson's quotation of Beckett's vagrant: "Il y avait longtemps que je n'avais eu vraiment envie de quelques chose[s] et l'effet sur moi fut horrible."[4] With Watson's appropriation of Beckett here, we are both at the limits of a dominant capitalist economy (in a figure of exclusion from property and the workforce) and at the limits of its symbolic economy. At the latter margin, the claim to self-possession, or submission to possession by another, can seem to belong to some alien, unreal, or unacknowledged other world, and to produce a language of propriety and exchange that is strange and challenging. Indeed, it will be my argument that there is another economy here, which—owing to its essential role in both Watson's and Beckett's writing, one that correlates with its predominant role in tribal literatures—I will soon refer to as an aboriginal economy. Only in cosmopolitan modernism, however, does this aboriginal economy appear simultaneously essential and abject.[5]

II

I take the view that Watson's work, like Beckett's, is conditioned by a familiar modernist vision of an alienated world, one stripped of those social ties (person to person, and person to nature) that are carefully reproduced in aboriginal societies, and which give life and writing, in whatever historical circumstances, their meaning. This vision is similarly represented in Beckett and Watson in the modernist mode of a black-comic literature of the absurd. More specifically, I will suggest that for both writers there arises—out of a modern sense of a catastrophic negation of aboriginal and archaic tradition, especially as tradition is articulated by a powerful economy of kinship ties—a sort of implicit primitivism. I am adapting the latter term to refer, in this literary context, to any counter-discourse of an idealized world of human bonds, referenced to pre-modern (re modern as defined above) ways of life. Primitivism will today suggest the aestheticization, itself alienated, of such traditions; but this does not extend equally to all modernist interests in the aboriginal, and I use the term warily, to mark the centrality of what I will call aboriginal discourse in the work of the two writers. This is a discourse not limited in reference to Native peoples' modernity or heritage but relevant to aspects of non-Native or indeed imperialist social formations as well; it involves any language or system that aligns kinship ties with a gift-dominated economy and dependency upon a native land.

I have said that I consider modernism to be defined in part in relation to a global process of modernization, and briefly sketched the latter in sociological terms. It will be evident that British imperialism, articulated across a vast array of cultural, political, and economic institutions, is the condition of possibility, a kind of host body for modernity as such in the Irish situation as well as the Canadian (and in both, the decades around the turn of the century mark a national or "post-colonial" turning point). So much for a diachronic framework; I will need also, however hastily, to sketch out a synchronic dimension to it, for social formations, imperial, national, or tribal, cannot be characterized by the rise and fall of single economic systems. Rather, I will draw on the model suggested by anthropologist Chris Gregory, which differentiates between three basic, regulatory economic systems that may coexist in any society: those of House, State, and Market. Each of these institutional fields marks value and organizes its possession and exchange in different ways. The Market refers to the production of value and rules of exchange of alienable possessions, or *commodities*, and is familiar to us as the central mechanism of value production under capitalism. The House refers to "a corporate body who owns an estate consisting of land, tools and livestock, and intangibles such as family stories, names, titles, religious powers, and character." This is where inalienable possessions are produced (that is, valued as such) and either kept out of circulation or exchanged according to the non-commodity organization of what anthropologists have called the *gift* economy.[6] The institutions are not, of course, exclusive, nor are their objects fixed in value: "A material object such as silver is now a *commodity*, now a *gift*, now a *good* depending upon the specific context of a transaction. If *commodities* are those values that arise as things pass from House to Market, then *gifts* are those values that pass between Houses and *goods* the inalienable keepsakes that are stored within a single House" (11). House and Market operate in virtually all societies, but the ubiquity of State, as Gregory defines it, is debatable: "The distinguishing feature of the State is the token money it creates. These tokens are created by marking *commodities* such as gold, silver, copper, or paper with a sign such as $, £, ¥, Rs and recognizing the product so created as legal tender within a clearly defined territory" (12). While all three institutions clearly operate together—Gregory uses the term "coevally" (7–10)—in modern societies of imperialist heritage, the presence of a State economy in tribal societies would depend upon population densities and regional histories, and might extend to tokens not marked by graphic signs (for example, shells) or to tokens not so marked at the commodity stage (for example, coppers). For present purposes, I will call aboriginal that economy in which the House has pre-eminent strength in assigning social identity and power to its members. I will call capitalist that society in which the Market has such strength. To speak of aboriginal modernity is to refer, then, to the experience of those social formations in which the aboriginal heritage of a strong House meets the combined forces of capitalist Markets and imperialist States, resulting in material and cultural conflicts, and the struggle of the House to retain its regulatory power over modern social change. To speak of imperialist modernity is to refer to the rise of the strength of the capitalist State over and against the House, the regulatory economy of the latter withdrawing to an increasingly "private sphere" of the nuclear family (and indeed, under continuing patriarchy, into a domestic sphere coded feminine), and of sentimental ties (elective affinities; friendship). Hence, when I say that an aboriginal discourse aligns kinship ties with a gift-dominated economy and dependency upon a local land (what Gregory would call a good), I am referring to the symbolic order of a world regulated by strong Houses. Aboriginal modernity registers the holistic, open collision of this symbolic order with that articulated instead by a strong Market and State. Cosmopolitan modernity, on the other hand, is the name we give precisely to the marginal containment and suppression of the power of the House, and the recognition of a symbolic order in which kinship and land are no longer the most powerful bases for identity, power, wealth, and historical transformation. Cosmopolitan modernism, I would suggest, does not merely express this symbolic order, but is contradictorily at one and at odds with it: seeking radically to rewrite it, to escape or to alter it, and often enough to transvalue the degraded or repressed symbolics of the House—available both in the interstices of its own world and in what a growing ethnography is telling of other worlds—in order to do so.

III

Beckett's first mention in Watson's journals is in two quotations from *Godot,* which she bought and read in the spring of 1956 (2 March). Both quotations are clearly transcribed for their relevance to her own life: an emotionally lacerating love triangle involving her husband Wilfred and the woman with whom he was having an affair. Wilfred struggled to convince Sheila to divorce him; she refused. She attempted in her journal to justify the decision, for she was continually reminded of the suffering she caused, and was accused of acting selfishly (2 March, and elsewhere). It is with this other woman in mind that Watson's quotation of Pozzo's assertion—"The tears of the world are a constant quantity. For each one who begins to weep somewhere else another stops"—has its poignancy. It reflects her own sense of the irremediable condition of the situation and, beyond that, of the unjustifiable brokenness of life itself; her biographer has called this her "acceptance of incoherence and inequity" (Flahiff, *Sheila Watson* ts. 93).[7] The only way to reduce suffering, she decides in another journal entry (12 April 1956), is to accept it. What must immediately be noticed as nearly too obvious to mention is that what is breaking up here is an essential form of kinship; her husband has become her family but now fails symmetrically to recognize this relationship; and there are no children (see Flahiff, *Sheila Watson* ts. 82). Whether there were similar betrayals in the past is unclear, but this marriage fracture was by 1956 at least three years old (Flahiff, *Sheila Watson* ts. 105). In other words, what Beckett calls "the breakdown of the object" confronted by the modernist artist (*Disjecta* 70) is in Watson's journals understood intimately, focused on the contours of the breakdown of a basic affiliation (so too in her interpolations of Eliot, 25 March 1954 and elsewhere). Her anxiety is never about herself as an independent identity but about herself as constituting a ground with others and vice versa.

Such a concern is arguably both central and increasingly unadorned in her writing life, in which the breakdown of affiliations, or basic kinship relations, is variously explored: the plot of her first novel, *Deep Hollow Creek,* turns on cuckoldry; the plot of her second, *The Double Hook,* turns on the murder of a mother and the failure to recognize paternity; and her short story sequence, *Five Stories*, plays on references to the Oedipus cycle, a powerful archetype for Western broken kinship narratives (as Gerald Vizenor has suggested in "Reversal of Fortunes" 219).[8] There is also a short story by Madeleine Ferron that Watson translated as "Be Fruitful and Multiply" (1974), which follows a woman's life from her marriage as a young girl to old age, giving birth to so many children (and to so many subsequent families and relationships) that she can no longer be sure she is not related to anyone she meets, or that others are not so related. The story resonates ambiguously with both Jesus's affirmation of his spiritual family in Matthew 12: 46–50 and, in its haunting closing lines, Cain's misrecognition of it in Genesis 4: 9. Watson claimed that she would have given all she had written to have written that one story (Flahiff, *Sheila Watson* ts. 348).

Turning back to Beckett's work, we see some striking parallels, and I will suggest that an aboriginal discourse is common to *The Double Hook* and Beckett's Trilogy in particular. In the latter also, we see an unremitting desire to strip both characterization and plot down to sequences, criss-crossings, and layerings of thought, feeling, action, and word whose only and inadequate common ground lies in existential duration—and finally and metafictionally, as F.T. Flahiff has observed of *The Double Hook*, in the duration of the reader ("Afterword" 125; see also re Watson and Beckett, *Sheila Watson* ts. 87, 235). Stripped away, too, are stable kinship ties, by marriage and blood alike. As in *The Double Hook*, the Trilogy begins with the absence of a mother and is haunted by this absence throughout (turning to violent fantasies of her death only near the end). This is the point of origin in the Trilogy for its well-nigh total stripping away of the self from all but fluid and fictional ties to others, to the endlessly deferred limit of a lonely core of the self, unnameable and dark, nearly identical with mere absence. Beckett's narrator is a kind of parodic James Potter, who has spiritually burned down his home—his House—yet has no other, and circles its dead on a clunky bicycle rather than a horse, and with Irish loquacity rather than Canadian reserve. For both Watson and Beckett, the narrative turns upon the problem of substitutions in the empty space left by the dead or estranged mother, a space haunted by both fear and desire. But there also appears to be that which *cannot* be substituted: in Beckett's English texts, it may be a native land (as argued by Eoin O'Brien's photographic essay in *The Beckett Country*) or a native voice—what various critics have called an unmistakably Irish voice (if not, moreover, that of an Irish storytelling genre); in Watson's texts, it is a native place, the childhood landscapes of the short stories, or the aboriginal territory, "In the folds of the hills / under Coyote's eye," of *The Double Hook* (11). The discourses of a native language and of a native land are connected to kinship in aboriginal discourses because together they define a House economy of gifts, goods, commodities, and social relations alternative to the dominant economy and social culture of modernity's capitalist and imperialist heritage.

The world of *The Double Hook* is a representation, not of the subtraction of civilization toward some "natural" or cliché "primitive" substratum of the human signified by its matter-of-factly violent plot, its regional desertification, and its aboriginal myth, even though this is the way the novel may be read by those who, like the novel's first scholarly advocate, Frederick Salter, see a kind of modernist existentialism in the work, what Raymond Williams called the ideology of "modern tragedy." Salter felt that as Shakespeare does with Lear, Watson "disaccommodates man" in order to "stud[y] him" stripped of the "garments" that "shelter us from the dark and the void of the universe" (qtd. in Flahiff "Afterword," 123). Although I think this "modern tragedy" reading of the novel is likely responsible for its canonization in Canadian literature as departing from the more apparently sentimental or earnest types of Canadian realism, I believe this reading actually inverts the novel's meaning and misrecognizes its achievement. Rather than stripping away civilization to reveal a primitive essence, this novel strips away the primitive—or, properly speaking, displaces the aboriginal—to reveal a stark residue of the civilized.

In a journal entry of 5 February 1956, thinking about the circus as a symbol of the absurdity of life and of the world, Watson is led to complain: "This is what Mr. Salter didn't understand about 'The Double Hook'—He thought that my people were stripped of society—conceived of as progressive[;] I meant that they were stripped of their bridges or centre, roots traditions" which, she goes on to say, Simone Weil describes as bridges "between earth & sky—and between one another even." Here, what Watson says she *is* saying, which accords well with her published statements, is clarified greatly by what she says she is *not* saying. She does not strip her characters of "society" *tout court*, as if society were responsible for constructing the artifice of civility and "progress" (or in terms proper to the novel's plot, duty, and justice) over the libido, savagery, or indifferent chaos of the human being without society. If we deny that such society is stripped away, then what we should infer is that society—perhaps not progressive, but society as itself an unexpectedly dark, chaotic form—is yet integral to the life of *The Double Hook*. This reading aligns itself with a modernism that sees society as a degenerated or degraded form—and if we ask degenerated from what, then we discover the primitivist aboriginal as a positive foil. In this case, the value of the primitive is inverted from the "modern tragedy" reading: the aboriginal is a prior (and displaced or marginalized) network of social relations, a whole economy of duties and obligations encoded in (verbal, labour, and property) exchange, that has been stripped away to produce the estranged anomie of the modern world.[9]

We see such kinship-economic "bridges" in the set of relations that determine the positive movement at the end of the novel. These relations, in what Flahiff has called a "silent consensus" (*Sheila Watson* ts. 440), all prohibit the possibility of individual identity separating itself from a ground in gestures of reciprocity and return: James's giving up "the price of his escape" (95) to the prostitutes, his giving his will to his horse and thus to his land (106–07), and Lenchen's giving of her child to James, in her naming of James to James, thus enunciating how she sees him in relation to their child, at the very end (117). It is in reparation for all of James's betrayed "bridges" (with the prostitutes as well as the stable-owner he cannot immediately pay, with his murdered mother and, proleptically, his dead sister, and with his child's mother, Lenchen) that he realizes: "There are times when a man spends more than he has and must go on credit.... Unless a man defaults ... a debt is a sort of bond" (106). The notion of debt (and of return: "a person only escapes in circles" [116]) is perhaps the central and certainly the clearest explicit sign in the text of its justice, its logic of closure, the logic of how and why the minimal restoration of families and obligations occurs.[10] We see the notion of debt developed even more elaborately in relation to gifts and exchanges in Watson's earlier novel, *Deep Hollow Creek*. I have discussed this in some detail elsewhere (see Willmott), but what is important to the present context is the aboriginal discourse—quite explicit in the earlier novel and tied to the indigenous Coyote—that is associated with those debts and returns. In *The Double Hook*, Watson has said she intended to address that which is "indigenous" but not "ethnic"—which I take to mean aboriginal, in my use of the term here (the House dominating social relations) (qtd. in Meyer and O'Riordan

159). Specifically, she wished to address the displacement or loss of those aboriginal "bridges" of tradition or ritual—not only in religious, but in everyday family and economic life—that is a part of modern history.

Nor were the colonialist politics of aboriginal modernity lost upon Watson. At the same time she was reading Beckett and completing *The Double Hook*, the journals tell us, she was reading Paul Radin's *The Trickster* (1956) alongside Octave Mannoni's *The Psychology of Colonization* (1950; English trans. 1956) regarding African colonialism, attending to the Algerian revolutionary war, and taking an interest in the history of the West Indies.[11] So, I suggest, *The Double Hook* attempts to encode an aboriginal economy at the dimly recognized limits (past, present, and future) of both Native and non-Native lives in the novel. This economy is linked as much to James, an apparently but not certainly non-Native character (in an earlier manuscript he is described as mixed-blood[12]), as it is, for example, to Angel, an apparently but not certainly Native character (see her faith in a spiritual Coyote throughout and the reference to her "fish camp" [29]). Indeed, Angel is arguably the only character with an active sense of community, however pessimistic; she brings characters together in the end, she returns to Felix in a parallel movement to that of James, and she orchestrates the birth of Lenchen's child. She is also, like Kip, most strongly connected to an awareness and wariness of Coyote in the text. Coyote himself is of course an aboriginal figure, the "trickster" who represents the absurdity of individualistically following one's own desires, of betraying or misrecognizing one's ground in others and in place—in order to reveal (and in some traditions, hence to teach) the suffering that must result. In other words, Watson imagines not only non-Native but Native society unaccommodated, stripped of its wealth of symbols and powers, its diversity of spirits, that are its own relational bridges, leaving only the trickster behind. This is the paradox of the aboriginal figure in *The Double Hook*: the trickster, the proper pedagogical figure of a figure-without-a-ground, is itself dispossessed of its ground, and becomes a ground *as such* (appropriately left to circle round and round a desolate land).[13] The appropriation, the uprooting and isolation of Coyote from the symbolic and social organization of the Shuswap House, serves Watson as a figure of the cosmopolitan of imperialist heritage itself, but estranged by its disturbing provenance—its incomplete address, its unfinished pedagogy—in an aboriginal language. As Native writers have often warned us,[14] and as Watson here affirms, it is a terrible world that is left only to the trickster—or to the modernist artist—to watch over.

IV

One might like Watson to have more consistently historicized this notion of a "disaccommodated" or "unaccommodated" modernity, to distinguish it not only from social formations existing outside of and alternative to those driven by capitalist empires (such as pre-colonial tribal cultures), but from those inside the range of modern capitalism as well, in order to register alterities and differences developing within modernity (such as modern aboriginal cultures themselves). But in her journals she wrote that the absurdity of the world, in which "there is no message" but only "the impossible" (5 February 1956), produces worlds like that of *The Double Hook* that are impervious to historical change and are simply "insoluble in human terms" (6 March 1956). What she says of her marriage at the outset of her Paris journal bleeds into her response to the absurd suffering world at large registered by Beckett: one can only, with Eliot, "be still, and wait without hope" (25 March 1954). Watson appears to have entertained feelings and commitments that could be both historicist and revolutionary, and essentialist and resigned: another double hook. Echoing the European avant-garde's fascination with the circus, she writes in her journal:

> It is across the absurdity of the world, conceived of and suffered as an absurdity not only that man finds the Kingdom which is not of this world but also that the artist finds his world of discourse.
>
> The circus becomes the symbol of life for the writer—for me at least—There is no message—there is the impossible—and men lifting it like a weight or jumping through it like a hoop—or trying to tame it—torn faces, falls from the tight rope—spectacular manipulations—tigers bowing humbly before men—clowns drooling.
> (5 February 1956)

It must be evident, however, that the absurdity and suffering of which she writes here—I mean as something intrinsic to the world and as the basic discourse of the artist rather than as a mere possibility for the artist to negotiate and overcome—is nowhere really echoed in aboriginal discourses, while it is everywhere echoed across a wide range of modernist responses to a capitalist modernity.

What is unique in Watson's achievement is to turn the "impossible" nostalgia of cosmopolitan modernism for an aboriginal world—that is, for a world of absurd obligations and debts, as opposed to absurd rivalries and profits—a nostalgia that is only implicitly historical in Beckett, into a complex, explicit dialogue. This dialogue may be considered more particularly as a dialogic heteroglossia, a literary concept developed by Mikhail Bakhtin to describe mutually contestatory discourses, arising from different social groups, coexisting in the novel form.[15] Those contestatory discourses would here be those of cosmopolitan modernism of the capitalist imperialist heritage, and of aboriginal discourses, historical and legendary. The result is a dialogue between resigned nostalgia (tradition is lost; tradition contradicts modernity; hope must be transcendental) and miraculous, actual transformation (tradition is ongoing; tradition inhabits modernity; hope may be historical). Such a paradoxical or even incoherent interplay is not a fault of the novel—much less the failure to assimilate cosmopolitan modernism to non-cosmopolitan worlds—but would seem to mirror an authentic crisis, and a productive one, in the depths of our time. The modern world must be suffered. This Watson demands that we acknowledge; hence the monumental importance of Beckett to her work. But in that suffering world, the ground from which restitutions arise—or even social changes—if perhaps that ground be repressed, can never be cut away. In her paradoxical articulation of this double movement, both toward the general inevitability of suffering and toward its modern contingency (in the not inevitable repression of the House), Watson thus both assimilates the lessons of cosmopolitan modernism and reaches beyond them toward an unrepresented future. Specifically, she forces upon us all the fateful powers and deprivals of modernity, yet at the same times adheres to what may be called an aboriginal perspective of and faith in their limits. In this sense, her work may be regarded as genuinely *post-cosmopolitan*, and invites us to think what that might mean for ourselves.

NOTES

[1] Pound's phrase appears in various places in his writing. It is the title of a 1934 collection of his essays, whose title page reproduces the Chinese characters from which he translated the phrase. The phrase and its Chinese context are spelled out in Canto LIII. See Pound, *Make It New* and *The Cantos* (265).

[2] See T.S. Eliot, "The Metaphysical Poets":

> Our civilization comprehends great variety and complexity, and this variety and complexity, playing upon a refined sensibility, must produce various and complex results. The poet must become more and more comprehensive, more allusive, more indirect, in order to force, to dislocate if necessary, language into its meaning. (289)

[3] Watson's journals quoted with permission.

[4] From Beckett, "The End" (1946; English translation, 1955): "It was long since I had longed for anything and the effect on me was horrible" (*Complete* 82).

[5] I refer here to Julia Kristeva's suggestion that objects washed with primal desire may inspire antagonism and horror, to put it over simply, in a kind of revenge for what has been lost in the progress of individuation. That this applies to Beckett's work is clear enough in the figure of the mother in the Trilogy, and I am developing this in a separate study; the application to *The Double Hook* refers to the (however positively interpreted, as I will argue in my conclusion) reduction of Coyote to a rather more negative figure than is proper to its significance in any aboriginal discourse.

[6] I refer to the tradition of analysis and debate in anthropology and more recently in cultural studies initiated by Marcel Mauss's *Essai sur le don, forme archaïque de l'échange* (1925), translated by Ian Cunnison as *The Gift: Forms and Functions of Exchange in Archaic Societies* (1967).

[7] F.T. Flahiff has graciously given permission to quote from the typescript (dated 15 March 2003) of his forthcoming biography, *Sheila Watson: A Life*. All citations of the biography will refer to page numbers in the typescript.

[8] Dates of composition for Watson's writings are uncertain. Her first novel was likely written in the 1930s; her second was written in the 1950s. Of the Oedipus cycle stories in *Five Stories*, "Antigone," "Brother Oedipus," and "The Black Farm" also date from the 1950s, while "The Rumble Seat" dates from the 1960s.

[9] Such an alternative economy is encoded not only in the Native figure of Coyote but in the traces of the Church that surface in fragments, like an archaic dream language, in Felix's struggle for words of hospitality or ejection when Lenchen arrives at his house.

[10] In the *In Their Words* interview, Watson says *The Double Hook* is about "community reduced almost to a single unit" (163) rather than about family. I take this to mean that "family" is too narrow a term for the problem of social and kinship "bridges" that are reduced to fragments at the threshold of family amidst wider community formations.

[11] That these readings mingled creatively in her mind is suggested, for example, by

her noting and transcribing a rare political reference in the Trilogy, in which the narrator compares himself (unfavourably) to the Haitian revolutionary, Toussaint l'Ouverture (29 July 1956).

[12] I am grateful to F.T. Flahiff for this information.

[13] In "What I'm Going to Do," Watson describes the characters of *The Double Hook* as "figures in a ground, from which they could not be separated" (183).

[14] See, for example, Keeshig-Tobias for the extensive figuration of the trickster as imperialist.

[15] Bakhtin spells this out in general terms, in advance of specific readings, in the "Discourse in Poetry and Discourse in the Novel" section (275–300) of *The Dialogic Imagination*.

WORKS CITED

Bakhtin, M.M. *The Dialogic Imagination: Four Essays*. Trans. Caryl Emerson and Michael Holquist. Austin: U of Texas P, 1981.

Beckett, Samuel. *The Complete Short Prose, 1929–1989*. Ed. S.E. Gontarski. New York: Grove, 1995.

———. *Disjecta: Miscellaneous Writings and a Dramatic Fragment*. Ed. Ruby Cohn. New York: Grove, 1984.

———. *Three Novels: Molloy, Malone Dies, The Unnamable*. French first editions, 1951–53; English first editions, 1955–58. New York: Grove P, 1991.

Cronin, Anthony. *Samuel Beckett: The Last Modernist*. London: HarperCollins, 1996.

Eliot, T.S. "The Metaphysical Poets." 1921. *Selected Essays*. 3rd ed. London: Faber and Faber, 1951. 281–91.

Ferron, Madeleine. "Be Fruitful and Multiply." 1966. Trans. Sheila Watson. 1974. *From Ink Lake: An Anthology of Canadian Short Stories*. Ed. Michael Ondaatje. Toronto: Penguin, 1990. 203–06.

Flahiff, F.T. "Afterword." Watson, *The Double Hook* 119–30.

———. *Sheila Watson: A Life*. Edmonton: NeWest, forthcoming.

Gregory, C.A. *Savage Money: The Anthropology and Politics of Commodity Exchange*. Amsterdam: Harwood Academic Publishers, 2000.

Keeshig-Tobias, Lenore. "Trickster Beyond 1992: Our Relationship." *Indigena: Contemporary Native Perspectives*. Ed. Gerald McMaster and Lee-Ann Martin. Vancouver: Douglas and McIntyre, 1992. 101–12.

Kristeva, Julia. *Powers of Horror: An Essay on Abjection*. Trans. Leon S. Roudiez. New York: Columbia UP, 1982.

Mauss, Marcel. *Essai sur le don, forme archaïque de l'échange*. 1925. Trans. Ian Cunison. *The Gift: Forms and Functions of Exchange in Archaic Societies*. New York: Norton, 1967.

Meyer, Bruce, and Brian O'Riordan, eds. *In Their Words: Interviews with Fourteen Canadian Writers*. Toronto: Anansi, 1984.

O'Brien, Eoin. *The Beckett Country: Samuel Beckett's Ireland*. Monkstown, co. Dublin: Black Cat Press; London: Faber and Faber, 1986.

Pound, Ezra. *The Cantos of Ezra Pound*. New York: New Directions, 1970.

———. "Hugh Selwyn Mauberley." 1920. *Personae*. New York: New Directions, 1990. 183–225.

———. *Make It New: Essays*. London: Faber and Faber, 1934.

Vizenor, Gerald. "Reversal of Fortunes." *Shadow Distance: A Gerald Vizenor Reader*. Hanover: Wesleyan UP, 1994. 219–26.

Watson, Sheila. *The Double Hook*. 1959. Toronto: McClelland and Stewart, 1989.

———. Journals, 1954–57. Sheila Watson Archives. In process of being established at St. Michael's College, University of Toronto.

———. "What I'm Going to Do." *Sheila Watson: A Collection. Open Letter* 3rd ser.1 (winter 1974–75): 181–83.

Williams, Raymond. *Modern Tragedy*. Stanford: Stanford UP, 1966.

Willmott, Glenn. "The Nature of Modernism in Sheila Watson's *Deep Hollow Creek*." *Canadian Literature* 146 (1995): 30–48.

ECLECTIC TRAVELLERS: FROM PETERBOROUGH TO PARIS

A.J.M. Smith's
Eclectic Surrealism

BRIAN TREHEARNE

A.J.M. SMITH EXPLICITLY rejected any identification of his poetry with Surrealism. When a conservative reviewer of *The Book of Canadian Poetry*, William Arthur Deacon, casually identified him as a poet of the Canadian "surrealist school," Smith vituperated on Deacon's obtuseness in a letter to A.M. Klein[1] and was still resentful thirty-five years later when he penned his "Confessions of a Compulsive Anthologist" (7–8). These protests notwithstanding, several of Smith's poems of the 1930s and early 1940s, especially those published from 1934 to 1936 during the Surrealist craze in London, show his distinct attraction to Surrealist ideas and effects, including imagery and its associative accumulation; automatic writing; surreal treatments of setting and landscape; the notion of "black humour"; and a cryptic but clearly emancipatory politics refusing alignment, like André Breton's, with the right, left or soft left demanded by the times. Smith more or less deliberately obscured his Surrealist experimentation by reprinting these poems haphazardly at best (only half survive in *The Classic Shade* of 1978), and his diffidence has helped to impoverish our narratives of his development, narratives that dwell almost exclusively on his relation to Anglo-American modernism and the Metaphysicals and that sport a vocabulary of "austerity," "classicism," and "difficulty" with which I for one am simply bored—and to judge by his steadily dwindling place in the canon,[2] I'm not alone. Smith's intermittent Surrealist practice would appear to offer a refreshing critical alternative to that overworked consensus, one that might make us interested once again in this alert, conflicted, self-deprecating modernist.

In an article published near the end of Smith's life Leon Edel remarked that his friend had early on "frolicked with the surreal and knew how [André] Breton was trying to trap the wit and humour of the unconscious" (202). No one found the hint suggestive; of the poems I will cite only "Noctambule" has been linked to Surrealism, in brief asides by Leo Kennedy (17), Sandra Djwa (20), and John Ferns (56). "Noctambule" was composed by 1932;[3] it first appeared in a Wisconsin campus publication in the spring of 1935 and was reprinted in London's *New Verse* in August–September 1936 and in every Smith volume. In the previous issue of *New Verse* W.H. Auden had published "Honest Doubt," a request for clarification of essential Surrealist doctrine;[4] earlier *New Verse* items surveyed the Surrealist imitators in England,[5] reviewed Surrealist publications from France,[6] and translated the poems of Paul Eluard and Jean Arp.[7] Surrealism was clearly that summer's rage, with the International Surrealist Exhibition taking place at the New Burlington Galleries in London in June.[8] Although these *New Verse* items were not free of skepticism, the appearance of "Noctambule" among them would have made the poem's Surrealism readily legible to a contemporary reader.

The poem's superficial features certainly justify such a reading. The "*a* of *b*" formula I first identified in the poetry of P.K. Page (*Montreal Forties* 74–75) and later recognized as a Surrealist mannerism[9] is prominent in "Noctambule," with its "flag of this pneumatic moon," "hulk of witless night," "pockethandkerchief / Of 6 a.m.," and "warcry of treacherous daytime." Smith's images, sharply juxtapositive, and with a latent violence typical of the mannerism, accumulate in a restless parataxis that begins to hint by the closing lines at the unconscious coherences of automatic writing, the free-associative compositional method that Breton identified early on as the essence of Surrealist artistic activity:[10]

> So mewed the lion,
> Until mouse roared once and after lashed
> His tail: Shellshock came on again, his skin
> Twitched in the rancid margarine, his eye
> Like a lake isle in a florist's window:

Reality at two removes, and mouse and moon
Successful.[11]

The broad result is a cryptic urban nightscape, with a "pneumatic moon" like a "wetwash snotrag," a looming figurative "Othello" overhead, a whiff of "horsemeat," and mice twitching in the margarine. If we surrender to an impulse to read "Noctambule" as a verbal painting, the Surrealist composition of Smith's canvas seems apparent.

That temptation can be misleading, though, because a brilliant ekphrasis of a Surrealist painting would not itself be a work of Surrealist art at all, since the poet would have had to accept a fixed mimetic motive that runs counter to the spontaneity of Surrealist creation. Running a little deeper than Smith's striking imagery and scene are epistemological emphases that situate "Noctambule" more clearly and intriguingly on the Surrealist horizon. The more French than English title[12] asks us to think of the whole vision as that of someone in a state between waking and dream. The inducement and articulation of such liminal states was of course a fundamental Surrealist activity,[13] and the art that results is not supposed to be aesthetically comfortable. Much as we might be glad to dismiss this brightly-faked world as merely "dreamed," Smith's hallucinatory imagery insists on its own absolute reality and demands that we internalize it as such, even as it refuses us the comfortable perspectives of neutral description. His famous remark that "a poem is not the description of an experience, it is itself an experience, and it awakens in the mind of the alert and receptive reader a new experience analogous to the one in the mind of the poet..." ("Refining Fire" 353) is brilliantly enacted in "Noctambule," which surely offers no coherent standpoint from which we might describe the kind of experience we are forced to appropriate as we read. This scorn for description is another facet of the poem's Surrealist sensibility, which radically opposed the mere description of dream to dream's *enactment* in art and saw realist description as the proof of literature's subservience to a hegemonic reason.[14]

Finally, Sandra Djwa's suggestion that the speaker of "Noctambule" may be a demobilized soldier suffering from residual "Shellshock" (20–21) offers another potential Surrealist context for Smith's poem. It is only coincidental that an initiatory moment of French Surrealism was the young André Breton's treatment of shell-shocked soldiers in World War I; his attempt to apply the ideas of Freud to their traumas helped to convince him of the complexity and power of the unconscious (Matthews 13–17). If Smith's poem *is* enacting such trauma, nevertheless, he is showing a typically Surrealist interest in the unique cast of mind and liberated perceptions of the mentally ill. His treatment here, hovering between sympathy and a disconcerting black humour, reflects the enduring Surrealist ambivalence over the real value of mental illness as a paradigm for the artist.[15]

Despite its prominence in the Smith canon and its unique gestures, "Noctambule" must have seemed an eccentric tour de force in *News of the Phoenix* in 1943, where it lacked the contextual thematic support of several comparably Surrealist poems from the mid-1930s. Smith's "Political Intelligence" and "The Resurrection of Arp," for example, were excluded from *News of the Phoenix*[16] and only redeemed by Smith for *A Sort of Ecstasy* in 1954. There and in all subsequent collections he placed the three poems in proximity, an implicit acknowledgment of their shared orientation. The Surrealist credentials of "Political Intelligence" are impeccable: first published in November 1936 in *Contemporary Poetry and Prose*, a short-lived London periodical closely associated with the British Surrealist school, it was later selected by Edward Germain for his anthology *Surrealist Poetry in English*, where it remains available in its original form. While "Political Intelligence" shuns the Surrealist concatenations of imagery prominent in "Noctambule," it develops that poem's mock-theatrical landscape and black humour with a hilarious pungency that keeps it unhappily relevant in a "post"-war climate today:

> Nobody said Apples for nearly a minute—
> I thought I should die.
> Finally, though, the second sardine
> from the end, on the left,
> converted a try.
> (It brought down the house.
> The noise was terrific.
> I dropped my glass eye.) (PNC 107)

This is a Smith we have apparently forgotten, this guffawing and scandalized political observer with a keen appetite for angry nonsense. The absurd military display, in which glass-eyed sardines play rugby for the Prime

Minister (who intones "Keep calm there is no cause for alarm" as, on the poem's margins, Germany occupies the Rhineland and Spain collapses into civil war), is distinctly Surrealist in its juxtapositions and its refusal to rationalize them.[17] But the humour of the poem takes on a more malign dissonance in the final stanza, where the bodily maiming hinted at in that "glass eye" suddenly defines the atmosphere:

> Two soldiers' crutches
> crossed up a little bit of fluff
> from a lint bandage
> in the firing chamber of a 12-inch gun.
> People agreed not to notice.
> The band played a little bit louder.
> It was all very British. (130–31)[18]

The layered Surrealist object rendered here—a cannon jammed with two crutches and a *femme enfant*, the child-woman of so much Surrealist representation[19]—is impossible to paraphrase.[20] Smith's simultaneous demands for visceral shock and sardonic laughter are exemplary of Surrealist black humour, an anarchic mode (but also "une attitude de l'esprit ... une attitude devant la vie..." [Le Brun 100–01]) in which the instincts of pleasure and play confront the violent fact of death. Black humour is partly defensive, like all laughter; but in its comic deconstructions of the absurd real world, it is offensive, a humour of subversion that protects the self from oppression and disintegration and exposes the fatuity of its opponents.[21] These are ideas of action and engagement—and fun—that are not usually pursued in Smith's poetry.

"Political Intelligence" may have been kept out of *News of the Phoenix* because that volume appeared in wartime, but "Resurrection of Arp" surely would have offended the Methodist-oriented Ryerson Press with its blasphemous treatment of the risen Christ as media darling, dealing soundbites to a frenzied audience of "saints" and "converts" who celebrate his return with "sexual intercourse (dancing) and eats" (PNC 94–95). I do not consider Smith's protagonist to have much to do with Jean Arp, the Dutch Dadaist and later Surrealist painter, poet, collagist and sculptor, because nothing I have yet grasped in the poem develops the connection, but Smith's borrowing of the surname may signal his familiarity as of April 1934[22] with

Surrealist work on the continent. A Surrealist reading of "Resurrection" is certainly possible, but as it is well known to those who know Smith at all and readily available in *The Classic Shade*, I prefer to get at its implications through a second "Arp" poem, "Arp's Randy Rant in the Comfy Confession Box," which made its lone appearance in *New Verse* in December 1935. Here we leave the canon altogether; Smith himself asked Djwa, "What is Arp's Randy Rant? Where was it published? I have no recollection of it. Will you send me a copy?"[23]

"Arp's Randy Rant" is in deliberately faulty heroic couplets, a regimen that confounds the spontaneous composition natural to Surrealism. We recur nevertheless to the false moon of "Noctambule," here an "old powdered wetnurse, Mother Moon," whose dripping milk is "bittersweet and goatish," and to the distempered "dreams" and "fancies" of another "young insomniac," rendered in an automatist barrage of inscrutably associated images that break angrily from their formal constraints:

> In narrow cot doth such an one abide,
> Himself the baited hook, himself the bride
> He dreams the green translucent future keeps
> To gasp beside him, and make deep his sleeps.
> He finds the moonmilk bittersweet and goatish.
> Alas! I find it brackish, something brutish.
> If I, on raspy canvas tossing sleepless,
> Oozing a clammy itchy sweat, keep less
> Than weepless eyes, keep bloody humpy back,
> It is to weep the most what most I lack....[24]

The persona goes on to confess not his sins but sins "craftily avoided" by denying "the incalculable debt / Of the mind to the swine's snout" and leaving "the natural heart perversely vilified"—lines that (in the context of the title, and *pace* the allusion to Browning's "Soliloquy of the Spanish Cloister") suggest the Surrealist desire to free the whole force of our emotional, bodily, and imaginative experience from the hegemony of the Church.[25]

But the more interesting implication here lies in Sandra Djwa's suggestion that "Arp's Randy Rant" was reworked for the 1940 poem "A Portrait, and a Prophecy," in which she finds Smith's "exasperation with Eliot" for his "religious conversion and [his] determination to subordinate the secular to the religious, as expressed in his 1935 lecture 'Religion and Literature'" (27). The two poems do share a central contrast between uncommitted "sins of youth" and too readily forgiven "sins of age," and Smith's having forgotten "Arp's Randy Rant" so completely may indicate that he indeed thought of it as no more than a draft of a later successful poem. The relation of either to Eliot's religious criticism is less certain, however: an early typescript of "A Portrait" was mailed to critic W.E. Collin in November 1933,[26] two years before Eliot's lecture was delivered, and the typescript version is in the first person (thus beginning, "Indeed *I* have sinned..." [emphasis added]). Smith could still of course have been reacting more generally to Eliot's conversion in 1927 and speaking ironically in his voice. In any case Djwa's suggestion raises the intriguing possibility that both "Arp" poems, and thus the Surrealist phase more generally, reflect Smith's desire to disburden himself of the legacy of Eliot that had been transparent in his work prior to 1934.[27] In this light the mid-decade Surrealist poems can be seen in part as a search for new models for his unshakeable modernism—and as a pioneering body of internationalist experiment that made possible the later Surrealist inventiveness of poets as diverse as P.K. Page, Irving Layton, and Leonard Cohen.

The evidence of Smith's actual contact with Surrealism has so far been circumstantial. I have claimed Surrealist techniques and themes in four poems, remarked his appearance in a British Surrealist periodical and anthologization as a Surrealist poet, and noted his titular allusions to a Surrealist artist.[28] Later in life he could place the Surrealists lucidly in a survey of French theories of artistic creation (see "The Poetic Process" 357), but even this gives no guarantee of conscious *creative* engagement with their ideas. It is only when we recover another forgotten periodical poem that Smith's recognition of and pleasure in his Surrealist project is made evident. "Surrealism in the Service of Christ" is a scathing vision of the Church, Nazism, misogyny, and the media, and of their collusion, that appeared in *Poetry* in April 1941.[29] His title parodies that of a Paris Surrealist periodical, *Le Surréalisme au service de la révolution*, that ran under the editorship of Breton from 1930 to 1933. Here the spate of Surrealist images strongly suggests a true automatic composition:

Collars are worn reversed across the privates
Or screwed to the navel with scallops of crepe:
You ought to see Judas in samite!

Anyway, they stoned the roll away,
And what do you think?
Only two storm troopers had the right time:
    Three merry widows in three
    Quarter time
    For you and
    Time for me and
    Three heil Marys on St. Stephansplatz.

Rubber Stocking came in with a lilt
And a penetrating skewer
And the headsman in black.

The controlled press agreed that she died rather well. (9–10)

Note too the mockery of Eliot, whose "Prufrock" (and possibly the more recent "Burnt Norton") gives Smith his play on "Time." The accumulation of images is loosely integrated by the Nazi icons and the apparent sacrifice of a woman and/or her virginity (the poem is strewn with words like "erect" and "penetrating," and "Rubber Stocking" may be an anthropomorphic condom). Smith treats her sacrifice with modernist irony rather than explicit outrage, but the male Surrealist's supposed indifference to his distortive constructions of women's bodies is not obvious here.[30] His scorn is instead reserved for a casuistical latter-day Aquinas, an "Angelic Doctor" who intones coldly "that having no form / … Neither had she, therefore, any death, / Either good, bad or indifferent" (10), as well as for all the minor functionaries who support such violent casuistry. Smith's chance premonition of Doctor Mengele, the "Angel of Death" in the extermination camps, is uncanny.

The poem's parodic title nevertheless raises the possibility that Smith assaults Surrealism here for inadvertent "service" to the very Church it means to undermine—in that the Surrealist appeal to perfect imaginative freedom risks perversion into violent, sacrificial ritual. Given the poem's extreme obscurity, this matter of Smith's intention may be impossible to resolve, partly because Surrealism enters the text proper only through his technique, and certainly not as an object of satire on a par with the "Angelic Doctor."[31] The bitter mockery of the Church and of Fascism seems indisputable in the poem, while Smith's ready and seemingly pleasurable exploitation of Surrealism as a style would make him a potential accomplice in any of its excesses as a politics. This hermeneutic indeterminacy is best understood, in my view, as a part of the poem's intense black humour, which incidentally received early formulation in the very journal to which Smith's title alludes:[32] an uncomfortable fusion of absurdist pantomime and ethical vacuity makes our position as readers profoundly problematic. Whereas in "Noctambule" and the two "Arps" Smith felt compelled to intervene with clarifying abstract remarks, he gives the meaning of "Surrealism in the Service of Christ" no such constraint. Some readers may wish he had, where the deaths of women and the actions of Nazis are concerned; for a committed modernist, however, this impersonality would have given the poem peculiar political agency, and the invitation to squeamish laughter would not cancel it. To read the poem at all, I am forced to resist its ambiguities, to assess inscrutable violent actions and react fully and freshly to the ambient propaganda. A rhetoric in which these decisions were made for me might leave me more certain that the poet shared all my views—but would also leave me passive and complacent in those views, and for that kind of ethics and that kind of art Breton himself had nothing but scorn. Early in the "Second Manifesto" he went so far as to say that "Surrealism attempted to provoke, from the intellectual and moral point of view, *an attack of conscience*, of the most general and serious kind, and ... the extent to which this was or was not accomplished alone can determine its historical success or failure" (*Manifestoes* 123–24). Smith's intuition of this polemical thrust may have encouraged his turn to Surrealist methods at a time when most of his Canadian contemporaries were taking up a much more explicit and reductive notion of political verse. Time will tell which wears better.[33]

"Surrealism in the Service of Christ," then, is good evidence of Smith's direct contact with and responsiveness to Surrealist ideas, but it is far more important as a lost document in the emergence of his political vision. The other poems in which Smith turned Surrealist visions to political ends are not quite as obscured as the last two on which I have drawn, but they are not in *The Classic Shade,* and one has not reappeared since 1943. This is "The Face," a poem of 1936 he liked well enough to put in the first edition of the *Book of Canadian Poetry* and in *News of the Phoenix* and to quote from thirty years later in one of his last poems.[34] Its opaque vision is of a demagogue whose political rhetoric disempowers his susceptible and passive audience:

> The man with the acid face
> Under the hammer of glass
> Imperils the pure place.
> The emotion of the mass,
> Inverted, seems to ask
> The jack queen king and ace
> To do the task. (*News of the Phoenix* 35)

As he disperses a conceit likening political revolution to a manic card game, Smith rejects both capitalist glad-handing ("Whose safe will you crack / With a pat on the back?") and the stark political alternatives that at the time appeared definitive:

> Each shall choose his place,
> Be Dead, or Red.
> The cards are no way stacked,
> And he may live by grace
> Who wills to act.

While this closure again shows Smith's need to batten down the anarchy of his own visions, the poem refuses to identify the demagogue with the extreme left or right, and it gains by the refusal. Most of the French Surrealists—Louis Aragon and Paul Eluard, for example—were led by devout anti-Fascism to sustain their commitment to the Communist Party even after it flatly condemned Surrealist ideas as a bourgeois obfuscation in the debates of 1935.[35] Smith's anti-Fascism was equally doctrinal, but he clearly believed that poetry could play no part in that contest if it accepted the reductive polarities Fascism had forced into political life in the 1930s. His ambiguity here, as in "Political Intelligence" and "Surrealism in the Service of Christ," is more like that of André Breton, expelled from the

French Communist Party in 1933, whose political writings—including the tract *Pour un art révolutionnaire indépendant*, co-authored with Leon Trotsky in 1938—sought "to justify endlessly the non-domestication of his spirit" ("Political Position of Surrealism," *Manifestoes* 209) and who therefore condemned both Communism's devolution into the brutalities of Stalin and the promised atrocities of Nazism. Both men lost friends and influence for spurning the political wishbone on which their peers were pulling so violently; both stand out in retrospect as artists of exceptional foresight and principle.

Taken together, "Political Intelligence," "The Face," and "Surrealism in the Service of Christ" show us a Smith almost unrecognizable from the anthologies: a citizen-poet who affirmed his radical art's function in the exposure and cauterization of global injustice and state violence. When I consider that he began the great anti-war "Ode: The Eumenides" roughly as the last of these appeared, I conclude that Surrealism intervened to vital effect between the last lingering poems of *Waste Land* despair and Smith's later production of passionate political verse, so much of which excoriates the Cold War posturing and hypocrisy that brought the entire world close to the brink of nuclear annihilation.[36] Smith, as the author of a substantial body of anti-propagandistic, anti-militaristic, and above all anti-war poetry, has an enduring part to play today in Canadian public discourse—a part we deny him by continuing to purvey a canon limited by his own later, prejudicial self-representations. Smith's Surrealism and the politics it helped him to formulate deserve a greater recognition, perhaps especially so from the generation now rising in concern not unlike his with the fundamental nexus between unchecked corporatism and incipient global war.

As forceful as its effects may have been, the sources of Smith's Surrealism are not entirely apparent. The Surrealist commentaries and translations available to him in *New Verse* from 1933–36 no doubt added to his understanding of the movement, but they cannot gloss "Noctambule," his earliest Surrealist poem, which was close to its final form in 1932. Continental periodicals are a more likely source of his earliest experiments in the vein. His 1941 parody of the title of a French periodical does not guarantee that he had actually read any issues of *Le Surréalisme au service de la révolution* as they appeared from 1930–33, but if he had it would help to explain the curious French asides in "Noctambule." And Smith was, in common with most of the *McGill Fortnightly Review* alumni, an occasional reader of *transition* (1927–38),[37] in which most of the major French Surrealists (Breton, Louis Aragon, Paul Eluard, Phillippe Soupault, and others) were to appear in the late 1920s.[38] Smith's visit to Leon Edel in Paris for New Year's 1929, a debauch which later gave rise to the wistfully bawdy "Souvenirs du Temps Perdu," would surely have given him other opportunities to follow the latest developments in French poetry and painting. All these points of contact remain potential, however: Smith's subsequent letters to Edel make no Surrealist references. But it is hard to believe that a young man who, on his first trip to London at the age of sixteen, had found Harold Monro's Poetry Bookshop, where Yeats, Pound and Eliot gave readings (Compton 59), could have missed, as an established poet and emerging critic, the ambience of Parisian modernism. His earliest Surrealist poems, at any rate, have as yet no better explanation.

Why, though, did Smith suppress or tolerate the suppression of so much of the Surrealist experimentation of his early maturity? My title's allusion to Smith's seminal essay "Eclectic Detachment"[39] was meant to acknowledge the possibility that his Surrealism was short-lived because his attraction to it was more a matter of creative curiosity and opportunity than personal or philosophical commitment. To borrow the essay's curiously instrumental idiom of influence, Smith certainly "selected" much that was "useful" in Surrealism. It helped move him away from Eliot's example, invited a new spontaneity, construction, and intensity of image—arguably the last period of extended formal and technical innovation in his career—and gave him some confidence in his instinctive distrust of the political affiliations of his contemporaries, as well as an alternative method of engagement. But he emulated Surrealist techniques openly for a limited time, as one might whose attractions were more "eclectic" than compulsive, perhaps because he recognized that the Surrealist revolt against reason, apotheosis of the imagination, and determination "to penetrate the deepest layers of the mental,"[40] including and perhaps especially the erotic life, would eventually demand a greater flaunting of the self than he was prepared to indulge.

That having been said, a final glimpse of the older poet at work suggests that the anarchic creative spirit of Surrealism remained attractive to this famously fastidious craftsman. On 16 September 1964, between 4:15 and 4:40 in the afternoon, Smith typed out two dozen short, random lines. On the bottom of the typescript[41] he wrote the date, the time, and a single short phrase: "automatic writing." The intensely associative poem was eventually published as "Those Are Pearls &c" but, like so much of Smith's work in the Surrealist manner, was never reprinted. Once again he was facing a falling off of his poetic output, and once again a Surrealist response recommended itself. His career as a poet was winding down, but we can take the hint he left us and revitalize it. A less familiar and more exuberant Smith, and a more various Canadian modernism—for he was always at its centre—await our recovery.

NOTES

[1] Deacon's review appeared in the *Globe and Mail* on 30 October 1943; he said that Smith had given too much room in his anthology to the members of "our surrealist school, including, prominently, A.J.M. Smith himself." Smith, quoting the review to Klein in a letter of 17 November 1943, inserted "!!!" between Deacon's words "surrealist" and "school" (A.J.M. Smith Papers, Trent University, Peterborough, Ontario [hereafter *SPTU*], acc. 80-005, box 1, file 9). The letter to Klein was penned shortly after the appearance of Smith's notably titled "Surrealism in the Service of Christ" in 1941 in *Poetry* (discussed later). If Deacon had seen the poem (and he might well have perused this special Canadian issue), it is hardly surprising that he identified Smith with its mannerism. See below.

[2] In Donna Bennett and Russell Brown's *New Anthology of Canadian Literature in English*, A.J.M. Smith's poetry covers three pages; that of Stephanie Bolster, a promising young poet whose first book appeared five years ago, covers twelve. The last new item of Smith criticism—Ann Compton's *A.J.M. Smith: Canadian Metaphysical*—appeared eleven years ago.

[3] My research for a forthcoming edition of Smith's complete poems has turned up a 1932 typescript collection entitled *Nineteen Poems*, in which "Noctambule" appears (W.E. Collin Papers, Talman Regional Collection, University of Western Ontario, London, ON, box marked "White Savannahs," second Smith folder).

[4] The item is signed "J.B." and identified as Auden's by Ray (107). See *New Verse* 21 (June–July 1936): 14–16.

[5] C.H. Madge, "Surrealism for the English," *New Verse* 6 (Dec. 1933): 14–18, and Hugh Sykes Davies, "Sympathies with Surrealism," *New Verse* 20 (Apr.–May 1936): 15–21.

[6] Charles Madge, review of *Petite Anthologie Poétique du Surréalisme*, *New Verse* 10 (Aug. 1934): 13–15, and D.E.G. (probably David Gascoyne), "On Spontaneity," a review of Paul Eluard's *Facile*, *New Verse* 18 (Dec. 1935): 19.

[7] Hans [Jean] Arp, "The Domestic Stones," and Paul Eluard, "At Present," trans. David Gascoyne, *New Verse* 21 (June–July 1936): 7–8, 9.

[8] Ray offers an excellent summary of the Exhibition's program and the many anarchic deviations from it (134–66).

[9] In "Page and Surrealism" 47. The formula's invitation to swift and unarticulated connections lent itself readily to the Surrealist desire to emulate the psychoanalytic practice of free association. See Matthews 91; Chénieux-Gendron 65.

[10] In the first "Manifesto," in *Manifestoes* (22–24). Valuable discussions of automatism and automatic writing are in Chénieux-Gendron (47–60) and Riffaterre (221–39).

[11] *Poems New and Collected* 92. Hereafter PNC.

[12] The French resonance of Smith's title has not been remarked: in English "noctambule" is extremely rare, but a "noctambulist" is the same as a "somnambulist," a sleep-walker; whereas the French sense is of a more willing and conscious and even playful night-walker (*Larousse* translates it, for example, as "night-owl"). We might note as well that he deliberately mentions *rosbif*, not roast beef, when he wants to evoke a lost pleasure of the shattered past. The word choices suggest a French subtext to "Noctambule" that needs to be articulated. Smith's strong and deep relation to French modernism more generally is a rich topic awaiting investigation.

[13] In the first "Manifesto" Breton had written, "I believe in the resolution of these two states, dream and reality, which are seemingly so contradictory, into a kind of absolute reality, a *surreality*, if one may so speak" (*Manifestoes* 14).

[14] For the Surrealist revolt against description see Chénieux-Gendron 2, Ray 7. Breton's attack on realism in Dostoyevsky in the first "Manifesto of Surrealism" is a foundational example of the attitude (*Manifestoes* 6–8). For a startling coincidence of wording, compare Smith's phrases with those of Ray in *The Surrealist Movement in England*: the Surrealists, he says, underscored the "crucial distinction between the description of an experience, and the experience itself" (214–15).

[15] These issues are treated thoroughly in Matthews, *Surrealism, Insanity and Poetry*.

[16] In a review of *News of the Phoenix* in 1944 Tom Boggs "notes the publisher's editorial decision not to include two 'robust ms. poems' in the collection" (Burke 342). Boggs must have had inside information. In a letter of 5 April 1943 Lorne Pierce, director of the Ryerson Press, wrote to Smith about the *Phoenix* manuscript he had received:

> There are two or three poems which in my judgment would be much better left out. They are not essential, I think, and they would involve the publication in such a riot of talk on the wrong thing in the book … the so-called Christian reader might regard these as sacrilege and throw the whole thing out the window…. (A.J.M. Smith Papers,

Thomas Fisher Rare Book Library, University of Toronto, Toronto, ON, box 2, file 75.

In Sandra Campbell's view (in "'Tempting Satan and the Bailiff'"), Pierce is referring to "Ballade un Peu Banale" and "Between Two Wars" (a variant title for "Political Intelligence"), although the latter offers nothing in particular to offend the "Christian reader."

[17] Surrealism's doctrinal anti-rationalism is only a counter to my general argument in this paper if we accept the canonical and reductive version of Smith as a poet simply of the "intelligence." The nature of Smith's rationalism—and the ways in which he too resists the excesses of dogmatic reason—needs much more careful treatment in the criticism.

[18] The 1936 version is variant here: "Two soldiers' crutches had sexual intercourse / on the spot with a little bit of fluff / from a lint bandage in the firing chamber / of a 12 inch gun…" The variant confirms that the "bit of fluff" surviving in the final version should be taken in its slang meaning—a sexually available and probably naive young woman.

[19] See Chadwick 33ff. She later notes that despite the repetition of this misogynistic trope *in* Surrealist art, "Surrealism offered the woman *artist* a self-image that united her roles as woman and creator in a way that neither the concept of the *femme-enfant* nor that of erotic muse could" (182; emphasis added).

[20] Breton wrote in the *Manifesto of Surrealism*, "For me, their [Surrealist images'] greatest virtue, I must confess, is the one that is arbitrary to the highest degree, the one that takes the longest time to translate into practical language, either because it contains an immense amount of seeming contradiction or because one of its terms is strangely concealed…" (*Manifestoes* 38).

[21] Breton admitted that a full definition of black humour will always escape us ("Preface" 10) and left readers of his *Anthologie de l'humour noir* to the further clarification available from his selections. Valuable discussions of the concept, from which I have profited substantially, are in Chénieux-Gendron (88–93), de Cortanze (130–31), and Le Brun, "*L'humour noir.*"

[22] In *New Verse*; it was reprinted in *Bozart* 9.1–*Westminster* 24.1 (spring/summer 1935), presumably to respond to the emerging Surrealist fad in London.

[23] Among his notes on a draft of her article "A.J.M. Smith: Of Metaphysics and Dry Bones," in *SPTU*, acc. 81-019, box 1, file 12.

[24] The reference to a "canvas" with which the insomniac speaker's world is confused doesn't really support an allusion to Jean Arp, since Arp is not so much known for his early paintings as for later paper, cardboard, wood and stone constructions.

[25] Compare the more emphatic conclusion of Smith's much better known "To the Christian Doctors," which first appeared in the *Canadian Forum* a year later

in December 1936: it is the end of our human "flame" "to burn sensation's lode, / With animal intensity, to Mind," and the "Christian Doctors" who seek "civil tears" and "denials of the blood" are the opponents of that wholeness (PNC 23). Cf. Breton, "Second Manifesto of Surrealism": "the idea of Surrealism aims quite simply at the total recovery of our psychic force by a means which is nothing other than the dizzying descent into ourselves, the systematic illumination of hidden places..." (Manifestoes 136–37). For Surrealism's anti-clericalism see de Cortanze's pithy summary, 17–18.

[26] See W.E. Collin Papers, box marked "White Savannahs," first Smith folder.

[27] Eliot's own relation to Surrealism is an irony of this hypothesis: Smith had arguably been primed for a Surrealist period by the pre-conversion works of the very master he was now trying to supersede. See Skaff, The Philosophy of T.S. Eliot, and Ray's discussion of Eliot's early poetry (264–69). Smith's wish to avoid further association with Eliot may also explain why one of his very few allusions to Wallace Stevens appears in "Arp's Randy Rant": compare his fourth line, "Whipping the curdlike fancies to delight," with Stevens's "The Emperor of Ice Cream" lines 2–3: "bid him whip / In kitchen cups concupiscent curds" (Palm 79). Stevens was not to become an alternative to Eliot for Smith, though the relation between the two deserves much more study.

[28] In addition, the French poet Smith chose to translate most often, Jacques Prévert, was himself associated with Surrealism from 1926 to 1929 (de Cortanze 179). Apart from "May Song," which appeared in PNC, Smith translated four other Prévert pieces. He published "The Important Personage and the Guardian Angel" and "Keys of the City" with Georges Joyaux in 1954, and left unpublished among his papers "Old Song" and "Song of the Shoeshine Boys" (both in SPTU, acc. 78-007, box 5, file 13). The Prévert poems that attracted Smith were all from a single volume, Histoires, which appeared in 1946, so his affection for them adds little to our knowledge of his Surrealist reading in the 1930s.

[29] The single typescript of this poem (SPTU, acc. 78-007, box 5, file 11) gives no clue as to the date of composition, but the invitation to ridicule Nazism rather than to vilify it suggests a pre-war composition, by analogy with A.M. Klein's satirical Hitleriad. It is a commonplace to remark that Klein's epic attempt was immediately dated by his ignorance at the time of its composition of the full scale of the Holocaust, the news of which was surfacing as the poem appeared and made its jibes seem inadequate to the evil newly apparent to all.

[30] For a contemporary recital of this familiar condemnation see Belton, The Beribboned Bomb. Recent feminist scholars of Surrealism have emphasized both the movement's inherent antifeminism and the opportunities it paradoxically offered women artists; see for example Chadwick (5) and Conley (3).

[31] In letters to Leon Edel, Smith referred to "Surrealism in the Service of Christ" as

a "bawdy religious poem" (17 March 1941) and as one of several pieces that were "longer, more spectacular, but probably not quite so good" as the poems that had been collected in *News of the Phoenix* (28 July 1944).

[32] Chénieux-Gendron cites several such items from *Le Surréalisme au service de la révolution* in her discussion of black humour (88–93).

[33] In the midst of his Surrealist practice Smith wrote the "Rejected Preface" for *New Provinces*. Here he claims that "the artist who is concerned with the most intense of experiences must be concerned with the world situation in which, whether he likes it or not, he finds himself. For the moment at least he has something more important to do than to record his private emotions. He must try to perfect a technique that will combine power with simplicity and sympathy with intelligence so that he may play his part in developing mental and emotional attitudes that will facilitate the creation of a more practical social system" (9). In the last sentence quoted one hears the burden Smith had placed upon himself at this critical moment in his development; it is not deeply contradictory of his attraction to Surrealism.

[34] See "Lines Written on the Occasion of President Nixon's Address to the Nation, May 8, 1972."

[35] See Chénieux-Gendron 71–73, and the various Breton polemics of 1935 in defence of Surrealism against such Marxist critique, in *Manifestoes* 205–78.

[36] See, for example, the sonnet trilogy "Business as Usual 1946," "Fear as Normal 1954" (in PNC) and "Universal Peace 19—" (in the *Collected Poems*), as well as "Lines Written on the Occasion of President Nixon's Address to the Nation, May 8, 1972."

[37] *transition* is among the international modernist literature Leo Kennedy recommends in "The Future of Canadian Literature" to the "young men" writing in Canada (36). My thanks to the editor of the present volume for the suggestion that *transition* was a likely source of A.J.M. Smith's early knowledge of Surrealism, and for this and other references to *transition* in Smith's correspondence with Leon Edel.

[38] See Smith's letter of 24 October 1928 to Leon Edel, then in Paris, in which he comments on a Graeme Taylor story in the June issue. Taylor was John Glassco's travel companion during the Montparnasse adventures and later housemate in the village of Foster, Quebec; his literary aspirations went unfulfilled, despite the early recognition by *transition*.

[39] In the essay Smith proposed that the Canadian poet had an unique means of seeking and accepting literary influences:

> He stands apart and, as all Canadian writers must do, he selects and rejects. He selects those elements from varied and often disparate sources that are useful to him, and rejects those that are not. Useful to

him. This brings in the personal. Detachment surely does not imply in this context detachment from the Self or from personality. (8)

The article is chiefly useful today as a way of thinking about Smith's own negotiation of literary influences.

[40] Breton, "Surrealist Situation of the Object" (*Manifestoes* 274).

[41] In *SPTU,* acc. 78-007, box 5, file 5.

WORKS CITED

Belton, Robert. *The Beribboned Bomb: The Image of Woman in Male Surrealist Art.* Calgary: U of Calgary P, 1995.

Bennett, Donna, and Russell Brown, eds. *A New Anthology of Canadian Literature in English.* Don Mills, ON: Oxford, 2002.

Breton, André. *Manifestoes of Surrealism.* Trans. Richard Seaver and Helen R. Lane. Ann Arbor: U of Michigan P, 1969.

———. "Preface." *Anthologie de l'Humour Noir.* Paris: Jean-Jacques Fauvert, 1940.

Burke, Anne. "A.J.M. Smith: An Annotated Bibliography." *The Annotated Bibliography of Canada's Major Authors.* Vol. 4. Ed. Robert Lecker and Jack David. Toronto: ECW, 1983. 267–366.

Campbell, Sandra. "'Tempting Satan and the Bailiff': Lorne Pierce as Unacknowledged Patron of A.J.M. Smith, F.R. Scott, and Irving Layton." "The Canadian Modernists Meet: A Symposium." University of Ottawa, Ottawa, ON, 9–11 May 2003.

Chadwick, Whitney. *Women Artists and the Surrealist Movement.* London: Thames and Hudson, 1985.

Chénieux-Gendron, Jacqueline. *Surrealism.* Trans. Vivian Folkenflik. New York: Columbia UP, 1990.

Collin, W.E. W.E. Collin Papers. Talman Regional Collection, D.B. Weldon Library, University of Western Ontario, London, ON. Uncatalogued.

Compton, Anne. *A.J.M. Smith: Canadian Metaphysical.* Toronto: ECW, 1994.

Conley, Katharine. *Automatic Woman: The Representation of Woman in Surrealism.* Lincoln: U of Nebraska P, 1996.

[Deacon, William Arthur.] "A.J.M. Smith's Anthology Is Both Antiquarian and Modernistic." *Globe and Mail* 30 Oct. 1943: 20.

de Cortanze, Gérard. *Le Surréalisme.* Paris: MA Editions, 1985.

Djwa, Sandra. "A.J.M. Smith: Of Metaphysics and Dry Bones." *Studies in Canadian Literature* 3 (winter 1978): 17–34.

Edel, Leon. Leon Edel Papers. Department of Rare Books and Special Collections, McGill University, Montreal, QC. Uncatalogued.

———. "The Worldly Muse of A.J.M. Smith." *University of Toronto Quarterly* 47 (spring 1978): 200–13.

Ellenwood, Ray. *Egregore: A History of the Montréal Automatist Movement.* Toronto: Exile Editions, 1992.

Ferns, John. *A.J.M. Smith.* Twayne's World Authors Series. Boston: Twayne, 1979.

Germain, Edward B., ed. *Surrealist Poetry in English.* Harmondsworth, UK: Penguin, 1978.

Kennedy, Leo. "Direction for Canadian Poets." *New Frontier* 1.3 (June 1936): 21–24. Rpt. in Stevens, ed. 11–19.

———. "The Future of Canadian Literature." *Canadian Mercury* 5–6 (Dec. 1928): 99–100; rpt. in *The Making of Modern Poetry in Canada: Essential Articles on Contemporary Canadian Poetry in English.* Ed. Louis Dudek and Michael Gnarowski. Toronto: Ryerson, 1970. 34–37.

Le Brun, Annie. "*L'humour noir.*" *Entretiens sur le Surréalisme.* Ed. Ferdinand Alquié. Paris: Mouton, 1968. 99–113.

Matthews, J.H. *Surrealism, Insanity, and Poetry.* Syracuse, NY: Syracuse UP, 1982.

Ray, Paul C. *The Surrealist Movement in England.* Ithaca: Cornell UP, 1971.

Riffaterre, Michael. *Text Production.* Trans. Therese Lyons. New York: Columbia UP, 1985.

Skaff, William. *The Philosophy of T.S. Eliot: From Skepticism to a Surrealist Poetic, 1909–1927.* Philadelphia: U of Pennsylvania P, 1986.

Smith, A.J.M. A.J.M. Smith Papers. Bata Library, Trent University, Peterborough, ON. Accessions 78-007, 80-005, 81-019.

———. A.J.M. Smith Papers. Thomas Fisher Rare Book Library, University of Toronto, Toronto, ON. Ms. coll. 15.

———. "Arp's Randy Rant in the Comfy Confession Box." *New Verse* 18 (Dec. 1935): 11.

———. *The Classic Shade.* Toronto: McClelland and Stewart, 1978.

———. *Collected Poems.* Toronto: Oxford UP, 1962.

———. "Confessions of a Compulsive Anthologist." *Journal of Canadian Studies* 11 (May 1976): 4–14.

———. "Eclectic Detachment: Aspects of Identity in Canadian Poetry." *Canadian Literature* 9 (summer 1961): 6–14.

———. Letter to Leon Edel. 24 Oct. 1928. Edel, Leon Edel Papers.

———. Letter to Leon Edel. 17 Mar. 1941. Edel, Leon Edel Papers.

———. Letter to Leon Edel. 28 July 1944. Edel, Leon Edel Papers.

———. "Lines Written on the Occasion of President Nixon's Address to the Nation, May 8, 1972." *Poetry* [Chicago] 120 (Sept. 1972): 335–36.

————. *News of the Phoenix*. Toronto: Ryerson, 1943.

————. "The Poetic Process: Of the Making of Poems." *Centennial Review of Arts and Science* 8 (fall 1964): 353–70.

————. "Political Intelligence" [as "Political Note"]. *Contemporary Poetry and Prose* (Nov. 1936): 130–31.

————. "Refining Fire: The Meaning and Use of Poetry." *Queen's Quarterly* 61 (1954): 353–64.

————. "A Rejected Preface." *Canadian Literature* 24 (spring 1965): 6–9.

————. "Surrealism in the Service of Christ." *Poetry* [Chicago] 58 (Apr. 1941): 9–10.

Stevens, Peter, ed. *The McGill Movement: A.J.M. Smith, F.R. Scott and Leo Kennedy*. Toronto: Ryerson, 1969.

Stevens, Wallace. *The Palm at the End of the Mind: Selected Poems and a Play*. New York: Vintage, 1972.

Trehearne, Brian. *The Montreal Forties: Modernist Poetry in Transition*. Toronto, Buffalo, London: UTP, 1999.

————. "P.K. Page and Surrealism." *Journal of Canadian Studies* 38.1 (winter 2004): 46–64.

Samizdat Odyssey: *Ulysses* above the 42nd Parallel

TIM CONLEY

I

WHEN WE LOOK at the trinity of books on modernism that the late Hugh Kenner wrote after *The Pound Era* (namely, *A Homemade World* [1975], *A Colder Eye* [1983], and *A Sinking Island* [1988]) we note how each is, respectively, a study of American, Irish, and English modern writers. Given his Peterborough roots, one might wonder where Kenner's book on Canadian modernism is. Kenner's passing in 2003 is certainly a loss both for Canadian letters and, specifically, for students of modernism, but given this combination it is worth remarking how his career represents an example of a potentially worrying separation between modernism elsewhere and modernism in Canada. If the Anglo-modernism of Europe is a natural formation (a sinking island) or bodily condition (a colder eye) and the American variation is a "homemade" affair (recalling Ezra Pound's appraisal of a young American Eliot as someone who had modernized himself [Pound 40]), what is Canadian modernism? The answer to how and when Canada became modern (that is, was modernized or modernized itself) depends on who you ask: in the CBC's colourful view of history, Trudeaumania and Expo 67 were the glorious moments of a Canada made new; on the other hand, poets, literary historians, and critics might point to the founding of a journal such as the *Canadian Mercury* in 1928, whose editors claimed as allies "all those whose literary schooling has survived the Confederation, and whose thought and verse is not afraid of being called free" (qtd. in Gnarowski 218). The disparity between these answers points to a useful way of thinking about Canadian modernism: with the recognition that neither answer is fully correct nor entirely invalid comes the appreciation that the divide (concerning both the *how* and *when*) between these perspectives may itself be essential to the conception of a Canadian modernism. I would like to suggest that choosing to study a significant event in the history of literary modernism between 1928 and 1967 that can be readily compared to similar events in the United States and Europe may provide valuable insights into the meaning of this divide for notions of modern literature in Canada. In particular (and this is where my over-weighted title comes to cast its shadow), I propose that the 1949 legalization of James Joyce's *Ulysses* in Canada makes for a uniquely fertile choice

Responding to a questionnaire from Raymond Souster in 1946, A.M. Klein proffers three significant assertions worth connecting, and I would like to re-present them in the order in which they appear in the text. The first concerns influences: Klein shrugs at the hoary invitation to choose a preference between English and American writing, in this case posed as a question of "the healthiest influence" (a metaphor to which I will return). He says that he has "never really made a distinction—except for the Customs department—between the one and the other" (*Literary* 217). Singling out Customs as the sole point of difference between the countries is only partly disingenuous, for Klein has in mind a special sort of difference roughly administered by Customs agents. Later in the same text, replying to questions about the standards of criticism in Canada and whether "commercialism has invaded the literary field to a high degree," Klein displays irritation that *Ulysses*, "the masterpiece of our century," is "still not purchasable in our country" (221). This claim is not altogether accurate, as I will explain in a moment, but the complaint is serious. The third point of Klein's I would like to highlight concerns the expression of Canadian "consciousness":

> I do not think we have yet arrived, in writing, at a "Canadian consciousness." Thus far all we have had is a Canadian subconsciousness—made up of colonialism, Victorianism, etc.—and that has been illustrated, not expressed—it takes more skill to express the subconsciousness than the consciousness—by all our organized bardlings and psittacean rhapsodists. (221)

Klein's answer has more ambivalent and intriguing loose ends than I am at liberty to pull here, but bearing in mind that this is a writer who appeared in the *Canadian Mercury* and so is someone who might well be expected to claim that a distinctly modern "Canadian consciousness"—something that moves beyond or contends with the attitudes of colonialism and Victorianism—had been achieved or was burgeoning, we find instead that Klein's criteria for the moment of a modern Canada focuses on a requisite foreign import: *Ulysses*.

The basis for Klein's chagrin concerning Customs is certainly solid enough. Only a full twenty-six years after Judge Woolsey's famous verdict in the United States, the same year the last holdout province entered into confederation, Joyce's *Ulysses* was removed from Canada's prohibited importations list. However, the book already enjoyed a rich life as an illegal immigrant: quite an active immigrant, as a matter of fact.[1] As American Customs officials kept their focus on overseas imports, potentially filled with morally decadent and politically dangerous works of modern art, Canada sometimes served as a conduit for the banned novel's surreptitious entry into the continent. With the cunning of contemporary liquor smugglers, writers and readers together contrived to dupe inspectors, whether by disguising the book with dustcovers featuring ironic titles like *"Shakespeare's Works, Complete in One Volume"* and *"Merry Tales for Little Folks"* or by concealing volumes in places where prudish officials dared not pry (Fitch 119). Here we tread into regions of apocrypha and anecdotal testimony, to be sure, but the social history of literature (particularly its unofficial sides) is made of such things. Stan Gébler Davies's account of such performances, for example, offers some useful details but has at least one significant error:

> Forty copies [of the novel] were smuggled across the Ontario border by Barnet Braverman, a friend of Hemingway's (the Canadians had unaccountably failed to ban *Ulysses*). Mr Braverman crossed by ferry from Windsor to Detroit once a day with two copies making an alarming bulge front and rear of him, eyed suspiciously by US Customs. (251)

Sylvia Beach later nicknamed Braverman, in a slight error of her own, her "Saint Bernard" (Fitch 119).[2]

The influence—it is altogether too weak a term—of Joyce's novel upon Klein's own work has been carefully documented by such critics as D.M.R. Bentley and Zailig Pollock.[3] In deference to these studies, I here submit one amendment relevant to the connection between *Ulysses* and Klein's characterization of that modern "Canadian consciousness." Pollock's critical study of Klein maps a thematic link between *Ulysses* and *The Second Scroll*: "the search for a kinsman" (238–39). The search for Uncle Melech is at once a struggle against oppressive taboos ("that person's name" is banned in the narrator's Canadian home from the novel's outset [17]) and a pursuit of lost texts, fugitive pieces, and concealed documents. First and foremost a struggle to fathom the Holocaust, this "epistolary dilemma" (77) also reflects Klein's frustration *as a Canadian* with cultural prohibitions and the remove from a "modern" identity and sensibility. *Ulysses* had provided Klein a taste of a possible "consciousness" and, as his rigorously, almost painfully detailed analysis of the "Oxen of the Sun" episode demonstrates (*Literary* 289–325), he wanted to experience it fully for himself. As we shall see, he was not alone in this desire.

II

Ulysses, in its samizdat odyssey, altered what Marshall McLuhan, Kenner's teacher, called "the interior landscape" (the title he gave his 1969 collection of literary essays): it was a kind of virus that infected various writers and artists and, in turn, the "consciousness" these Canadians would express. As I have suggested with the example of Klein, merely calling *Ulysses* influential is not the sum of these observations. What is really striking to note is (1) how the influence of Joyce's modernism in Canada is illegitimate, and (2) how Canada's position as transmitter of *Ulysses* to the United States suggests that Canada's modernism is not tertiary or "after" European and then American modernisms, but "between" them. For Canadian writers who intercepted *Ulysses*, the forbidden quality of that text thereafter applied to modernism as both import and export. This intriguing dynamic is also, of course, an understated response of difference to the more clamorous and famous struggles of law and opinion in the United States.

In his 1998 book *James Joyce and Censorship*, Paul Vanderham demonstrates careful study of the readings of *Ulysses* by lawyers, witnesses, and judges in the different American hearings and trials, from the early prosecution of the *Little Review* to the 1934 upholding of the Woolsey decision by Judges Learned Hand and Augustus Hand (Judge Martin Manton dissenting). Vanderham concludes by advocating the need to admit *Ulysses* (or indeed, any literary work) can be obscene rather than denying it this quality in a misguided ploy to defend the novel from censorship. In this regard the puritanism exhibited in these American trials, where art and obscenity are almost always mutually exclusive categories, appears in contrast to the quietly hungry reception of *Ulysses* by certain Canadian writers. We can think of how little Klein seems to care about how "healthy" a given influence is, and may observe further that, indeed, part of the attraction of *Ulysses* and modernism for such writers was precisely their forbidden aspect.

Vanderham observes that the habitual model for American censorship discourse, the basis of the so-called Hicklin rule, is the fearful image of the book in question falling into the hands of a young person (this quaint expression is found in the legislation). This same model was employed in the case of *Ulysses*. Part of John Quinn's strategy for the defence of the *Little Review* in the 1921 trial was to suggest that the sheer complexity of *Ulysses* prohibited gratification: it was, if you will, too big and dense to be read with one hand. John Cowper Powys, Quinn's first witness, agreed with this assessment and called the novel "a beautiful piece of work in no way capable of corrupting the minds of young girls" (qtd. in Vanderham 48).

Powys did not know Canadian "girls." Travelling in Sweden and Germany, Elizabeth Smart records in her journal on 19 July 1933 that she has begun to read *Ulysses* (*Necessary* 40). It is a proud first statement to the day's entry. Smart is not quite twenty years old. In the same month she was winning disapproval from adults for reading *Lady Chatterley's Lover* and recording in her diary that reading Woolf's *To the Lighthouse* "makes me remember all the things that have made me blush" (*Necessary* 37). Young Smart is irritated by the view of her chaperone, Mrs. Watt, that it is "perfectly disgusting to want to read a book my country won't allow" (45). Although "perfectly disgusting" is a formulation worth reckoning with, the salient part of this statement is the authority given "my country": in this case, Mrs. Watt's England, whose moral authority represents the most resilient vestiges of imperial dominion (at one point in *Ulysses*, England is called the empire "on which the sun never rises" [427]). The influences of English modernists such as Lawrence, Mansfield, and of course Woolf have achieved the status of standard mention in discussions of Smart's writing, but it is interesting to consider her reading *Ulysses*—by which I mean both her interpretation of the novel and the historical fact of her opening it in the first place. Admittedly I do not know whether Smart later that summer or ever finished *Ulysses* (though as Jacques Derrida will attest, there may be no such state as having "read Joyce" [see Derrida 145–58]). Nor do I know precisely what she thought of it—Rosemary Sullivan's *By Heart* makes no mention of Joyce or the novel, and I note that she titles the chapter in which these significant instances of exposure to modernism occur "Kissing the Dead Lips of Emily Brontë"—but I can trace out a few plausible suggestions as to its meaning for her.

The first is, as I have already been implying, the overt wish to be corrupted. But what reading *Ulysses* offers is, in distinction to reading *Lady Chatterley*, an experience that is indecent not only to the English but to the new empire, the same America whose puritanism she would most fiercely reject in the fourth part of *By Grand Central Station I Sat Down and Wept*. Recall that Smart's proud announcement of her beginning to read *Ulysses* is made at the same point in time the legal proceedings that would ultimately legalize the novel's sale in the United States were under way. So by choosing to pick up *Ulysses*—and I would very much like to know where she did pick it up, and where that copy of the book ended up when she returned to Ottawa—Smart is deliberately looking for the most contemporary sort of trouble, as reviled by English *and* American authorities. Children grow "contrary as trees," she writes in *By Grand Central Station*, "blown by a fatal wind their parents never envisaged" (55). "Children" here may be taken as generally synonymous, I think, with the creative or artistic temperament as Smart envisions it, and specifically reflective of her own response to the protective Ottawa-middle-class upbringing she experienced.

I do not know what her justification is for this hypothesis, but Sullivan suggests that when Smart picked up George Barker's volume of poetry it may have been his poem "Daedalus" that caught her eye (2). This is not a connection that bears overplaying—it is hard to countenance that Smart's lust for Barker is part of a hunt for a Stephen Dedalus of her own to bring home and bathe as Molly Bloom fancies doing—but I would suggest that the association of flying past nets and being corrupted resonates with this possibility. The best argument for a palpable influence (this word is exact in this case: a "flowing-into") of *Ulysses* within *By Grand Central Station* centres upon the untrammelled expression of desire, particularly as voiced by a woman. The following juxtaposition of Joyce's famous conclusion and the opening of the third part of Smart's novel is illuminating:

> O that awful deepdown torrent O and the sea the sea crimson some-times like fire and the glorious sunsets and the figtrees in the Alameda gardens yes … and how he kissed me under the Moorish wall and I thought well as well him as another and then I asked him with my eyes to ask again yes and he asked me would I yes to say yes my mountain flower and first I put my arms around him yes and drew him down to me so he could feel my breasts all perfume yes and his heart was going like mad and yes I said yes I will yes. (*Ulysses* 932–33)

> O the water of love that floods everything over, so there is nothing the eye sees that is not covered in. There is no angle the world can assume which the love in my eye cannot make into a symbol of love. Even the precise geometry of his hand, when I gaze at it, dissolves me into water and I flow away in a flood of love.
>   Everything flows like the Mississippi over a devastated earth, which drinks unsurfeited, and augments the liquid with waterfalls of gratitude; which raises a sound of praise to deafen all doubters forever; to burst their shamed eardrums with the roar of proof, louder than bombs or screams or the inside ticking of remorse. Not all the poisonous tides of the blood I have spilt can influence these tidals of love. (*By Grand* 39)

Not only has Molly's all-encompassing, all-affirming flood here become a rhetorical strategy for Smart (or possibly more than that: "The overflow drenches all my implements of trivial intercourse" [39]), but the modernist aesthetic principle of the artist's perception of the world as transformation of that world, which Joyce tends to articulate in alchemical terms, becomes in *By Grand Central Station* the "love in my eye" that can reread and rewrite the signatures of all things. It is also hard to deny that Molly's lusty prag-matism of "well as well him as another" would hold considerable appeal for someone who chooses her lifelong "love object" (Sullivan 153) sight unseen. Since Smart chose Barker from the pages of a book, it may be no more implausible to speculate whether she might have culled the matter-of-fact way of setting her heart on him from the pages of another.

The censorship of *By Grand Central Station*, initiated by Smart's scandal-ized mother calling in favours from government chums, may be fruitfully studied in light of this connection. Like ships passing each other, *Ulysses* is mysteriously removed from the list of banned imports just as Smart's novel takes a place on it: "Whether it was officially banned will never be certain," writes Sullivan, "but for decades the book was effectively kept out of Canada" (229). The uncertainty on this important point—and the biographer's use of "never" sounds a resolute note of defeatism—connects the two banned texts. As we shall see when we look at how Canada Customs decided to allow *Ulysses* entry into Canada, that matter of qualifying "officially" is crucial to an appreciation of Canadian modernism as a cultural and explic-itly material mediation between the "homemade world" (Kenner) of the United States and the European nexus of exiles and expatriates. *By Grand Central Station*, whose very title bespeaks a point of transition, mediated the foreign modernisms by becoming itself a homemade sort of exile.

III

In the same year that Smart announces her beginning *Ulysses* and the American trial begins, Marshall McLuhan sits his graduate student exams in English literature at Cambridge, an experience Glenn Willmott paints as instrumental to McLuhan's concentration in all his work on reception and his ultimate theoretical coup of erasing the distinction between content and consumer, between text and reception (6). McLuhan has a prominent position in that CBC version of Canada's coming to modern conscious-ness, something akin to "the high priest of popcult and metaphysician of media" (as no less a tasteful institution as *Playboy* crowned him [McLuhan, "Playboy" 233]): this is partly why I arrive at him now. The various effects of Joyce on McLuhan have been repeatedly examined and I would like to limit my comments on the subject to one word, more or less: obscenity. Obscenity, McLuhan once quipped—and everything McLuhan said he quipped—is linguistic violence on the frontier of reality.

It is interesting to note that "linguistic violence" might well define a number of the usual charges brought against McLuhan by his critics. That sharp degree of hucksterism, that fascination with surface and surface alone, and that perverse knack for polymorphous aphorism were the trade-marks of an intellectual who, like Stephen Dedalus in *Ulysses*, refused to endorse his own critical theories by believing them. New Criticism balked at his emphasis on material history in a way that is bizarrely analogous to Customs rejections of a banned text like Joyce's novel: in both cases the opposition stems from the (accurate) acknowledgement that there are no ideas but in things, and every thing is also its own idea. McLuhan, radiant in the pages of *Playboy*, flirts with being himself a kind of obscenity, and admits in that interview that what writers such as Joyce taught him is that the movement "from trash to treasures" is a relatively simple but powerful one, and with that lesson, he says, "I ceased being a moralist and became a student" (265).

Paul Boyer has remarked upon how the 1933 Woolsey decision was presented as "America's answer to Hitler's repressions" (272); the American legitimation of modernism (at least in this safety-inspected incarnation) thus counters fascist denigrations of art and persecutions of artists and writers. The obscenity, Nazism, is far away, at the frontier or at a remove, in the case pointed at and labelled such by the United States in officiating its culture as a moral absolute with this legal decision. Canada's response to Joyce's book, on the other hand, is conspicuously less certain, and so too is its own style of modernism. Looking back at these examples of the official recognitions of *Ulysses* and the subversive readings of it by Canadian writers, the character of Canadian modernism assumes a revealing dialectical form: at the same time that it exists as a kind of "mediation" between European and American modernisms, it (perhaps necessarily, in the interest of differentiation) refuses total legitimation. There is something of the wish to remain illicit, without legal definition. Klein's opposition of "consciousness" with "subconsciousness" fits very well, since each is provisional and requires the other, just as the idea of "Canada" in *Ulysses* (see, for example, *Ulysses* 417) has varying, often slyly comic associations with colonialism (a component of Klein's "subconsciousness," remember) and swindling (the fraudulent or unofficial). "Canadian modernism" as a subject may assume a modest or even subservient, implicitly colonial pose, but this is just its "subconscious" manner; wide awake it is in revolt against convention and repression.

However disconcerting or even embarrassing it may feel to reflect that Canada was, of all English-language nations, the last holdout for a ban on *Ulysses*, it is probably more valuable and even, perhaps, more necessary to ask, in an attempt to understand modernism and the Canadian consciousness, why the novel was finally exempted at all. Angelo Merola, the assistant curator of the Canada Customs museum, and Anne Klein, an official at the prohibited importations division of Customs, inform me that no records for so ancient a date as 1949 survive—another, rather eerie, sign of the illegitimacy of modernism in Canada—but assure me that the removal of *Ulysses* must have been the result of either an internal revision of guidelines or a reinterpretation of a given piece of legislation by Customs officials. Given the undisclosed criteria and methods by which these judgements are summarily made or reversed, it is hard to take seriously the apologists for such practices, like Mark Cohen, who would make the processes no less rarified by replacing Customs officials with "expert readers" (157), a specialized class of which Cohen himself is presumably an example member. The abilities to censor, for Cohen, are synonymous with the critical skills

> practised and taught in English departments at universities across the country. Graduate students and English professors are too often accused of inhabiting an ivory tower, of being out of touch with the practical realities of our society; I believe that censorship disputes offer them the perfect opportunity to apply the skills they have acquired and, in so doing, contribute to censorship judgments that are more just. (156)

Please note that the operative phrase is "more just" and not simply "just." I quote Cohen here—despite the litter of clichés that is his prose—to conclude in a necessarily un-reassuring way, and to take up, after a fashion, the invitation to participate as an English professor in "censorship debates."

To the extent that the forbidden entry of *Ulysses* into Canada "modernized" its writers and readers, we may feel wrongly complacent in our reading of the fraught history only partially presented here. Book seizures at the border continue and the temptation to abandon the role of student and revert to that of the moralist remains. The non-extant archive of Canada Customs and Cohen's call for literary academics to legitimate themselves in a most literal and heinous manner together cast into doubt the claims to "Canadian consciousness" as Klein conceives of it: if we do not have within the purview of this "consciousness" a functioning collective memory and the freedom to recognize and brave the "practical realities of our society" on our own terms, such "consciousness" seems little worth having. "No wonder we insulate ourselves from wonders," writes Elizabeth Smart: "Poetry is like this, it is life moving, terrible, vivid. Look the other way when you write, or you might faint" (*In the Meantime* 51). This insight was significantly nurtured by the stigma of *Ulysses* and Smart's decisive transgression of that judgement.

Although Kenner did not include Canada as one of the "Three Provinces" of "International Modernism" (*A Sinking Island* 4), he did on occasion offer comment on his native country's bewilderment at its own identity and culture.[4] In an article published in the second issue of *here and now*, Kenner concludes his consideration of the "Canadian laconicism," which Chester Duncan describes as "a kind of dumbness, a frustration, *a betweenness*," by expressing hope that "the tortured Canadian face" that had hitherto been avoided or concealed "is at last being illuminated" ("The Case of the Missing Face" 74 [emphasis added], 78). The timing of this statement should not be missed: "The Case of the Missing Face" appeared in 1948, two years after Klein suggested that "Canadian consciousness" had not yet been achieved and a year before the Confederation finally embraced the entire country and Kenner's and Klein's favourite novel was at long last decriminalized. The samizdat odyssey of *Ulysses* is only one example of the "illegitimate" character of Canadian modernism, but a most instructive one. The movements of that suspect book highlight that space between complacency, colonialism, unconsciousness and unlawfulness, rebelliousness, and consciousness that is Canadian modernism.

NOTES

[1] Note that Klein himself, of course, had a copy of the book. His annotated copy of *Ulysses* (Paris: Shakespeare and Co., 1928) is in the A.M. Klein Fonds, National Archives of Canada, MG30 D167, vol. 38, file 6.

[2] A fascinating nexus of associations is to be had in the fact that Braverman worked as "copywriter, advertising-research man, and part-time salesman for the Curtis Company, an advertising agency in Windsor" (Fitch 119), for he shares his trade (and his being Jewish) not only with Joyce's hero, Leopold Bloom, but also with Harry Pollock, "a partner in Grosberg, Pollock and Gwartzman, Ltd., an ad agency that sells girdles, pickles, machines and a few other things" (Fulford 19). Pollock founded the James Joyce Society in Toronto, whose roughly seventy members first met on 14 February 1964, and wrote and performed stage adaptations of Joyce's work. His "Lots of Fun at Finnegan's Wake" (1964) included McLuhan in the cast (as himself—a dozen years before he would rematerialize in *Annie Hall*).

[3] Pollock's editorial presence in Klein scholarship is redoubtable (see Pollock); see also Bentley, whose essay is repeatedly cited with good reason. Also of interest is Harold Heft's unpublished dissertation, "The Presence of James Joyce in the Poetry and Prose of A.M. Klein."

[4] That the *Globe and Mail* only ran an obituary of Kenner, that superb explicator, advocate, and ambassador of modernism, nearly two weeks after his death (Csillag) and almost as long after those run in both American and British newspapers such as the *New York Times* and the *Guardian* is a disappointing suggestion that Canada's significant "between" position within and contribution to international modernism is as yet insufficiently acknowledged in Canada.

WORKS CITED

Bentley, D.M.R. "A Nightmare Ordered: A.M. Klein's 'Portrait of the Poet as Landscape.'" *Essays on Canadian Writing* 28 (spring 1984): 1–45.

Boyer, Paul. *Purity in Print.* New York: Scribner's, 1968.

Cohen, Mark. *Censorship in Canadian Literature.* Montreal: McGill-Queen's UP, 2001.

Csillag, Ron. "A true renaissance man." *Globe and Mail* 6 Dec. 2003: F10.

Davies, Stan Gébler. *James Joyce: A Portrait of the Artist.* New York: Stein and Day, 1975.

Derrida, Jacques. "Two Words for Joyce." Trans. Geoff Bennington. *Post-structuralist Joyce: Essays from the French.* Ed. Derek Attridge and Daniel Ferrer. Cambridge: Cambridge UP, 1984. 145–58.

Fitch, Noel Riley. *Sylvia Beach and the Lost Generation: A History of Literary Paris in the Twenties and Thirties.* New York: Norton, 1983.

Fulford, Robert. "Irish by Joyce." *Toronto Star* 1 Dec. 1964: 19.

Gnarowski, Michael. "The Role of 'Little Magazines' in the Development of Poetry in English in Montreal." *The Making of Modern Poetry in Canada: Essential Articles on Contemporary Canadian Poetry in English.* Ed. Louis Dudek and Gnarowski. Toronto: Ryerson, 1968. 212–22.

Joyce, James. *Ulysses.* London: Penguin, 1992.

Kenner, Hugh. "The Case of the Missing Face." *here and now* 2 (May 1948): 74–78.

———. *A Colder Eye: The Modern Irish Writers.* New York: Penguin, 1984.

———. *A Homemade World: The American Modernist Writers.* New York: Knopf, 1975.

———. *A Sinking Island: The Modern English Writers.* New York: Knopf, 1988.

Klein, A.M. *Literary Essays and Reviews.* Ed. Usher Caplan and M.W. Steinberg. Toronto: UTP, 1987.

————. *The Second Scroll*. 1951. Toronto: McClelland and Stewart, 1969.

McLuhan, Marshall. *The Interior Landscape: The Literary Criticism of Marshall McLuhan 1943–1962*. Ed. Eugene McNamara. New York: McGraw-Hill, 1969.

————. "Playboy Interview." 1969. *Essential McLuhan*. Ed. Eric McLuhan and Frank Zingrone. Concord: Anansi, 1995. 233–69.

Pollock, Zailig. *A.M. Klein: The Story of the Poet*. Toronto: UTP, 1994.

Pound, Ezra. *Selected Letters of Ezra Pound*. Ed. D.D. Paige. New York: Harcourt, 1950.

Smart, Elizabeth. *By Grand Central Station I Sat Down and Wept*. 1945. London: HarperCollins, 1991.

————. *In the Meantime*. Ottawa: Deneau, 1984.

————. *Necessary Secrets: The Journals of Elizabeth Smart*. Ed. Alice Van Wart. Toronto: Deneau, 1988.

Vanderham, Paul. *James Joyce and Censorship: The Trials of Ulysses*. London: Macmillan, 1998.

Willmott, Glenn. *McLuhan, or Modernism in Reverse*. Toronto: UTP, 1996.

"a widening of the northern coterie": The Cross-Border Cultural Politics of Ezra Pound, Marshall McLuhan, and Louis Dudek

TONY TREMBLAY

I

THERE IS NO better measure of the ambiguity surrounding Canadian modernism than the fact that the only uncontested understanding shared by critics on the matter is an almost universal familiarity with the postmodernist position that we *did not have any* modernism in Canada: that, according to Robert Kroetsch, our literature evolved from E.J. Pratt's late Victorian aesthetic to parodic postmodernism (1), and that, according to George Bowering, Canadian modernism began and ended with Sheila Watson's *The Double Hook* (4). Around this presumption has developed a conventional, albeit late-forming, wisdom in Canada that our writers leapfrogged the search for order amid moral uncertainty that preoccupied most of the developed world's artists in the early years of the twentieth century. The general reluctance of our critics to contest Kroetsch's and Bowering's oversights, which now seem more related to myth-making than careful scholarship, is symptomatic of the difficult, perhaps even dialectical, nature of our modernism, its multiple loci, and entanglement with other social forces in this country. As Marshall McLuhan's aptly described "borderline case" ("Canada" 226), Canada more often received and mediated innovations like modernism than exported them, at least in our early years. Thus, while key moments in our social history such as the formation of the Canadian Authors Association in 1921 complemented the cultural work being done by John Grierson at the National Film Board and Gerald

Noxon at the Canadian Broadcasting Corporation,[1] there was only limited concentration of nationalist cultural interests until the release of the Massey *Report* in 1951. Until that time, our cultural nationalism was fragmented across regional vortices of energy as diverse as the realist schools of war and landscape artists, the west-coast radio experiments of young poets, the small-magazine culture in and around McGill University, and scattered groups of increasingly demanding Canadian readers, who in small pockets across the country celebrated the legalization of Joyce's *Ulysses* in 1949, almost thirty years after its first release.[2] Though all these modernizing energies were important, none managed to achieve the authority of being univocal, which is perhaps why Hugh Kenner, both a Canadian and the world's foremost modernist scholar, never wrote a book on Canadian modernism. The stars shone brightly, but the constellations, if the critics are to be believed, never formed.

As we look back now to assess these modernizing energies, one mid-century association in particular emerges as vital, mostly because of its concreteness in a literary past that we continue to insist was equivocal. The association I am referring to is the important and often-overlooked intellectual association between the leading American modernist Ezra Pound and the two leading second-generation Canadian modernists Marshall McLuhan and Louis Dudek. Why such an obvious association has been consistently overlooked is a curiosity related to the nature of Canadian modernism outlined above: in short, because critics like Bowering and Kroetsch have popularized the idea that our modernism was indeed ambiguous, more a mirage that was fleeting than a movement with roots, branches, and presence. In this essay I challenge the "ambiguity thesis" by making a number of observations about literary ethos and practice that stem from this important association between Pound and the two Canadians: that the relationship between McLuhan/Dudek and Pound was an integral point of entry for American-styled modernism into Canada at mid-century, that McLuhan and Dudek adapted different strands of Pound's dialectical modernism to their work in Canada, and, finally, that the impetus for and implications of their associations for Canada arrived at an especially important time in our cultural history.

I must stress, however, that I am *not* suggesting that McLuhan and Dudek were the first purveyors of American or, for that matter, continental modernism in Canada. E.J. Pratt's letters when he was editor of *Canadian*

Poetry Magazine from 1936–43 reveal that Canadian poets *were* emulating American and British models early in the twentieth century. Specifically, W.W.E. Ross's close study of Marianne Moore's forms, as well as the publication of his Imagist poems in the *Dial* in the late 1920s, indicates that Canadian poets, in seeking alternatives to the conventional monotones of the Confederation group, were aware of developments from afar. Canadian critics such as E.K. Brown were likewise aware of the modernizing energies affecting the "experiment[al]" work of A.J.M. Smith, F.R. Scott, and A.M. Klein (43). What I *am* suggesting is that McLuhan and Dudek were the first to *systematically* apply Pound's cultural politics to Canada. My thesis is that much of the cultural direction that McLuhan and Dudek provided for an increasingly self-conscious Canadian discourse, one both critical and literary, can be found in Pound's brand of republican/technological modernism.

II

Pound's status as the leading and most vocal of the pioneering modernists is, now, rarely challenged, even in revisionist projects such as those of John Carey and Bob Perelman that seek to question the motives behind Pound's and T.S. Eliot's reactionary canonizing. Though they are critical of the self-promotional tendencies of the early modernists, Carey and Perelman take it largely for granted that having harnessed the twin energies of formal experimentation and Flaubert-like realism in European sculpture and art, Pound became the most ambitious theorist of avant-garde modernism in the west. They also concede that, "in spite of Pound himself" (Perelman 228), the totality of his work—his doctrinaire books of required reading and poetics; his impressive historical, linguistic, and intellectual reach; and his brash Yankee energy—gave him the kind of Arnoldian authority that the new century seemed to demand. "A Yank among the Georgians" (Reck 11), Pound's was the voice that consolidated the otherwise fragmentary modernist intonations of Wyndham Lewis, Ford Madox Ford, F.S. Flint, and T.E. Hulme. Without him, these other theorists and technicians would have been figures without a ground. Pound's sometimes reckless enunciations of their various formulae for poetic immanence and social change, however, often blurred his own basic intention: namely, that modernism was a programme of renewal across a unified field, affecting not only literary artists, but, through them, nationhood and civilization as wholes.

While there is abundant evidence to conclude that Pound was merely a great sponge, borrowing ideas, often carelessly, from painting, architecture, music, sinology, and assorted other disconnected movements swirling around him, few critics contest that he was a flashpoint among poets, thinkers, and social reformers for a radical new poetics. As K.L. Goodwin wrote in *The Influence of Ezra Pound*, "[h]is influence has [been] ... unparalleled in English literature, it has been a deliberate influence, a conscious attempt to set up the equivalent of a Berlitz or extra-mural course in poetics" (219).

By mid-century, though, after his voluminous periodical publishing of the 1930s and after his Italian wartime broadcasts had earned him imprisonment back home at St. Elizabeths Hospital for the Criminally Insane in Washington, DC, his contact with the outside world changed dramatically. What had been three decades of restless movement westward was reduced, suddenly, to stasis. Letter writing and receiving visitors became his public work. It was in this period of stasis, and coincident with Washington's proximity to Canada, that McLuhan and Dudek, then unknown to each other, both formed close alliances with Pound. They were the first and only Canadians[3] to have any significant contact—that is, a deeply engaged and lasting working relationship—with the foremost member of the early modernist group that Wyndham Lewis called the "Men of 1914" (*Blasting* 9).

What prompted McLuhan and Dudek to seek out the incarcerated Pound at St. Elizabeths is itself interesting, providing a telling footnote to the intellectual climate in Canada in the 1930s and 1940s. In this period, with the advent of the modernist magazine *First Statement* (1942–45), Dudek's Montreal was just beginning to emerge from the grip of ultramontane parochialism. Dudek's contact with the intellectual underground of both language groups in Montreal—with the *joual* revival of Jean Narrache and the publishing activism of Yves Thériault and John Sutherland—was, however, insufficient to offset the overriding regimental politics of Maurice Duplessis's old Quebec. Even Dudek's undergraduate education at McGill was wanting, requiring him to discover "Eliot, Pound, and Joyce" in his own independent reading (*1941 Diary* 4). Dudek's departure for Columbia University in New York in 1944 was therefore not surprising, nor was it surprising that he chose history as his study, the discipline that would open up provincialism for broader, diachronic consideration. "I wanted to deal with a huge subject," he wrote, "whose findings were everywhere to be seen, like the ruins of Ozymandias, and whose history embraced everything written and published from classical times to the present" ("Louis Dudek: 1918–" 130). Hiding his eastern European ancestry and Catholicism to secure social advantage, preferring the company of French Canadians and Jewish immigrants in his east-end neighbourhood, and finding few outlets to engage his bookishness, Dudek's early experience of Montreal was that of secrecy and limitation. He thus sought the breadth of history and the dynamism of New York as antidotes to the smothering insularity of feudal Quebec.

McLuhan's experience of intellectual enervation in Canada was remarkably similar to Dudek's, which is striking given McLuhan's upbringing on the "real" western frontier. Not only did the young McLuhan have to contend with Manitoba summers of "lethal boredom" (Gordon 18), but when he finally began to study literature at the University of Manitoba in the fall of 1929, "no one," states his first biographer, was "aware of [the] momentous shift in literary consciousness" (Marchand 17) that had taken place; "it was as if Joyce, Eliot, and Pound did not exist" (18). And so it was not until McLuhan attended Cambridge University in 1934 that he would encounter the moderns and shake off the Edwardian ideal of gentleman scholar—and with it the well-learned colonial disdain for all things modern, capitalist, and industrial, the very things, curiously, that would later support his lifetime of critical reflection. In early letters to his mother from Cambridge he was often disconsolate about Canada, joking that he would "tear the hide right off Canada some day and rub salt into it" (*Letters* 86). Even when his own self-concept strengthened and he returned home, he continued to lament "the mental vacuum that is Canada" (*Letters* 165, 236, 241), acknowledging the country's benefits as an "anti-environment" (*Letters* 321), but continuing to despair about its self-effacing intellectual vacuity (*Letters* 525). My point here is not to disparage Canada for its lack of sophistication in the 1930s and 1940s, but to suggest that the embrace of Poundian energy and dicta was a countermand to the colonial and ecclesiastical insularity that sent both Dudek and McLuhan into exile from Canada in the first place. When as young men they did encounter Pound, he provided the means and aims to overcoming resentments that they were just starting to understand.

McLuhan was the first of the two to encounter Pound at St. Elizabeths, meeting him in June 1948 on an aborted trip to enlist Cleanth Brooks's help in enrolling Hugh Kenner in the PhD program at Yale (*Mazes* 296). This second mention of Kenner, who would become in the years after meeting McLuhan the world's foremost modernist scholar, must pass here largely unqualified, except to say that his pioneering work on Pound, Joyce, Eliot, and Lewis owed much to McLuhan's tutelage, which began at the University of Toronto in the summer of 1946.[4] Dudek's route to Pound was less haphazard, involving a longer gestation of interest and a much deeper familiarity with Pound's cultural activism by the time Dudek met him in June 1950. Dudek's greater interest in Pound's activist agenda— reflected in his offer to be of service to Pound while studying in New York (*Dk/* 13)—meant that in terms of cultural praxis, Dudek, who had literally studied at what James Laughlin has called the "Ezuversity" (3), was the more deliberate proponent of Pound's ideas in Canada. His "higher educa- tion in the reality of modern poetry" ("Louis Dudek: 1918–" 130) was admittedly Poundian, a reality that involved top-down, often polemical, renewal; small-press publishing and literary activism; and the recruitment of select bands of serious characters who would reaffirm the centrality of poetry for civic ends. For McLuhan, by contrast, Pound was a personality first and then always something of a curiosity, more of the strong poet from whom one learns first principles than a teacher whose lessons extend over a lifetime.

One final curiosity of McLuhan's and Dudek's associations with Pound bears consideration: the near-identical trajectory of their post-visit rela- tionships with the incarcerated poet. Both visited Pound only once at St. Elizabeths; both visits precipitated a flurry of letters between 1950 and 1953 (over 100 letters each); both correspondences deeply affected the scholar- ship and teaching of the two young Canadians at formative times in their academic careers; and both associations lapsed in 1953 as a result of Pound's increasing paranoia[5] and McLuhan's and Dudek's increasing confidence in their own independent undertakings. It was as if both Canadians had to get through Pound—that is, encounter, assimilate, and reject him—to proceed with their own cultural work. Dudek's admonishment of Pound that follows was typical of this impulse, its degree of bombast reflecting the closeness Dudek felt to his mentor and the difficulty of eliminating "echoes of the master" (Dudek, Letter to Ezra Pound, 10 October 1957):

Note that the difference in Canada is, we don't mess with preten-
tious revivals of the Renaissance ... nor catalogues of world literature. We're hitting at the particulars right here: The Shearer Mansion
on Mt. Royal; Premier Duplessis (Quebec, benighted licker of Fr.
Canadian sentimental prejudices & religiosity); the Canadian Legion
and tourist trade; Toronto puritanism; commercialism; advertising;
importation of Oxford accents to Can universities, to spout cultured
inanities, tradition & Eliotism. (Dudek, Letter to Ezra Pound, 4
January 1955)

Shortly after they became permanently ensconced at Canadian universities at mid-century (McLuhan at the University of Toronto and Dudek
at McGill), both proceeded to adapt the generalities of Pound to "the
particulars right here." If we were therefore to isolate key interactions in
the deepening of Canada's commitment to not merely the principles but
also the operations of literary modernism, we would have to include the
heated if short-lived epistolary conversations between the three (Pound,
McLuhan, and Dudek) at mid-century. I use the *un*grammatical construction "between the three" because, despite promptings from Pound that his
two most significant Canadian protégés join forces to effect "a widening of
the northern coterie" (Pound, Letter to Marshall McLuhan, 20 June 1951),
they never did; instead, each used Pound's ideas to go in opposite directions. It is these different directions that bear thinking about in terms of
our own national cultural development, for second-generation Canadian
modernism was not monolithic and univocal, but was a complex of often-
divergent ideas that, in Dudek's and McLuhan's hands, were manifest as
both high-cultural and low-cultural practice. In other words, Pound's
multivalent modernism was as useful to Dudek's guardianship of civilization-building and the tradition as it was to McLuhan's non-canonical
probes into popular and mass culture.

One way to understand this important divergence in McLuhan's and
Dudek's embrace of separate strands in Pound's pluralistic modernism
(and, in fact, the ways in which Canadian artists and thinkers mediated
what Peter Nicholls calls "modernisms" [vii]) is to consider one of the key
fundaments of that modernism: its syncretic republican base. I use the
term "republican" to suggest that Pound's aesthetic modernism reflected

the political philosophy of turn-of-the-century America, the America that had evolved through revolutionary wars to accommodate the competing polarities of classical republicanism and eighteenth-century Lockean liberalism. The "America" of Pound's Quaker/entrepreneur father was a hybrid of both streams of thought—that of classical republicans who advanced *civic* humanism as the ideal social order, in which citizens subverted private interests to the public good, and that of Lockean liberals who took up the cause of individual rights and the freedoms of the marketplace, arguing that economic self-interest was the more appropriate social ground for the full flowering of emergent republics. The tension between these two opposing forces has characterized much of the political debate in America since the Revolution and, more importantly, the *synthesis* of these two forces has determined the special nature of American democracy. Social historians such as Robert Shalhope believe that so complete was this synthesis that "Americans … never had a sense of having to choose between two starkly contrasting traditions—liberalism and republicanism. Instead, they domesticated classical republicanism to fit their contemporary needs…, [amalgamating] inherited assumptions with their liberal actions" (471). Regardless of the exact circumstances of their conjunction, the result of this synthesis was a hybrid democratic ideology, an enlightened or syncretic republicanism, that harmonized these liberal and classical tendencies in the text of the American constitution, thus allowing the new republic to function as a workable rather than balkanized state.

In corroborating what us political historians are now calling America's "intermediate status" between the extremes of Hobbesian despotism and classical Greek renunciation (Rahe 602), Shalhope and other theorists could be describing Pound, who had emerged from working-class Protestant dissent to espouse the Jeffersonian ideals of the virtuous state. In being syncretic, reaching a détente, that is, between rival Old and New World paradigms, Pound's republicanism (and the influential modernism that emerged from it) was thus typically American. It was simultaneously elitist, hierarchical, nostalgic, and classical—proffering "the tradition" as the great civilizing inheritance through history—and it was also individualist, egalitarian, reactionary, and liberal, believing in the work of non-conforming artists/intellectuals to both "make it new" (*Confucius* 36) and uncover "some of the vital facts which the powers of hell and corruption have been hiding under the blackout of history" (Pound, Letter to

Marshall McLuhan, 4 January 1955). Pound's alleged treachery against his own country's interests in broadcasting on Mussolini's Italian airwaves can be more fully understood when considered in the light of this political hybridity. As Pound wrote to his son-in-law, Boris de Rachewiltz, "E.P. has … [n]o interest in Italian politics … NOT his job as american" (17 June 1954) and "EP not dazzled by Muss/ and never ceded an inch of his principles…. [Rather] EP a constructive critic of Fascism FROM the Jefferson-Adams U.S. constitutional angle" (27 December 1955). Following from this, good government, for Pound, involved the elimination of overt, meddling bureaucracies (a liberal position shared by the "horse-thieves" on his mother's side of the family) and the transfer of good will from leaders to the interests of their citizens (a goal of the conservatives of the classical *ancien regime* that Pound so admired).[6] In insisting that the two duties of government were to "conserve its human resources" ("Patria Mia" 120) and to censure the bureaucrats bent on "destroy[ing those]" ("Bureaucracy" 217), Pound was merely enunciating the balanced American position, that mix of frugality and idealism, that informed the culture of Jefferson and Adams, namely, "'Low Living High Thinking'" ("Economic Nature" 174).

I belabour the consideration of the wellspring of Pound's modernism to make the point that the elbow room in Pound's political philosophy that allowed two exiled Canadians to arrive at vastly different conclusions as to how to effect cultural renewal back home was indeed abundant. McLuhan found ample room and precedent in Pound's thought to embark on an initial investigation of commercial heresies in *The Mechanical Bride* (1951), modelling his *sottisier* on Pound's own catalogues in *The Cantos* of some of the fools in history, not to mention fashioning the original title of the book, *Guide to Chaos*, after Pound's *Guide to Kulchur* (1938), the book McLuhan judged to be a gloss for *The Cantos*.[7] In McLuhan's mind, *Guide to Chaos/The Mechanical Bride* would continue what Pound had started by updating some of the later crimes of the century. Laughlin's observation that "the voice of the *Cantos* is explaining everything except science and technology" (112) reveals the space that McLuhan would certainly have seen for himself within the broader frame of Pound's work. Dudek found equivalent space and guidance in Pound's work to launch a mid-century revolution in the arts that involved the Poundian mechanics for civilization-building: mobilization of poets in small-press publishing, institutional incursion for the purposes of curricular reform, and the use of electronic and print media for public intellectualizing. Coming only four years after *The Mechanical Bride*, Dudek's "Literature and the Press" (1955), his doctoral thesis at Columbia, also redoubled Pound's efforts to find a basis in history for how the commercial media first encroached upon then silenced the independent voices of non-aligned writers and thinkers. Dudek's small magazines and presses of the 1950s and 1960s were but the concrete means by which these independent voices could be vindicated.

The first substantial pieces of independent work produced by McLuhan and Dudek in Canada were Poundian in execution, theme, structure, and scope. Both books were reactionary, conservative, and declarative in their articulation of the different paths each Canadian would pursue: McLuhan's the path of the guide, that of daring toward emancipating discovery, and Dudek's the path of the guardian, that of fidelity to sustaining classical ideals.[8] What is key for the purposes of this study is to point out that both paths of insight and action find expression in a multivalent modernism that rests atop a uniquely American syncretic republican base. I am not aware of any equivalent European or British admixture of classical aims and reactionary means that ever hit Canadian shores, nor am I aware of any other authority or conduit that mediated that syncretic modernism in Canada. By mid-century, then, the systematic application, not merely proximate influence, of Pound's uniquely *American* modernism altered what had been the historical pattern of east/west exchange between Canada and Europe. While the *McGill Fortnightly Review*'s first editorial (November 1925) provides abundant evidence that Smith and Scott were aware of the programme of modernist renewal in the 1920s (Djwa 83), and while Earle Birney, Dorothy Livesay, Irving Layton, Ralph Gustafson, and W.W.E. Ross, the poets of the intermediate period of the 1930s who slightly preceded or were contemporaries of Dudek and McLuhan, all knew of Pound's work,[9] none made close studies of Pound's poetics nor incorporated those poetics into their work to the extent that Dudek and McLuhan did. Theirs was a totality of embrace and application disproportionate to anything that had come before.

There remains, within what is reasonable in the space of an essay, the deeper consideration of what the two Canadians did with what they learned from Pound. Of the two, McLuhan was the bolder interpreter of Pound's thought, which is to say that he had no wish to explicate or advance Pound's work (he would leave that to Kenner), but to apply the logic and some of the inference of that thought to his own investigations of culture. In so doing, McLuhan was among the first critics in the world to recognize the broader application of Pound's ideas. Beginning with the insight that Pound's modernist "aesthetic … was widely sought and found in the contemplation of mechanical tools and devices" ("Pound's Critical Prose" 77), McLuhan then applied Pound's theories of poetics—theories of how to manipulate the formal properties of language for literary effect—to the contemplation of media forms, thus not only treating cultural utterance as text (whether an advertisement or a situation-comedy or a fashion item) but, far more profoundly, pioneering a way in which Canadians could understand and theorize their relationship with the media behemoth to the south. As Glenn Willmott argues, "the extension of the metaphor [of *technique*][10] under modernist formalist poetics to totalizing cultural descriptions" was a trademark of "the polymathic projects of Ezra Pound" (48). McLuhan's advance was merely to take Pound's totalizing theories seriously—that is, to treat *parole* as constitutive of *langue*—thereby treating culture in all its forms as a symptom of language. Culture/*parole* was thus part of a great poem-in-progress/*langue* that could most profitably be analyzed and dissected by the literary critic. The idea that linguistic form or *technique* governed all media became for McLuhan the first "law" that he had sought from his early days (Marchand 19). Pound's technological modernism allowed McLuhan to finally formulate that law in social terms:

> For the purposes of the present book [*The Mechanical Bride*] it is also important to detect this "law" at work all around us because of the intelligibility it releases from such diverse situations. As the unity of the modern world becomes increasingly a technological rather than a social affair, the techniques of the arts provide the most valuable means of insight into the real direction of our own collective purposes. (87)

While it is true that McLuhan encountered the rudiments of these ideas at Cambridge (especially in Richards's lectures on "practical criticism" and Leavis's *Culture and Environment: The Training of Critical Awareness* [1933]), it was Pound's early criticism that he used (as the New Critics had before him) to operationalize his theories of media forms. Pound's

1910 *Spirit of Romance* was especially interesting to McLuhan as a model of the poet's analysis of culture through language. Pound's discussion in that book of the "mediumistic properties" of the style of the troubadours leading "to an exteriorization of the sensibility" (*Romance* 94) prompted McLuhan to wonder years later if the new electronic technologies were initiating a similar "outering or extension of [man's] central nervous system" (*Understanding Media* 252). Pound's numerous injunctions concerning the primacy of forms—what he termed "the beauty of the means" versus "the beauty of the thing" ("Osiris" 41)—became for McLuhan a lifetime study of effects before causes and media before messages.

McLuhan's obsession with Poundian "technical precision" ("Pound's Critical Prose" 75), "exact juxtaposition," and "analogical presentation" (79) also betray his overriding interest in *technique*, in finding a formal apparatus to carry his own criticism in a world grown blind to the rhetorical connection between style and thought. Rhetorical style, he argued, was merely the technologizing of one's ideas, thus appropriate to the times. Suffice it to say that the famous McLuhan "mosaic" or "galaxy" configuration—that of discontinuity, aphorism, disengagement, and intellectual iconoclasm—also found precedent in Pound's ideogrammic methodology, his "rendering of complex actualities" (80) by formal homology. McLuhan's method became similarly polyphonic and representational, the ideal rhetorical form for a world that, by the 1960s, had become "a great multimedia poem" (Nevitt 231), best apprehended "by means of a discontinuous and discursive presentation of quotations, … aphorisms, metaphors, [and] analogies" (*Letters* 176). McLuhan donned a fragmentary rhetoric in order to speak of fragmentation, much as Pound had used cacophonous verbal forms to capture the "accelerated grimace" ("Hugh Selwyn Mauberley" 61) of a cheapening civilization.

The greater effect of this metaphorical style and method placed McLuhan on the periphery, where observation and detachment from the ownership, and therefore defence, of ideas gave him a "cool" new authority in an accelerated, postwar world that had indeed become, like a symbolist poem, another total-field environment. McLuhan's new authority to speak about popular and mass culture from such an engaged periphery became Canada's own, finally privileging our position on the edge of two titanic cultures. Neither British nor American, we could exist as something *other*, a kind of "interface culture" (Johnson 26) whose independence was bound up in the act of mediation, an act that came with a new kind of moral authority not unlike McLuhan's own (that disinterested study provided "civil defense against media fallout" [*Understanding Media* 305]). For a country with comparatively little mythology, history, or cultural production, lacks that gave rise to Frye's oft-quoted question "Where is here?" (220), this new authority was tailor-made, particularly when the alternative was the rather minuscule exercise of political sovereignty on the world stage. In real terms, then, McLuhan's extension of Pound's poetics from literary to cultural pioneered a way in which Canada could become a new kind of authority in a world increasingly technological and post-national, something more than a partisan colony or fifty-first state. Perhaps this explains Pierre Trudeau's fascination with McLuhan.

But McLuhan's reading of Pound's *American* modernism did not only influence a national style; his peculiar inflection also influenced what our literary artists were doing within our own borders. In *Future Indicative* (1987) and *Studies on Canadian Literature* (1990), two books that sought to assess the programme of theorizing *Canada* that began with the postmodernist generation of the 1970s, Barbara Godard and Barry Cameron isolate McLuhan as the key figure behind Robert Kroetsch, Frank Davey, George Bowering, and other anti-thematists of the post-*Survival* period. Cameron cites McLuhan's influence on Frank Davey's "Surviving the Paraphrase" (1976), the revolutionary essay that led to a shift in Canadian criticism from an emphasis on theme to an emphasis on text (137); and Godard cites McLuhan's influence on the ground-breaking *Studies in Canadian Literature* issue "Minus Canadian" (1977), which, in privileging experimentation with form over colonial mimesis, anticipated the unique voice of the "new new critic[al]" Canadian literature ("Structuralism" 27, 26). Tracing Kroetsch's phenomenological orientation to McLuhan, Davey writes that in the new literary consciousness of Canada "perception not only takes precedent over argument, but often replaces argument" (*Surviving* 7), a statement that places McLuhan's method at the centre of Canada's new wave of the 1970s.

Dudek's lading of Poundism into Canada was, in contrast to McLuhan's, far more direct. Because Dudek's relationship with Pound was essentially a meeting of minds—both were poets, after all, concerned primarily with creating an optimal space for the broadcast and reception of their art— the transfer of Pound's *American* modernism to Canada via Dudek was much more a literary than experimental affair. Dudek was certainly not the free interpreter of Pound that McLuhan was. Rather, his oft-stated and unashamed intention was to embark on a close study of Pound's cultural poetics in order that those principles might be imported to Canada to modernize our literature. As he wrote to Pound just after arriving in Montreal to teach at McGill, "There aren't many defects in Canad [sic] poetry that could not be corrected by application of your critical standards and directive" (28 August 1951). "Standards" and "directive" are the key words, for the overhaul of Canadian poetry that Dudek engineered in the 1950s and 1960s was a combination of the editorial and small-press activism of Pound *and* the overarching orthodoxy of his conservatism—the belief, that is, in what Dudek called "the right order of values" ("Louis Dudek: 1918–" 124). While McLuhan, then, was attracted to the liberalizing inducements of Pound's formal experiments, seeking even the occult laws that inhered invisibly in the alchemy, Dudek identified with Pound's classical values, entertaining dynamism only in practical terms and only in as much as it opened the field for the arts. Though it would be inaccurate to say that Dudek was unconcerned with Pound's formal renderings (even after his dismissal of Pound's theory of particulars in the important essay "The Theory of the Image in Modern Poetry"), Dudek was certainly far less concerned with Pound's formalist alchemy than was McLuhan. Taking positions on Pound opposite to McLuhan's own, Dudek was critical of what he perceived as the bohemian in Pound—scolding him as "an actor [who] does not appear in his own character" (*1941 Diary* 78)—and he was distrustful of where Pound's concentration on *technique* might lead. *Technique*, Dudek argued, was not an end in itself, but a seduction of the modern, one that recasts the poet/thinker as servo-mechanism. As he explained in a short description of his visit to the American Pavilion at Expo 67:

> the new technology is against old art; it demands a new kind of art that comes straight out of the new technology. The old principles of individual creativity and expression are replaced by new impersonal and functional products. The result is a state of crisis in all the arts, a kind of hysteria that seems ready to abandon all known distinctions between art and non-art, all aesthetic principles, and yields to the process of mechanical transformation. ("The American Pavilion" 54)

The warning seems aimed directly at McLuhan's (borrowed) ideogrammic method, suggesting that one could not casually "put on" the servo-mechanistic apparatus of mass man, that "cool" new style of theoretic-rhetorical detachment, without being reduced accordingly. The "con" of McLuhan's Menippean satire, because it was both homologous and parodic of fragmentation, might just as easily become a contagion, leading to a corresponding fragmentation of one's ethical base.[11] The concern prompted Dudek to ask if it was "too much to hope that McLuhan, hardening into radio's Mechanical Groom, ... will wake up and face the job to be done?" (*CIV/n* 91).

Part of what Dudek considered the danger of believing that *technique* constituted one of the deep structures of proto-scientific modernist society was that the formalist obsession that frequently followed (as it did in McLuhan's case) was undiscriminating, allowing for just the divestiture from "the right order of values" that McLuhan displayed. For Dudek, this divestiture from what ultimately was the responsibility of the poet/thinker in society (to expound on what was good or bad in culture), marked the error of structuralism, its swerve from the ordering principles of high-modernism.[12] To sidestep the structuralist error, Dudek rejected Pound's notion of messy anthropological "kulchur"—that which, said Pound, "occurs in or above the stinking manure heap, and can not [*sic*] be honestly defined without recognition of the dung-heap" (*Selected Letters* 294)—and adopted an elitist stance on aristocratic culture that was Ciceronian and republican in its desire for the transcendent, thus in fundamental opposition to the masses. Classical democracy was elitist, Dudek argued, intended as "a raising up of individuals so that they might aspire to the great hierarchy of values" ("American Literature" 222). When *he* wrote of the dung-heap, Dudek rejected both McLuhan and that aspect of Pound that licensed such crass, undignified, and ultimately irresponsible slumming:

> My various discussions of McLuhan in *CIV/n* and elsewhere were highly critical because I saw him as compounding with Madison Avenue instead of making a radical criticism of illiterate culture; and also as turning away from the major arts to an exaggerated concern with the vaporous media, treating them, rather than the traditional arts, as the shaping forces of society. The Venerable Bede might as well

> have turned his attention to the dunghill in Anglo-Saxon England
> as begin the true education of his people with Latin and the Bible.
> (*Dk*/ 110)

In contrast to Dudek's insistence that civil order, ethical conduct, and the aesthetic values of beauty and truth be paramount in society if culture is to stand a chance against commercial interests, McLuhan's fetish for vulgar formalism was a regressive contagion. For Dudek, the high seriousness with which one considered art should not be shared or compromised, nor should the poet/critic concern himself with anything other than building a better and more just civilization. "It is obviously civilization," wrote Dudek, "that modern society most desperately needs" ("American Literature" 223), for "only where you have afflatus—a touch of divine inspiration—do [you] get the ephemeral that is worth preserving…. [I]t is the difference between a culture that knows nothing but rubbish and one that knows, or desires, the permanent lost in the scrabble of things. Those cultures that do, and that achieve it … are called civilizations. The rest is barbarism" ("Questions" 23).

Dudek's literary activism, small-press publishing, and curricular reform were, then, a corrective to the further fragmentation of McLuhan's modernism and the material means to a greater end: that, in raising the project of artists to that of great citizens, civilization might advance beyond the crass and impermanent. The most tangible result of this application of Pound's reactionary conservatism was unprecedented support for those whose labour was civil and creative, thus reversing in Canada some of the social stigmas of being a poet and creating spaces in which poets could showcase their art. In de-institutionalizing literary publishing, Dudek, on top of heavy teaching and writing loads,[13] took the lead role at Contact Press to publish the early (in some cases, the first) works of the now best-known poets in Canada: Al Purdy, Alden Nowlan, John Newlove, F.R. Scott, Phyllis Webb, Eli Mandel, D.G. Jones, W.W.E. Ross, Gwendolyn MacEwen, R.G. Everson, George Bowering, Milton Acorn, and Margaret Atwood. Through the university, he began the McGill Poetry Series, publishing the first collections of a number of his most promising students, including Leonard Cohen, Daryl Hine, David Solway, and Seymour Mayne. He joined with editor Aileen Collins to help with the literary magazine *cıv/n*, and, in 1957, he purchased his own printing press and founded the magazine *Delta*, which he edited (and printed in his basement) until 1966. None of this activity was undirected; rather, it was, as the following letter to Pound indicates, the crystallization of a vision of literary renewal that was no less than a unifying theology: "Our hope, if any, is to cultivate and enlarge the small magazines, get them an audience slowly, so that in a generation or two we may have a solid minority which will be immune and embattled against the surrounding sea of plebeian mindlessness and ignorance" (Dudek, Letter to Ezra Pound, 16 April 1951). What makes Dudek's programme coherent is this theology of enlightened high modernism. Simply put, he construed this unity as a response to the vulgar modernism to which he saw Pound's formalism leading.

As poet, critic, publisher, editor, professor, anthologist, translator, and, as Frank Davey wrote, "the first to follow Arnold and Pound in combining poetry, polemical editing, and cultural criticism into one multi-faceted cultural vision" ("Introduction" 7), Dudek turned poetics into literary practice. Working from Pound's directive that there "MUST be correlation between the honest few ... and concerted attempt to penetrate the CHANNELS of communication print and air" (Pound, Letter to Louis Dudek, 11 April 1951), Dudek instituted a practical apparatus through which civilization might grow in this country, thus placing himself (and the rudiments of Pound's cultural poetics) at the centre of the Canadian literary awakening of the 1960s. It would not overstate the matter to say that our literary heritage is part of Dudek's creation, for he was the one who put the material structures in place that allowed our writers to speak and to develop the small but important later presses that further carried the project of defining Canada (Anansi, Coach House, Oberon, Talonbooks, Black Moss, and Quarry). As Terry Goldie wrote, "*Delta* and the various presses with which Dudek was associated were a major part of the development of contemporary Canadian literature ... of the 1950s and 1960s" (51).

While McLuhan's work, then, extended the theoretical boundaries of Pound's *technological* modernism, Dudek's work instituted the practical apparatus of Pound's *kulturmorphologie*, the drift or transfer of ideas from writer to writer. Because this project was utopian, Dudek was necessarily reactionary, giving equal time to the dismissal of McLuhan and the commercial interests that his method validated, as to the celebration of enlightened alternatives to a cheapening civilization, including establishing the physical structures by which this could happen. "What Pound opened up for me," wrote Dudek, "was a great curiosity about contemporary poetry—and its engagement with the cause of civilization" ("Louis Dudek: 1918–" 131). In operationalizing reactionary modernism in Canada—thus testing Pound's notion that "the history of a culture is the history of ideas going into action" (*Kulchur* 44)—Dudek became one of the great cultural architects of the twentieth century.

III

In an important essay written in *Open Letter* in 1992, Barbara Godard proposes, as an alternative to the "biased" theorizing of Canada, "a more productive strategy [that would] pay systematic attention to the highly selective processes of appropriation and realignment that have taken place throughout the history of the Canadian literatures" ("Canadian?" 10). In other words, Godard invites a more far-ranging investigation into the "veritable patch-works of theories borrowed, rewritten and used for new ends" that have "invent[ed] Canadian literature" (10). It is in light of Godard's direction that this investigation of our modernist inheritance has proceeded.

While *Future Indicative* and *Studies on Canadian Literature*, among the most ambitious critical studies that "theorize" Canadian modernism, do indeed focus on the centrality of McLuhan and Dudek to the project of mid-century literary renewal, neither collection ties the work of the two Canadians to the cultural politics of Pound. This is not a result of critical malaise but of the aforementioned ambiguous nature of our modernism. Establishing the influence of Pound's uniquely *American* modernism for a Canadian sense of voice and nationhood indebted to McLuhan's pioneering studies of media forms and Dudek's literary and small-press activism eliminates some of that ambiguity, for the intimacy of McLuhan's and Dudek's connections with the incarcerated poet and the systematic ways they applied his ideas constitute a set of historically measurable exchanges much more tangible than the sporadic emulation of strong poets or the incidental absorption of radio signals and cinematic developments from afar.

In privileging form over content (thus opening the way for the media/technology critique that McLuhan popularized, as well as his influential "interface" equipoise); in envisioning the artist/critic as a cultural crusader (thus elevating the thinker to the status of public intellectual that McLuhan and Dudek both exercised); in showing poets how to expose and counter mediocrity with tools and resources (thus providing Dudek with the aims and means for cultural renewal); and in expanding the nineteenth-century definition of text to include a broad range of styles and expressions in music, literature, and visual art (thus informing the inter-disciplinary nature of the Canadian small-magazine and mixed-media experiments of the 1960s)—Pound's ideas resound. The modernism that McLuhan and Dudek imported into Canada was not "troubled within itself" (210), as Gail McDonald describes the expatriate modernism of Americans abroad, but a dialectical modernism of multiple possibilities. Modernism's some-times warring tendencies of tradition and innovation reached a working détente in Canada, allowing two of our most influential mid-century modernists to be radicals in their own right, transforming culture in mark-edly different ways while also being deeply conservative at their cores.

NOTES

Unpublished letters from Dudek to Pound have been used by permission of Michael Gnarowski and Gregory Dudek (copyright © 2004 by Michael Gnarowski). Unpublished letters from Pound to Dudek, McLuhan, and Boris de Rachewiltz have been used by permission of New Directions Publishing Corporation (copy-right © 2004 by Mary de Rachewiltz and Omar S. Pound).

[1] My knowledge of the early cultural (radio and film) modernists in Canada comes from Paul Tiessen's article "From Literary Modernism to the Tantramar Marshes: Anticipating McLuhan in British and Canadian Media Theory and Practice."

[2] For the history of the legalization of *Ulysses* in Canada, see Conley.

[3] Pound's knowledge of and acquaintance with other Canadians—with the social creditors "Bible Bill" Aberhart and the Anglican clergyman Rev. Henry Swabey, with whom he corresponded in the 1930s—never even remotely approached the scope or intensity of the McLuhan and Dudek associations. Pound's relationship with the Peterborough, Ontario-born Hugh Kenner, though similar in scope and engagement to the McLuhan/Dudek associations, reflected the different interests of Kenner, whose work, based entirely in the United States, was much more schol-arly than cultural or national.

[4] Kenner has always been reserved about his relationship with McLuhan, admit-ting indebtedness but never clearly delineating McLuhan's influence. In a 1984 article for *Harper's* magazine, reprinted in the essay collection *Mazes*, Kenner did

admit that "Marshall McLuhan was my first mentor" (*Mazes* 223), and in an earlier 1981 remembrance of McLuhan for the *National Review*, also reprinted in *Mazes*, he admitted that "I've been going on from extemporizations of Marshall's for thirty years" (297). But aside from those comments, his dedication of *The Poetry of Ezra Pound* (1951) to McLuhan—which reads "To Marshall McLuhan, A catalogue, his jewels of conversation"—and the following notes to Marchand to aid his biographical account of McLuhan, Kenner has divulged little else that would help us make sense of the McLuhan/Kenner association: "He pushed at me T.S. Eliot, who'd been the type of unintelligibility to my Toronto profs. And he had me read Richards'[s] *Practical Criticism*, Leavis's *New Bearings in English Poetry*, and (eventually) the entire file of *Scrutiny*. He kept mentioning Wyndham Lewis, whom I'd never heard of, notwithstanding that for two years I'd lived half a mile away from him [in Toronto].... So many windows opened!" (qtd. in Marchand 93).

[5] See Carpenter 760.

[6] Pound wrote that "the culture of Adams and Jefferson is a Latin culture with a mixture of Greek" ("Economic Nature" 174).

[7] Pound's correspondence with McLuhan reveals the older poet's fascination with McLuhan's desire for a Canadian cultural revolution grounded theoretically in his *ABC of Reading* (1934) and *Guide to Kulchur*.

[8] For the Eliade metaphors of "guide" and "guardian," I am indebted to George Sanderson.

[9] In an interview in *Essays on Canadian Writing*, Dudek remarked that "Pound meant a lot to me, but not to anyone else. That is, amongst the people I moved around with, nobody was very much influenced [by] or much concerned with Ezra Pound. Not Layton, not Souster, not Earle Birney. What he was for me, I would say, was a kind of synthesis or focus for all the problems that I saw in poetry, beginning with the aesthetic position, the notion of art in poetry" (qtd. in Goldie 8). Gustafson agreed, writing that "Others have poetically descended from Ezra Pound but none has practiced Pound with more affinity and cogency than Dudek" (308). Livesay's encounters with Pound were proximate to her independent readings of H.D. in Toronto in the late 1920s, and largely scrapped because of differences over politics. For Ross's knowledge of Pound, described as "little," see *A Literary Friendship* 22. For more on McLuhan's uptake of Pound, see Willmott 50, and McLuhan's biographer, Marchand, who wrote about his subject that "Of all the twentieth-century literary giants, Pound was closest to being a soul mate of McLuhan's" (96).

[10] Willmott actually uses the Greek term *techne* to describe the totalizing belief system that characterized the Greek's understanding of the practical arts. This belief, adopted by Pound in *Guide to Kulchur*, amalgamated all things made by creative impulse—whether arts or crafts, poems or machines—into one category.

Techne, then, includes all things made. I prefer and have used Jacques Ellul's term *technique*, which means something quite different than *techne*. As defined by Ellul and later Neil Postman, *technique* involves the method of doing things, especially those methods that are the most efficient. Efficiency thus becomes divorced from craft and the intentions of the artist. I prefer *technique* to *techne* because the former term implies an animation of process and not merely an identification of the constituents of process. McLuhan believed that *technique* animated culture, thus could be harnessed; Dudek that *technique* was the animus of culture, thus must be stopped. *Techne* is a term too passive to use in these contexts.

[11] Though he never spoke of his disagreements with McLuhan in Catholic terms, Dudek seemed especially perturbed by what he perceived as McLuhan's swerve from Catholic pedagogical obligations as Aquinas and Newman would have defined those. McLuhan's formal and lexical bravura seemed at odds with his private convictions (he converted to Catholicism in 1937 and was devout throughout his life) and were certainly different from Dudek's, who, as a lapsed Catholic, still held to the early Catholic principle that art was a revelation of the sacred amidst the profane. One of the ironies of their quarrels is that, publicly, the lapsed Dudek was more Catholic than the zealous convert McLuhan.

[12] The difference in McLuhan's and Dudek's graduate-school experiences may have affected their attitudes to structuralism. While McLuhan studied at the feet of the New Critics at Cambridge, and came to know Mansfield Forbes and Leavis as friends, Dudek's strongest influences at Columbia were Emery Neff and Lionel Trilling, both historically inclined, both believing in the primacy of the "moral imagination." Trilling, especially, writes Nathan Glick, "raised questions about how we live our lives, about the nature of good and evil … about our ambivalence in making moral choices" (86). Dudek remained committed to Trilling's brand of moral conservatism throughout his life. I thank Sandra Djwa for bringing Trilling's importance to my attention.

[13] His classes at McGill were so popular in the late 1950s and 1960s that they often neared 500 students, yet during this period he managed frequent radio talks and an exhausting programme of literary journalism. Between 1958 and 1969, he contributed over 300 critical essays and reviews to the *Montreal Star*, the *Gazette* (Montreal), and the *Globe and Mail*, working, he said, to create a literate Canadian audience receptive to poetry and the arts.

WORKS CITED

Bowering, George. *Imaginary Hand: Essays by George Bowering*. Edmonton: NeWest, 1988.

Brown, E.K. "The Development of Poetry in Canada." *Poetry* 58 (Apr. 1941): 43–45.

Cameron, Barry. "English Critical Discourse in/on Canada." *Studies on Canadian Literature*. Ed. Arnold E. Davidson. New York: MLA, 1990. 124–43.

Carey, John. *The Intellectual and the Masses: Pride and Prejudice among the Literary Intelligentsia, 1880–1939*. London: Faber and Faber, 1992.

Carpenter, Humphrey. *A Serious Character: The Life of Ezra Pound*. New York: Delta, 1988.

Conley, Tim. "Samizdat Odyssey: *Ulysses* above the 42nd Parallel." *The Canadian Modernists Meet*. Ed. Dean Irvine. Ottawa: U of Ottawa P, 2005. 139–51.

Davey, Frank. "Introduction." *Louis Dudek: Texts & Essays*. Spec. issue of *Open Letter*. Ed. Frank Davey and bpNichol. 4th ser. 8–9 (1981): 7–8.

———. *Surviving the Paraphrase: Eleven Essays on Canadian Literature*. Winnipeg: Turnstone, 1983.

Djwa, Sandra. *The Politics of the Imagination: A Life of F.R. Scott*. Toronto: McClelland and Stewart, 1987.

Dudek, Louis. "The American Pavilion at Expo 67." *In Defence of Art: Critical Essays & Reviews*. Ed. Aileen Collins. Kingston: Quarry, 1988. 54–55.

———. *CIV/n: A Literary Magazine of the 50's*. Ed. Aileen Collins. Montreal: Véhicule, 1983.

——— , ed. *Dk/ Some Letters of Ezra Pound*. Montreal: DC Books, 1974.

———. "Is American Literature Coming of Age?" *Louis Dudek: Texts & Essays*. Spec. issue of *Open Letter*. Ed. Frank Davey and bpNichol. 4th ser. 8–9 (1981): 217–23.

———. Letter to Ezra Pound, 16 Apr. 1951. Louis Dudek Fonds. National Library of Canada, Ottawa. LMS-0167. Ser. 2, box 16.

———. Letter to Ezra Pound, 4 Jan. 1955. Louis Dudek Fonds. National Library of Canada, Ottawa. LMS-0167. Ser. 2, box 16.

———. Letter to Ezra Pound, 10 Oct. 1957. Louis Dudek Fonds. National Library of Canada, Ottawa. LMS-0167. Ser. 2, box 16.

———. *Literature and the Press: A History of Printing, Printed Media, and Their Relation to Literature*. Diss. Columbia University, 1955. Rev. Toronto: Ryerson and Contact, 1960.

———. "Louis Dudek: 1918–" *Contemporary Authors Autobiography Series*. Vol. 14. Ed. Joyce Nakamura. Detroit: Gale, 1991. 121–42.

———. *1941 Diary*. Ed. Aileen Collins. Montreal: Empyreal, 1996.

———. "Questions (Some Answers)." *Louis Dudek: Texts & Essays*. Spec. issue of *Open Letter*. Ed. Frank Davey and bpNichol. 4th ser. 8–9 (1981): 9–38.

———. "The Theory of the Image in Modern Poetry." *Louis Dudek: Texts & Essays*. Spec. issue of *Open Letter*. Ed. Frank Davey and bpNichol. 4th ser. 8–9 (1981): 263–82.

Frye, Northrop. *The Bush Garden: Essays on the Canadian Imagination*. Toronto: Anansi, 1971.

Glick, Nathan. "The Last Great Critic." *Atlantic Monthly* July 2000: 86.

Godard, Barbara. "Canadian? Literary? Theory?" *Open Letter*. 8th ser. 3 (spring 1992): 5–27.

———. "Structuralism/Post-Structuralism: Language, Reality and Canadian Literature." *Future Indicative: Literary Theory and Canadian Literature*. Ed. John Moss. Ottawa: U of Ottawa P, 1987. 25–48.

Goldie, Terry. *Louis Dudek and His Work*. Toronto: ECW, 1984.

Goodwin, K.L. *The Influence of Ezra Pound*. London: Oxford, 1968.

Gordon, W. Terrence. *Marshall McLuhan: Escape into Understanding*. Toronto: Stoddart, 1997.

Gustafson, Ralph. "Louis Dudek." *Contemporary Poets of the English Language*. Ed. Rosalie Murphy. London: St. James, 1970. 308–10.

Johnson, Steven. *Interface Culture: How New Technology Transforms the Way We Create and Communicate*. San Francisco: Basic Books, 1997.

Kenner, Hugh. *Mazes*. San Francisco: North Point, 1989.

Kroetsch, Robert. "A Canadian Issue." *Boundary 2* 3 (fall 1974): 1–2.

Laughlin, James. *Pound as Wuz: Essays and Lectures on Ezra Pound*. 1985. Saint Paul, MN: Graywolf, 1987.

Lewis, Wyndham. *Blasting and Bombardiering: An Autobiography (1914–1926)*. 1937. London: Calder and Boyars, 1967.

Marchand, Philip. *Marshall McLuhan: The Medium and the Messenger*. Toronto: Random House, 1989.

McDonald, Gail. *Learning to be Modern: Pound, Eliot, and the American University*. Oxford: Clarendon, 1993.

McLuhan, Marshall. "Canada: The Borderline Case." *The Canadian Imagination: Dimensions of a Literary Culture*. Ed. David Staines. Cambridge: Harvard UP, 1972. 226–48.

———. *The Letters of Marshall McLuhan*. Ed. Matie Molinaro, Corrine McLuhan, and William Toye. Toronto: Oxford UP, 1987.

———. *The Mechanical Bride: Folklore of Industrial Man*. New York: Vanguard, 1951.

———. "Pound's Critical Prose." *The Interior Landscape: The Literary Criticism of Marshall McLuhan, 1943–1962*. Ed. Eugene McNamara. Toronto: McGraw-Hill, 1969.

———. *Understanding Media: The Extensions of Man*. New York: McGraw-Hill, 1964.

Nevitt, Barrington, and Maurice McLuhan, et al. *Who Was Marshall McLuhan?* Toronto: Comprehensivist, 1994.

Nicholls, Peter. *Modernisms: A Literary Guide*. Berkeley: U of California P, 1995.

Perelman, Bob. *The Trouble with Genius: Reading Pound, Joyce, Stein, and Zukofsky*. Berkeley: U of California P, 1994.

Pound, Ezra. "Bureaucracy the Flail of Jehovah." *Selected Prose: 1909–1965*. Ed. William Cookson. New York: New Directions, 1973. 217–21.

———. *Confucius: The Unwobbling Pivot, The Great Digest, The Analects*. 1928. New York: New Directions, 1969.

———. *Guide to Kulchur*. 1938. New York: New Directions, 1970.

———. "Hugh Selwyn Mauberley." *Selected Poems of Ezra Pound*. New York: New Directions, 1957. 61–77.

———. "I Gather the Limbs of Osiris." *Selected Prose: 1909–1965*. Ed. William Cookson. New York: New Directions, 1973. 21–43.

———. "An Introduction to the Economic Nature of the United States." *Selected Prose: 1909–1965*. Ed. William Cookson. New York: New Directions, 1973. 167–85.

———. Letter to Boris de Rachewiltz, 17 June 1954. Ezra Pound Fonds. William Berg Collection. New York Public Library. Folder 5.

———. Letter to Boris de Rachewiltz, 27 Dec. 1955. Ezra Pound Fonds. William Berg Collection. New York Public Library. Folder 14.

———. Letter to Louis Dudek, 11 Apr. 1951. Louis Dudek Fonds. National Library of Canada, Ottawa. LMS-0167. Ser. 2, box 16.

———. Letter to Marshall McLuhan, 20 June 1951. H. Marshall McLuhan Fonds. National Library of Canada, Ottawa. MG31 D156, vol. 34.

———. Letter to Marshall McLuhan, 4 Jan. 1955. H. Marshall McLuhan Fonds. National Library of Canada, Ottawa. MG31 D156, vol. 34.

———. "Patria Mia." *Selected Prose: 1909–1965*. Ed. William Cookson. New York: New Directions, 1973. 101–41.

———. *The Selected Letters of Ezra Pound: 1907–1941*. 1950. Ed. D.D. Paige. New York: New Directions, 1971.

———. *The Spirit of Romance*. 1910. New York: New Directions, 1968.

Rahe, Paul A. *Republics Ancient and Modern: Classical Republicanism and the American Revolution*. Chapel Hill: U of North Carolina P, 1992.

Reck, Michael. *Ezra Pound: A Close-Up*. 1967. New York: McGraw-Hill, 1973.

Ross, W.W.E., and Ralph Gustafson. *A Literary Friendship: The Correspondence of Ralph Gustafson and W.W.E. Ross*. Ed. Bruce Whiteman. Toronto: ECW, 1984.

Shalhope, Robert E. "In Search of the Elusive Republic." Rev. of *Republicanism and Bourgeois Radicalism: Political Ideology in Late Eighteenth-Century England and America*, by Isaac Kramnick. *Reviews in American History* 19 (1991): 468–73.

Tiessen, Paul. "From Literary Modernism to the Tantramar Marshes: Anticipating McLuhan in British and Canadian Media Theory and Practice." *Canadian Journal of Communications* 18.4 (1993): 1–14.

Tremblay, Tony. "'git yr / eye off Canada / and onto internat criteria /': Exploring the Influence of Ezra Pound on the Cultural Production of Louis Dudek." *Essays on Canadian Writing* 74 (fall 2001): 26–52.

————. "'The Literary Occult' in the Letters of Marshall McLuhan and Ezra Pound." *Paideuma: A Journal Devoted to Ezra Pound Scholarship*. 27.2–3 (fall–winter 1998): 107–27.

Willmott, Glenn. *McLuhan, or Modernism in Reverse*. Toronto: UTP, 1996.

POLITICAL BODIES: STAGES AND STATIONS, CASTS AND BROADCASTS

Modernism's Red Stage: Theatre and the Left in the 1930s

CANDIDA RIFKIND

I. SOCIALIST THEATRE IN THE 1930S

THE SEMIOTIC FLEXIBILITY of the word "stage" offers a productive entry into the field of English-Canadian socialist theatre in the 1930s. On the one hand, the Depression era produced a theatrical encounter between modernism and socialism on stages organized by the Canadian left. On the other hand, this convergence catalyzed multiple aesthetic and ideological transformations, and thus it demands readings that can account for the stages of socialist theatre over the course of the decade. While the category of literary modernism may seem relatively homogeneous, this illusion is achieved through a progressivist narrative of development. Therefore, modernism's red stage is an aesthetic and a generic descriptor, a periodizing and a political category. Although modernist theatre experienced multiple and different phases in each of its national incarnations, during the interwar period there was a striking convergence of avant-garde theatres and militant working-class movements in both Europe and North America (Williams 87).[1] Throughout the 1930s, theatre was a vital cultural site for Canadian socialists across the left, from the Communist Party of Canada (CPC), to the social democrats of the Cooperative Commonwealth Federation (CCF), to unionists and unaligned leftists. This ideologically and aesthetically diverse theatre was part of a broader culture of performativity in 1930s socialism characterized by the ephemeral and "elative performances" of political sociability found in parades, rallies, pageants, picnics, parties, summer camps, festivals, and even funerals (Filewod, "Performance" 72). Just as it overlaps with the political cultures of socialism, so does leftist theatre have affiliations with the literary cultures of the period. The socialist theatres of this decade are one site of a larger aesthetic of political commitment that extended across the arts. In poetry and fiction, it produced the radical documentaries, critical realisms, and fierce satires of Irene Baird, Leo Kennedy, A.M. Klein, Kenneth Leslie, Dorothy Livesay, L.A. Mackay, F.R. Scott, and A.M. Stephen, among others. Although the leftist theatre is distinct in some important ways—not least the number of working-class participants who swelled the ranks of sympathetic middle-class writers—it participates in a broader Marxist belief that aesthetic representation operates through, but also on, political representation. The economic and political strains of the Depression compelled both workers and bourgeois dissidents to take to the Canadian amateur stage, so that in the performing arts the lines were often blurred between aesthetics and politics, realism and expressionism, actor and audience. Canadian leftist theatre in the 1930s is consequently best understood as a collective effort to create an experiential and an experimental space, in which everyday life is denaturalized and estranged to reveal the structural historical forces that shape it.

The 1970s witnessed a surge of interest in the 1930s literary and theatrical left as writers, historians, and surviving participants republished some of the original texts and produced memoirs and surveys of the leftwing cultural scene (see Gordon Ryan; Livesay; Robertson; Souchotte; Waddington; Wright and Endres). More recent scholarship has relied on these sources but also returned to the archives and situated the English-Canadian literary left within an international frame. James Doyle's book, *Progressive Heritage: The Evolution of a Politically Radical Literary Tradition in Canada* (2002), focuses on Communist-affiliated literature produced throughout the twentieth century and provides an important commentary on how debates within the left shaped national literary history. Doyle's study makes a significant contribution to the biographical and bibliographical gaps in the scholarship, yet he admits in his introduction that his centre of gravity is the CPC and that he is interested in literary rather than theatrical activity (9–10). I therefore want to build on Doyle's summary of anglophone Communist scripts from the early 1930s by considering the whole decade, as well as a spectrum of leftist ideologies, within the theoretical contexts of performance studies and the field of cultural production.

I am indebted in this approach to the work of Alan Filewod, whose recovery and criticism of the Communist Workers' Theatres in the early 1930s has implications for studying all of the decade's leftist theatre. In his 1997 article "National Theatre / National Obsession," Filewod insists that the 1930s theatrical left must be reintegrated into the narrative of Canadian drama because it was the closest the country has ever come to a "true national theatre" (20). He concludes that the relegation of the Workers' Theatre and its successors outside the canon of Canadian theatre proves "its [own] fundamental assertion that theatre in Canada was an expression of class interests" ("National Theatre" 21). However, in his 2003 article "Performance and Memory in the Party: Dismembering the Workers' Theatre Movement," Filewod revises some of his own and other critics' earlier assertions that the Workers' Theatre was an authentic moment of an imagined past in Canadian theatre. While he admits that there is enough material in the historical record to support claims that the 1930s produced a radical theatre that intervened in national culture in productive ways, he now believes these recoverable texts are misleading because "they evidence not the work of a movement but the situational tactics of the strategic attempt to organize a movement" (61). He remembers and dismembers the Communist-affiliated Workers' Theatres of the Third Period by contextualizing their statements and productions within the larger field of CPC elative performances. These "generated an embodied, physiological rapture through spectacle" by which "the party performed itself as a simulacrum of the revolution" (75). Filewod concludes that within this wider field of performativity, the Workers' Theatre was "relatively inconsequential" (75). Yet, it has entered the canonical spaces of national theatre history in part because it won the internal CPC struggles among agitprop movements, and in part because of postwar detachments of leftist cultural productions from their Party origins. The Workers' Theatre has been preserved and commemorated despite the erosion and failures of Communism (75). My essay casts a wider net than Filewod's focus on the Third Period Worker's Theatre to examine a multiplicity of socialist stages in the 1930s, and to consider them as a national field of positions and position-takings intersected by international performances of the left as well as hierarchies of class, ethnicity, and gender. It remains mindful, however, of the political and performance pressures at work in the exchanges between actors and audiences on the 1930s left.

The field of 1930s socialist theatre needs to be understood around a central mid-decade shift when geopolitical upheavals were registered in socialist politics as well as leftist dramaturgy. Between 1929 and 1934, the Third Period policies of the Communist International (Comintern) were manifested in Stalin's militant class warfare as well as the agitational-propaganda (agitprop) performances of a European-inspired workers' theatre. This gave way mid-decade to the coalitionist statements of the Popular Front period, from 1935–39, when the Communist Party opened up to former adversaries on the left to forge a united front against fascism.[2] In English Canada, formerly militant Communist theatre turned, with only a few exceptions, to an American-influenced naturalist humanism. On the social-democratic front, the CCF nurtured a range of cultural activities, including drama clubs. In Vancouver, participant Arthur Turner recalled that by the mid-1930s the lower mainland CCF had a total of ten play-reading groups, comprised mostly of unemployed volunteers. The success of borrowed and original plays among CCF actors and audiences led to the creation in the early 1930s of a workers' drama festival in New Westminster, BC. By the late 1930s, Popular Front theatre often involved both Communists and CCF members in productions that represented the international events of the Japanese invasion of Manchuria or the Spanish Civil War as often as the national ones of dustbowl scarcity or urban protest. Throughout the decade and across the left, albeit in different ways, the theatre acted out what Perry Anderson calls socialism's and modernism's "imaginative proximity" (34). At this point, the stage is a space in which the seemingly competing discourses, ideologies, and aesthetics of socialism and modernism converge to produce a field structured by competition as well as complementarity. It is in Pierre Bourdieu's sense of the field, then, that we can understand the ways in which the productive antagonisms of 1930s socialist theatre in Canada constitute a "space of positions and the space of position-takings" (30). These competitions among agents in the field are fundamental to the social relations that structure the field of cultural production and its determinations of artistic value, which are also always intersected by the field of political power.

II. THE PARTIALITY OF THE PEOPLE'S STAGE

It is often lamented that the majority of Canadian plays written and performed have never been published. This dismal situation found a temporary reprieve among the literary left of the 1930s. Its cultural journals, *Masses* (1932–34) and *New Frontier* (1936–37), commissioned, printed, and circulated original scripts. The New Hogtown anthology *Eight Men Speak and Other Plays from the Canadian Workers' Theatre* (1976) joins with two collective memoirs, Dorothy Livesay's *Right Hand Left Hand* (1977) and Toby Gordon Ryan's *Stage Left* (1981), to reproduce the texts and contexts of this movement. This has led in turn to a critical preference, forced in part by many large gaps in the archive, for Communist-affiliated productions. However, not all socialist theatre troupes were urban, anglophone, or Communist. Throughout 1930s periodicals, there are references to the socialist plays of non-anglophone immigrant communities, including the Finnish, German, Icelandic, Polish, Yiddish, and Ukrainian radical theatres across the country. Some groups wrote their own material, including the Finnish workers' theatre of Kivikoski (a farming centre north of Port Arthur) and the Youth Section of the Ukrainian Labour Farmer Temple Association in Moose Jaw ("Workers' Theatre"). Significantly, the latter began to translate their plays into English because their audiences expanded with interested anglophone workers ("Workers' Theatre in Action"). In other cases one immigrant community's cultural activities would attract interest from another non-anglophone group because of the general feeling that life in English Canada was divided between Anglo-Saxons and the "others." Ester Reiter's description of the rich Yiddish culture forged by radical Jewish immigrants in several Canadian cities includes examples of how members of these communities reached out to other labour-oriented and leftist ethnic organizations (see Reiter).

One mainstream record of this immigrant theatrical left indicates the extent to which studies of modernism's red stage can only ever be partial. A 1929 *Saturday Night* article on a Ukrainian Bolshevist playwright in Winnipeg, Miroslav Irchan, claims that by sheer performance and audience numbers alone he must be the most popular and prolific playwright in Canada (Roslin 77). His plays demanded large casts of amateur actors and include such titles as "The Unemployed," "The Awakening of the Workers," "Spies and the Communist Party," and "The Tragedy of the First of May" (Roslin 74–77). Performed in Ukrainian for a loyal western-Canadian audience, these plays enjoyed a wider popularity than any English-Canadian plays. Just as there is a wealth of leftist poetry and fiction produced by these immigrant communities in the 1920s and 1930s, so too did they cultivate a lively socialist theatre, little of which has been sufficiently translated or studied. The production of French-language socialist theatre is equally difficult to examine. According to Emile Talbot, the dominance of religious ideology led 1930s Québécois literature to demonize Communists and socialists as potent threats to traditional values, even though some of their ideas accorded with papal teachings and the Church's anti-capitalist stance (76). However, that there were some francophone Montreal Communists and that they were interested in theatre is evident in a 1934 *Masses* appeal they sent out to their comrades, asking for agitprop scripts relevant to their local struggles and in their own language ("Workers' Theatre").

These linguistic barriers to remembering the socialist stages of 1930s Canada are compounded by ideological barriers, both within the period and later. The proliferation of immigrant leftist theatres, the number of new immigrants who joined anglophone companies, and the appropriation of international models for Canadian stages combine to taint modern socialist theatre as foreign. At the time, however, anglophone leftists were both aware of and sometimes involved in the non-anglophone cultural left. In *Right Hand Left Hand*, Livesay recalls that while living in Montreal in 1933–34 she was assigned the task of helping to create "an ethnic festival of working class plays and songs" (74). She contacted labour organizations from the Ukrainian, Russian, Latvian, Swedish, Finnish, and French communities to arrange for singers, dancers, and actors to compete in the festival. The remorse of her comment, "I wish I had kept the programmes!" is a common feeling among the participants of the 1930s theatrical left when it later came time to document and evaluate that movement (74).[3]

Studies in Canadian theatre history and historiography reveal that there has long been a powerful notion that Canadian theatre must serve national interests, that the well-made play is the exemplum of the well-made modern nation (Salter 73). Canadian theatre has tended to organize itself around what Alan Filewod sets out as a syllogism: "if we have a Canadian nation, then a Canadian drama must be one of its proofs; therefore we must have a national theatre to advance the national drama" ("National Theatre" 15). Moreover, the dominant definition of the nation since the nineteenth century has been exclusive and colonial in ways that muffle and even silence the voices of minority communities and non-dominant aesthetics (Salter 73). Ioan Davies seeks a corrective to this when he observes that the variety of non-English theatre, prior to the public cultural debates of the

Massey Commission (1949–51) and its published *Report* (1951), should invite critics to rethink that document's powerful and lingering assumption that Canadian culture in the first half of the twentieth century was the product of an urban English-Canadian middle class (7). Davies asks that contemporary critics look to the cultural workers of the 1930s left because, among these artists and writers, "the idea that culture had an ethnic as well as a class component was prominent, and thus the concept of what constituted culture was pulled out of its immediately colonial origins" (7).

It is in all senses of the word, then, that the socialist stages of the 1930s, as well as our efforts to reconstruct it, need to be acknowledged today as always partial. Race, understood as a temporally specific construction of otherness and not only an index of skin colour, joins with class to locate this leftist theatre beyond the pale of national literary history. It also suffers from a broader critical narrative that reads the 1930s as the doldrums between two storms of modernist activity in the 1920s and 1940s. The effect is to devalue the 1930s literary left as a temporary outburst of youthful idealism that would come to its artistic and political senses during the Cold War. Linguistic, nationalistic, and periodizing ideologies of the socialist stage, and of modernist stages, thus impose a force on the theatrical field that tilts the scholarship off balance and diminishes, if not occludes, the variety and complexity of the moment of cultural production itself. Cary Nelson's comment about the repression and recovery of American radical modernist poetry reverberates in this context: "we no longer know the history of the poetry of the first half of this century; most of us, moreover, do not know that the knowledge is gone" (4). Nelson provokes critics into recognizing the politics of forgetfulness as much as he wants the literary institution to analyze the canonizing effects of remembering. His comment applies equally well to the history of modernist leftist theatre in Canada because, in a number of ways, we do not know how much has been forgotten.

III. "A PROPERTYLESS THEATRE FOR THE PROPERTYLESS CLASS"

The internationalism of the 1930s theatrical left was able to take root because the national ground was fertile. The economic crash that led to structural unemployment created a large body of people, particularly men, inhabiting public spaces and desperate for something to do. This forced leisure created a ready-made audience on which many socialists were opportunistic, in the sense that they appealed to bourgeois subjects as a necessary tactic to achieve socialism. The economic depression also provided a pool of potential actors eager to recuperate the individual and collective identities denied them by unemployment. The growth of anglophone leftist theatre was also helped by several decades of organized amateur dramatics across the country. This was formalized in 1932 when Governor General Lord Bessborough initiated the Dominion Drama Festival (DDF). The DDF was a nationwide competition primarily for the groups of the Little Theatre movement. It was a nationalist forum holding a position in the field of theatre akin to that occupied by the Canadian Authors Association (CAA) in the field of literature (the DDF and the CAA even shared members on their organizing committees, including critic and editor B.K. Sandwell of *Saturday Night* and publisher Hugh Eayrs of Macmillan). Although it was a celebration of amateur productions, the absence of professional companies during the Depression overturned the usual dynamics of the field. The DDF and the Little Theatres, which might ordinarily have been dismissed as the hobbies of amateur dabblers, attracted out-of-work theatre professionals; their competitions temporarily replaced commercial productions as the most lively and symbolically powerful sites of the national stage. The Little Theatres tended to favour Shakespeare and the playwrights of an earlier European modernism, including Ibsen, Strindberg, and Gogol, but they also encouraged an indigenous naturalism modelled on the Irish literary renaissance in the works of Merrill Denison, John Coulter, and Gwen Pharis Ringwood, among others. Some of these plays documented local social problems, but they rarely offered solutions. This would be the task undertaken by socialist stages.

The modern innovations of a Canadian agitprop theatre were inspired by Soviet and German models featuring a completely mobile stage, neutral costumes augmented by simple props to signify character types (a top hat for an industrialist, a cloth cap for a worker, and so on), direct addresses to the audience, and mass recitations. Toby Gordon Ryan describes seeing a German-American workers' troupe perform in New York as an artistic epiphany. As she recalls, it "shed light for me on a new and dynamic form of theatre. The experience certainly helped broaden my own view of the stage as a potent instrument for change and a voice through which one could reach and affect people" (*Stage Left* 22). She returned to Canada in 1932 eager to start an agitprop movement, and recruited Dorothy Livesay, their friend Jim (Jean) Watts, cartoonist Avrom Yanovsky, and others from the Toronto student and Communist arts scene to foster a network of workers' experimental theatres through the newly created Progressive Arts Clubs (PACS). *Masses* reports that by 1934 there were PACS in Halifax, Montreal, Toronto, London (Ontario), Winnipeg, Edmonton, and Vancouver ("Workers' Theatre"). There were many CCF drama clubs across the country, too, as well as independent groups such as Toronto's Miracle Players of Seaton House, Hamilton's Rebel Arts Players, and the theatre section of the Edmonton Unemployed Married Men's Association.

One of the aesthetic and political goals of this diverse movement was to prove to Canadian audiences that the national theatre was in the stranglehold of liberal–bourgeois culture, that theatre was another site of the class struggle. This message takes aesthetic form in the most common feature of Third Period agitprop: mass recitations. Sometimes performed as parts of concert evenings, mass recitations were also mobile performances that could occur on sidewalks, in picket lines, before and after meetings, and at public demonstrations. Many of the scripts are lost but, ironically, records of performances are available in the RCMP reports filed by undercover officers who infiltrated the left, contributing to the very climate of repression expressed on stage.[4] "Theatre—Our Weapon" was the first published script of the Toronto PAC's Workers' Experimental Theatre, which changed its name by the end of 1932 to the Workers' Theatre.[5] Its form and title are borrowed from a script published in *New Red Stage*, the organ of the British Workers' Theatre Movement (WTM) spearheaded by Tom Thomas and Ewan McColl.[6] A key aesthetic shift adopted by Canadian cultural activists was the British WTM's proclamation that theirs was an avant-garde but also a vanguard theatre. In England and in Canada, workers' theatres opposed the dominant bourgeois stage when they shifted from realistic to symbolic representations, dispensed with traditional staging and the mystifications of the curtain, and struggled to transcend the logocentrism of literary drama with swirling movement, acrobatics, athletics, and the sounds of modern machines and the city (Samuel 42). In Britain, Tom Thomas described the Hackney Labour Dramatic Group, which provided scripts to Communist and CCF theatre groups in Canada, as forging a "propertyless theatre for the propertyless class" (77).

This is articulated in the choral proclamations of "Theatre—Our Weapon" as it moves from political to meta-theatrical statements:

1st: Down with the theatre where the bourgeois comes to digest his
heavy meal!
2nd: Down with the theatre where the idle parasites come to amuse
themselves!
3rd: Down with the theatre where drunken debauchery dopes the
minds of the masters and their obedient slaves!
4th: Down with the theatre which lulls the indignation of the
hungry slaves of capitalism!
Chorus: DOWN WITH IT! (2)

The flag raised over the denounced and moribund body of bourgeois theatre
belongs to the workers' theatre, forged in the revolution and "tempered in
the flames of the class war" (3). But this is not just a Canadian workers'
theatre; it is, as the Chorus proclaims, "THE WORKERS' THEATRE
INTERNATIONAL!" (3). The workers' theatre performs the utterances
of revolution that, in their very performance, bind together workers from
disparate nations and define their struggle against a single-class enemy.

Mass recitations use stock characters through which workers act out
Marxist theories of political change. Players speak some lines alone and
others in unison in complex vocal arrangements that stage the political
process of bringing the working classes to consciousness. Some mass
recitations were written and performed for particular local events, such
as the RCMP murder of Montreal immigrant worker Nick Zynchuk or the
imprisonment of Young Communist League organizer Joe Derry. Dorothy
Livesay's mass recitation is one of at least three titled "Joe Derry." Hers
is unusual in that it is also a pantomime acted by and for children, who
become the chorus of the Canadian working class as they act out adult
conflicts. Prior to the first speech, a group of children enter the stage and
play with a spinning top, roller skate, cards, and other innocent pastimes.
The pantomime lasts for about a minute and then it is replaced by the
voice of a single child. In these first lines, the speaker hails an audience
of "children of the working class" to suture them into a collective revolutionary subject (107). The initial juxtaposition of mimed activity and
recitation is repeated throughout the script as groups of children silently
act out the story of Joe Derry's impoverished childhood, coming to class
consciousness, organization of the workers, and unfair arrest for protesting
bad working conditions.

Livesay's script extends beyond the purely vocal to fold in the radical performance techniques favoured by agitprop companies experimenting with mass movement and changing tempos. In the second section, the stage directions call for the children to perform a mechanistic ballet: "The children enter and form a straight line, as if at a row of machines. Their hands make a monotonous repetitive gesture in unison. Their bodies move back and forth in time to the movement of their hands. They look as if they were all of one piece. They remain on stage while the child continues talking" (108). The children act out the factory labour Joe Derry was sent to do while still a child. Their stylized mass movements are a formal innovation of the proletarian stage seeking to denaturalize capitalist production. Although it appeals directly to other children and provides them with a proletarian education, Livesay's use of children and her directions for them to depart from any realistic or individuated characterizations estranges scenarios that dominant discourse would represent as both natural and inevitable. The very process of making this theatre is a revolutionary education that achieves the transformations in its actors it also hopes to inspire in its audiences.

Mass recitations often ended with the audience joining the actors in chants demanding retribution for the dead or the imprisoned. They function to channel grief, outrage, and anger in collective performances that mourn and memorialize as much as they agitate and provoke. Consequently, they hold a key place in the production of a national working-class culture and its martyrs, as well as in the deconstruction of conventional dramaturgy. Mass recitations documented Canadian experiences, and to do so they dispensed with dramatic realism in favour of the symbolic gestures, episodic montages, and alienation effects favoured by the European socialist stages of the interwar period. Although Livesay would later describe it as "a Brechtian or 'guerrilla' theatre," this attribution is largely retrospective ("Interview" 93). At the time, Bertolt Brecht's theoretical writings had not yet been sufficiently translated and he had much less influence on the Canadian agitprop movement than his antecedents, notably the Russian constructivist Vsevolod Meyerhold and the German Communist Erwin Piscator.[7] Despite the embrace of these foreign influences, the participants felt that the workers' theatre was also a national theatre. Communist cultural and political leader Ed Cecil-Smith makes this point in a 1934 article in the *Canadian Forum*:

> Very Canadian in the problems with which it has to deal and the
> difficulties which it must overcome, this new movement does not
> cut itself off from the international scene in the way which the
> nationalistic amateur "drama leagues" must do, in order to prove its
> Canadianism. Its themes, its plots, its stage difficulties and technique,
> its authors and its players—these and many other things clearly
> stamp it as truly Canadian. (68)

Cecil-Smith hopes to find common ground between his own Communist
Party and the social-democratic readers of the *Canadian Forum* on two
issues: the plight of Canadian workers and the plight of Canadian theatre.
He is emphatic that the revolutionary working classes may transform
both.

The adaptation of European theatrical experimentation to Canadian
experience is particularly clear in the collaboratively written *Eight Men
Speak*, a 1934 play about the unjust imprisonment of eight leaders of
the Communist Party in Kingston Penitentiary and the shooting of their
leader, Tim Buck, in his jail cell by a prison guard. The play itself presents
the dialectical operations of socialist content and modernist form. Act II
uses combinations of spotlights and blackouts to mark the shifts from a
mass recitation of prisoners' demands, to dialogues between media types
concocting false stories of Communist violence, to conversations between
members of the bourgeoisie that reveal their class and ethnic prejudices.
The stage directions require a two-second blackout between each of these
short scenes. The movement between scenes is quick and the dialogue
within them would take no more than one or two minutes to deliver, so
the effect is that of a series of film shots flashed in fast tempo. The mass
recitation of prisoners' voices in Act II.i ends with a chorus demanding
state accountability for their treatment by the guards. The voices repeat
the choral cry, "Investigation!" (Ryan et al. 42). The prisoners want to use
the state apparatus to protect their interests, whereas characters representing the Canadian bourgeoisie want to eject the Communists from the
country altogether in order to have the state protect their own interests.
This montage of scenes shines the light on typical scenarios of bourgeois
fears of socialism in particularly Canadian settings. Ideological complicity
between the oppressive anti-Communism of the state and a public fearful

of anything it deems foreign is achieved through the content of the lines but also through the structure of Act II. Form and content operate dialectically to expose and transform the contradictions of bourgeois culture and monopoly capitalism.

In order to expose the decadence and degeneracy of the bourgeoisie, *Eight Men Speak* draws on gender stereotypes circulating in popular culture and makes only a limited effort to estrange them from their normal usage. The play opens with a satire of bourgeois domestic life to expose middle-class hypocrisies by using the familiar sexual stereotypes of popular culture harnessed to the leftist trope of a feminized and degenerate bourgeoisie. Three different kinds of female stock characters (femme fatale, feisty adventuress, and jealous wife) triangulate around three male characters similar in their susceptibility to female desire. In Act I, the prison warden and his privileged coterie are debased by their sexual urges, while in Act III the Workers' Court is rendered on a higher moral plane by its relative absence of individual sexual desire and female threats to masculine self-possession. It is notable that, in the trial scene, the prosecutor of capitalism is the CLDL (Canadian Labour Defense League) Organizer. In the original production, this character was played by female actor Toby Gordon Ryan. Doyle interprets this as a sign "of the feminist influences in the Communist literary community that made this milieu so congenial to writers like Dorothy Livesay and *New Frontiers* editor Margaret Gould" (131). However, as historian Joan Sangster has shown, women who took on the real roles represented by Gordon Ryan in this play, especially campaigning and fundraising work for party leaders and the CLDL, entered a tributary of Communist labour that rarely flowed into positions of political leadership (Sangster 58). Revolutionary socialism worked to draw women into the struggle against capitalism in ways that often depended on an iconography of the bourgeoisie as feminine and the working classes as masculine. As a result, women's participation in socialist culture is not necessarily a sign that the culture itself promoted a feminist consciousness. This play thus needs to be situated as a document of a particular political event achieved through modernist techniques, and as a document of how Third Period revolutionary culture performed class and ethnic struggles on a stage made comprehensible by its reliance on popular culture's gender codes.

IV. THE POLITICS OF POPULARITY

The workers' theatre movement and its principle form of agitprop were relatively short-lived. In some ways, 1934 was both the international height of the movement and the year it began to decline (Friedman 116). Many of the participants in Britain, the United States, and Canada cite similar artistic reasons for the general turn away from agitprop: its limited theatrical possibilities, its inability to engage an audience growing tired of repetitive performances, and the players' desires to work on full-length scripts and to establish stationary and semi-professional stages. But this theatrical shift took place in the context of a major political shift from the anti-capitalism of the Third Period to the anti-fascism of the Popular Front. The triumph of fascism in Europe, particularly in Germany in 1933, demanded urgent changes to Communist organizing. The movement towards uniting all parties and forces that could fight fascism has its analogue in the workers' theatre's attempts to seek alliances with social-democratic and liberal theatre professionals (Friedman 117). This also led to a return to more conventional staging and the search for naturalistic plays that would appeal to a broader audience. However, I want to conclude by showing how the Popular Front stage, in spite of the emergence of a new theory and praxis of theatre that disavowed its recent militant heritage, nevertheless retained residues of the symbolic economies of agitprop.

The popular aspect of the Popular Front amplified what was already a vexed issue for leftists across the arts. In agitprop, the players relied on stock figures from popular culture, including the older forms of vaudeville, melodrama, pantomime, the musical review, and morality play, as well as newer idioms derived from radio, cabaret, and film (Hyman 209). In this sense, agitprop was a hybrid form, drawing bits and pieces from popular culture only to estrange them, but presenting them as part of what Sergei Eisenstein termed in film a "montage of attractions" (230–33). Anxieties about the ideological freight carried by these popular forms would grow throughout the decade. Popular culture was considered to be both an obstacle and a resource, not only a bourgeois narcotic to pacify the people but also a recognizable framework in which to insert radical content. A problem with socialist appropriations of popular forms, evident in the clichéd female roles in Act I of *Eight Men Speak*, is that revisions of popular class and ethnic images often uphold traditional gender stereotypes. Socialist culture in 1930s Canada, although frequently spearheaded by women, tends to gender the class struggle in images of the virile masculine proletariat and the parasitic feminine bourgeoise. This leftist iconography co-operates with dominant gender discourses to contain feminist opposition in plays from across the left. On the non-Communist labour and CCF front, Vancouver's Harold Griffen, Calgary's William Irvine, and Sarnia's Eric Harris all wrote plays in which female dependence is draining, while female independence is seductive but ultimately threatening to public men as well as political progress.[8] So, although the Canadian leftist stage was often supported and administered by both Communist and social-democrat women, feminist oppositional politics were subordinated time and again in productions that mobilized gendered stereotypes to highlight class and ethnic inequities. Indeed, that so many women assumed prominence in socialist cultural circles while relatively few rose to the political leadership may itself signal a gendered division of labour between political work addressed to power versus cultural work addressed to the dispossessed and therefore designated as educative and caring.

This gendered division of labour is a structuring principle of the field of leftist theatrical production throughout the 1930s. The United States Federal Theatre Project, one mid-decade initiative of Roosevelt's New Deal, had no small impact on the Canadian stage. By 1935, the PACs rearranged themselves under new banners: the Theatres of Action in Toronto and Vancouver, and the New Theatres of Montreal and Winnipeg. Following this rebranding into Popular Front companies, and the recruitment of liberals as well as socialists, the most popular full-length productions were American Federal Theatre plays. The best-known of these is the Vancouver Progressive Arts' Players version of Clifford Odets's *Waiting for Lefty*, which won the 1936 prize at the Dominion Drama Festival in Ottawa. There were many other productions of *Waiting for Lefty* across the country, and often Odets's setting of a New York taxi drivers' strike was localized to regional labour struggles.[9] There are two other Federal Theatre plays that circulated in interesting ways on the Canadian Popular Front stage. One is Irwin Shaw's *Bury the Dead*, an anti-war play that draws on the surrealist uncanny. It begins with a group of dead soldiers who refuse to be buried because they were too young to be sacrificed for a general's war of profit. When their generals eventually order them to be shot again, the living soldiers assert solidarity with the dead men and collectively they rise up in resistance. Unlike the more naturalistic social dramas of this period, *Bury the*

Dead shares elements with militant agitprop. It includes an extended mass recitation that mourns and memorializes at the same time that it demands retribution for wrongful deaths at the hands of a corrupt military–industrial class. When he represents the ghostly figures of dead soldiers haunting the present, Shaw also folds in an allusion to the famous preamble to *The Communist Manifesto*, that "[a] spectre is haunting Europe—the spectre of Communism" (Marx and Engels 218). Its combined realism and surrealism, humanism and socialism, were popular with audiences who may not have subscribed to a cosmopolitan modernism but who were anxious about the prospect of another disastrous world war.

The national differences between the United States and Canada are glossed over in *Bury the Dead*, but in other plays they are at the forefront. The Toronto Theatre of Action's production of Sinclair Lewis's *It Can't Happen Here*, which Lewis himself travelled to see in rehearsal, was based on a script of the American author's 1935 speculative novel of the same title about the rise of a fascist government in the United States. This play was also produced by the Montreal New Theatre Group, which proclaimed Lewis's script as nearly universal in its "deep note of sympathy for simple, trusting folk facing an insidious and sinister force and their inability to think their way through the confusion" (*It Can't Happen Here*). Lewis's message about the need for international anti-fascist struggle is particular to Popular Front culture, but his satire depends on stock characters and oppositions inherited from Third Period agitprop.[10] Towards the end of the play, the protagonist, Doremus Jessup, wakes up from his liberal belief in individual freedom to recognize the need for an organized armed movement. He flees with his comrade-wife to Canada to establish a resistance movement from across the border.

Although the play represents the possibility of a fascist American regime, its incorporation of Canada as a setting of refuge invites a range of responses from Canadian audiences, from recognition to rejection. Liberal audiences may have agreed with the play's projection of their nation as a democratic asylum, while those further left would have resisted this idealization and received it as a cautionary tale about all forms of corrupt government, regardless of nationality. In either case, to perform *It Can't Happen Here* in Canada, in a decade that had witnessed the severe state repression of many forms of dissent, is to call in the particularities of national difference through the seeming universality of an American cultural product. This is evident in a local mutation of Lewis's text into a song with the same title written for the much bawdier venue of the Winnipeg New Theatre's "Beer and Skits" cabaret nights. The lyrics to this catchy polka tune, possibly written by Joe Zuken, suggest how relevant Lewis's vision was to Canadian circumstances:

> It can't happen here
> It can't happen here
> It can happen over there
> But it can't happen here
> Oompah, Oompah, etc.
>
> Down on the Ford Assembly plant
> A certain guy named Jones
> Went on the picket line
> And six policemen broke his bones. (qtd. in Ryan, *Stage Left* 227)[11]

The Federal Theatre's prominence on the Canadian Popular Front stage has invited some critics to lament it as another instance of American cultural imperialism. Yet, the particular plays selected by Canadian groups, their resonance with an earlier phase of radical theatre, and their active rather than passive consumption suggest that working through American leftist culture was one way that the Canadian leftist stage could work against American imperialism.[12]

While 1930s leftist theatre was part of a wider culture of socialist performativity, it is also important to note that some plays, including Livesay's "Joe Derry," seem to have had few if any stage performances. Without diminishing the importance of performativity to leftist culture, it is nevertheless crucial to recognize that many plays circulated in publications working to build class consciousness through textual study and literary discussion. Reading plays as well as going to them is an activity promoted in 1930s leftist periodicals as part of modern Marxist culture. When interested readers outside of large cities did have a chance to see a live performance, it was sometimes the first theatre production of any kind—professional or amateur, bourgeois or socialist—that they had ever seen (Cecil-Smith 69). The circulation of plays in print thus combines with their performance histories to suggest that the leftist theatre of the 1930s is distinctive in the decade's cultural production because it constructs both a discursive community bound together by written textual circulation, and a public speech community bound together by an immediate performative event. The seeds of political sociability and modernist aesthetics planted in each of these differently constituted but overlapping publics are nourished by plays experimenting in different ways throughout the decade to document and transform lived experience.

As much as there is a split in the socialist stages of modern Canada, there are also thematic and formal continuities. The Popular Front period seems to repeat an earlier moment during the Third Period when artists looked outside the country for a radical modernist dramaturgy, but these foreign models did not remain the same once they travelled across and within the national borders. A field of Canadian leftist theatre existed in the 1930s and, despite its internal competitions and struggles, it invites a reconsideration of how the borders have hitherto been drawn around the field of Canadian literary modernism. In one sense, the red stage of modernism may be understood as a theatre of formal innovation and socialist message. In another sense, it is also a stage of red modernism in which the spirit of international solidarity was not necessarily the mark of colonial mimicry. In each sense, the English-Canadian socialist stage of the 1930s forged a space at once historical, social, and artistic in which experiences of the nation were re-imagined at the nexus of modernist experiment and Marxist hope.

NOTES

[1] This is not to deny the prior existence of working-class and socialist theatres and performances, such as the dramatics club the Toronto Young Socialists formed earlier in the century, or the International Workers of the World (iww) skits performed for strikes and in pageants commemorating labour's past (Scott 58). One forerunner of 1930s leftist theatre in Canada is J.S. Woodsworth's offshoot of his Winnipeg All People's Mission, "The People's Forum." Operating out of that city's Grand Theatre in the 1920s, "The People's Forum" included lectures on social issues as well as evening performances by various ethnic and immigrant arts groups (Longfield 79). Another precedent for the workers' theatre movement in English Canada is the suffragist mock parliaments staged in Manitoba, Ontario, and British Columbia between the 1870s and 1920s. In these sell-out perfor-

mances, some written by Nellie McClung and Lillian Thomas, female suffragists parodied the political discourse of public men intent on denying women the vote. The mock parliaments formed a loose network of political performances in several provinces. They transformed material from daily life into plays aiming to change women's experiences of citizenship (Longfield 92). Like the satires of the socialist stage, these mock parliaments used role reversal to denaturalize and deflate official performances in the nation's legislative halls.

[2] During the Third Period at the beginning of the decade, many Canadian Communist artists and organizers denounced social democrats and other non-Communist leftists as anti-revolutionary. Third Period sectarianism was officially left behind by the Popular Front in 1935 when the Comintern encouraged Communists everywhere to seek alliances with the non-Communist working and middle classes and form a united front against fascism. Although a socialist international remained the ultimate goal, CPC leaders asked their members to recognize that at least the bourgeois democratic traditions of the Canadian state granted the freedoms of expression and association denied by fascist governments in Europe (Manley 61). Despite these public utterances of solidarity, however, sectarianism continued to simmer on the left and any provisional alliances among the CCF and the CPC on either political or artistic fronts remained fragile.

[3] Gordon Ryan hints at her group's knowledge and appreciation of immigrant leftist stages when she admits to an interviewer how difficult it was to gather material for her memoir that would speak to the diversity of 1930s leftist theatre. She echoes Livesay when she admits how difficult it is to account for the number of Ukrainian and Finnish organizations producing leftist scripts ("Interview" 27). Filewod also highlights the ethnic language theatres as a center of activity that went largely unrecorded. He argues that the most active groups claimed as part of the Third Period Workers' Theatre were part of the CPC's ethnic organizations, but their diverse cultural and theatrical practices were often received as non-normative by the party's anglophone leadership ("Performance" 67–68).

[4] See the volumes of RCMP Security Bulletins edited by Kealey and Whitaker.

[5] By the time "Theatre—Our Weapon" appeared in the December 1932 issue of *Masses* it had already received at least one performance at a PAC social. Notices of its reprise appear throughout *Masses* and it remains a popular mass recitation for the run of the magazine.

[6] The British WTM moved away from older notions that the working classes should be exposed to Shakespeare, dramatizations of Dickens, and other English classics. Instead, they offered to Canadian artists a celebration of working-class culture in zesty and parodic plays about syndicalism and class struggle inherited from the IWW. Arthur Turner describes adapting their version of *The Ragged Trousered Philanthropists* (a play based on Robert Tressell's 1914 socialist novel of the same name) for British Columbia audiences.

[7] Robertson confirms that this was the case in his footnote that Piscator had an immediate effect on North American workers' theatre but Brecht did not (25). Meyerhold influenced Brecht with the idea that social attitudes are "quotable through the stylization of the gesture or vocal expression" (Stourac and McCreery 9). This gestic approach is fundamental to the agitprop theory that the stage quotes rather than represents reality. Also of influence was Piscator's Weimar Republic Proletarian Theatre, which sent over 200 agitprop troupes across Germany in the late 1920s, under the sponsorship of the German Communist Party (KPD) (Robertson 25). Piscator innovated a socialist–modernist stage of revolutionary content enacted in the formal experiments of episodic montage, speech choruses, symbolic gestures, alienation effects, mechanical sets, and cinematic projections (Stourac and McCreery 91–101).

[8] The educational mandate of the CCF clubs also meant that they became a site of political and cultural activism for women, since the party ideology tended to view them as more suited to behind-the-scenes political and educational work than public leadership (Sangster 101).

[9] For more on *Waiting for Lefty* see Bray and Filewod.

[10] *It Can't Happen Here* was the flagship of the newly created Federal Theatre Program, which organized twenty-one simultaneous openings of the play across the United States in October of 1936, leading over 20,000 people to see what MGM studios considered too militant a script for film production (Melosh 15).

[11] Gordon Ryan reprints an excerpt from this song but its full and much longer version is located in the Toby Gordon Ryan Collection ("It Can't Happen Here").

[12] Doyle describes the decline of Third Period agitprop as the result of Communist "compromises with socialists, liberals, and other movements that preferred more moderate and subtle forms of socially critical art" (131). Filewod's analysis of the Canadian Popular Front theatre cites performances of Clifford Odets's *Waiting for Lefty* as a site of struggle between oppositional practices that has been subject to revisionism within cultural history by a normalizing imperial discourse. For him, this play is an exemplary moment of American neo-colonialism:

> Less than 12 hours by train from New York, Toronto was the cultural centre of the closest satellite in the emerging American imperial sphere, and the demographic, social, and linguistic affinities between anglophone Canada and the United States made cultural exchange sufficiently easy that the border seemed to disappear in the popular imaginary. ("Qualified" 124)

While I agree that the Theatres of Action, and the Popular Front stage more generally, worked to distance themselves from the revolutionary politics and practices of the Third Period, many of the Federal Theatre plays performed in Canada deserve fuller study for the complex ways in which the border between Canada and the United States contracted and expanded around national and international leftist imaginaries.

WORKS CITED

Anderson, Perry. *A Zone of Engagement*. London: Verso, 1992.

Bourdieu, Pierre. *The Field of Cultural Production*. Ed. Randal Johnson. New York: Columbia UP, 1993.

Bray, Bonita. "Against All Odds: The Progressive Arts Club's Production of *Waiting for Lefty*." *Canadian Working Class History*. 2nd ed. Ed. Laurel Sefton MacDowell and Ian Radforth. Toronto: Canadian Scholars' P, 2000. 489–504.

Cecil-Smith, E. "The Workers' Theatre in Canada." *Canadian Forum* Nov. 1933: 68–70.

Davies, Ioan. "Theory and Creativity in English Canadian Magazines of the State and Cultural Movement." *Journal of Canadian Studies* 30.1 (1995): 5–19.

Eisenstein, Sergei. *The Film Sense*. Trans. Jay Leyda. New York: Harcourt Brace, 1947.

Filewod, Alan. "National Theatre / National Obsession." *New Contexts of Canadian Criticism*. Ed. Ajay Heble, Donna Palmateer Penee, and J.R. Struthers. Toronto: Broadview, 1997. 15–23.

———. "Performance and Memory in the Party: Dismembering the Workers' Theatre Movement." *Essays on Canadian Writing* 80 (fall 2003): 59–81.

———. "'A Qualified Workers Theatre Art': *Waiting for Lefty* and the (Re)Formation of Popular Front Theatres." *Essays in Theatre / Études théâtrales* 17.2 (1999): 111–28.

Friedman, Daniel. "A Brief Description of the Workers' Theatre Movement of the Thirties." *Theatre for Working-Class Audiences in the United States, 1830–1980*. Ed. Bruce A. McConachie and Daniel Friedman. London: Greenwood, 1985. 111–20.

Griffen, Harold. *Embargo: A Play in One* Act. Ms. Play File. Harold Griffen Archives.

———. *Hostage: A One Act Play in One Scene*. Ms. Play File. Harold Griffen Archives.

Harold Griffen Archives. Special Collections, Simon Fraser University.

Harris, Eric W. *Such Harmony*. Canadian Playwright Series. Toronto: Samuel French, 1936.

———. *Twenty-Five Cents*. Canadian Playwright Series. Toronto: Samuel French, 1936.

Hyman, Colette A. "Politics Meet Popular Entertainment in the Workers' Theater of the 1930s." *Radical Revisions: Rereading 1930s Culture.* Ed. Bill Mullen and Sherry Linkon. Chicago: U of Illinois P, 1996. 208–24.

Irvine, William. *The Brains We Trust.* Toronto: Thomas Nelson, 1935.

Irvine, William, and Elsie Park Gowan. *You Can't Do That.* Toronto: Thomas Nelson, 1936.

"It Can't Happen Here." Ts. Winnipeg New Theatre File. Toby Gordon Ryan Collection.

It Can't Happen Here. Program. Montreal New Theatre Group. Stage Left File. Toby Gordon Ryan Collection.

Kealey, Gregory S., and Reg Whitaker. *R.C.M.P. Security Bulletins: The Depression Years, Part I, 1933–1934.* St. John's, NL: Canadian Committee on Labour History, 1993.

Lewis, Sinclair, and John Moffitt. *It Can't Happen Here.* New York: Dramatists Play Service, 1938.

Livesay, Dorothy. "An Interview with Dorothy Livesay." By Doug Beardsley and Rosemary Sullivan. *Canadian Poetry* 3 (1978): 87–91.

———. "Joe Derry." *Masses* 2.10 (Sept. 1933): 14–15. Rpt. in Wright and Endres, eds. 107–12.

———. *Right Hand Left Hand: A True Life of the Thirties: Paris, Toronto, Montreal, the West and Vancouver. Love, Politics, the Depression and Feminism.* Erin, ON: Porcépic, 1977.

Longfield, Kevin. *From Fire to Flood: A History of Theatre in Manitoba.* Winnipeg: Signature, 2001.

Manley, John. "'Communists Love Canada!': The Communist Party of Canada, the 'People' and the Popular Front, 1933–1939." *Journal of Canadian Studies / Revue d'études canadiennes* 36.4 (2002): 59–84.

Marx, Karl, and Friedrich Engels. *The Communist Manifesto.* 1888. Ed. Gareth Stedman Jones. London: Penguin, 2002.

Melosh, Barbara. *Engendering Culture: Manhood and Womanhood in New Deal Public Art and Theatre.* Washington: Smithsonian, 1991.

Nelson, Cary. *Repression and Recovery: Modern American Poetry and the Politics of Cultural Memory 1910–1945.* Madison: U of Wisconsin P, 1989.

Odets, Clifford. "Waiting for Lefty." *Proletarian Literature in the United States.* Ed. Granville Hicks et al. New York: International, 1935. 276–97.

Reiter, Ester. "Secular Yiddishkait: Left Politics, *Culturem* and Community." *Labour/Le Travail* 49 (2002): 121–46.

Robertson, Clive. "Canadian Agit-Prop and Workers' Theatre in the 30's." *Fuse* May/June 1982: 25–34.

Roslin, Charles. "Canada's Bolshevist Drama." *Saturday Night* 9 Feb. 1929: 2, 5. Rpt.

in *Prophets and Proletarians: Documents on the History of the Rise and Decline of Ukrainian Communism in Canada*. Ed. John Kolasky. Edmonton: Canadian Institute of Ukrainian Studies P, U of Alberta, 1990. 72–77.

Ryan, Oscar et al. *Eight Men Speak: A Political Play in Six Acts*. Toronto: Progressive Arts' Club, [1934]. Rpt. in Wright and Endres, eds. 21–89.

Ryan, Toby Gordon. Interview with Clive Robertson. "Canadian Agit-Prop and Workers' Theatre in the 30's." *Fuse* May/June 1982: 27–32.

———. *Stage Left: Canadian Theatre in the Thirties: A Memoir*. Toronto: CTR, 1981.

Salter, Denis. "The Idea of a National Theatre." *Canadian Canons: Essays in Literary Value*. Ed. Robert Lecker. Toronto: UTP, 1991. 70–90.

Samuel, Raphael. "Theatre and Socialism in Britain (1880–1935)." *Theatres of the Left 1880–1935: Workers' Theatre Movements in Britain and America*. Ed. Raphael Samuel, Ewan MacColl, and Stuart Cosgrove. London: Routledge, 1985. 3–76.

Sangster, Joan. *Dreams of Equality: Women on the Canadian Left, 1920–1950*. Canadian Social History Series. Toronto: McClelland and Stewart, 1989.

Scott, Robert B. "Professional Performers and Companies." *Later Stages: Essays in Ontario Theatre from the First World War to the 1970s*. Ed. Ann Saddlemyer and Richard Plant. Toronto: UTP, 1997. 13–120.

Shaw, Irwin. "Bury the Dead." *New Theatre and Film 1934 to 1937*. Ed. Herbert Kline. New York: Harcourt Brace, 1985. 130–64.

Souchotte, Sandra. "Workers' Theatre in the Thirties Part I." *This Magazine* 9.2 (May–June 1975): 3–5.

———. "Workers' Theatre in the Thirties Part II." *This Magazine* 9.3 (July–Aug. 1975): 3–6.

Stourac, Richard, and Kathleen McCreery. *Theatre as a Weapon: Workers' Theatre in the Soviet Union, Germany and Britain, 1917–1934*. London: Routledge, 1986.

Talbot, Emile. "Literature and Ideology in the Thirties: Fictional Representations of Communism in Québec." *International Journal of Canadian Studies* 20 (1999): 53–66.

"Theatre—Our Weapon." *Masses* 1.7 (Dec. 1932): n. pag. Rpt. in Wright and Endres, eds. 1–4.

Thomas, Tom. "A Propertyless Theatre for the Propertyless Class." *Theatres of the Left 1880–1935: Workers' Theatre Movements in Britain and America*. Ed. Raphael Samuel, Ewan MacColl, and Stuart Cosgrove. London: Routledge, 1985. 77–98.

Toby Gordon Ryan Collection. Archival and Special Collections, McLaughlin Library, University of Guelph.

Turner, Arthur. *Trade Unionism and Social Democracy*. Interview with Marlene

Karnouk. 10 Dec. 1973. Ts. of tape 251. Rare Books and Special Collections, University of British Columbia.

Waddington, Miriam. "The Cloudless Day: Klein's Radical Poems." *Apartment Seven: Essays Selected and New.* Toronto: Oxford UP, 1989. 120–38.

Williams, Raymond. *The Politics of Modernism: Against the New Conformists.* Ed. Tony Pinkney. New York: Verso, 1989.

"Workers' Theatre." *Masses* 2.11 (Jan. 1934): 13.

"Workers' Theatre in Action." *Masses* 2.9 (May–June 1933): 13.

Wright, Richard, and Robin Endres, eds. *Eight Men Speak and Other Plays from the Canadian Workers' Theatre.* Toronto: New Hogtown, 1976.

Dorothy Livesay, the "Housewife," and the Radio in 1951: Modernist Embodiments of Audience

PAUL TIESSEN

... is there enough program planning in the daily housewife's portion
of listening; are people listening?
—Livesay, *Dorothy Livesay and the* CBC (1)

Shake off, shake off your radio-trained ears.
—Livesay, "Invitation to Silence" (*Archive* 48)

I

WHEN RADIO PROGRAMMING began in the early 1920s, radio's disembodied
voice suggested to the public a live announcer's or entertainer's spatial
proximity yet simultaneously drew attention to that person's corporeal
absence. Radio's foregrounding of the voice at the expense of the body also
produced the listener's sense of disembodiment. As late as 1939, modernist
writer Malcolm Lowry spoke of a radio listener's experience as though it
mapped an "ultimate Unreality." In an essay for the Vancouver *Province*,[1]
Lowry emphasized what John Durham Peters calls radio's "uncanniness
quotient" (211), the material insubstantiality of bodies loosed from space
and place. Lowry, who had just visited Hollywood, drew on news reports
of the early days of World War II to describe a surrealism that inevitably
affected radio's audience, linking it simultaneously to the workings of
cinema on its audience. "Somewhere in Hollywood a soldier leaned against
a radio. Round his head was a bloodstained bandage. In his muddy uniform
he seemed rigid with listening," Lowry began; "[t]his man, an extra, despite
his unlikelihood, was real. So was what he heard from Warsaw. His look,
as of one who sees into hell but doesn't believe it, was real too." But in a
town where "unreal" fragments of history were in fact the norm, and where
NBC and CBS loudspeakers in 1939 caused more than the usual pandemo-

nium, an observer now "was forced to wonder whether or not our extra, or anyone else in Hollywood listening to the radio, was convinced that the war was real at all. Did it not seem, perhaps, on the contrary, an ultimate Unreality?" (Lowry, "Hollywood" 4–5).

In his "history of the idea of communication" *Speaking into the Air,* Peters reminds us of the anxiety about radio's socio-political effects during the politically-charged interwar years. He recalls that "[r]adio carried what Rudolf Arnheim in 1936 called 'voices without bodies' and breached limits of space, time, and audibility that had once seemed natural" (211). Radio's acoustical space seemed unnatural. Throughout the 1920s and 1930s, the social disorientation that accompanied the loss of the body was strong enough that deliberate measures were taken—through programming, genre creation, and other institutional forms—to develop a new sense of the normal within society where radio had intruded. Political and commercial interests sought to re-embody the radio listener: "Organizing radio's connection to the bodies of the communicants was a chief prerequisite of its naturalization into daily life" (Peters 211). Program directors created stylistic gestures to overcome the underlying difficulty caused by the apparent immateriality of even the most realistic appeals. Of course, just a year before Lowry's comments, Orson Welles with his *War of the Worlds* broadcast pushed to the extreme the very conventions that had been established—including what Paul Heyer calls *radio vérité*—and played havoc with audiences' responses (154). Welles's approach recalls Leni Riefenstahl's approximations of *cinéma vérité* in her exploitation of the documentary film genre only three years before, in *Triumph of the Will* (1935). Both Welles and Riefenstahl used the documentary's apparent authority of seeming to embody the image/voice that it represented.

Throughout the 1930s and 1940s both radio and film surged to the fore of critical consciousness because national and international propagandists on all sides were using these media to further political interests, and were doing so with seemingly enormous success amongst the "mass audience," those classes among whom modernists did not imagine finding their readership, nor people with whom they might like to stand in line at a movie theatre. But it was especially during the period after World War II that intellectuals, in Canada as elsewhere, revealed the extent to which they had inherited a complex suspicion of both film and radio, and of their audiences—a wariness about the ease with which populations might be rendered "passive" and readily manipulated. Postwar consumerism, the Cold War, and the bomb only intensified cultural elites' fears of the manipulation of stultified "masses" (Litt 95).

For followers of literary modernism, an anxiety about new media such as film and radio had begun in the early 1920s. Above all, in those days, it was cinema—with its "mass audiences"—that was gaining the cultural attention that it was to receive for decades. For example, book reviewers turned to film when they sought metaphors for the new literary forms that were making a strong appearance, especially in the form of the stream-of-consciousness novel. What reviewers and others said about film (particularly, here, the commercial rather than the art cinema) is in some measure instructive—once we make a series of historical and other adjustments—for our understanding of aspects of modernists' reception of radio (notably, here, Dorothy Livesay's response to national public radio in Canada).[2] Film, like the radio that Lowry noted in his 1939 piece, was obviously unnatural or unreal yet largely based its methods and appeal on audiences' expectations about the behaviour of "reality." W.L. George in 1920, for example, claimed that writers such as James Joyce, Wyndham Lewis, Dorothy Richardson, and Virginia Woolf were producing visual impressions that would "compare ill with the product of a cinema camera man" (234). In 1922 John Middleton Murry dismissively observed of a new volume of Dorothy Richardson's *Pilgrimage* that it was as "tiring as a twenty-four-hour cinematograph without interval or plot" (298).[3]

When radio programming began to develop, Dorothy Livesay (1909–96) was already entering her teen years. She turned toward radio-based activities fairly early in her career as a poet. Already, in the 1930s, she was organizing poetry readings on radio and writing poetic drama. During the 1940s and 1950s, carrying on as a contributor, she also was (as she put it in 1951) a housewife active as a radio listener. And "[l]ike most housewives," she pointed out, reflecting the specifics of her place in a family with one husband and two children, she was "more frequently a daytime than an evening listener" (*Dorothy Livesay* 10).

Livesay's housewife, a citizen passionate about a Canadian cultural agenda, was also a radio listener who asserted the primacy of the self, of the sensate listener in real space. At the same time, her housewife is given to "the business of listening" (*Dorothy Livesay* 15) and, thus, has some roots among those high modernists who in their roles as members of the film audience in the 1920s and early 1930s registered an awareness of their own place within "the mass." Among those, certain modernists took decidedly subversive approaches to the fashionable view among the cultural elite who identified new media as mechanized products of a late industrial modernity characterized by values contrary to high modernism and by stupendous success in getting "inside the collective public mind" and paralyzing it (McLuhan, *The Mechanical Bride* v). As I shall suggest, writers such as these offered "themselves" as challenges to the belief that new media brought about not only a dematerializing of the body but also, through the dissolving of the body and the unity of its sensorium, a disintegration of tradition and meaning. These modernists—particularly women writers such as Dorothy Richardson, Virginia Woolf, and H.D. (Hilda Doolittle)—argued against technological absolutes and suggested that the body could thrive as an undiminished whole even when faced with mechanized institutions and forms. To dramatize their point, they inserted themselves physically and socially among the feared and presumably disembodied "masses" of the day, about whom there was general anxiety and even feelings of revulsion among intellectuals.

Livesay's critical interest in media also overlaps with those of literary modernists—Wyndham Lewis, Malcolm Lowry—whose impact was experienced more directly by writers in Canada. As I shall point out, both Lewis and Lowry brought to Canada from Europe some of the presuppositions that lay behind modernists' debates in the 1920s and 1930s about new-media audiences. Livesay's links with Lewis and Lowry remind us not only that Canada's was an international modernism but also that it included visiting players. I shall note, too, that from Livesay's generation—not only Marshall McLuhan (whom, if our terminology is elastic enough, we can readily regard as a literary modernist) but also, in particular, the virtually unknown writer Vernon van Sickle, as well as Earle Birney, Wilfred Watson, and Gerald Noxon, all of whom in varying ways had connections with each other through Vancouver-based communities, or, in McLuhan's case, came from western Canada—paid attention to the social effects of new media, and helped to expand our understanding of one of Canadian modernism's priorities, notably its commitment to responding critically and creatively to new media.

Modernism in Canada registered and absorbed a deep uneasiness about the effects on the body—including the body politic—of media such as radio and film. In *McLuhan Studies*, looking at modernism in general, Joe Galbo points out that "[w]ithin this new discourse, the body becomes the arena in which society's anxieties about fakery, decay, corruption, the blunting of sensibility, and most important, about the nature of consciousness itself, came to be expressed" (104). New media bring to the fore new forms of "discarnate existence," a threat of "phantom bod[ies]" that parallel and parody "the real body" (Galbo 104). Joe G. Keogh observes in the same journal issue that electric technology, for which the creation of "mass man" is ever imminent, has the power "to strip men and women of their bodies and even their identities" (184 n2) and threatens to bring about their dematerialization, their complete disembodiment. Mass man, writes Keogh, "was first noticed as a phenomenon in the age of radio" (184).

Livesay's housewife challenges the McLuhanesque convention described by Keogh: "[w]hen man is … 'on the air,' moving electrically at the speed of light, he has no physical body" (184). Her housewife is an embodiment, an actual member, of the radio audience. To some extent she is a materialization of the phantom Other that through the dominant discourse of the day many modernists such as Lewis—from the 1920s on—tended to disown. More generally, Livesay's housewife reminds us that Livesay is one of those literary practitioners who, independent of McLuhan's influence, began to define non-literary media as part of the Canadian modernist project.

II

Within British and English-Canadian literary modernism there were numerous ongoing if scattered efforts to define itself in relation to those media—first, film, then to a lesser extent, radio—that came into prominence in the first half of the twentieth century. First in England and subsequently in Canada (and often as a direct consequence of developments in England) literary modernists became preoccupied with assessing media effects. They pursued their concern from myriad positions, spurred sometimes by hostile anxiety, sometimes by hopeful anticipation. It is inevitable that their reactions to new media, because they have been persistent and distinctive, should determine our multiple definitions of modernism itself.[4]

In the late 1920s, in their critique of film as art and as medium for a mass audience (with the attendant questions of that audience's gender, class, and race), a significant concentration of British modernists produced, however unsystematically, a body of work that in scope and significance rivals that of the Frankfurt School. Further—especially through Wyndham Lewis, who was an opponent of popular film partly because of what he saw as its disincarnational effects, of what he felt was its disorienting and debilitating impact on the individual intellect and on the mass—they created categories of assessment and analysis that directly anticipated McLuhan's approaches to the effects of media on the individual and social body. Indeed, much British modernist analysis from 1925 to 1933 looks forward to work in Canada from the 1930s to the 1960s, most notably to McLuhan's work of the 1950s and 1960s.[5]

During the modernists' stormy debates about film in the late 1920s, positions such as Lewis's were understood as dominant among intellectuals. For Lewis, the primary film audience was a mass audience, modernism's anaesthetized and feminized Other—a "gum-chewing World-pit," a "robot-rabble," "box-office gulls" (Lewis, *Filibusters* 100, 101, 104)—at which he looked askance and only from a distance.[6] However, among modernists, the other side began to show itself by the late 1920s. Often it was women modernists who sought for oppositional ways to alleviate the hostility, to undo the distance and disdain of a Lewis; they showed that they were prepared to act in good faith with the mass audience, even identifying with it, enwrapping themselves in the very world that Lewis denounced. Performing audience roles that included not only intelligent analysis but also their appearance at the box office with the robot-rabble, they began to liberate the film audience from the constraints imposed by intellectual orthodoxy and dogma. Attending the movies themselves, they showed that they could survive quite nicely with their transgressive flouting of social borders. For example, Dorothy Richardson inserted herself right into the audience, describing her experience in her film essays from 1927 to 1933, in effect countering Lewis. "The cinema … is now a part of our lives," she proclaimed in 1927. "We go. No longer in secret and in taxis and alone, but openly in parties in the car" ("Increasing Congregation" 61–62).[7]

In a 1927 letter to Bryher (Winifred Ellerman) about what she elsewhere labelled the "Big Bugs" (*Letters* 139), Richardson suggested drolly that Bryher might get a "big bug" like D.H. Lawrence to write something for her film journal, *Close Up*: "You know Lawrence *loathes* films? *Foams* about them. I'm sure he'd foam for you" (*Letters* 135). Like Richardson, Woolf, in an essay prominently published, without blushing presented herself (in

1926) as having been in attendance at the movies "the other day," where she was stimulated into anticipating for the cinema an exciting future (350). For her part, H.D. dismissed the threat of bodily death by technological tyranny that writers such as Lewis claimed was affecting the sensorium by scoffing at "high-brow" arguments that cinema was "a Juggernaught [*sic*] crushing out mind and perception in one vast orgy of the senses" (23). She, too, was determined to install the human at the cinema where for Lewis only phantoms ran amok.

Lewis, of course, brought his Orwellian side of the modernist debate directly to Canada when he arrived in Toronto in September 1939. And if there was a modernist who brought to Canada something of the women novelists' interventionist spirit, it was Malcolm Lowry, arriving only a month or two ahead of Lewis and settling first in Vancouver, where Livesay had moved in 1936. Had Livesay been watching the Vancouver *Province* in December 1939, she might have noticed Lowry's gentle and sympathetic attention to the effects of radio's and cinema's adjustment of various people's places within the accustomed axes of time and space (from which I briefly quote, above).

As I have noted, in Lowry's brief article about radio and film, his interest (like Lewis's) included the audience; unlike Lewis, Lowry did not treat the audience with derision or disrespect. Thus, in a 1949 film script (really a metascript about film and related media, written in an attempt to revive Hollywood fare) that he wrote for Hollywood while he was living in Vancouver, we find Lowry deliberately and sympathetically drawing on the common man and woman, members of the very audience that Hollywood had created, as strategies that guided him while he created his *tour de force*.[8] Indeed, in his novels from the early 1930s to the 1950s, where to be sure we sometimes do find a film-going "rabble" of rather indeterminate origin, Lowry tended to treat his characters who went to the movies with considerable tenderness. Writing from Canada in 1950, he castigated fellow writers who accepted Hollywood's invitations to sign on to the studios' payrolls, and who then turned against Hollywood for what they alleged were its superficial values; he felt that they were hypocritical in exhibiting an elitism typical of modernists, but one that was for him morally repugnant. Further, he felt that they were betraying their obligation as serious writers to Hollywood and its audiences, merely contenting themselves by adding their "tithe to all the other obvious things that have been said in that great

American pastime, the criticism and abuse of Hollywood" (Lowry and Lowry 6–7). Striving against a patriarchy that carelessly drew its strength from vestiges of Matthew Arnold's division of culture and anarchy, Lowry would have joined Richardson in defending the diverse film goers she identified in the late 1920s and early 1930s, from the "starveling" to the "pleasant intellectual," from "happy childhood" to "happy youth" to "weary women of all classes for whom at home there is no resting-place" ("The Increasing Congregation" 64). Richardson's "weary women" were creations of new media, each woman simultaneously not only the effect (as Lewis and later McLuhan would stress) but also (as Richardson and Lowry—and Livesay—might add) the vibrant co-producer of those media.

When McLuhan in effect revived debates of the 1920s much later, he became preoccupied with renewing in systematic terms the modernists' unsystematic concern about the identity of the individual or group as a function of new media. From the 1950s onward, McLuhan searched for historic and contemporary traces of media effects on the body, whether taken at the level of the sensorium or the social. What McLuhan found were multiple severances and an underlying longing for wholeness. It was for him the printing press that had severed the eye from a sensorium that had once flourished within a unified universe. For some modernists back in the 1920s—notably Lewis—it was the cinema (and photographic technique more generally) that had severed the eye from the sensorium, and most overwhelmingly had severed it from the hand. For some—as we have seen in the example from Lowry—the ear had been severed from the other senses by radio (and, some decades earlier, by the phonograph). Thus, modernists from the 1920s on—recognizing that within Western culture not only the place of the book but also the location of its reader and the reader's body were being altered—came to understand and define film and radio (and also television—though I do not attend to television in this essay) not simply in terms of its content or its medium, but in terms of an economy of the body, an economy of personal and social spaces.[9] The mythically resonating cultural impression that we have inherited of an 1895 film audience ducking or scattering before the rush of the Lumières' train gave us a starting point for observing the individual or collective body "in action" in the face of a new medium whose "body" seemed to have run amok.

III

Livesay made her mark as a modernist writer in Canada with the publication of her first two volumes of poetry, *Green Pitcher* (1928) and *Signpost* (1932). By 1932, after studies in Toronto and Paris, Livesay—active in the 1930s as a social worker in Montreal (1933–34), Englewood, New Jersey (1934–35), and Vancouver (starting in 1936)—began to shift much of her attention from aesthetic modernism to a modernism of political action.[10] As poet, she began seeking for herself a public voice in the context of a committed and, in effect, collaborative audience—a community. She turned to left-wing political causes, and wrote agitational-propaganda pieces such as "Joe Derry," a text performed by children that mixed pantomime and recitation. It was first published in 1933 in *Masses*.[11]

"Joe Derry" prefigured what became Livesay's long-lasting interest in writing for and performing on radio, and in defining and connecting with radio audiences, an interest that took hold once she moved to Vancouver in 1936 (the year that the Canadian Broadcasting Corporation [CBC] was founded).[12] Even though Livesay's work evolved "from communist idealism in the thirties to social realism in the forties" (Irvine 225), we still find structural and thematic vestiges of "Joe Derry" in later work. For example, "Joe Derry" draws our attention to Livesay's great achievement of 1950, when the CBC produced one of her major works for radio on its Trans-Canada network as part of its *Summer Theatre* series: "If the World Were Mine," a radio play about racial and religious prejudice.[13] Like "Joe Derry," it exploits what Livesay called "montage effect," a modernist style recalling both T.S. Eliot and Sergei Eisenstein, and addresses the destructiveness of societal divisions that are based on class and (in "If the World Were Mine") on race, ethnicity, and gender. It was also at this time (in 1950 and in the two years following) that Livesay did her best and most detailed polemical writing about radio. She wrote with the authority not only of a "warm" radio listener and active practitioner and apologist in a country where CBC radio was making an effort to bring writers to audiences but also of an acclaimed poet who had just shortly before won two Governor General's Awards for her poetry.[14] She wrote, also, out of the experience of a community—Vancouver—in which creative radio work flourished in the years that she lived there.[15]

In the 1940s and 1950s, Livesay's active interest in and commitment to radio flew in the face of strong arguments that the "proper business" of poets was the writing of books, and not the "frittering" away of their talent on what one Toronto book reviewer—referring to radio drama and documentary poetry for radio such as Livesay's—called "the second rate."[16] During the 1960s and 1970s, once some of the battles about "the second rate" had been laid aside, Livesay continued to engage questions raised by the potential of radio, and, through these, draw attention to film and television.[17] She actively opposed producer Robert Weaver's use of professional actors in reading her poems on CBC radio because they turned them into something impersonal: "'the rhythms are so personal to me,'" she argued, "'that [only] I can render them effectively'" (qtd. in Tiessen and Tiessen, Introduction xxi). On one occasion in 1967, when she managed to have her poems recorded in her own voice at a CBC studio, she mailed the package to Weaver in Toronto, taunting him with an enclosed note: "I nearly sang the first poem, 'The Woman I Am,'" she said, "because that is what I do on a platform; but I thought this might cause you real agony, so I refrained [from singing]" (qtd. in Tiessen and Tiessen, Introduction xxii). Livesay was trying to impart to Weaver a sense of the importance of the presence of the performer within a space that contained both performer and audience. She was literally seeking an interventionist space for her voice, through which she might declare the corporeality of her work. She was resisting the mechanizing and normalizing—for her, the anaesthetizing—tyrannies of radio programming, of "'the mysteries,'" as she put it, of "'the air goddess'" (qtd. in Tiessen and Tiessen, Introduction xxi). She argued that institutionalized radio—which, overall, she very much relied on and vigorously supported—exacted too high a price with the absolutizing effects of its regulatory practices. Unlike McLuhan, who downplayed critics' concern with media programming and who instead foregrounded the medium itself as message, Livesay always kept alive an emphasis on programming in her discussions of a medium. Perhaps her attention to content (as well as medium) gave her scope to remain less absolutist than McLuhan about the effects of a medium. At various points in her career, she was prepared to argue directly with CBC management, with the expectation that her strategies would be persuasive.

Livesay's chafing at the CBC's use of officialese in controlling her proposals to read her own work or, often, in rejecting her submissions as too formal, too lacking in narrative line and human interest, must certainly have been affected by Vernon van Sickle and, through him, Wyndham Lewis.

Van Sickle discovered Lewis around 1930,[18] seemingly in the stacks of the Vancouver Public Library. By 1937, Livesay and van Sickle had joined the writers' group at the West End Community Centre in Vancouver. Van Sickle, a dominant figure whom Livesay thought of as an "iconoclast," according to her "seemed to be well read in contemporary English criticism, but he had little respect for [Livesay's] views"; indeed, he "crushed [and] intimidated" her (and behind her back irreverently referred to her as "the Duchess") (Livesay, *Journey* 159).[19]

Van Sickle would read sections from his novel-in-progress, *Vaudeville* (a modernist—or postmodernist—comic satire that he lugged around with him and that by the 1950s had grown into a 464-page typescript),[20] to the West End writers, all the while holding forth about the work of Lewis, in whose thinking *Vaudeville* is steeped. Indeed, the novel is sprinkled with direct quotations from Lewis's cultural analyses of the late 1920s and early 1930s, notably *The Art of Being Ruled* (1926), *Time and Western Man* (1927), and *Men Without Art* (1934).[21] We feel the caustic presence of Lewis also in van Sickle's satiric parodies in his novel of policies defended by the CBC and the NFB, agencies that van Sickle felt were too impersonal and dogmatic, too high-handed and regimented in their treatment of the individual artist, the contemporary writer.

To be sure, van Sickle took government-supported agencies such as the CBC and the NFB as the logical extension of American mass media and American popular culture, not only because these Canadian institutions had their own hegemonic grip on affecting individual destinies within artistic communities in Canada but also because their policy relied so fully on the apparent threat of the American presence. Further, like American radio or film production organizations, the CBC and the NFB too were in search of a mass audience, one to which they sought to deliver a very particular message. Certainly, from the 1920s on, van Sickle's mentor Lewis was constant in his observation that new media hegemonies—radio, film, television, the press—allowed no place for individual subjectivity and identity, that they rendered the individual's body and mind unintelligible while maiming also the body politic.

In 1946 Lowry, through his and van Sickle's common interest in international cinema, got to know van Sickle personally in Vancouver, and they stayed in touch for some time. In 1947 Lowry met Livesay and they became personal friends.[22] In 1949 Lowry began his ten-month corrective project for Hollywood on behalf of the frustrated people with whom he claimed to have mingled in cinemas where they all longed for better fare to come along: "there is a sense of frustration one has seen expressed in a thousand gestures of impatience in cinema lobbies, a thousand exclamations of … it's 'just another movie,' a thousand interruptions by people … with no train to catch, and who have not seen the film through, but yet who go out before the end" (Lowry and Lowry 11). And it was in 1949 that he invited Livesay to use his and his wife Margerie's cabin at Dollarton, so that Livesay might spend time alone to write what became her best-known and most successful radio script for national radio, her documentary poem, "Call My People Home."[23] Lowry, who had himself become involved in radio projects in Canada earlier in the 1940s, encouraged Livesay in her work for radio. Indeed, two Canadians—Gerald Noxon and Fletcher Markle—had with his support only months before put his own work, *Under the Volcano*, on the Columbia Broadcasting System's Studio One radio program in New York.[24]

IV

Situated between the British modernists' media theorizing during the late 1920s and early 1930s and the development of media analysis in Canada after World War II, fascism changed the coordinates, and the urgency, of questions involving media and audience from 1933 on. For one thing— during their domination of both radio and film in Germany after 1933— the fascists (as I have noted) vigorously appropriated documentary film form, producing simulacra of spontaneity and unity in the recording of human activity in such works as *Triumph of the Will* (1935).[25] By 1951 in Canada, underneath the nervousness about new media, and tremors about their manifest content, lay a new politically sensitive anxiety that drew on questions about the individual and society, about rational thinking and orderly behaviour, about individual action and the mood of the body politic. It was an anxiety about power and control, an anxiety that for the cultural and intellectual elite in Canada found expression on the basis of class difference: "The image of mass culture as monolithic, homogenizing, and authoritarian pervaded the intelligentsia" (Litt 97).

It was more difficult than it might seem, however, for progressive thinkers in Canada to develop and articulate an analysis that adequately addressed questions raised by the media's apparent control of the audience. For example, when about forty intellectuals, farmers, and urban labourers met in 1944 and 1945 in Saskatoon and Winnipeg at sessions of a short-lived organization of cultural critics and activists, the Prairie School for Social Advance, and tried to extend some of the cultural analysis such as that undertaken by the New School for Social Research in New York (an extension of the Frankfurt School), they were unable to find a necessary critical language, unable to make media visible either as figure or as ground. As part of their program, they tried to take aim at the German fascists' *faux*-human uses of radio and film during the 1930s and 1940s, but had difficulty finding the mark. Perhaps they did succeed symbolically: by drawing on gestures that they felt functioned on a humane level, from learning the folk music of various lands to initiating the small-enrollment study group as a means of addressing the new age of postwar plenty, they gave themselves some sense of control at least at the micro-level, if not beyond their own numbers. Livesay did not attend these meetings, and likely did not know about them; in any case, perhaps in 1944 she too would not have been as articulate about issues of media effects as she later became. Certainly, the delegates—though committed to orality and dialogue as antidote to contemporary mass media—seemed ill-prepared to make explicit the kind of trenchant media analyses that were to follow shortly in Canada, in and around 1951.[26]

The year 1951 was pivotal for a modernist writer such as Livesay reflecting on new media. Major events occurred. McLuhan published *The Mechanical Bride*. The Massey Commission (1949–51)—much preoccupied with national and international developments in both radio and film, and anticipating the vast expansion of television—issued its report on the future of cultural development in Canada.[27] Harold Innis published *The Bias of Communication*. Privately, Malcolm Lowry, in epistolary conversation with James Agee, Jay Leyda, Christopher Isherwood, and others, was revelling in their responses to his analysis of the impact on audiences of cinema, the press, advertising, and other media that he had developed in the course of writing his Hollywood metascript, exactly while Vincent Massey was undertaking his cross-country conversations in Canada (see Lowry, *Selected Letters* 441–44). In Canada in 1951, assessments of the effects of the relatively new but widely entrenched media—magazine advertising, radio, film—shot to the top of various agendas of the day.

McLuhan's stance quickly became provocative, so that by 1954, in his Lewisian *Counterblast*, McLuhan stated flatly that with movies and TV "we have abolished writing" and have "regained our WHOLENESS."[28] Livesay, too, though in her own terms, was prepared to focus on the effects that media had on "our WHOLENESS." Although she never turned her attention to a sustained analysis of new media, she was attentive and insightful. For example, if we glance at Dean Irvine's recent recovery of hitherto unpublished and uncollected work from all points in her career, we see (especially in the second half of her career, after 1951) that she was quick to explore the problem of traditional subjectivity in a world governed by simulacra, where space and time seemed to have become commodities that are arbitrary and mass produced. Thus, in "McLuhan Criticized" (1970), her speaker is tormented by the split between her memory of the human body and society's restricted access, via celluloid recollections, to the body, to celluloid images only, that produce false hope and desire for what Livesay calls "the loneliness / of the outdistanced / masses" (*Archive* 190). The narrator's eyes and cheeks and smile in the poem "Self on TV" (1980) "are so unlike / the way I feel" (*Archive* 239). In "Between a Thousand" (1967–68), identity flits among "a thousand photographs" and the "places / no place" of television images (*Archive* 164). When the woman in "Incognito" (1955–56) "lights a cigarette / As if a camera recorded her," Livesay shows us a movie star, or an advertising-magazine model, walking among simulacra—"as if she might be recognized"—but walking ever separate and "alone," "Unable to be known" (*Archive* 101). Livesay's probes in these poems suggest the extent to which all along for her it was the not only the manifest content but also the medium that was the message.[29]

But it was in 1951, the year of the Massey Commission's *Report*[30] and of *The Mechanical Bride*, that Livesay—during a series of "Critically Speaking" presentations that ran from 1950 to 1952[31]—turned her attention to writing an apology for a national radio. Here she argued for national radio's improvement by lightly yet deftly putting forward her figure of the "housewife," someone who performed life corporeally and socially. Recalling other modernists who put forward the human figure, whether as victim or resistor, in the face of a gigantic technological facelessness—like Wilfred Watson, for example, finding in the movie theatre's pianist a human marker against the relentless image of silent movies that once had invaded all the world—Livesay put on the line a version of the intervening human figure to strengthen her apology and her argument. In addressing the widespread anxiety among Canadian intellectuals about slumbrous but volatile audiences, she (unlike, for example, the personae we have seen in Woolf or Richardson at the movies) did not use the image of the modernist writer but instead insisted on a more domestic and prosaic strategy. Livesay's housewife, engaged and independent-minded, stood in contrast to McLuhan's mechanical bride.[32] If anything, Livesay's housewife, however distracted with the business of family life in the 1950s, was like Edgar Allen Poe's sailor whom McLuhan evoked in his preface to *The Mechanical Bride*, someone capably negotiating the mass media's "whirling phantasmagoria" and eluding the media's grip on their "prey," on the "collective public mind" held in a helpless state by "the mechanical agencies of the press, radio, movies, and advertising" (v).

Livesay constructed her housewife with an eye on the audience— presumably the cultural elite, operating at a time when Canada was trying to secure housewives for their traditional place in the home, primarily the kitchen.[33] Like the Massey Commission, Livesay's housewife, a figure in an urban community of homes and homemakers, put broadcast policy at the top of her agenda; again like the commissioners—in an elitist gesture that recalls high modernism's own predilections—Livesay herself was prepared to offer "high culture as a panacea for the ills of modernity" for all social classes (Litt 103). But her technique—her persona—was disarming, and suggested at the same time a social egalitarianism in its identification with and sympathy for "the people":

> Who are the listeners to the CBC? Does the Corporation really know? … I have no geiger counter either, to determine who is listening! But I live in an ordinary town, an ordinary neighbourhood, amongst parents of growing children. From listening at open windows—and from mixing at parent get-togethers—it is clear to me that most of the people in my area are not listening to the CBC. (*Dorothy Livesay* 7–8)

Claiming to be concerned about the missed opportunities at "the people's own radio system," Livesay (echoing van Sickle's attacks on CBC rhetoric) objected to the CBC's false construction of an implied or fictive audience that it called "the masses" (*Dorothy Livesay* 8). The CBC, she said, "at present is not reaching the masses; yet the great majority of week-day programs are apparently levelled at a mass audience" (*Dorothy Livesay* 8). Making explicit a position more likely to be taken up by Woolf or Richardson or H.D. than by Lewis in London twenty or twenty-five years earlier, Livesay stated firmly: "There is no mass audience" (*Dorothy Livesay* 8). Perhaps recalling with some mixture of nostalgia and frustration her own work for *Masses* eighteen years earlier, she claimed now that the "mass audience" was "the great twentieth century myth" (*Dorothy Livesay* 8).[34] In this respect interrogating the agenda of the Massey Commission, she was prepared to deconstruct the "mass" as a threatening abstraction and reveal instead the presence of the individual, active in body and in mind. She pointed to young children and teenagers as examples of engaged listeners, actively choosing from among myriad commercial stations.

Contradictorily, Livesay simultaneously took refuge in the Massey Commission's assertion of a high-culture agenda. She seemed to express the sentiments of the culture lobby behind the Massey Commission that "despised" the low-brow tyranny that they felt pulsating within mass culture: "They believed that its inspiration was purely commercial rather than communal or critical" (Litt 85). And so she complained that serious adult listeners—those seeking modern poetic drama, fine music, and stimulating talks rather than "a bog of soap suds" (*Dorothy Livesay* 8)—were left in a frantic state by the clumsiness of CBC programmers, who indiscriminately mixed "corn" with "culture" (*Dorothy Livesay* 7). Livesay's culturally blessed but seemingly uncomplicated housewife, seeking sustained nourishment but resisting being reduced to a mechanical timepiece, is somewhat helplessly caught in space/time run amok, recalling Lowry's Hollywood extra. She had come to think of herself as hapless victim of the CBC's "hit and miss procedure, with only the newspaper hieroglyphics as a guide" for its imagined mass audience: "since I always have to run and turn off the soap serial, I often miss a good part of the next offering—just because I am not myself a clock!" (*Dorothy Livesay* 10). Livesay advised the CBC to attend to housewives' demands for "culture": "[s]erve the minority well—and the minority will swell!" (*Dorothy Livesay* 9).

With her housewife figure, Livesay addressed a Canadian cultural realm that felt increasingly unsteady in its sense of itself—insecure in its subjectivity—and she tried to shore up the sense of a stable space within the specifics of an interactive and coherent community, a utopian space in which a modernist sensibility might operate unimpeded in Canada. Yet even while she was exercising her vision of a housewife enlightened by a high culture that was user-friendly to one and all in middle-class Canada, McLuhan, as we see from his 1954 *Counterblast*, was getting ready to announce the end of "Canadian kulcha" as modernists had come to rely on it.

[1] The essay appeared in the *Province* on 12 December 1939, while Lowry was waiting for his manuscript of *Under the Volcano* to follow him from Los Angeles to Vancouver. This early version has been published as *The 1940 Under the Volcano* (see Lowry, *The 1940*). From 1941 to 1945 Lowry revised his manuscript and published it in New York and London in 1947. *Under the Volcano* immediately became one of the internationally best-known modernist novels written in Canada.

[2] My focus is on commercial (feature) films and not, for example, the highly experimental, avant-garde works of the late 1920s. My focus in radio is on the work of the CBC during the late 1940s and early 1950s. For avant-garde approaches to radio and related audio art in Europe and the United States, especially in the first half of the twentieth century, see Kahn and Whitehead.

[3] Richardson's multi-volume *Pilgrimage*, which began to appear in installments in 1915, attracted comparisons with film as early as 1919.

[4] I have identified portions of both British and subsequent English-Canadian phases of this tradition within modernism in my article on John Grierson, Wyndham Lewis, Graham Spry, and Gerald Noxon (see Tiessen, "From Literary"; see also Tiessen, "Film"). Concerning Livesay and radio, see Tiessen and Tiessen, "Dorothy Livesay," and "Livesay/Riel."

[5] McLuhan's work, representing as it does a Canadian modernist practice of the 1950s and 1960s that has particular roots in British modernisms of the 1920s, reminds us of some historical parallels. Britain-to-Canada migrations can be found in the ethos surrounding state-run radio, first the BBC and then the CBC; in John Grierson's British documentary film institutions' influence on the NFB; and in the London Film Society's influence on the 1930s and 1940s film society movement in Canada, not least in Vancouver.

[6] For Lewis's hostility to cinema, see Tiessen, "A New Year." See Sara Danius concerning modernism's "antitechnological bias," its discomfort with modernity, its "suppression, denial, or even a renunciation of the historical, social, and institutional conditions that brought it [modernism] into being" (40).

[7] For an overview of Richardson on cinema, see Marcus. Marcus's "Introduction" (150–59) precedes a re-printing of Richardson's film essays published in *Close Up*.

[8] Lowry's script (with Margerie Bonner Lowry) was ostensibly an adaptation of F.

Scott Fitzgerald's *Tender Is the Night*, but it became a text that vastly exceeded the style of a conventional filmscript. See Lowry, *Cinema*.

[9] McLuhan, unlike literary figures such as Lowry or Noxon, did not experience first-hand the European film/media debates of the late 1920s.

[10] David Arnason argues that Livesay's *Green Pitcher* and *Signpost* were the "first books of modernist poetry broadly available to a reading public in Canada, and written by a Canadian poet who was to develop a substantial reputation" (13). He notes that with her move toward "longer, more extended, socially committed poems" after 1932 (16), Livesay deliberately made an effort to separate herself from an Eliotic high modernism, and pursue a path closer to that of "Spender, C. Day Lewis, and sometimes Auden" (17).

[11] See *Masses* 2.10 (Sept. 1933): 14–15. For a reprint of "Joe Derry," see Livesay, *Dorothy Livesay* 25–29.

[12] For a detailed historical discussion of Livesay and radio see Tiessen and Tiessen, Introduction. For a note on Alan Crawley's collaboration with Livesay in presenting poetry readings on radio in Vancouver in 1939, see Crawley 120.

[13] "If the World Were Mine," a thirty-minute radio play, was produced by Raymond Whitehouse. It is possible that an earlier version was produced on CBC radio around 1940 or earlier. "If the World Were Mine" is published in Livesay, *Dorothy Livesay* 31–60. It has various versions and titles, including "'The Times Were Different'?" and "Personal History." See also "'The Times Were Different'?" in Livesay, *Right Hand* 132–50.

[14] Governor General's Awards for Poetry for *Day and Night* (1944) and *Poems for People* (1947).

[15] Before taking up duties on his CBC *Stage* series in Toronto in 1943–44, Andrew Allan (after a stint with BBC radio) worked from 1940 to 1943 for CBC radio in Vancouver. Fletcher Markle wrote radio drama for Allan in Vancouver, then Toronto. Birney and Livesay also came to work with Allan—the architect of Canada's "golden age" of radio drama (1944–55)—in Vancouver in the early 1940s. Malcolm and Margerie Lowry considered taking on work for Allan in Vancouver, and did write scripts for him when they lived in the Toronto area (in 1944–45). Noxon had done some radio writing in London for the BBC during the 1930s, and continued with the CBC in Toronto during the 1940s. For more information on radio work in Vancouver in the 1940s, see Tiessen, Introduction 16–18. For a discussion of the Lowrys' unfinished radio-drama adaptation of Melville's *Moby Dick*, and of Lowry's "Through the Panama" as mental radio, see Newton.

[16] See Scott. Earle Birney and Livesay both rejected Scott's charges.

[17] Simultaneously—and very notably in her 1969 essay on documentary—Livesay was suggesting reading strategies reflecting traditions planted in what was for her

a form allied to radio, namely, documentary film. In the essay's opening sentences, she links "documentary" in three media—film, radio, and television—and suggests that the roots of documentary lie in the 1940s work of John Grierson ("Documentary" 267). In 1952, she spoke highly of some of the history documentaries presented by CBC radio, and wished that CBC drama might inject "the same qualities of experimentation and admirable restraint that we find in the documentaries" (*Dorothy Livesay* 14). In the opening line of her "Critically Speaking" pieces in 1950, she contrasts radio (aural) and television (visual) forms (*Dorothy Livesay* 3).

[18] At about the same time, writers such as Douglas Adam and Leo Kennedy, embarking on their post-*McGill Fortnightly Review* careers, were encountering Lewis. At The Canadian Modernists Meet symposium at the University of Ottawa in 2003, David McKnight drew attention to Adam's reading, in 1928, a recent issue of Lewis's *The Enemy* (first two issues, 1927) and *The Wild Body* (1927), and at the same time searching for copies of *Time and Western Man* (1927) and *Tarr* (1918 and 1926). McKnight also noted Kennedy's reading, in December 1928, Lewis's *The Wild Body* and *The Childermass* (1928). I am grateful to McKnight for his conversation with me about Lewis, and for making available to me a copy of his paper.

McLuhan encountered Lewis's writing during his studies at Cambridge University around 1936. He met Lewis in 1943, in Windsor, Ontario, and began a personal association with him.

[19] Because van Sickle debunked her work, which (as she says) had moved from "agitprop poetry" to "ironic political poems along the lines of Auden, Spender and C. Day Lewis," Livesay turned in 1938 for support to Alan Crawley, who had recently moved to Vancouver. With Crawley as its editor, Livesay nurtured her commitment to *Contemporary Verse* (1941–52), a little magazine that she thought of as their "west-coast project" (see *Journey* 163–65). In a paper ("Modernism, Blindness, and *Contemporary Verse*") presented at The Canadian Modernists Meet symposium, Jason Wiens spelled out Crawley's central role in Canadian modernist publishing.

[20] An excerpt from *Vaudeville* appears in Tiessen, "Vernon van Sickle."

[21] Because van Sickle continued to expand and refine *Vaudeville* even in the 1950s, we find quoted in it Lewis's later works, too, such as *Rude Assignment* (1950). In 1956 van Sickle sent his manuscript to Lewis, who commented favourably on it. See Tiessen, "Film" 87–93.

[22] For an account of Livesay's and Lowry's friendship, see Livesay, *Journey* 167–71. See also Lowry, *Sursum Corda!* (76–77, 89, 618–19) for three letters (two from 1947, one from 1952) to Livesay. Through Livesay, Lowry also came to know *Contemporary Verse*, where Crawley published some of Lowry's poetry. See Lowry, *Sursum Corda!* (77–79, 103–04, 156–57) for letters of 1947 and 1949 to Crawley.

In 1947, the Lowrys and the Birneys became friends, too. During the late 1940s and early 1950s they sometimes attended Vancouver Film Society screenings together (see Tiessen and Mota 12–13). A year after McLuhan published *Understanding Media: The Extensions of Man*, Birney was exhorting university graduates to be mindful not just of books but also of films, in learning how to live "in this shaky global house of 1965." Addressing a convocation of the University of Alberta (at what was then its Calgary campus), he said: "You now know far more than most about the poems of ... Spenser, Milton, Pope, Wordsworth.... [Do you have] some acquaintance with the best films of, say, Bergman, or the contemporary Italian and Japanese film-makers?" (*Convocation*). Birney submitted to the CBC fourteen radio plays between 1946 and 1957. For eight of these plays, see Birney, *Words*.

[23] "Call My People Home" was Livesay's documentary poem for radio about the fate of Japanese Canadians during the 1940s.

[24] See Markle and Noxon.

[25] A 2003 exhibition at the Filmmuseum Berlin places stress on director Leni Riefenstahl's shrewd exploitation of the public's acceptance of documentary film idiom as authentic and reliable. Lewis pointed to the fascists' exploitation of documentary film form in his books on Hitler in the 1930s. See Tiessen and Tiessen, "Wyndham Lewis" 80–84.

[26] There had already been an extensive examination of the effects of media in Canada, particularly in the 1920s and early 1930s with respect to radio, and again in the late 1930s with respect to documentary film production (see Tiessen, "From Literary"). Documents describing the work of the Prairie School for Social Advance are held in the Bruce Peel Special Collections Library at the University of Alberta; I am grateful to the archivists at the University of Alberta for making them available to me.

[27] The Royal Commission on National Development in the Arts, Letters and Sciences began its investigation in April 1949, and submitted its final recommendations in June 1951. The cultural elites' reports to the commission were filled with angst about the individual's and the community's loss of a tactile, participatory culture (one that McLuhan brought forward under entirely new socio-cultural and intellectual auspices, with the aural universe of his village/tribe). The commission's anxiety about the effects of mass media—that a passive and easily manipulated public was made particularly vulnerable in the face of totalitarian pressures from the left or the right—"made broadcast policy the most important issue on the commission's agenda" (Litt 90). In 1951 (as with cultural elites' readings of cinema in the 1920s), the commission felt as though much was at stake: the "attacks on the culture of the masses can be seen as a form of class conflict fought on cultural ... grounds" (Litt 96). Litt concludes that the commission "offered high culture

as a panacea for the ills of modernity" (103). He notes that with *The Mechanical Bride* McLuhan offered a service parallel to that of Massey: "[McLuhan] synthesized many of the contemporary complaints about mass culture in *The Mechanical Bride* (1951), a critique of recurring icons of advertising in popular print media." Shortly after, McLuhan, increasingly less defensive in turning his attention to new media, was to give notice to a culture rooted since Gutenberg in the book, but shifting to new intellectual modes of experience and perception, and to human body parts and a sensorium subject to delirious extension and painful amputation. McLuhan then found himself uncomfortable with the Massey Commission's too bookish, too programmatic proposals for development in radio, film, and television. He used his *Counterblast 1954*—his explicit homage to Lewis's 1914 issue of *Blast*—to question the presuppositions of "the Massey Report damp cultural igloo for Canadian devotees of / TIME / & / LIFE" ([5]) and to suggest that the report represented a "HUGE RED HERRING for derailing canadian kulcha while it is absorbed by American ART & Technology" ([6]).

[28] In 1954 van Sickle, having moved east, picked up a copy of McLuhan's *Counterblast 1954* in a Toronto magazine shop and was aghast at what he took to be McLuhan's abandonment of Lewis's argument in favour of the culturally stable word, and told McLuhan so during their one or two visits in 1954–55.

[29] For an explanation of the dating of these poems, see Dean Irvine's notes in Livesay, *Archive* 273.

[30] Livesay herself, through the Canadian Writers Committee, had joined an elitist lobby that urged the Massey panel to avoid a parochial emphasis on Canadian culture (Litt 110). At the same time, with reference to programs such as the nightly "News round-up," she made it clear that the CBC should drop its primary focus on the "international scene" in favour of much a stronger emphasis on Canada— and thereby abandon its colonial parochialism: "Parochialism is still the curse of Canada," she said; "even though the CBC is the main agency working to break down that parochialism, its job seems to me to be spotty" (*Dorothy Livesay* 16). During her "Critically Speaking" talks, she made explicit reference to the Massey Commission (*Dorothy Livesay* 7).

[31] See Livesay, *Dorothy Livesay* 3–19.

[32] McLuhan's mechanical bride appeared in altered form in a 1960 play fragment by Wilfred Watson, a comic satire of consumerism that Watson titled "The Mechanical Bridegroom" (see Tiessen, "'Shall I say'").

[33] The "housewife" appearing in my first epigraph to this essay is taken from a letter to CBC officials, in which Livesay was referring to the "Critically Speaking" essays that she prepared for radio presentation during 1950–52 (*Dorothy Livesay* 1). In her "Critically Speaking" essays she, making clear also her role as "mother," included in two different versions of her text the two following sentences, implic-

itly seeming to link "housewife" with "woman": (1) "Like most housewives, I am more frequently a daytime than an evening listener." (2) "Like most women, I am more frequently a day listener than an evening listener" (*Dorothy Livesay* 10, 15). [34] Livesay, in denying the existence of the mass audience, was echoing the thoughts of an unnamed book reviewer whom she claims to have heard on radio the week before.

WORKS CITED

Arnason, David. "Dorothy Livesay and the Rise of Modernism in Canada." *A Public and Private Voice: Essays on the Life and Work of Dorothy Livesay.* Ed. Lindsay Dorney, Gerald Noonan, and Paul Tiessen. Waterloo, ON: U of Waterloo P, 1986. 5–18.

Birney, Earle. *Convocation Address.* Calgary, University of Alberta at Calgary, Nov. 1965.

————. *Words on Waves.* Kingston and Toronto: Quarry and CBC Enterprises, 1985.

Crawley, Alan. "Dorothy Livesay." *Leading Canadian Poets.* Ed. W.P. Percival. Toronto: Ryerson, 1948. 117–24.

Danius, Sara. *The Senses of Modernism: Technology, Perception, and Aesthetics.* Ithaca and London: Cornell UP, 2002.

Galbo, Joe. "McLuhan and Baudrillard: Notes on the Discarnate, Simulations and Tetrads." *McLuhan Studies* 1 (1991): 103–07.

George, W.L. "A Painter's Literature." *English Review* 30 (March 1920): 223–34.

Heyer, Paul. "America under Attack I: A Reassessment of Orson Welles' 1938 *War of the Worlds* Broadcast." *Canadian Journal of Communication* 28 (2003): 149–65.

H.D., "The Cinema and the Classics." *Close Up* 1 (July 1927): 22–33.

Irvine, Dean. "Editorial Postscript." Livesay, *Archive* 250–72.

Kahn, Douglas, and Gregory Whitehead, eds. *Wireless Imagination: Sound, Radio, and the Avant-Garde.* Cambridge, MA and London, UK: MIT P, 1994.

Keogh, Joe G. "Laureate among the Shades: Tennyson and the Phonograph." *McLuhan Studies* 1 (1991): 181–6.

Lewis, Wyndham. *Filibusters in Barbary.* London: Grayson and Grayson, 1932.

Litt, Paul. *The Muses, The Masses, and the Massey Commission.* Toronto: UTP, 1992.

Livesay, Dorothy. *Archive for Our Times: Previously Uncollected and Unpublished Poems of Dorothy Livesay.* Ed. Dean Irvine. Vancouver: Arsenal Pulp, 1998.

————. "The Documentary Poem: A Canadian Genre." *Contexts of Canadian Criticism: A Collection of Critical Essays.* Ed. Eli Mandel. Chicago and London: U of Chicago P, 1971. 267–81.

———. *Dorothy Livesay and the* CBC: *Early Texts for Radio*. Ed. Paul Tiessen and Hildi Froese Tiessen. Waterloo, ON: MLR Editions Canada, 1994.

———. *Journey with My Selves: A Memoir 1909–1963*. Vancouver: Douglas and McIntyre, 1991.

———. *Right Hand Left Hand*. Erin, ON: Porcépic, 1977.

Lowry, Malcolm. *The Cinema of Malcolm Lowry: A Scholarly Edition of Lowry's 'Tender Is the Night.'* Ed. Paul Tiessen and Miguel Mota. Vancouver: UBC P, 1990.

———. "Hollywood and the War." *Malcolm Lowry Newsletter* 11 (fall 1982): 4–6.

———. *The 1940 Under the Volcano*. Ed. Tiessen and Mota. Waterloo, ON: MLR Editions Canada, 1994.

———. *Selected Letters of Malcolm Lowry*. Ed. Harvey Breit and Margerie Bonner Lowry. Philadelphia and New York: Lippincott, 1965.

———. *Sursum Corda! The Collected Letters of Malcolm Lowry. Volume II: 1947– 1957*. Ed. Sherrill E. Grace. Toronto: UTP, 1996.

Lowry, Malcolm, and Margerie Lowry. "A Few Items Culled From What Started Out to be a Sort of Preface to a Film-script." *White Pelican* 4.2 (spring 1974): 2–20.

Marcus, Laura. Introduction. *Close Up 1927–1933: Cinema and Modernism*. Ed. James Donald, Anne Friedberg, and Laura Marcus. Princeton: Princeton UP, 1998. 150–59.

Markle, Fletcher, and Gerald Noxon. "Under the Volcano: A Radio Drama." *Malcolm Lowry and Conrad Aiken Adapted*. Ed. Paul Tiessen. Waterloo, ON: Malcolm Lowry Review [MLR Editions Canada], 1992. 1–63.

McKnight, David. "Geniuses Together: The McGill Movement and Montparnasse." "The Canadian Modernists Meet: A Symposium." Ottawa, University of Ottawa, 9–11 May 2003.

McLuhan, Marshall. *Counterblast 1954*. Toronto: Private publication, 1954.

———. *The Mechanical Bride: Folklore of Industrial Man*. 1951. Boston: Beacon, 1967.

Murry, John Middleton. "The Break-Up of the Novel." *Yale Review* XII (Oct. 1922): 288–304.

Newton, Norman. "Malcolm Lowry and the Radiophonic Imagination." *Malcolm Lowry Review* 36–37 (spring-fall 1995): 56–95.

Peters, John Durham. *Speaking into the Air: A History of the Idea of Communication*. Chicago and London: U of Chicago P, 1999.

Richardson, Dorothy. "Continuous Performance, VI: The Increasing Congregation." *Close Up* 1.6 (Dec. 1927): 61–65.

———. *Windows on Modernism: Selected Letters of Dorothy Richardson*. Ed. Gloria G. Fromm. Athens and London: U of Georgia P, 1995.

Scott, James. "Radio and Writers: West Coast Replies." *Telegram* 27 Jan. 1951: 4.

Tiessen, Paul. "Film, Culture Criticism and Institutional Form, 1936–1956: The Work of Vernon van Sickle." *Canadian Journal of Film Studies* 9.1 (spring 2000): 80–100.

———. "From Literary Modernism to the Tantramar Marshes: Anticipating McLuhan in British and Canadian Media Theory and Practice." *Canadian Journal of Communication* 18.4 (autumn 1993): 451–67.

———. Introduction. *The Letters of Malcolm Lowry and Gerald Noxon, 1940–1952.* Ed. Paul Tiessen. Vancouver: UBC P, 1988. 1–21.

———. "A New Year One: Film as Metaphor in the Writings of Wyndham Lewis." *Words and Moving Images: Essays on Verbal and Visual Expression in Film and Television.* Ed. W.C. Wees and M. Dorland. Montreal: Mediatexte, 1984. 151–69.

———. "'Shall I say, it is necessary to restore the dialogue?' Wilfred Watson's encounter with Marshall McLuhan, 1957–1998." *At the Speed of Light There Is Only Illumination: A Reappraisal of Marshall McLuhan.* Ed. Linda Morra and John Moss. Ottawa: U of Ottawa P, 2004. 95–145.

———. "Vernon van Sickle and Malcolm Lowry: Some Connections." *Malcolm Lowry Review* 40 (spring 1997): 111–26.

Tiessen, Paul, and Miguel Mota. Introduction. Lowry, *Cinema* 3–38.

Tiessen, Paul, and Hildi Froese Tiessen. "Dorothy Livesay and the Politics of Radio." *A Public and Private Voice: Essays on the Life and Work of Dorothy Livesay.* Ed. Lindsay Dorney, Gerald Noonan, and Paul Tiessen. Waterloo, ON: U of Waterloo P, 1986. 71–86.

———. Introduction. Livesay, *Dorothy Livesay* xi–xxviii.

———. "Livesay/Riel." *Images of Louis Riel in Canadian Culture.* Ed. Ramon Hathorn and Patrick Holland. Queenston: Mellen, 1992. 311–25.

———. "Wyndham Lewis and Documentary Film in the 1920s and 1930s." *Varieties of Filmic Expression.* Kent: Romance Languages Department, Kent State U, 1989. 80–84.

Wiens, Jason. "Modernism, Blindness, and *Contemporary Verse*." "The Canadian Modernists Meet: A Symposium." Ottawa, University of Ottawa, 9–11 May 2003.

Woolf, Virginia. "The Cinema." *The Essays of Virginia Woolf, Volume IV: 1925–1928.* Ed. Andrew McNeillie. London: Hogarth, 1994.

MODERNISM'S ARCHIVES AND LEDGERS

The Literary Archive and the Telling of Modernist Lives: Retrieving Anne Marriott

MARILYN ROSE

LITERARY CRITIC DONALD BARTHELME speaks of "not-knowing" as instrumental in the production of fiction. He argues that "the scanning process engendered by not-knowing" frees the mind to move in "unanticipated directions" so that powerful "invention" may ensue (11). Barthelme's sense of the fecundity of a writer's "not knowing" is relevant to the writing of nonfiction as well, and particularly to the production of literary biography. Writing history of any kind requires the practitioner to be true to what passes for fact at a given moment in time, while admitting to those inevitable gaps, fissures, and speaking positions that ultimately mark historical discourse as hypothetical. Certainly in the case of biography, the "telling of lives," scholars can produce only hypothesis, the best that can be conjectured given the knowledge available at the time, some parts of which inevitably will be challenged by new frameworks and new discoveries in the future.

The centrality of archives to the process of literary biography is undeniable. Archives must be plumbed and it is only when every relevant archive with respect to a subject has been mined that the work of writing can begin. In fact, because they are so substantial and so important to the work of telling lives, a sense of reverence tends to accrue to the archive, especially for those literary historians working on modernist archives—those developed during a time of archival consciousness, during which writers have tended assiduously to save all of their potentially important papers with archival preservation in mind. For modern biographers, archives are typically seen as ample, plenteous, abundantly testimonial, and legitimate,as rich archaeological sources, in short, which belong in unproblematic ways to the institutions that own and manage them, which are made available to properly credentialed researchers, and which offer those researchers authorized and incontestable truths about the past. Such attitudes are evident in the hushed and almost devotional language that is used to describe archival research. We speak of *visiting* the archives, of being *authorized* to do so, of finding *evidence* therein, of *confirming* facts through archival fonds, and of issues of *proprietorship* and the *legitimate use* of archival materials.

Yet so partial, in every sense of the word, are archives and archival work that the archive must be theorized and unthinking veneration challenged. Telling lives based on archival scholarship inevitably involves telling plausible fictions that elide inevitable but significant gaps in knowing, and do so with an authority that is far from infallible. In fact the most an archival scholar can aim for is *attempted* fidelity to his or her subject as glimpsed through the distorting lens of the archival repository, while recognizing that the textual body that is the archive is remarkably wilful, remarkably resistant to all attempts to contain it. Even in the case of a modernist poet such as Anne Marriott—whose rather small repository reflects an abbreviated working life—the archive can be seen to testify to no singular Anne but rather myriad Marriotts, each dependent upon the reading position (and perhaps the unacknowledged desires) of the archival reader. For the archival reader/writer is also a complex being, one who writes from a complicated perspective; after all, as Jerome McGann observes, every author is "plural," himself or herself a multiply constituted manifestation of a socially constituted identity (75).

That archives are problematic as historical testimony has been acknowledged on many fronts over the past several decades. In recent years, archivists themselves have engaged in heated debate over the incursions of theory into their discipline, and particularly contemporary notions of history and textuality that challenge the traditional sense of the archive as, in Tom Nesmith's words, existing "fully in a state of nature, outside of or prior to communications process" (144). In the end, most have found it impossible not to acknowledge that archives are at best compromised sites, consisting of *mediated* experience that has been fundamentally shaped by the "social and technical process of inscription, transmission, and contextualization" that converts raw deposits into ordered fonds (Nesmith 143).[1] Archivist Terry Eastwood acknowledges such difficulties as challenging the foundational principles of archive building and archive maintenance: "[Archival] discipline stands on two propositions, which certainly need extensive contemplation: that archival documents attest to facts and acts, and that their trustworthiness is dependent upon the circumstances of their generation and preservation" (126). If neither the authenticity of archival materials nor the disinterestedness of their management can be guaranteed, then much indeed is thrown into question.

Such observations raise the question of power relations within the community within which the archive exists. Whom, or what, do archives serve in their organizational principles and usage, if not the dominant discourses under whose aegis they are formed and regulated? Eastwood's use of the word "discipline" and his reminder, as a practising archivist, that archives are rooted in legal and administrative principles—that they were intended originally to "extend memory, to bear evidence of acts forward in time" as potential testimony in support of future claims (125)—supports contemporary theoretical notions of the archive as a hegemonic institution linked in powerful but unspoken ways to notions of legitimacy and hence the status quo. Michel Foucault defines the archive as a "discursive formation" that constitutes legal authority and imbeds legal power through its "discursive apparatus," its systems of regulation. In saving certain things, and erasing or suppressing others, the archive establishes "the law of what can be said" in a given economy, and thereby reinforces dominant systems of power (126–29). For Jacques Derrida, the archive is a "*place* from which order is *given*," and the "*archon*" who is given the power to interpret the archive is "a vested authority" inalterably aligned with "hermeneutic power," as he or she works within the archive's protocols (9–10). Thus, as Paul Voss and Marina Werner note in "Towards a Poetics of the Archive," though once imagined as "a space of pure knowledge," the archive must now be recognized as "an ideologically-charged space." It confers order through "bibliographical determination," so that "an official record of the past" may seem to be "preserved and transmitted intact" within its boundaries, yet the history of the archive is always "on the one hand a history of conservation," and on the other "a history of loss." Its "logic" is "paradoxical": "[t]he archive preserves and reserves, protects and patrols, regulates and suppresses," and through "the architecture of the archive and the sentinels who control access to its interior ... the conservation and transmission of knowledge" becomes "the prerogative of a few chosen agents, of a coterie of privileged insiders" (i).

The focus in such observations is on the archive as selective and incomplete, but on the whole stable and orderly, owing to archival management. Canadian theorist Pamela Banting, however, shifts attention to the slippery nature of the archive itself, construing the archive as a "literary genre." Archival materials, she suggests, are elusive, perhaps even mischievous. They offer different faces, different "masks," to different researchers as those scholars attempt to discipline, through interpretation, the repository's various bits and pieces. Individual researchers call certain archival elements into *play*, in her view: they make the archive *perform* in ways that suit their own needs in terms of the cultural *productions* they wish to mount (119–22). In doing so, as David Greetham observes in "The Cultural Poetics of Archival Exclusion," the notion of neutrality must be abandoned, although this may be less because certain elements are selected, taken up, or played up by interested users, than because "the concept of unrelated themes" or "unwanted materials"—of exclusion, in other words—is "clearly ... as powerful an agency of selection" as is inclusion (12). To foreground is to repress, and specifically to repress, as Derrida suggests, that which is fearsome or otherwise intolerable to the otherwise aligned archon.

And here the theoretical focus shifts again, since an archive is clearly at best a repository of *possible* truths that are available to the situated archival reader, rather than *the* truth about anything or anybody, least of all its ostensible subject. Thus much depends upon the personal, intellectual, and cultural climate into which the "buried treasures" are retrieved. The reading/interpretation of archives, through the practices of history or life writing, will certainly inevitably testify as much to the inclinations and aspirations of the researcher as to the truth of that wickedly resistant archival body that we like to imagine as being full of "data," of evidentiary facts. Here the archivist may shrug his shoulders and bow out. Terry Eastwood, for example, acknowledges that the interpreter's use of archival documents may "complicate what truth can be derived from the document," but states that "So long as the use does not corrupt the document, such fidelity to the event as it possesses remains undiminished" (127). In other words, there is documentary truth in the archive, in his view, however unfortunate it is that its interpreters may be tainted by bias, despite their heartfelt desire to recover and disseminate archival truths with veracity.

Eastwood's elevation of the archive above its usage (the notion that as long as the archive is not corrupted, it matters little if writing about it is biased) is not likely to sit well with literary biographers whose deepest desire, surely, is to tell the truth, the whole truth, and nothing but the truth. Such biographers, like all others, yearn to tell lives without telling lies. They sincerely wish to recover the silenced and give voice—like the crusading coroner who promises to speak for the dead—to those who cannot speak for themselves. Basically, or so it seems to me, biographers are inherently programmed for the chase. They cannot help but buy into the paradigm of detection, the idea of solving mysteries through the aggressive pursuit of facts, with the goal of compiling textual evidence in such a way that the ultimate assemblage of the shards leads to a proper intuition of the whole that they are seeking to reconstruct. Biographers assume that at some point they will know enough to compensate for what they cannot know—in other words, that what is known will *properly* elide and thereby silence the gaps that remain. Such assumptions beg the question, of course, of whether absences can ever be silenced or whether they perpetually haunt and threaten to "out" even the most informed of assertions.

Nonetheless, the goals of literary biography, with its rootedness in the assumptions about the validity of information to be found in archives, are seductive given the nobility that attaches itself to the enterprise: we who bio/graph imagine, I think, subjects who need our kindly ministrations, who would champion (if they could) our liberatory tactics. Contemporary biographers are not naive: we are properly fearful of slipping into voyeurism, and we worry about invasiveness. We genuinely hope that as we come to know intimate detail about those whom we research we will succeed in separating "telling" from "telling all," an issue that Christl Verduyn raises, for example, in dealing with the *cahiers* of Marian Engel (93), as does Mary Rubio in her work with the journals of L.M. Montgomery. And we are on the whole wary, I think, of reductionism, concurring with Marian Engel's observation in warning readers of her journals that "Only fictional characters can satisfy our desire for perfect consistency" (qtd. in Verduyn 93). Nor can we deny, in keeping with Pamela Banting's argument, that the archive is a *genre*, with conventions (like all genres) that govern presentation, selectivity, and imaginative construal of whatever "reality" inheres in its representation of the real that it purports to reflect.

And yet, as self-conscious as we may be, I wonder how many of us succeed in avoiding the language of positivistic detection and of our own authority as we speak of our "field work." I am struck, for example, by the language adopted by formidable Canadian biographer Phyllis Grosskurth, whose romantic and idealistic language mirrors my own as I began my work on Marriott and other Canadian women poets of the modern period more than a decade ago. In the Toronto *Globe and Mail* (March 1997), Grosskurth writes of her archival work on the diary and letters of Annabella Milbanke, Lord Byron's first wife, which are to be found in the Lovelace Papers in the Bodleian Library. Grosskurth configures herself as a cross between a literary detective and a conjurer of the dead. She speaks of the large cardboard folders brought to her desk at the library, of the "trembling fingers" with which she opens them, of her unwillingness to take lunch or tea as the folders "pile up" around her, of her near-oblivion as she stumbles, rapt, into each Oxford evening, still wrapped in her archival pursuits. She speaks of being lost in time, her reading-room days stretching into weeks and the weeks into months. She mentions her subsequent travels to Portugal, Spain, Greece, Italy, and Switzerland in a "determined quest" for "atmosphere redolent of Byron's exile." Her identification with her subject is tangible: in "handling those family letters," she says, "some of them tear-stained, I felt that I was touching a part of the past." Grosskurth's admitted obsession with her subject does not detract from her confidence, however, that she *can* arrive at truth through the evidence "documented in these family pages," that she *can* reconstruct the past with a fair degree of accuracy in the end, through the application of what Agatha Christie's Hercule Poirot refers to as one's "little grey cells," for in the end Grosskurth asserts that she was indeed able "… by weeks of careful comparison, of sorting through the evidence of friends and foes of all the parties concerned, … to form some sort of balanced judgment." The confluence of the words "document," "evidence" and "judgment" demonstrate her allegiance to the model of biographer as detective, a proclivity that all life writers, I imagine, are likely to need to own up to.

A number of Canadian scholars have addressed problems particular to the archives of Canadian women writers. Prominent theorists of the archive, such as Helen Buss, Marlene Kadar, and Carole Gerson, point, for example, to problems of institutional bias with respect to women writers: in Buss and Kadar's *Working in Women's Archives* (2001), for example, biographers lament the paucity of records kept relating to women writers, and the way in which materials related to women's lives are scattered across archives and too often poorly documented in archival catalogues. Drawing upon new directions in the discipline of anthropology, particularly its emphasis on inequities of power that exist between the researcher and the observed subject, such scholars warn as well of the difficulties surrounding the attempt to speak for archival subjects, whose voices may be compromised by filters through which researchers retrieve materials into a veritable network of power relations that may or may not be acknowledged. The interesting lack of focus on the archives of modern Canadian women writers in this collection indicates another kind of institutional bias related to archives, moreover: the way in which archival problems are assumed to be prevalent only in the case of pre-modern writers, whose archives were assembled and preserved less consciously or deliberately than those of the modern period and later, even though many of the problems signalled (paucity, scattered records, poor documentation) plague the archives of more contemporary women as well.

At times, however, it is a different problem, the very richness of the modernist writer's archive, that hampers the literary biographer, a tendency that Carol Shields speaks of in the building of her own repository. In contrast to the paucity, or to use Gwendolyn Davies's word, the "silences" (35), that characterize the holdings of many early Canadian women writers, Shields reminds us of why modern and contemporary women's archives tend to be dauntingly full. She confesses that once she had made arrangements for the donation of her papers to the National Library of Canada, she was advised to "save everything, with the possible exception of what we might have jotted down on a paper napkin in a coffee shop—and even that depended on who we were and what the jotted-down words were." In consequence, she began to save not only what she "considered to be serious documents that directly intersected with [her] writing life" but, gradually, a great deal of extraneous matter—personal papers, family materials, and even notations to herself about possible ideas for projects "that never in the end came to anything." In the end, Shields admits, the ministrations of the archivists, in sorting and preserving whatever she donated to them, served to dignify and legitimize her bits and pieces, and to create a charming fiction of an ordered life: "My motley papers were now arranged in beautiful acid-free, lignin-free folders.... Looking at them I was amazed to see that my disorganized, untidy, and unexamined life had contained all sorts of recognizable patterns, … a life that gave every outward impression of direction and shape." While clearly amused by the way in which her archive mis/represents her life that it sets out to document, Shields's words are a reminder of the insufficiency of the archive in general, its inadequacy in the face of the excess that is a life lived, an experience to which it bears only partial witness and distorts, in the end, through the imposition of its own categories and ligatures.

Quite apart from the ways in which the archive as a self-standing body is compromised by principles of collection and selection, there is much to think of in terms of archival usage and the kinds of bias brought to the archive and imported into its reading by the researcher. I speak here of the often unconscious levels of subjectivity that one brings to archives in reading and writing about them, and particularly the tendency of biographers, however enlightened their theoretical frameworks, to foreground those elements in the subject's life that correspond directly or indirectly to aspects of their own. Can we deny the tendency of the biographers to blur the boundary between biography and auto/biography, by writing lives that, in simple or complicated ways, address or authorize their own? A turning point for me, in approaching archives with a view to life writing, was an off-hand comment made some years ago at a conference when Gloria Erlich, the prize-winning biographer of Nathaniel Hawthorne, spoke of the way in which, well after her completion of her Hawthorne biography—*Family Themes and Hawthorne's Fiction: The Tenacious Web* (1984)[2]—she began to recognize, with considerable surprise, the shape of her own subjectivities in having approached his papers in a certain way in the course of her research and reconstruction. In retrospect it became apparent to her that, from all of the sometimes contradictory fragments available to her, she had constructed a Hawthorne family romance that in covert ways paralleled her own family history: she had selected and strung together "data" that authorized not only his behaviour but hers. She had failed to notice this at the time, she said, but clearly biography was quite simply a species of auto/biography—and hereafter she would expect such a propensity in her work and see it in the works of others. I, of course, secretly vowed never to participate in that particular biographical fallacy.

I turn now to my own work, with a wry sense of what would seem to be the failure of that earlier avowal. The papers of Anne Marriott (1913–97) are held by the University of British Columbia, with archival remnants scattered elsewhere—at Queen's University, the University of Toronto, and the National Library of Canada, where bits and pieces can be found in the collections of others. The UBC Marriott archive is small but various, and includes everything from letters, manuscripts, and journals to greeting cards, pamphlets, church bulletins, and minutes of meetings of volunteer associations, not to mention children's report cards, medical and eyeglass prescriptions, and even the dog Cassie's health records—the detritus of a busy and multiplex life. It is also incomplete, since a second accession, following Marriott's death, is anticipated but has not yet arrived. Particular aspects of Marriott's life, then, as Shields suggests, are now slotted into archival boxes and folders that contain her manuscripts, her correspondence, and various artefacts relating to her family life. The files are full, though incomplete, and her life apparently preserved, ordered, and dignified—again as Shields observed about the contours of the archival body—through the shaping of her archive in ways that invite the discovery of patterns by the scholarly reader. The patterns seen, however, will depend upon the proclivities that mark the biographer's gaze.

My own view of Anne Marriott, based on work with all of the Canadian archives that bear her traces, is of Marriott as a too little-known Canadian poet of the modernist period, despite the fact that she produced nine books of poetry, beginning with *The Wind Our Enemy* (1939) and ending with her last collection, *Aqua* (1991), which was published almost a half-century later. She has also left a substantial body of poetry that appeared in literary periodicals during her lifetime but has never been collected and published in book form. In short, her oeuvre, the substantial product of a lifetime of writing, has not been collected, and a critical biography has yet to be written. That Marriott's life and work are not better known is attributable in good part to her long and mysterious poetic silence between the publication of *Sandstone and Other Poems* (1945) and *Countries* (1971), the most obvious of the "patterns," to use Shields's word, that become evident through the chronological arrangement of the archive. That period of silence tends to be questioned by all who examine Marriott's working life, given her meteoric rise. As a young poet living in obscurity in Victoria at the western edge of Canada, Marriott had catapulted to a position of national prominence at the age of twenty-six on the strength of the publication of the chapbook *The Wind Our Enemy* (published by

Ryerson Press in 1939)—a triumph closely followed by her reception of the Governor General's Award for Poetry in 1941 for her second collection, *Calling Adventurers!* By 1945, however, with the publication of her fourth poetry collection, Marriott apparently entered a dry period, and failed to produce a single volume of poetry for more than thirty-five years. And when Marriott did re-emerge as a poet with *Countries* in 1971, it was as a different kind of poet, as a lyric poet of edges and margins rather than as one reflecting the Canadian modernist mainstream that she left, in effect, in the 1940s.

In attempting to account for the trajectory of Marriott's life as a modernist poet, I read Joyce Anne Marriott McLellan as a complicated person and poet (indeed the complexity of the name alone signifies the multiplicity of identities and the slipperiness one encounters in her archive).[3] The story of Joyce Anne Marriott begins with a young woman who was, though unknown at the centre of Canada, rather well connected to the emerging modernist community on the west coast. A member of the Canadian Authors Association in Victoria, she attracted the attention of powerful male mentors, including Dorothy Livesay's father, J.F.B. Livesay, who brought that initial long poem sequence, *The Wind Our Enemy*, to the attention of Lorne Pierce of Ryerson Press in Toronto. Well-received at that time, this long poem of the prairies—written after Marriott visited relatives for a few weeks in 1937 during the period of the Great Depression in Saskatchewan—remains powerful to this day, and "Prairie Graveyard," an excerpt from it, still stands as Marriott's most-often anthologized work. The book attracted letters of support from E.J. Pratt and from Sir Charles G.D. Roberts, both of whom were known for their encouragement of women poets who seemed to them to bridge Victorian and modern sensibilities, and whose support must have been both gratifying and helpful in advancing Marriott's career. By 1941, when she won the Governor General's Award for *Calling Adventurers!* a collection featuring verse choruses from a CBC radio documentary called *Payload* (1940) that focused on the Canadian north, Marriott had become well-established in west-coast poetry circles, as a founding member—with Dorothy Livesay, Floris McLaren, Doris Ferne, and Alan Crawley—of the literary magazine *Contemporary Verse* in Victoria in 1941, and as a contributor (along with Livesay and McLaren) to *Poetry* (Chicago), the modernist American magazine on which *Contemporary Verse* intended to model itself. She also served as an associate editor of *Canadian Poetry Magazine* under Earle Birney's editorship in the mid-1940s.

Yet, by the mid-1940s, Marriott was struggling in terms of her own enterprise as a serious modern poet. Subsequent to *Calling Adventurers!* her next two books, *Salt Marsh* (1942) and *Sandstone and Other Poems* (1945), proved difficult for Marriott to produce. Her Toronto editor Lorne Pierce was not enthusiastic about either manuscript, though Ryerson published both in the end. And, within the *Contemporary Verse* group, as Dean Irvine points out in his unpublished dissertation, "Little Histories: Modernist and Leftist Women Poets and Magazine Editors in Canada, 1926–56," Alan Crawley was urging Marriott to return to the long-poem form with which she had known much success—and not the short lyric that appeared to be her preference by this time (100). That Marriott failed to conform to the tastes of the modernist literary establishment at this time, managing to please neither her Toronto editor Pierce nor her west-coast mentor, the acute Crawley, invites speculation. Was she, as Irvine suggests, too inter-ested in developing a popular reputation—as Marriott's having published more than two hundred, often slight poems in popular magazines between 1934 and 1945 (96) would appear to suggest? Was she simply too distracted by the availability of other kinds of work during her middle years—given the fact that she was the poetry columnist for the Victoria *Daily Times* (1943–44), worked as a scriptwriter for the National Film Board of Canada in Ottawa in the mid-1940s, produced more than seventy-five broadcast scripts for CBC radio (as well as locally, in British Columbia) over the years, including many "school broadcasts," taught creative writing in the schools, spent a great deal of time writing short stories and failed novels rather than poetry, and spent much of her life patching together a necessary but tenuous freelance income?

Certainly much of Marriott's absence from modernist publishing venues (Irvine notes that she published only twenty-seven poems in literary maga-zines between 1945 and 1960 [96]) is attributable to family demands. By 1947 Marriott had married Gerald McLellan and returned to British Columbia from her brief sojourn in Ottawa; thereafter she would spend most of the rest of her life caring for a family of three adopted children and an almost blind father, difficulties compounded by her early and penurious widow-hood. Owing to Gerald's work, she spent a number of years in northern British Columbia, particularly Prince George (where she served as Women's

Editor for the *Prince George Citizen*, 1950–53), and upon returning to the lower mainland, the family relocated to North Vancouver, where Marriott remained on the margins of Vancouver's literary culture. Much of her time was spent in community work of various kinds, including leading poetry workshops for elementary schoolchildren, and much of her energy clearly went into the raising of her rambunctious, often-challenging adolescent children on her own, difficulties that are well-documented in the archive. It is quite possible that Marriott's family demands were compounded by a crisis of confidence after her early editors and mentors had left the literary scene. Certainly Marriott's archive testifies to fears on her part of unsustainability with respect to her early promise as a poet—the sense that her muse might have deserted her. But then why did Marriott return to writing poetry in the 1970s after more than three decades of poetic silence, and produce at that point a very different kind of poetry?

The Marriott archive, then, poses a number of questions in response to which different narratives—depending upon the predilections of different biographers—might be developed. One such narrative might focus on marginality, if not outright exclusion, as the central fact of Marriott's working life. While Marriott was taken up early by male mentors and had achieved much success by the age of thirty-six, she clearly fell from favour, for one reason or another, by the mid-1940s, perhaps most particularly because of her resistance to producing sustained work in the long-poem format, which *The Wind Our Enemy* had employed and to which many of the expectations surrounding her work were tied. A degree of isolation from women poets and their community ensued as well. In her early years, Marriott's close contacts with Ferne, McLaren, and Livesay of *Contemporary Verse*, her acquaintance with P.K. Page (whom she knew in Ottawa and later on the west coast), and her connections with Miriam Waddington and Kay Smith, with whom she corresponded, appear to have sustained her. In moving away from Victoria, first to Ottawa, then to Prince George and later to North Vancouver, largely owing to her husband's work and family demands, Marriott became severed, to a great extent, from the women who had formed her writing community in her early years. Indeed by mid-life, when her peers were attending conferences across Canada, Marriott, without the funds or the freedom to travel, seems to have been unable to capitalize on her relations with better-connected poets such as Livesay—who used Marriott to cover her own classes at times so that she could travel to conferences and the like.

In addition, Marriott did not fare well at the hands of modernist male anthologists over the years of poetic "canon-building" in Canada. Pre-eminent Canadian anthologist A.J.M. Smith included two selections from *The Wind Our Enemy* ("The Wind Our Enemy" and "Prairie Graveyard") in three successive editions of his *Book of Canadian Poetry* (1943, 1948, 1957), but by 1960, in the *Oxford Book of Canadian Verse*, his Marriott selections were reduced from two to one. By the time of his 1967 edition of *Modern Canadian Verse in English and French*, she had disappeared entirely. Other modernist anthologists, such as Ralph Gustafson (*Anthology of Canadian Poetry [English]* [1942]) and Earle Birney (*Twentieth-Century Poetry* [1953]), selected a poem or two by Marriott, including "Woodyards in the Rain," from *Sandstone*, while pre-modernist anthologists Bliss Carman, Lorne Pierce, and V.B. Rhodenizer included four Marriott poems in their *Canadian Poetry in English*, published in Toronto by Ryerson Press in 1954. Yet by 1960, just as Canadian literature was emerging as a field and Canadian poetry anthologies were becoming teaching anthologies, Marriott's presence as a modern Canadian poet had been virtually erased. Not only had Smith omitted Marriott in his post-1960 anthologies of Canadian poetry, but Gustafson's *Penguin Book of Canadian Verse* (1967) omits Marriott as well, and Marriott's anthological exile persists to this day. The pre-eminent teaching anthologies of our times, the *Anthology of Canadian Literature in English* series, edited by Russell Brown and Donna Bennett (two volumes [1982], abridged single volume [1990], and the revised edition [2002]), omits Marriott's work entirely, as do *15 Canadian Poets x 3* (2001), edited by Gary Geddes, *The New Canadian Anthology* (1988), edited by Robert Lecker and Jack David, and the earlier *Oxford Anthology of Canadian Literature* (1973), edited by Robert Weaver and William Toye. Women and regional editors have tended to nod in her direction, as in Margaret Atwood's *New Oxford Book of Canadian Verse* in 1982 and Rosemary Sullivan's *Poetry by Canadian Women* (1989), as does Daniel Lenoski's western collection, *A/long Prairie Lines* (1989). But none of these collections features more than a few of her poems, and the same three are habitually selected: "The Wind Our Enemy," "Prairie Graveyard," and "Countries." Her poetry collections are all out of print, with the nominal exception of *Aqua* (1991), which is difficult to locate.

Marriott's progressive erasure from the modernist mainstream, then, is evident, and her own poetry of the 1970s and after would appear to bear further witness to the narrative of marginality and marginalization that I have been developing in my biographical sketch. By this time, Marriott's domestic pressures had eased. Her children had left home and her time and income were her own again. At the same time, she appears to have developed a sense of once again having something to say in the medium of poetry—about aging, illness, death, and life on the margins. It is as if, after such a long hiatus, Marriott feels liberated at this point from earlier expectations and freed in particular from the long-poem pressures to which her earlier mentors had subjected her. She begins to concentrate once again, with increasing confidence, on the short lyric—informed by modernist interests in economy, aestheticism, and imagism—that may have always been her true but unacknowledged métier. Indeed, one might argue that at this point Marriott had finally come to terms with her own liminality, so that the marginality that had always been her bane became a boon, as she discovered a "poetics of the margin" that proved to served her well in her declining years. My own sense is that Marriott was never at heart the kind of poet her mentors wished her to be. She was fiercely independent and drawn to the imagistic lyric from the start—as is evident in the way that individual poems from the sequence *The Wind Our Enemy* can be so easily excerpted without loss of resonance. Critical expectations of long poems and poems offering regional "atmosphere" ran counter to the pared-down poems of contemplation—of brief, cool encounters with borders, edges, and particularly the strand/the sea—that mark her later work.

Such a construal of Marriott's life privileges certain elements over others. The Marriott I have presented here is a poet taken up early, then deserted by senior male mentors, most of whom served her ill in the end by demanding from her a kind of writing that served their purposes rather than her own. I have noted the ways in which Marriott was a woman to whom female community was important but, again, that this proved elusive and at best something of a mixed blessing. I have attended to her struggles as a mother, a woman for whom adoptive parenthood was a challenge (and perhaps a more guilt-ridden venture than "normal" parenthood tends to be). I see her as a woman with a too-various professional life, which was very much a part of her needing to generate income, but also an aspect of her need to involve herself in local affairs, and in her local community, from schools and churches to radio stations and newspapers—as if thereby to authorize herself as a fully engaged citizen. Most of all, I see Marriott as a woman who had to struggle to find her own voice and march to her own professional drummer. Her primary gifts as a poet were lyrical, I argue, but it took a long time for her to find and develop confidence in the modernist mode most true to her voice and her vision, the short modernist lyric. In the end, what is most remarkable about my Anne Marriott is that she ultimately managed to read her own liminality as positive, and produce a substantial poetry of edges and margins late in her life, a body of work that is, at the very least, much more rich and rewarding than has been acknowledged thus far by the literary-critical modernist establishment in Canada.

To speak of "my Marriott," however, is telling, for there are certainly "other Marriotts" under current investigation. Dean Irvine's dissertation, for example, reads Marriott very differently, and convincingly, in the context of the role of women in modernist little-magazine culture in Canada in the 1930s through the 1950s. Others are reportedly writing on Marriott as a participant in leftist discourse in Canada during the modern period. Clearly, as Gloria Erlich notes in observing herself writing a life of Hawthorne, we take from the literary archives that which aligns itself with ourselves as cultural constituents, as individuals who are multiply and socially constituted, as McGann has pointed out. While I cannot address the inclinations of others in approaching Marriott's life and work, I can confess, at least retrospectively, to my own subjectivities. Is it an accident that I see Marriott as early taken up and then dropped by powerful male mentors, that I foreground her struggle as a mother of adopted children, often distracted from her professional life by family demands, that I valorize her insistence on turning from prescribed paths in order to be true to her own sense of her writing self, or that I respond to the way in which she makes a silk purse out of the sow's ear of liminality? I would have to admit, as did Erlich—as uncomfortable as such public self-disclosure may be—that in identifying such patterns in Marriott's life and valorizing her struggle to realize herself against significant odds, I have to some extent mirrored my own life and circumstances, as if to somehow authorize myself in the process of construing another through the ostensibly objective tools of archival research. Evidently, then, archival work is fraught with difficulty and writers of modernist lives face great challenges in dealing with the literary archive, which—however it may appear to be orderly—is fundamentally undisciplined, perhaps even intractable. Two responses are possible. One is to abandon the attempt to distill, rationalize, and univocalize the archived life, to stop trying to make complete sense of it. The scholar can simply revel in the archive's seductive contradictions, celebrate its "polyphonic textuality" and "carnivalesque irreverence," as Pamela Banting appears to suggest (122). To do so is to resist the urge to subdue the "contestatory voices and counter-discourses," to quote Dominick LaCapra (132), which clearly inhere in archival records—in the interests of avoiding monologic, thesis-driven, or otherwise expedient arguments. Alternatively, researchers can confess partiality up front, and insert themselves into the archival record in an attempt to equalize the unequal relation between biographer and "subject" by foregrounding the subjectivity of himself or herself as reader. This is the response of Helen Buss, for example, who writes her own "maternal body" into her depiction of the life of Catherine Neil, as a way of addressing lacunae in Neil's "Jocastan" journal.[4]

In a sense, however, literary archival scholars are simply entering into the dialogue that characterizes historical and historiographical theory in our time. In "The Manx Peril: Archival Theory in Light of Recent American Historiography," Peter Russell maintains that in the conflict between the claims of those who see history as an objective account of the past and the arguments of those who argue that all history is tainted by the contemporary concerns of those writing it, the "relativists" appear to have won (131). He then goes on to speak of James Kloppenberg's positing of a "third way"— what Kloppenberg calls "a moderate historicism" in which "communities of the competent" write from a shared perspective, a body of cherished principles, while "recognizing that these are rooted in convention rather than timeless truth" (qtd. in Russell 131). It is a consoling thought, but one that perhaps elides "the contingencies of value surrounding the very institution of the archive," in Carole Gerson's words, the existence of the archives as a product of institutional politics and hence hardly a "neutral zone" in any sense of that word (7). It also requires a reversal of what LaCapra describes as a still powerful confidence in a "documentary" or "objectivist" model of knowledge that is "typically blind to its own rhetoric" (17). Enlightened self-consciousness and a willingness to acknowledge the tentativeness of all uses of the archive, including those that attempt to recover and re/cover lives, is perhaps the most we can hope for.

NOTES

[1] See, for example, Roberts; MacNeil; Heald; Dodge; Cook.

[2] See also Erlich, "Subjectivity."

[3] In working with the archive, the researcher encounters numerous versions of her signature. Christened Joyce Anne Marriott, she later marries Gerald McLellan and takes his surname. Documents exist signed variously as "Anne Marriott," "Anne Marriott McLellan," "Joyce McLellan," "Mrs. Gerald J.A. McLellan," and "Mrs. Joyce A. (Marriott) McLellan."

[4] Here Buss is attempting to avoid what Shirley Neuman has called the "Jocasta" syndrome—which is to say the erasure of the maternal body from auto/biographical accounts of women's lives (qtd. in Buss 200).

WORKS CITED

Atwood, Margaret, ed. *New Oxford Book of Canadian Verse*. Toronto: Oxford UP, 1982.

Banting, Pamela. "The Archive as a Literary Genre: Some Theoretical Speculations." *Archivaria* 23 (1986–87): 119–22.

Barthelme, Donald. "Not-Knowing." *Not-Knowing: The Essays and Interviews of Donald Barthelme*. Ed. Kim Herzinger. New York: Random House, 1997. 11–25.

Birney, Earle, ed. *Twentieth-Century Canadian Poetry: An Anthology*. Toronto: Ryerson, 1953.

Brown, Russell, and Donna Bennett, eds. *A New Anthology of Canadian Literature in English*. Toronto: Oxford UP, 2002.

Buss, Helen. "Listening to the Ground Noise of Canadian Women Settler's Memoirs: A Maternal Intercourse of Discourses." *Essays on Canadian Writing* 60 (winter 1996): 199–215.

Carman, Bliss, Lorne Pierce, and V.B. Rhodenizer, eds. *Canadian Poetry in English*. Toronto: Ryerson, 1954.

Cook, Terry. "Fashionable Nonsense or Professional Rebirth: Postmodernism and the Practice of Archives." *Archivaria* 51 (spring 2001): 14–35.

Davies, Gwendolyn. "Researching Eighteenth-Century Maritime Women Writers: Deborah How Cottnam—a Case Study." *Working in Women's Archives: Researching Women's Private Literature and Archival Documents*. Ed. Helen M. Buss and Marlene Kadar. Waterloo, ON: Wilfred Laurier UP, 2001. 35–50.

Derrida, Jacques. *Archive Fever: A Freudian Impression*. Trans. Eric Prenowitz. Chicago: U of Chicago P, 1996.

Dodge, Bernadine. "Places Apart: Archives in Dissolving Space and Time." *Archivaria* 44 (fall 1997): 118–31.

Eastwood, Terry. "What is Archival Theory and Why is it Important?" *Archivaria* 37 (spring 1994): 122–30.

Erlich, Gloria. *Family Themes and Hawthorne's Fiction: The Tenacious Web*. New Brunswick, NJ: Rutgers UP, 1984.

———. "Subjectivity and Speculation in Thematic Biography: Nathaniel Hawthorne and Edith Wharton." *Biography and Source Studies*. Ed. Frederick R. Karl. Ser. no. 2. New York: AMS, 1996. 79–96.

Foucault, Michel. *The Archeology of Knowledge*. Trans. A.M. Sheridan Smith. New York: Pantheon, 1972.

Geddes, Gary, ed. *15 Canadian Poets x 3*. Toronto: Oxford UP, 2001.

Gerson, Carole. "Locating the Female Subject in the Archives." *Working in Women's Archives: Researching Women's Private Literature and Archival Documents*. Ed. Helen M. Buss and Marlene Kadar. Waterloo, ON: Wilfred Laurier UP, 2001. 7–22.

Greetham, David. "'Who's In, Who's Out': The Cultural Poetics of Archival Inclusion." *Studies in the Literary Imagination* 32.1 (spring 1999): 1–28.

Grosskurth, Phyllis. "Scenes from a Regency Marriage." *Globe and Mail* 22 Mar. 1997: D9.

Gustafson, Ralph. *Anthology of Canadian Poetry (English)*. Toronto: Penguin, 1942.

———, ed. *Penguin Book of Canadian Verse*. Toronto: Penguin, 1967.

Heald, Carolyn. "Is There Room for Archives in the Postmodern World?" *The American Archivist* 59.1 (winter 1996): 88–101.

Irvine, Dean. "Little Histories: Modernist and Leftist Women Poets and Magazine Editors in Canada, 1926–56." Diss. McGill University, 2001.

LaCapra, Dominick. *History and Criticism*. Ithaca and London: Cornell UP, 1985.

Lecker, Robert, and Jack David, eds. *The New Canadian Anthology*. Scarborough, ON: Nelson, 1988.

Lenoski, Daniel, ed. *A/long Prairie Lines*. Winnipeg: Turnstone, 1989.

MacNeil, Heather. "Archival Theory and Practice: Between Two Paradigms." *Archivaria* 37 (spring 1994): 6–20.

Marriott, Anne. *Aqua*. Toronto : Wolsak & Wynn, 1991.

———. *Calling Adventurers!* Toronto: Ryerson, 1941.

———. *The Circular Coast*. Oakville, ON: Mosaic, 1981.

———. *Countries*. Fredericton, NB: Fiddlehead Poetry Books, 1971.

———. *Letters from Some Islands*. Oakville, ON: Mosaic, 1986

———. *Salt Marsh*. Toronto: Ryerson, 1942.

———. *Sandstone and Other Poems*. Toronto: Ryerson, 1945.

———. *This West Shore*. Toronto: League of Canadian Poets, 1981.

———. *The Wind Our Enemy*. Toronto: Ryerson, 1939.

McGann, Jerome. *The Textual Condition*. Princeton, NJ: Princeton UP, 1991.

Nesmith, Tom. "Still Fuzzy, but More Accurate: Some Thoughts on the 'Ghosts' of Archival Theory." *Archivaria* 47 (spring 1999): 131–50.

Roberts, John W. "A Debate on the Validity of Archival Theory." *Archivaria* 37 (spring 1994): 111–21.

Rubio, Mary. "'A Dusting Off': An Anecdotal Account of Editing the L.M. Montgomery Journals." *Working in Women's Archives: Researching Women's Private Literature and Archival Documents*. Ed. Helen M. Buss and Marlene Kadar. Waterloo, ON: Wilfred Laurier UP, 2001. 51–78.

Russell, Peter A. "The Manx Peril: Archival Theory in Light of Recent American Historiography." *Archivaria* 32 (summer 1991): 124–37.

Shields, Carol. "Giving Your Literary Papers Away." *Quill & Quire* Nov. 1998: 43.

Smith, A.J.M., ed. *The Book of Canadian Poetry*. Chicago: Chicago UP, 1943. Rev. ed. 1948. 3rd ed. Toronto: Gage, 1957.

———, ed. *Modern Canadian Verse in English and French*. Toronto: Oxford UP, 1967.

———, ed. *Oxford Book of Canadian Verse in English and French*. Toronto: Oxford UP, 1960.

Sullivan, Rosemary, ed. *Poetry by Canadian Women*. Toronto: Oxford UP, 1989.

Verduyn, Christl. "Personal Papers: Putting Lives on the Line—Working with the Marian Engel Archive." *Working in Women's Archives: Researching Women's Private Literature and Archival Documents*. Ed. Helen M. Buss and Marlene Kadar. Waterloo, ON: Wilfred Laurier UP, 2001. 91–101.

Voss, Paul J., and Marta L. Werner. "Towards a Poetics of the Archive." *Studies in the Literary Imagination* 32.1 (spring 1999): i–viii.

Weaver, Robert, and William Toye, eds. *Oxford Anthology of Canadian Literature* Toronto: Oxford UP, 1973.

As For Me and My Blueprint: Sinclair Ross's Debt to Arthur Stringer

COLIN HILL

CRITICS HAVE OFTEN called Sinclair Ross's *As For Me and My House* a pivotal text in our literature. Robert Kroetsch declares, for example, that "Mrs. Bentley...writes the beginning of contemporary Canadian fiction" (217). Ross's novel has certainly been the subject of some of Canada's most innovative and sophisticated literary criticism, and its influence on some of our best writers is well-documented.[1] As David Stouck summarizes in his introduction to *Sinclair Ross's As For Me and My House: Five Decades of Criticism*:

> more often than any other novel, *As For Me and My House* has been named by other writers as a seminal work in the development of Canadian fiction. Margaret Laurence, Margaret Atwood, and Robert Kroetsch have all referred to *As For Me and My House* as an originary text, similar to the way Hemingway spoke of *Huckleberry Finn* in American literature. Again, more than any other Canadian novel, *As For Me and My House* has provided the occasion for this country's critics to write and test the limits of new literary theory.... (6)

Much of the well-deserved attention granted *As For Me and My House* is undoubtedly a consequence of its technical complexity and accomplishment relative to most other well-known Canadian novels of its period. It avoids almost entirely both the technical fumbling evident even in some of the most canonical and overtly realist works of its time—including, most infamously perhaps, the novels of Frederick Philip Grove—and the excesses of much early twentieth-century romantic fiction from Canada and beyond. It bears more formal resemblance to much-celebrated foreign modernist models than almost any Canadian novel published before 1950. It is among the few Canadian novels of its period written in a first-person voice, and critics sometimes place it among the first novels from this country to foreground the human mind epistemologically, and to emphasize the writerly problems associated with modern storytelling. *As For Me and My House* is sometimes called the first Canadian novel deliberately to feature an unreliable narrator, to obscure its central concerns with ambiguous symbolism, and to communicate primarily by inference, indirection, and implication. Ross's critics also frequently draw attention to the meaning and ambiguity that result from his creative manipulation of the diary form, and his problematic creation of a female narrator who confesses personal thoughts about marriage, pregnancy, sexuality, infidelity, and her body image. For all of these reasons, Ross's novel is the central text in Canadian modernist fiction.

These general assertions about *As For Me and My House* as a groundbreaking and landmark Canadian novel are now almost a given, and interest in Ross's work shows no sign of abating.[2] Yet despite the attention critics are paying to Ross, it is inaccurate to suggest that his novel is truly "originary" in any of the aforementioned respects: in fact, most of its major formal, thematic, symbolic, and even modernist elements were borrowed from Arthur Stringer's almost unknown prairie trilogy—*The Prairie Wife* (1915), *The Prairie Mother* (1920), and *The Prairie Child* (1922)—which began publication two and a half decades before Ross's novel first appeared. Although Dick Harrison briefly compares *As For Me and My House* to Stringer's trilogy in *Unnamed Country: The Struggle for a Canadian Prairie Fiction*,[3] critics and writers have not yet recognized that the most written about pre-contemporary Canadian novel is to a remarkable, indeed almost scandalous, extent derived from these earlier works. Ross himself never publicly acknowledged his debt to Arthur Stringer, although he had several opportunities to do so. In interviews published in 1972 and 1977, when questioned about the origins of his first novel, he offered the now often-cited story of how he arrived at his material independently after failing in earlier attempts to write a story with Philip Bentley as the central character (qtd. in McMullen 44). In Keath Fraser's *As For Me and My Body: A Memoir of Sinclair Ross*, published a year after Ross's death in 1996, we find a portrait of a writer who is startlingly frank about most aspects of his life and career. But when Fraser queried him about the origins of his best-known work, he supposedly insisted that he could hardly remember writing it: "Ross said the only time he could distinctly remember writing *As For Me and My House* was during a two-week summer vacation in a cottage he rented with 'another boy' on Lake Winnipeg" (45). In fact, Ross only ever directly endorsed one study of his influences, D.M.R. Bentley's "*As For Me* and Significant Form,"[4] and his critics have usually shown far more interest in exploring his impact on others than in identifying his sources and early affinities.

While Ross never publicly admitted knowledge of Stringer's prairie novels, there is solid unpublished evidence that he encountered the trilogy between 1924 and 1928, long before he wrote *As For Me and My House*. John O'Connor, author of a forthcoming biography of Ross, asked him about the trilogy in 1994 and he admitted to having read and enjoyed it, although he stopped far short of revealing its influence on his finest novel.[5] While I acknowledge some striking differences between the styles and methods of Ross and Stringer, I believe that the prairie trilogy inarguably provided a blueprint for *As For Me and My House*: it is written in a diary form and narrative voice that are for the most part markedly similar to Mrs. Bentley's, and it is clearly the source for numerous symbols, motifs, events, philosophical concerns, and structural devices found in Ross's novel. I believe that Ross's borrowing has been so extensive as to require a critical re-evaluation of the contribution of both writers to the development of Canadian fiction. Although Stringer's trilogy has only exerted its influence on later writers and critics indirectly through Ross, it nevertheless deserves belated recognition as the origin of many aspects of *As For Me and My House* that critics have deemed most significant. At the same time, a recognition of Stringer's influence sheds much light on Ross's problematic modernist aesthetic and the ambiguous structural and symbolic facets of his novel that have perplexed readers, and it necessitates a re-examination of many critical statements about his work, including some by Canada's leading critics. I am not, however, suggesting that *As For Me and My House* ought to be supplanted by Stringer's vastly inferior work or jettisoned from the canon: on the contrary, a recognition of Ross's borrowing from an earlier source adds yet another layer of meaning to his enigmatic novel, and, for what it is worth, further entrenches it in a Canadian literary tradition that it has helped to shape. It is also not my intention to take Ross's many critics to task for missing an obscure if indisputable influence. Rather, this essay aims, in a general way, to expose the considerable and unacknowledged debt that Ross owes to his forerunner, and to suggest briefly some possible points of departure for a reconsideration of his novel and the critical discourse that surrounds it.

Although the similarities between the works of Ross and Stringer are glaringly obvious if one reads them side by side, it is not altogether surprising that they have been overlooked for decades. Stringer's prairie novels have never been the subject of more than passing critical attention, and for some very good reasons: they are largely sensational, evanescent, insincere, and certainly not in the same league as Ross's comparatively literary and serious effort. The few critics to notice Stringer's work have at very best offered muted praise. In 1949 Edward McCourt, writing in the first major study of prairie writing, *The Canadian West in Fiction*, set the stage for future disregard of the prairie novels by denying Stringer status as a serious writer: "Stringer's trilogy does not rise above the level of the ephemeral popular success" (78). Wilfrid Eggleston, writing in his 1980 memoir, *Literary Friends*, recalls encountering the trilogy as a young man and aspiring prairie realist: "I was disappointed in his interpretation of the prairie *milieu*, and the prairie people; but I had to admit that [his prairie novels] were highly readable, witty, entertaining, diverting..." (25–26). In *The Literary History of Canada*, Gordon Roper, among the most generous critics of the trilogy, identifies an "honest realism" in relation to "some aspects of ranch life," but regrets the absence of "a living sense of ... farm environment and the moulding effect of that environment on ... characters" so important to nationalist critics of prairie fiction in the 1960s, 1970s, and 1980s (313). And the most recent study of his work, a chapter in Clarence Karr's *Authors and Audiences: Popular Canadian Fiction in the Early Twentieth Century*, arrives at a mixed evaluation: "Stringer sought to understand modern human consciousness, particularly women's consciousness and motivation.... Known for the diversity of his product, Stringer was no mere formula writer of popular fiction" (139).

Stringer's trilogy, then, probably needs some introduction. It begins when an unreliable prairie diarist, an eastern socialite named Chaddie McKail who bears a conspicuous resemblance to Mrs. Bentley, marries Duncan McKail, a Scottish-Canadian gentleman who shares many of his personality traits with Ross's Philip Bentley. After their marriage, Chaddie and her husband, whose unaffectionate broodiness is the subject of large portions of the confessional narrative, leave New York for the Canadian west where they experience difficulty adjusting to their new lives on a homestead. Much as the Bentleys' does, the McKails' marriage slowly deteriorates. The early parts of the trilogy are packed with dated and superficial references to New York fashion, high society, and culture that are sometimes inaccurate, make little sense to a contemporary reader, and are jarringly out of place in a novel of the Canadian west. As the trilogy progresses, the story becomes reminiscent of some of the earliest attempts at prairie realism that freely combine referential and romantic elements—Robert J.C. Stead's novels of the 1910s and early 1920s come to mind—only this story is much longer than other works: for 1100 pages, Chaddie tells us about her usually uneventful life, her psychological states, her failing marriage, and her family's struggle to make a new life on the prairie. Her ample descriptions of the minute details of everyday existence, and her confused, at times almost childlike emotions are explored side by side. They are also interwoven with much superficial chatter that proves especially irritating because Chaddie insists upon referring to her husband Duncan, son Elmer, and daughter Pauline as "Dinky Dunk," "Dinky Dink," and "Poppsy" respectively. But the most grating aspects of the trilogy on a contemporary reader arise from Stringer's persistent and almost misogynist structural irony: clearly he intends his audience to snicker at his naive narrator as she makes mistakes in her cultural references, misunderstands the sexual intentions (or disinterest) of the men around her, and writes out her wildly fluctuating emotional states. At the same time, she writes inane and prejudicial comments about women of the period, Native Canadians, and Chinese immigrants. She also voices what appear to be Stringer's own derisive thoughts about women writers of popular fiction. Stringer turns her into an hysterical, unreliable, emotional wreck during her first pregnancy, which she attempts to conceal from herself and her husband, either because of her infidelity or naivety: the author thankfully leaves this ambiguous.

The similarities between *As For Me and My House* and the prairie trilogy may have been overlooked because of their sometimes discordant tones and styles. Although Stringer's structural irony generally recedes as his trilogy progresses, past readers might be forgiven for failing to read far enough to notice the obvious parallels with Ross's novel. The opening sections of Chaddie's diary, which explain her reasons for writing and introduce her addressee, are exemplary of the worst parts of the trilogy:

> SPLASH! ... That's me, Matilda Anne! That's me falling plump into the pool of matrimony before I've had time to fall in love! And oh, Matilda Anne, Matilda Anne, I've *got* to talk to you.... I'd blow up and explode if I didn't express myself to some one ... it's so lonesome out here.... This isn't a twenty-part letter, and it isn't a diary. It's the coral ring I'm cutting my teeth of desolation on. For every so long, I've simply got to sit down and talk to some one, or I'd go mad....
> (*Prairie Wife* 1)

Despite the obvious contrast of Chaddie's early voice with Mrs. Bentley's, structural and thematic similarities between their diaries are immediately apparent: both are written in a desperate attempt to cope with isolation and loneliness, both have marital problems as their focus, and both hint at the psychological instability of their authors.

There are other reasons that may account for the critical oversight of Stringer's trilogy. While Ross's novel is surely one of the most serious and psychologically intense Canadian works of its time, Stringer's prairie novels are popular, humorous, escapist fiction, aimed at the mainstream audience of their day. Karr writes that "Stringer saw himself as a professional writer who wrote to entertain his readers with his crime, adventure, and romance stories" (138). Letters that Stringer wrote to his publishers in the 1910s, 1920s, and 1930s indicate that he considered his trilogy pulp fiction, and it was accordingly serialized in the widely-circulating *Saturday Evening Post* and *Pictorial Review* before being published by Bobbs-Merrill of Indianapolis.[6] Still, his trilogy apparently never enjoyed the popular success that its superficiality seemed to promise: Stringer's letters also reveal that he was displeased by his publisher's almost non-existent efforts to market his prairie books in Canada, and that they never had a wide reception in the country where they are set.[7] Although Stringer wrote about forty volumes of fiction in his lifetime, very few of them were set in

Canada; after publishing the last installment of the prairie trilogy in 1921, he left Canada for New Jersey and effectively became an American writer. There has been little incentive, then, for Canadian critics and literary historians to look closely at Stringer's work.

The sheer quantity of material from Stringer's trilogy that reappears in *As For Me and My House* provides the most incontrovertible evidence of influence. A comparative reading might usefully begin with a catalogue of the most obvious similarities between the two works. Both Ross's novel and Stringer's trilogy are, of course, written by men, and depict, with irony, "unreliable" women writing diaries about their repeated and unsuccessful attempts to win affection from their unhappy and unloving husbands; this likeness alone makes these works stand out from all other Canadian fiction of the period. Both female diarists are pianists who sacrifice "cultured" lives to support their husbands' interests, and guiltily (and perhaps passive-aggressively) use their music as an outlet for their repressed emotions, often to the irritation of their husbands who consider it a reminder of their own ineffectuality. Both stories are short on dramatic incident, but are emplotted instead over the decay of once happy marriages, and both painstakingly and repetitively detail awkward silences, tense mealtimes, marital quarrels, misguided and rebuffed attempts to communicate, aborted and sometimes manipulative attempts to show affection, and the ever-growing isolation and alienation of their authors. Both women also indirectly reveal their husbands' adulterous affairs, and respond to betrayal with a similar sense of resignation. Both women develop a romantic attachment to an intellectual neighbour to compensate for their husbands' lack of affection and companionship—Mrs. Bentley to Paul Kirby, Chaddie to Peter Ketley—and both diaries hint at, but never confirm, their authors' own adulterous affairs. Both diarists become increasingly unreliable during discussions of pregnancy and sexual matters. Both women write of pretending to be sleeping at night when their husbands come to bed, presumably to avoid sexual intimacy. Both women suffer the death of a child and refuse to confront it openly in their writing. Both women manipulate their children similarly in attempts to win affection from their husbands, and when unsuccessful they both admit to confusing their sons with their husbands in a disturbing form of psychological transference. Both women concede their waning physical attractiveness, and remark jealously upon the way in which their husbands regard other women. Both women have fits of rage during which they almost violently berate their husbands; later they both fail adequately to acknowledge doing this in their diaries. Both women describe their prairie houses and prairie weather in a manner that is symbolic of their own psychological states. Both husbands seclude themselves in their studies in order to avoid their wives who then resent the withdrawal and try to intrude. And both novels include a character who is an amateur etymologist.

These similarities will be apparent to anyone who knows *As For Me and My House* well and gives the trilogy even a cursory reading. Less obvious are Ross's various methods of reworking Stringer's material. Closer inspection of several passages from the two works reveals not just the extent of Ross's borrowing but also some of his creative methods and possible writerly motivations. It also demonstrates that some of the much-celebrated and "originary" modernist aspects of Ross's novel can be traced back to the trilogy. On the simplest level, there are several scenes in Ross's novel in which he rewrites melodramatic material from the trilogy while diffusing its emotionalism. Both women diarists, for example, detail in markedly similar ways their rebellious acts of playing the piano to stave off an encroaching and metaphorical silence. As Chaddie writes,

> [t]he hot white light of this open country makes my eyes ache and seems to dry my soul up.... I went to the piano and pounded out *Kennst Du Das Land* with all my soul, and I imagine it did me good. It at least bombarded the silence out of [the house]. The noise of life is so far away from you on the prairie! It is not utterly silent, just that dreamy and disembodied sigh of wind and grass against which a human call targets like a leaden bullet against metal. It is almost worse than silence. (*Prairie Wife* 234–35)

Although written mostly in an ironic and insincere tone, Stringer's trilogy contains numerous examples, such as this one, of striking psychological realism. In these sections, Stringer's tone begins to anticipate Ross's, and the ironic gap between author and narrator narrows dramatically. The sympathetic passages from the trilogy are usually those that appear rewritten in *As For Me and My House*, as this section of Mrs. Bentley's diary confirms:

> After supper when he went out I played awhile. Sedately, though, with the soft pedal down, for the house sits so close to the sidewalk that I

could hear every footstep going past…. I feel exposed, catch myself walking on tiptoe…. Tomorrow I must play the piano again, play it and hammer it and charge it with the town's complete annihilation. Even though Philip slams a door or two and starts his pacing. For both our sakes I must. (18)

Although Ross's lifting of Stringer's scene is hardly word for word, Mrs. Bentley links her piano playing to her psychological state much as Chaddie does, and while Ross's version is more subtle and convincing, it employs a tone and diction comparable to Stringer's.

In other instances, Ross seizes upon what appear to be minor, under-developed incidents from the trilogy and heightens their dramatic and psychological importance. In the following example, Ross takes an almost playful incident from *The Prairie Wife* and turns it into a powerful, almost cinematographic scene that conveys the sterility of the Bentley marriage. Chaddie writes the following account of an exchange with her husband:

"You don't seem to mellow with age," I announced with my eyebrows up. He flushed at that, quite plainly. Then he reached over and took hold of my hand. But he did it only with an effort, and after some tremendous inward struggle which was not altogether flattering to me.

"Please take your hand away so I can reach the dish-towel," I told him. And the hand went away like a shot. After I'd finished my work I got out my George Meredith and read *Modern Love*. Dinky-Dunk did not come to bed until late. I was awake when he came, but I didn't let him know it. (148–49)

Ross's version is less flippant but retains two tell-tale elements from Stringer's—the awkward and rebuffed attempt at tactile communication, and the diarist's defiant act of feigning sleep:

When at last he came into the bedroom I pretended to be asleep. For a long time after he had undressed and blown out the lamp he sat on the edge of the bed. I could see his profile, motionless as if it were painted there, against the lighter rectangle of the window. We both lay awake most of the night. I could feel the strain of his rigid, aching muscles. Once I pressed closer to him, as if I were stirring in my sleep, but when I put my hand on his arm there was a sharp little contraction against my touch, and after a minute I shifted again, and went back to my own pillow. (153)

Ross's transformation of such "throw away" scenes into psychological moments of crisis—usually at the expense of seemingly more significant and dramatic incidents from the trilogy—perhaps helps to explain the peculiar combination of intensity and monotony that many critics have associated with the novel.

Other scenes from Stringer's trilogy are reworked by Ross in an effort to heighten their symbolic importance. Chaddie's husband guiltily secludes himself in his study during difficult times in his financial dealings. Although these moments are indicative of Duncan's increasing inability and unwillingness to communicate with his wife owing to shame and fear of recrimination, they are neither as psychologically developed nor as central to the action of their story as are the scenes they anticipate in *As For Me and My House*. As Chaddie writes,

> I felt a bit audacious as I quietly pushed open that study door. I even weakened in my decision about pouncing on [my husband] from behind ... something in his pose, in fact, brought me up short. [He] was sitting with his head on his hand, staring at the wall-paper.... He was sitting there in a trance ... without speaking a word, [I] shrunk rather guiltily back through the doorway. It was a relief, in fact, to find that I was able to close the door without making a sound. (*Prairie Mother* 18–19)

In Ross's novel, the silent and apologetic opening and closing of Philip's study door becomes a full-fledged motif, and Mrs. Bentley's attempts to "reach" Philip as he retreats more frequently into his private space becomes a metaphor for the problems of communication in the Bentley marriage: "A few minutes ago I knocked at Philip's study and went in, but he didn't want me, and I came away again. It's nearly always like that; sometimes I wonder why I go" (57). Most of the key psychological symbols found in Ross's novel, in fact, can be traced back to episodes in Stringer's work where they are not exploited. In Ross's version, often through simple repetition, otherwise benign incidents become memorable psychological symbols.

Two of the best-known symbols in Ross's novel are the wind and the dust that seem inseparable from Mrs. Bentley's psychological states. In Stringer's work, the symbolically paired wind and snow function similarly, but again are neither fully developed nor ubiquitous. Rather than aiming to fuse a subjective perspective with objectivist referentiality, as Ross does in *As For Me and My House*, Stringer merely uses the wind and snow to reflect Chaddie's changing mental states in an at times elaborate form of pathetic fallacy. Despite these differences, numerous symbolic passages in Ross and Stringer are again strikingly similar. Chaddie writes,

> I scratched the frost off a window-pane, where feathery little drifts were seeping in through the sill-cracks…the wind blew harder and harder and the shack rocked and shook with tension. Oh, such a wind! It made a whining and wailing noise, with each note a little higher, and when you felt it couldn't possibly increase, that it simply *must* ease off, or the whole world would go smash … that whining note merely grew tenser and the wind grew stronger. (*Prairie Wife* 176)

Ross, in keeping with his Depression-era prairie setting, reworks this image of drifting snow into one of drifting dust, and in the process all but breaks down the barrier between Mrs. Bentley's descriptions of her environment and her own psychology:

> The sand and dust drifts everywhere…. In the morning it's half an inch deep on the window sills. Half an inch again by noon. Half an inch again by evening…. [I]f the wind has been high and they have outdrifted themselves, then I look at them incredulous, and feel a strange kind of satisfaction, as if such height were an achievement for which credit was coming to me…. The wind and the sawing eaves and the rattle of windows have made the house a cell. Sometimes it's as if we had taken shelter here, sometimes as if we were at the bottom of a deep moaning lake. (97)

Ross's development of the study, wind, and snow or dust motifs, then, is typical of his reworking of material from the trilogy: he takes promising but underdeveloped scenes and images and exploits their full, psycho-symbolic potential.

In other instances, however, he does almost the reverse: instead of expanding upon material from the trilogy, he takes relatively well-developed scenes and incidents from Stringer and condenses or fragments them, thus rendering them ambiguous. One such example appears at the peculiar ending of Ross's novel, where Mrs. Bentley infamously writes that she is looking forward to confusing her adulterous husband with his newly-adopted illegitimate son: "'Two of us in the same house you'll get mixed up. Sometimes you won't know which of us is which.' [new paragraph] That's right, Philip, I want it so" (216). This troubling conclusion has been criticized by some, and it certainly invites various interpretations and psychoanalytical probing. It becomes less ambiguous, but more disturbing perhaps, when we acknowledge that Ross is borrowing his ending from Stringer: the final installment of Stringer's trilogy, *The Prairie Child*, has as one of its central concerns Chaddie's deliberate confusion of her son with her husband. However, in Stringer's work, her reasons for doing are stated more explicitly. As she writes,

> I was made to love somebody—and my husband doesn't seem to want me to love him. So he has driven me to centering my thoughts on the child. I've got to have something to warm up to. And any love I may lavish on this prairie-chick of mine ... will not only be a help to the boy, but will be a help to me, the part of Me that I'm sometimes so terribly afraid of. Yet I can't help wondering if Duncan has any excuses for claiming that it's personal selfishness which prompts me to keep my boy close to my side. And am I harming him, without knowing it.... (*Prairie Child* 36)

Although Chaddie's conscious statements do not usually make it clear, we learn indirectly from her diary that she has developed a vaguely sexual attachment to her son Elmer that grows in intensity as her marriage decays. She begins calling him her "man-child," delights a little too much when he asserts that he wants to marry his mother when he grows up, feels rejected romantically when he asks her to stop bathing him, feels sadness that she will no longer be able to kiss his naked body during bath times, and becomes inappropriately jealous when he develops a love interest outside of the family. Of course we cannot assume that Ross is implying a similar possibility at the end his novel. But the similarities between these two situations must be more than coincidental, and Ross's reworking of this aspect of Stringer's trilogy would certainly be in keeping with the submerged sexual tension of his novel.

Most significantly, several of the overtly modernist characteristics of *As For Me and My House*—epistemological writing, unreliable narration, competing subjectivist and objectivist perspectives—appear to derive from the prairie trilogy. Ross's critics have frequently remarked upon his epistemological representation of female psychology. In "Mrs. Bentley and the Bicameral Mind: A Hermeneutical Encounter with *As For Me and My House*," John Moss writes that, "[a]ll that we receive as readers is the product of Mrs. Bentley's mind…. [I]n the best tradition of modernism from Joyce to the present, reality and consciousness share mutual boundaries" (139–40). In "Who Are You Mrs. Bentley? Feminist Re-vision and Sinclair Ross's *As For Me and My House*," Helen M. Buss argues that "Mrs. Bentley's sense of herself is almost completely dispersed in the lives of others … the diary offers an excellent form to express such a consciousness…" (203). Unlike so many of his realist contemporaries, Ross was not fundamentally interested in producing an "objective" portrait of Canadian life or landscape: his chief concern in *As For Me and My House*, and perhaps his most significant contribution to the development of Canadian fiction, was the creation of a credible, sustained, subjective interpretation of the world filtered through a single human consciousness. Yet Stringer, albeit with much less success, had quietly treaded this same ground more than a decade before. Karr links a kind of awkward modernity in Stringer's popular fiction to his interest in psychological writing and the representation of female consciousness:

> The most persistent claim for Stringer's uniqueness made by critics and readers was his ability not only to write successfully, on occasion, with a woman's voice, but also to probe women's consciousness so deeply and convincingly that many refused to believe he was a man…. For readers in the first two decades of the twentieth century, Stringer's fictional women were very aggressive and very modern. (144)

Ross, then, is not merely borrowing and reworking scenes, events, symbols, and motifs from Stringer: the very "originary" modernist, epistemological, diary form of *As For Me and My House* closely resembles that of the prairie trilogy.

One of the most distinctive formal and modernist elements of Ross's novel is the tension it sets up between an unreliable, female voice, and a barely detectable second voice, or authorial presence, that manipulates the reader's response to Mrs. Bentley's diary. This presence has been described by Ross's critics as both the impersonal, detached modernist author—"[t]he author is not to be seen; the proposition essential to the modernist [is]…that he does not exist" (Moss 140)—and a subjective, autobiographical bias—"Mrs. Bentley gave Ross a doubly safe disguise of his own situation" (Buss 203). Regardless of how this second voice is characterized, it clearly undermines Mrs. Bentley's credibility. D.M.R. Bentley argues that "[n]ear the core of Ross's novel lies a tension between the Romantic subjectivity of its narrator, Mrs. Bentley, and the modernistic detachment valued by her husband…" (18). In the trilogy, Stringer, perhaps unwittingly, sets up a similar tension between Chaddie's voice and an ironic authorial presence. While Stringer's early reviewers often found Chaddie's voice credible—in 1920, one wrote of *The Prairie Mother* that "[i]t is difficult to divest oneself of the notion that it is a woman who writes so knowingly and sympathetically of the intimate circumstances of a woman's life" (qtd. in Karr 144)—clearly the trilogy is intended in part as a satire of popular fiction by women of the period. Some of the most memorable, but unconvincing and unpalatable, portions of the trilogy are those in which Chaddie voices what appear to be Stringer's own thoughts about women writers: "I was terribly sea-sick, and those lady novelists who love to get their heroines off on a private yacht never dream in anything but duckpond weather the ordinary yacht at sea is about the meanest habitation between Heaven and earth" (*Prairie Wife* 5). In other entries, Stringer undermines the credibility of his prairie diarist by having her voice derogatory comments about women that are jarringly out of character: "But you're a woman, and before I go any further you'll want to know what Duncan looks like" (6). Stringer's structural irony suggests that he is participating in the traditional modernist critique of "sentimental" women's writing that Suzanne Clark has identified in *Sentimental Modernism: Women Writers and the Revolution of the Word*: "Modernism developed its antisentimentality into a contemptuous treatment of women, who had to struggle both internally and externally with this contempt" (4–5). Whether Stringer is a modernist in this respect or simply a popular writer with a chip on his shoulder is debatable, and Ross's possible motivations for reworking his material are even more open to speculation. But the fact that both Ross and Stringer set the subjective voice of a woman writer against the detached, authorial, male perspective, and voice what appear to be their own thoughts about modernist writing through these same women, is remarkable and surely not coincidental.

These, then, are a few of the most interesting points at which *As For Me and My House* and the prairie trilogy intersect. I believe that an awareness of Stringer's work is obligatory for Ross's future critics as there is scarcely an extant critical work on *As For Me and My House* that cannot be subjected to some re-evaluation with attention to its influence: this holds true even for some of the best works on Ross by Canada's foremost critics. One good example is the case of Frank Davey's "The Conflicting Signs of *As For Me and My House*," which was published in 1992 as part of John Moss's collection, *From the Heart of the Heartland: The Fiction of Sinclair Ross*. In this essay, Davey provides a convincing and largely post-structuralist reading of Ross's novel that, among other things, draws attention to "the kinds of constructions it offers, whether these be through its construction of Mrs. Bentley, through gaps, intrusions or contradictions it allows in her narration, or through other determinations" (26). In so doing, Davey draws attention to several flaws in Ross's diary that he considers obvious signposts of its textual construction:

> Mrs. Bentley is not an etymologist, yet both Paul and his reflections on words become parts of the novel; she has little interest in ranching, yet the male sexuality the text locates in horses at the Kirby ranch is still signalled by many of the names various horses and bulls in the novel carry. The text's presentation of itself as a diary [and] its killing of Judith in childbirth evade recuperation by appeal to her personality. (25–26)

Davey is right on all of these points. What he does not realize, however, is that the best evidence for his argument is provided by Stringer's trilogy: all of these inconsistencies pointing to the fact that Mrs. Bentley and her diary are part of a larger narrative construction exist only because of Ross's clumsy rewriting of Stringer's material. Stringer's Chaddie is, like Paul in *As For Me and My House*, an amateur etymologist, and her interest in words fits seamlessly into *her* diary; when Ross makes the etymologist a secondary character in his version he creates the problem that Davey identifies. Stringer's Chaddie takes up ranching as a profession during a separation from her husband, and her pages are filled with sexually suggestive renaming (usually of people); Ross gets into trouble when he keeps Stringer's ranching material and sexual naming, but denies his diarist a logical connection to or credible interest in ranching. Stringer "accounts" for Chaddie's diary by having its writer address her friend Matilda Anne directly at the start of the trilogy, and then at regular intervals throughout; in contrast, when Mrs. Bentley chooses to write well-emplotted history that she already knows too well it appears incredible because Ross has discarded the addressee. And the children in Stringer's work are not adopted but Chaddie's own, so Ross has to kill off Judith conveniently if he wishes to conclude his novel with Stringer's theme of father-son confusion.[8]

A less-convincing argument that might also be subjected to some reconsideration appears in Fraser's *As For Me and My Body*. This memoir presents Ross's homosexuality as a means of decoding aspects of his fiction, drawing numerous and often weakly supported links between Ross's life and art. We learn, for example, that Ross's mother "used to cover up for the fact that her son didn't seem interested in girls by telling outsiders: 'No girl is good enough for him,' or, 'Oh, he's an artist,'" and that "Mrs. Bentley uses the same excuse on more than one occasion" (46). Less tastefully, Fraser divulges biographical material that he considers a likely source for the homoerotic relationship between Philip and Steve in Ross's novel. After discussing Ross's early friendship with his piano teacher—"He [Ross] and Frank [Woodbury], a reputed pedophile, used to pal around" (47–48)—Fraser makes the case for a similar situation in Ross's fiction: "It's a kind of wish-fulfilment dream for Philip to have Steve in the same house with his wife's connivance, planning his bedroom, taking him alone for car rides, dressing him up, buying him treats and a pony. Ponies, horseplay, mannish women, trunkless men, stovepipes, tobacco pipes, Hereford bulls, hands on shoulders..." (49). And if this is not ample evidence that Ross is writing autobiography in *As For Me and My House*, Fraser offers a further, accusatory tidbit: "I happen to know that later on in his life Jim [Sinclair] also adopted a boy, far from Saskatchewan, and that his experience which began ideally like Philip's ended abruptly" (49).

Stringer's influence suggests that the homoerotic and vaguely improper relationship that perhaps exists between Philip and Steve may not be attributable solely, or even primarily, to Ross's life experience. One of the most peculiar aspects of the trilogy emerges in the final installment, *The Prairie Child*. As the McKail marriage decays, Chaddie takes in the local school teacher, Gershom Binks, because "it will be a great help to Dinkie in his studies" and "the mere presence of another male at Casa Grande seems to dilute the acids of home life" (40). Over the course of *The Prairie Child*,

Chaddie develops an increasingly affectionate attachment to Gershom, while at the same time her diary entries unwittingly reveal his growing and possibly improper attachment to her son, Dinky Dink. She admits to a "subliminal play of sex-attraction ... between Dinky and me" (73) and details Gershom's similar attachment to her son favourably: "I like him because he shares in my love of Dinkie" (84). These vague hints at Gershom's sexual interest in the boy are lent some support perhaps by a later scene recounted by Chaddie:

> I stood under the mistletoe, this morning, and dared Gershom to kiss me. He turned quite white and made for the door. But I caught him by the coat, like Potiphar's wife, and pulled him back to the authorizing berry-sprig and gave him a brazen big smack on the cheekbone.... The other day Suzie intimated that he was too homosexual and that it was the polygamous wretches who really kept the world going. (250)

Whether Stringer's text is deliberately homoerotic is debatable, and it is impossible to say for sure that the Gershom/Dinky relationship provided a model for that between Philip and Steve in *As For Me and My House*. Regardless, Stringer's influence would not necessarily invalidate Fraser's biographical thesis: it might even lend it credence by indicating one reason why Ross found the trilogy interesting in the first place. But this example suggests that some past readings of Ross's fiction, no matter how easily attributable they are to what we know about Ross's life and work, might valuably be reconsidered.

I am certainly not implying that an acknowledgement of Stringer's influence on Ross will invalidate the substantial criticism on *As For Me and My House*. Indeed, as these short examples suggest, it might actually solidify some claims that have yet to be firmly established. But admitting Ross's debt to Stringer does hold the promise of explaining some of the technical inconsistencies and ambiguities of his novel that have proven most difficult for his readers. It also raises a few questions that future studies, in my opinion, might usefully try to answer. How much of Ross's ambiguity in *As For Me and My House* is deliberate, and how much is an unintended consequence of his selective borrowing? What does it say about Canadian modernist fiction that its central text, published in 1941, is in fact based on a popular work from the 1910s and 1920s? Does Ross's borrowing displace *As For Me and My House* from the centre of our modernist canon or further entrench it in a national modernist tradition? How might we re-evaluate Ross's feminism by acknowledging that he reworks material from an at times misogynist source text? Does Ross's novel still deserve recognition as an "originary" work? Stringer's trilogy, which may now be exacting payment for Ross's debt by demanding rescue from an otherwise certain obscurity, may deny *As For Me and My House* some of the privileged status implied in the last question, but it will probably do little to curb the enthusiasm of critics for his work. I hope it invites us to continue writing about the most remarkable work of pre-contemporary Canadian fiction from new and innovative perspectives.

ACKNOWLEDGMENTS
I would like to express my gratitude to several people who helped me with this article. Brian Trehearne (McGill) and Dean Irvine (Dalhousie) offered insightful commentary on an earlier and much abbreviated version of this argument when it appeared in the third chapter of my dissertation, "The Modern-Realist Movement in English-Canadian Fiction, 1919–1950" (McGill University, 2003). D.M.R. Bentley (University of Western Ontario) offered helpful suggestions after hearing the conference version of this paper, and graciously allowed me to cite his unpublished correspondence with David Stouck. Nick Mount (University of Toronto) provided for my reference copies of his voluminous notes for his forthcoming book, which will include a substantial section on Stringer. Most importantly, John O'Connor (University of Toronto), author of a forthcoming biography of Ross, answered some of my biographical questions about his subject, and furnished direct and incontrovertible evidence that Ross read Stringer.

NOTES
[1] Margaret Laurence, for example, wrote the following in her afterword to the New Canadian Library edition of Ross's short story collection, *The Lamp at Noon and Other Stories*: "*As For Me and My House* ... had an enormous impact on me, for it seemed the only completely genuine [novel] I had ever read about my own people, my own place, my own time" (129).

[2] The body of criticism on *As For Me and My House* is now larger than that on any other single Canadian novel published before 1950, and a substantial amount of this work has been produced since 1990. This contemporary interest in Ross

contrasts sharply with the dramatically waning attention afforded his most famous contemporaries: Morley Callaghan, Frederick Philip Grove, and Hugh MacLennan. For a nearly complete and regularly updated bibliography of Ross criticism, see Andrew Lesk's "Sinclair Ross: A Bibliography."

[3] Harrison rightly notes that

> Stringer in his prairie trilogy may also have made direct contributions to Ross's *As For Me and My House*. His Chaddie McKail, along with Carol Kennicott in Sinclair Lewis's *Mainstreet*, may have provided an early model for Mrs. Bentley. There is no evidence that Ross ever read Stringer; the characters touch only at a few points. Yet … one cannot easily believe that the similarities are pure coincidence. (92–93)

He then offers a paragraph-long enumeration of a few of the most obvious similarities between the two works. Harrison, however, stops far short of exploring Ross's at times almost wholesale borrowing from Stringer, and no later study has built upon his discussion. Harrison also briefly mentions Stringer as a possible influence on Ross in his entry on the former in *The Oxford Companion to Canadian Literature*.

[4] Bentley's article indisputably demonstrates the influence of Roger Fry and Clive Bell, "the principal aesthetic theoreticians of Bloomsbury," on *As For Me and My House* (18). In a letter to Bentley, Stouck wrote the following: "The other day I took the article ["*As For Me* and Significant Form"] to the hospital to show him [Ross] and he said right away that you were exactly right in making those connections between the novel and the essays by Bell and Fry…. Yours is the only essay Ross has wholeheartedly endorsed as an accurate source and influence study" (Stouck to Bentley, 9 July 1994). This exchange indicates that, contrary to Fraser's account, Ross was able to recall something more about writing *As For Me and My House* than the romantic affair that perhaps took place at the same time. Ross's willingness to validate Bentley's argument also suggests that he was not deliberately trying to conceal his influences, and that his debt to Stringer may only have remained unacknowledged because no one asked him about it directly.

[5] O'Connor wrote the following in response to my letter requesting information about Ross's knowledge of Stringer's trilogy: "On 3 July 1994 when I arrived for my final visit of that particular trip to Vancouver, Ross was entertaining a young man who regularly visited him to discuss his life and work. The three of us chatted about many aspects of Ross's life, including his time in the Saskatchewan town of Lancer, where Ross worked for the Royal Bank from April 1928 to June 1929. Ross mentioned that one of his co-workers, the accountant, had a name like Stringer but not quite that—'a variant,' he said. This comment prompted me to ask him about Arthur Stringer and his trilogy. Ross replied, 'I liked it' and pointed out that he had

convinced his young visitor to read it. That seemed to me a little odd, since there are clearly so many better books he might have recommended, so I asked Ross to clarify his own opinion of the three books. 'It was a pleasant read,' he responded. 'I enjoyed them, but I was not enthusiastic. It was a world familiar to me.' I then asked him when he had read the books, and he answered that he had done so in Abbey. I know from my research and my conversations with Ross that he lived in or near that town twice: from December 1918 to June 1920, when he was an elementary student in the Abbey Public School; and from June 1924—when he had completed his secondary-school education in Indian Head and moved back to a farm near Abbey where his mother worked before Ross secured a position in November 1924 with the Union Bank of Canada (taken over by the Royal Bank in February 1925)—to April 1928, when he and his mother left their house in Abbey because of his transfer to the Royal Bank branch in Lancer. At that time Ross would either have bought or borrowed the three Stringer books, possibly in Swift Current if not Moose Jaw or Regina, or would have borrowed them from an up-to-date reader in the town, where he was in regular contact with the minister, the teachers, the doctor, and so on. It is clear, therefore, that Ross *did* read the Stringer books shortly after the final volume was published in 1922. Ross's precise memory for place and what happened there, combined with his especially keen powers of recall in July 1994, makes his recollection about reading Stringer's trilogy no later than April 1928 completely reliable."

[6] As Stringer wrote in a 24 May 1915 letter to his publishers at Bobbs-Merrill in defence of the title of his first installment, "I have given much thought to your suggestion with regard to the title of this novel. While I am only too willing to do anything to help along the sale of the book, I find it hard to see that a change of title would eventually prove expedient.... [T]he 'Prairie' part of the title surely to city folks stands as a sign of that 'escape' literature which they seem to hanker for" (194–95).

[7] An irritated Stringer wrote the following to Hewitt Hanson Howland at Bobbs-Merrill on 15 October 1915:

> Is 'The Prairie Wife' to get *no* newspaper advertising? Or is it to gumshoe its way surreptitiously out with the also-rans and die a-borning? Whether or not your office has strategic reasons for holding back its fire I can't say, but I can say I experience a distinct sense of disappointment at the singularly reticent manner of this book's launching. (203)

[8] Davey also notes the "construction of Steve as Catholic and 'Hungarian or Rumanian'" (26). This element of Ross's novel has no apparent origin in Stringer's work.

WORKS CITED

Bentley, D.M.R. "*As For Me* and Significant Form." *Canadian Notes and Queries* 48 (1994): 18–20.

Buss, Helen M. "Who Are You, Mrs. Bentley? Feminist Re-vision and Sinclair Ross's *As For Me and My House*." *From the Heart of the Heartland: The Fiction of Sinclair Ross*. Reappraisals: Canadian Writers. Ed. John Moss. Ottawa: U of Ottawa P, 1992. 190–209.

Clark, Suzanne. *Sentimental Modernism: Women Writers and the Revolution of the Word*. Bloomington: Indiana UP, 1991.

Davey, Frank. "The Conflicting Signs of *As For Me and My House*." *From the Heart of the Heartland: The Fiction of Sinclair Ross*. Reappraisals: Canadian Writers. Ed. John Moss. Ottawa: U of Ottawa P, 1992. 25–37.

Eggleston, Wilfrid. *Literary Friends*. Ottawa: Borealis, 1980.

Fraser, Keath. *As For Me and My Body: A Memoir of Sinclair Ross*. Toronto: ECW, 1997.

Harrison, Dick. "Stringer, Arthur (1874–1950)." *The Oxford Companion to Canadian Literature*. Ed. William Toye. Toronto: Oxford UP, 1983. 775.

———. *Unnamed Country: The Struggle for a Canadian Prairie Fiction*. Edmonton: U of Alberta P, 1977.

Karr, Clarence. *Authors and Audiences: Popular Canadian Fiction in the Early Twentieth Century*. Montreal: McGill-Queen's UP, 2000.

Kroetsch, Robert. Afterword. *As For Me and My House*. 1941. New Canadian Library. Toronto: McClelland and Stewart, 1989. 217–21.

Laurence, Margaret. Afterword. 1968. *Sinclair Ross: The Lamp at Noon and Other Stories*. New Canadian Library. Toronto: McClelland and Stewart, 1993. 129–35.

Lesk, Andrew. "Sinclair Ross: A Bibliography." Homepage. August 2003. <http://www.andrewlesk.com/sinclairross.html>.

McCourt, Edward. *The Canadian West in Fiction*. Toronto: Ryerson, 1949.

McMullen, Lorraine. *Sinclair Ross*. Ottawa: Tecumseh, 1991.

Moss, John. "Mrs. Bentley and the Bicameral Mind: A Hermeneutical Encounter with *As For Me and My House*." *Sinclair Ross's As For Me and My House: Five Decades of Criticism*. Ed. David Stouck. Toronto: UTP, 1991. 138–47.

O'Connor, John. E-mail to the author. 15 February 2004.

Roper, Gordon. "The Kinds of Fiction, 1880–1920." *Literary History of Canada: Canadian Literature in English*. Vol. 1. Ed. Carl F. Klinck. Toronto: UTP, 1965. 298–326.

Ross, Sinclair. *As For Me and My House*. 1941. New Canadian Library. Toronto: McClelland and Stewart, 1989.

Stouck, David. Introduction. *Sinclair Ross's As For Me and My House: Five Decades of Criticism*. Toronto: UTP, 1991. 3–12.

———. Letter to D.M.R. Bentley. 9 July 1994.

Stringer, Arthur. "To the Bobbs-Merrill Company." 24 May 1915. "Arthur Stringer as Man of Letters: A Selection of His Correspondence with a Critical Introduction." Ed. Barbara Wales Meadowcroft. Diss. McGill University, 1983. 194–95.

———. "To Hewitt Hanson Howland." 17 Oct. 1915. "Arthur Stringer as Man of Letters: A Selection of His Correspondence with a Critical Introduction." Ed. Barbara Wales Meadowcroft. Diss. McGill University, 1983. 203.

———. *The Prairie Child*. Indianapolis: Bobbs-Merrill, 1922.

———. *The Prairie Mother*. Indianapolis: Bobbs-Merrill, 1920.

———. *The Prairie Wife*. Indianapolis: Bobbs-Merrill, 1915.

BEYOND IMPERSONALITY

Elizabeth Smart and Cecil Buller: Engendering Experimental Modernism

ANNE QUÉMA

THE WRITINGS OF Elizabeth Smart and the wood engravings of Cecil Buller tend to have a similar effect on readers and viewers. In both cases their works are discovered with a shock of recognition. The shock stems from the realization that these mature and accomplished works deserve a place in the modernist pantheon, and that they were produced by women who remained in critical obscurity for a long time. Smart's writings were rediscovered in the late 1970s, and since the 1980s a number of critical works have appeared.[1] Cecil Buller is hardly known, and there are to my knowledge only two monographs analyzing and documenting her engravings.[2] In addition, the tendency among critics has been to categorize them in ways that remain very difficult to challenge. For a long time, Smart was perceived as the genius out of nowhere who wrote that book about her relationship with the British poet George Barker, while Cecil Buller still stands in the shadow of her American husband John J.A. Murphy who in the 1920s and 1930s was an acclaimed wood engraver. Although she won major American awards such as the Audubon Artists Society award and the Pennell award from the Library of Congress, Buller died in 1973 having had her one and only moment of Canadian recognition at an exhibition of her works organized by the Montreal Museum of Fine Arts in 1957. Born in 1886, Buller participated in the earlier phase of the modernist movement, while Smart produced her novel *By Grand Central Station I Sat Down and Wept* (1945) at the tail end of international modernism.

I propose to locate Buller and Smart in the modernist pantheon by taking Bonnie Kime Scott's typology of modernists and counter-modernists as my starting point. In *The Gender of Modernism*, Scott refers to the "tangled mesh of modernists" and defines the movement as the product of dialogical relations and counter-relations among writers and, by extension, artists of the same period (10). Scott's typology crosses national and gender boundaries and can be seen as a very useful critical tool to locate artists such as Buller and Smart who, by virtue of their career choices, belonged to an internationally defined modernism. Her definition of the modernist movement allows for a subtle and dynamic exploration of the different expressions that modernism assumed in the course of its complex development. Relying on her definition, I will argue that both Buller's and Smart's participation in modernism are best understood in terms of a dialogical relationship that led them not only to endorse modernist practices but also to challenge the dominant discourse of modernism. I will consider three levels of analysis to demonstrate Buller's and Smart's dialogical contribution to the modernist movement. To begin with, both artists defined their works in relation to the prevailing poetics of intertextuality and impersonality, or what in 1919 T.S. Eliot referred to as the relation between tradition and the individual talent. Both Smart and Buller revisited these poetics by incorporating in their works a rhetoric of pathos or affect that derived from their exploration of the body. This questioning has to be understood within the context of a predominantly masculinist culture in which women artists struggled to engender their visions of the world. At the same time, their practice of experimentalism locates Smart and Buller firmly in the modernist movement. Smart produced a text, the linguistic equivalent of some of the most abstract modernist paintings, challenging naturalistic conventions of writing and reading. Buller practised a subtle kind of experimentation, balancing figurative representation with abstraction. In both cases, experimental practices result in striking patterns of linguistic and visual texture. However, we need to interpret the significance of this experimental practice. Should we see Smart's text as the sheer expression of self-referential wordplay and Buller's textured abstractions as signs of autotelic art? The groundbreaking publication of *The Spiritual in Art: Abstract Painting 1890–1985* (1986) demonstrates persuasively that the interpretation of modernism as the production of formalist and self-referential art derives from a theoretical trend that began to develop in the

1930s, and that made abstraction of the fact that a substantial number of modernist artists were from the start engaged in formal experimentation to convey their spiritual quests. Smart and Buller should be regarded as such artists. At a time when the theorization of modernism was taking a formalist turn, they produced experimental works that were motivated by spiritual concerns.

Buller and Smart display their entangled and complex relationship to modernism in their approach to an experimental creativity that rests on a practice of intertextuality, which includes the relationships that Buller established between words and visual art as well as the relationships that Smart established between texts. In this sense I extend the definition of intertextuality that Julia Kristeva proposed in 1974 when she described the novel as the product of a redistribution of different systems of signs such as the carnivalesque, courtly romance, and scholastic discourse (59–60). It used to be argued that in the modernist paradigm literary allusions and poetics of impersonality go hand in hand. The model here is Eliot for whom intertextual references were a means of erasing romantic subjectivity for the sake of an impersonal self. However, Maud Ellmann long ago challenged the arbitrariness of the association, and demonstrated that Eliot's poetic practice does not necessarily support or illustrate his poetics of impersonality as stated in "Tradition and the Individual Talent."[3] Critics such as Shari Benstock and Suzanne Clark have argued that the challenge to the poetics of impersonality originated in the modernist period, and in part stemmed from women's attempts at defining and creating gender-inflected writing practices.[4] In this respect, Buller's and Smart's works constitute a fascinating critique of this modernist poetics, which they implicitly conducted through their gendered reappropriation of cultural references traditionally associated with patriarchy. Both artists use *The Song of Songs* in their work and succeed in breathing new life into tradition by producing a gendered subjectivity that has no truck with impersonality but that has much to do with individual talent.

Buller and Smart subscribed to the trend of modernism that, from Sigmund Freud and Havelock Ellis through D.H. Lawrence to Anais Nin, Henry Miller, Auguste Rodin, Henri Matisse, and Pablo Picasso, explored the body in its relation to the self, the phenomenological world, and modernity. It is in part this exploration of the body and eroticism from a gendered standpoint that determines their redefinition of tradition through verbal and visual intertextuality. In his introduction to an analysis of the biblical poem, Francis Landy argues that "sexual interpretations of the Song are both fascinating and boring; they exemplify the pornographic desire to name and appropriate pleasure, to have it at imaginative command, and they miss the point" (305). It could be argued that a similar interpretation of Buller's and Smart's use of the *Song* indicates the same shameful desire; yet, it is difficult to ignore the fact that their representations are powerfully erotic and that they were conceived at a time when women and men were questioning the Victorian heritage concerning sexuality. So, as a first stage of my argument, I suggest that both artists use intertextuality in order to reinterpret tradition from the standpoint of a gendered vision that offers a paean to physical pleasure and plenitude. At a further stage of my argument, I will demonstrate the way in which the intertextual reference to the *Song* has the effect of transfiguring the commonplace into something unique and ecstatic.

Smart's use of *The Song of Songs* to relate the passion between the two protagonists of her novel is well known and imparts a hyperbolic tone to the narrative, which questions the model of creativity that Scott has identified as a masculinist modernist poetics. "Modernism," Scott argues, "as caught in the mesh of gender is polyphonic, mobile, interactive, sexually charged" (4). It is Smart's rhetoric of the sublime that constitutes her contribution to the polyphony of modernism. *The Song of Songs* can be regarded as the ur-text that sets the pitch of the narrative. Although the *Song* is not overtly quoted until part four of the novel, its hyperbolic style and sublime reach are already evident in the following passage from part three: "O the water of love that floods everything over, so that there is nothing the eye sees that is not covered in. There is no angle the world can assume which the love in my eye cannot make into a symbol of love" (*By Grand* 39). The tone of the passage indicates a belief in and desire for a sense of totality that lifts the self above the pedestrian level of existence. Part four juxtaposes, on the one hand, the prosaic description of police interrogation at the Arizona border where the two lovers are under arrest for committing adultery and, on the other hand, the quotations from *The Song of Songs* to convey the protagonist's intense love for the man with whom she travels. Consider the opening passage from the exchange that is supposed to take place between the police and the culprits:

"What relation is this man to you? (My beloved is mine and I am his: he feedeth among the lilies.)

How long have you known him? (I am my beloved's and my beloved is mine: he feedeth among the lilies.)

Did you sleep in the same room? (Behold thou art fair, my love, behold thou art fair: thou hast dove's eyes.) ….

Did intercourse take place? (I sat down under his shadow with great delight and his fruit was sweet to my taste.) (*By Grand* 47)

Smart's sleight of hand is to draw upon an archetypal, biblical text to challenge what she perceived as the arbitrary and authoritarian culture of modern America. To a practice of surveillance and sexual discipline she opposes a celebration of sexual love by drawing upon the authority of a text that the wardens of moral tradition usually invoke.

The surfeited style of the novel may lead one to conclude that what we have here is the immature, wide-eyed expression of love to which only young people or, perhaps, women can succumb. In this respect, Smart's narrative fits Glenn Willmott's identification of the Canadian modernist novel as a recurrent *Bildungsroman* (17): the narrator-protagonist goes through the educational experience of passionate love and ends up in the prosaic and common situation of being pregnant and abandoned by her lover. However, the hyperbolic rhetoric of the narrative is too poetic and insistent not to be analyzed in other terms. More compelling than the mere statement of passion, Smart's style unfolds as if constantly drawing attention to its effects of sublime surfeit. It is as if the style itself possessed its own meaning, gesturing to some unsaid and perhaps unsayable message.

As I have argued elsewhere, Smart's novel and diaries of the period preceding World War II herald Hélène Cixous's concept of *écriture fémi-nine* in an attempt to reclaim the power of feminine sexuality, reproduction, and maternity.[5] This is evidenced by the metaphors of ovulation, pregnancy, waters, blood, and birth scattered throughout Smart's poetic narrative. For instance, the metaphor of birth applies to the nascent love between the narrator and the lover and to the transformative effect that this love has on the narrator's perception of the world. Referring to the lover's wife, the narrator states: "But her eyes pierced all the veils that protected my imagination against ruinous knowledge, to bleed me too in this catastrophic pool of birth" (*By Grand* 31). Smart's variations on the metaphor impart a sense of linguistic plasticity. The narrator goes on to evoke the generative power of love: "it has happened, the miracle has arrived, everything begins today, everything you touch is born; the new moon attended by two enormous stars; the sunny day fading with a glow to exhilaration" (*By Grand* 40). The narrator's pregnancy, which is not referred to until part nine, is not only part of the minimalist plot; it also functions as a metaphorical expression of the narrator's attempt to create herself as a creative voice in her own right. We have here, I suggest, the key to Smart's textual mystery and fascination. The insistent, self-referential aspect of her hyperbolic style stems in part from a heroic attempt to create a narrative persona that is gender-inflected and that is threatened by masculinist assumptions concerning creativity. The paradox of such an enterprise lies in the fact that, in claiming creative autonomy from masculinist assumptions, Smart nevertheless chose to write a narrative of what may appear to our modern and sophisticated feminist sensibility as female emotional dependency and sacrifice.

However, it is also possible to interpret the intensity and extremism of the narrator's emotions as a means of achieving a sense of self that only plenitude can create and sustain. Although we tend to associate the publication of the novel with the period of World War II, we should also consider that the text was in gestation in Smart's diaries dating from the late 1930s.[6] Her novel was not published until 1945, but Smart had completed a first handwritten draft by August 1941 (*Necessary Secrets* 268). Thus her novel stands between the nihilism of *The Waste Land* (1922) and the redemption of *Four Quartets* (1943) as two of the major cultural expressions of the crisis that western Europe underwent. In this context, the following lines may not sound as naive as one would assume:

> it is the lavishness of my feelings that feeds even the waifs and strays. There are not too many bereaved or wounded but I can comfort them, and those 5,000,000 who never stop dragging their feet and bundles and babies with bloated bellies across Europe, are not too many or too benighted for me to say, Here's a world of hope, I can spare a whole world for each and everyone, like a rich lady dispensing bags of candy at a poor children's Christmas feast. (*By Grand* 43)

To hollow men, Smart proffers a vision of fulfilment and abundance.[7]

Similarly, Buller's work on the *Song* allows her to break new ground within a well-established traditional framework in a series of eleven prints engraved in 1929 and reproduced in *Cantique des Cantiques* (1931) (Ainslie 32, 34). What identifies Buller as a modernist artist is the typical way in which her creativity feeds upon an intertextual reinterpretation of a traditional text. Buller draws on a textual and biblical tradition while using the traditional block-print technique which, as far as I have been able to establish, was not frequently associated with this specific biblical text. In *An Introduction to a History of Woodcut*, Arthur M. Hind demonstrates to what extent in Europe block printing and Christianity went hand in hand, going back to the medieval period.[8] One cannot assume that Hind's book catalogues all of the woodcuts produced by Christian culture, but tellingly enough, his extensive list of illustrations does not include any representation of *The Songs of Songs*. So Buller's selection of the *Song* seems to constitute an innovation in the field of block printing, which since the end of the eighteenth century has been redefined by Thomas Bewick's innovative use of end-grain wood to allow for a smoother technique of wood engraving (Sander 15).

In addition, Buller's engravings of the *Song* present a complex relationship between text and visual representation. Combining modern representation with textual tradition, she used Isaac Le Maistre de Sacy's seventeenth-century French translation of the *Song* (Martin 41). She also associated visual innovation with traditional technique by appending to her prints excerpts from the *Song*, therefore drawing on the long-established tradition of printing image and text side by side. In this respect, Buller's approach is rooted in the practices of block printing, which, as David M. Sander points out (19), was for centuries the only technology allowing the simultaneous printing of image and text on the same page. Buller captures this tradition, which coincided with the Gutenberg era, in her intriguing self-referential print entitled *Man-Machines* (1924) in which nude bodies of men and women are seen standing or lying down side by side the large and florid belts of a printing press.

Buller's intertextual reinterpretation of *The Song of Songs* shares with Smart's literary rendering an intense sense of eroticism and lushness, as is exemplified by the print entitled *I am my beloved's and my beloved is mine* (1929–31; see fig. 1). Everything breathes desire in Buller's prints as they are irradiated with erotic energy. Several elements contribute to the modernity of her interpretation: the daring and erotic positions of the two bodies that stretch and span open; the lush and erotic symbolism of the vegetation, with its foliage opening like wide vulvas; and the texture of the vegetation that makes her visual world vibrant with organicism. Critics such as Denis Martin (36–37) and Patricia Ainslie (20) invoke the influence of Maurice Denis, Paul Cézanne, and Matisse on Buller's treatment of nature and the body. Martin goes on to identify the specificity of Buller's representations in the following terms: "her female nudes express vitality and energy, communion with a world coursing with the lifeblood of Mother Earth" (37). To my mind, the reference to the topos of Mother Earth tends to euphemize the nature of Buller's representation. Her eleven prints are in part a narrative of sexual love, representing bodies tense and contorted with desire. Her representation of the *Song* does not display the abstract purism of Matisse's pictures; instead, it stands closer to the primitivism of D.H. Lawrence's exploration of sexuality. The gender inflection of her visual art does not derive from the fact that she chose eroticism as her main subject; rather, it stems from the cultural context in which she made the decision to visualize this topic. An analysis of this context reveals to what extent Buller's visual art establishes a dialogical relation with the dominant discourse of modernism by deviating from central, gender-biased dogmas.

This context concerns the cultural world of wood engraving, its practices, and its gender traditions at the beginning of the twentieth century. Buller had to make and leave her mark on the art of wood engraving. Sander reports that in the late nineteenth century wood engraving was the purview of male commercial craftsmen; however, women were encouraged to practise the art as a leisure activity (27–28). Only in the early twentieth century did women artists emerge as wood engravers. Artists such as Buller, Gwen Raverat, and Gertrude Hermes pulled women engravers out of the private, genteel sphere into the public and artistic sphere. Furthermore, these women asserted themselves as artists in their own right and gained the respect of their male contemporaries by creating feminine visions of life and reinterpretations of tradition.

The kind of gender bias with which Buller had to contend is illustrated by a statement Herbert Furst made in *The Modern Woodcut* (1924), where he reproduced one of Buller's wood engravings. In this statement, Furst comments on what he regards as the revolutionary impact of modern practices of block printing:

Today, the artist knows more consciously than ever before, that art consists in leaving out rather than in putting in; he will, therefore[,] seek to do with one stroke as much as his immediate forbears did with a hundred. But what distinguishes him, in common with all other truly modern workers, is that he feels himself the father of a potent future rather than the degenerate grandchild of a "glorious" past. (xxviii)

The diction Furst uses indicates an unquestioned patriarchal conception of wood engraving and creativity. The same self-proclaimed masculinist assumption concerning creativity appears in George Barker's critique of Smart's manuscript for her novel. The critique is meant to be helpful, but the androcentric bias of the commentary is blatant. Barker argues that her writing is marred by an indiscriminate use of metaphorical language, and proposes a corrective to what he sees as a fundamental flaw: "You gotta put powder on and gild the eyelids and lacquer the fingernails and use a good lipstick BUT ALL THIS IS USELESS UNLESS THE MARRIAGE SERVICE TAKES PLACE BETWEEN ALL THIS LITERARY PARAPHERNALIA AND THE MASCULINE METAPHORICAL. At present you have an immense masculine metaphorical and dozens of cosmetics i.e., images vocabularies etc. BUT NO BRIDE … she is the story or drama or history or happenings or events or what have you" (Smart, *Autobiographies* 76). Barker's critique reads like an extraordinary example of the way androcentrism determines the use of language and creates gender trouble for women artists like Smart. The style of his critique is brilliant and vigorous, but it is underscored by a division of labour that arbitrarily ascribes the metaphorical function of language to man and the narrative process to woman.

Smart was writing and publishing at a time when Canadian modernists were predominantly male, as the texts anthologized in Louis Dudek and Michael Gnarowski's *The Making of Modern Poetry in Canada* (1967) and Peter Stevens's *The McGill Movement* (1969) exemplify. Her period of exile in England (1942–86) is often interpreted in the light of her relationship with Barker,[9] but it is also possible to see in it an attempt to cut loose from a Canadian culture historically defined in specific gender terms. Rather than seeing her move to Britain as a sign of subservience to her companion or as a regressive move to the old imperial culture, one might argue that Smart was trying to reinvent herself outside of the familiar grounds of the culture in which she grew up. Her dislocation proved successful professionally as, according to Rosemary Sullivan, she became one of London's best-paid copywriters in the 1950s ("Tantalus Love" 111). However, her period of exile from creative writing lasted thirty-two years, until 1977 when she published a volume of poetry, *A Bonus*, and a prose work, *The Assumption of the Rogues and Rascals*. These states of personal and creative exile are, to a certain extent, anticipated by the plot of *By Grand Central Station*, which is partly based on a restless quest whose trajectory takes the narrator to the eastern and western coasts of the United States and to Canada.

The notion that Smart's exile in Britain should be interpreted as an attempt to cope with a gendered, cultural script is reinforced by the themes that surged again in her writing towards the end of her life. In a prose fragment entitled "Scenes One Never Forgets" (1979), Smart travels back to the place of origins associated with memories from her childhood. The fragment focuses on Smart's experience of isolation from her mother and the effect that this isolation had on her sense of identity. She writes: "Rejected, I ached to please, somehow, by hook or crook. I hoped to attain praise, if not warm encircling arms; approval, a light, a look in the eye, at me, at ME, to give me a place in the universe, to confirm my existence, as I stood there shivering with doubt and fear, and nowhere to go" (*In the Meantime* 15). This passage reveals that, in her attempt to create herself as an artist, Smart was operating under two constraints. Not only did she develop as a writer in a literary field that was predominantly masculine, but she also struggled to define herself while experiencing her mother as a distant yet dominating figure. Thus Smart's selection of *The Song of Songs* is no coincidence. What attracted her to the biblical text was its intertwining of the themes of love and exile. The *Song* offered her the opportunity to explore the dynamic between the originary exile from maternal love and the narrator's attempt to fashion a creative, maternal, and sexual identity by subverting as well as moving away from a society determined by gender strictures. The fact that the mother figure haunts her final writings implies that the decision to live in exile never brought a full resolution to the problem, and that the move to England in part redoubled the originary experience of dissociation and isolation. What in "In the Meantime: Diary of a Blockage" Smart refers to as "Mother thought" (*In the Meantime* 133) signals the thematic continuum that links the biographical complexities of her relation to her mother, the central representation of motherhood in *By Grand Central Station*, and the narrator's perpetual flight from cultures regulated by patriarchal norms.

Our assessment of Smart's and Buller's contributions to modernist experimentation should therefore take account of the patriarchal bias that Furst's and Barker's texts betray. The concept of modernist experimentalism has become a critical commonplace and has traditionally been associated with male writers such as James Joyce, T.S. Eliot, Ezra Pound, and Wyndham Lewis—the Men of 1914—and with male visual artists such as Cézanne, Picasso, and George Braque (see Kenner). Both Smart and Buller participated in modernism by practising techniques of experimentation that foregrounded their gendered vision of passionate bodies.

The aim of Smart's experimental writing is to create a type of language that will circumvent linearity. Buller's approach to visual representation combines a powerful sense of the line and a keen eye for detail. In both cases, the creative outcome consists of works that are characterized by either linguistic or visual texture. Smart aimed at transforming the conventions of the realist novel at the levels of plot and narrative language. Stylistic and structural experiments in her text are motivated by the imperative to give birth to the narrator's self on the white page against all historical and apocalyptic odds. Her use of intertextuality does not lead to the erasure of personality; rather, it participates in a process of self-creation that involves the refashioning of language and temporality. *By Grand Central Station* begets what Cixous later referred to as the newly born woman by maintaining a sublime and apostrophic rhetoric.[10] The novelist who strives to capture the effects of the sublime must create a new temporal paradigm that unhinges temporal norms. One means of achieving this new sense of time is best described by Smart when in her journal she refers to her habit of producing a "plot squashed into penny size" (*In the Meantime* 140). Although the plot is reduced to its bare minimum, the implicit temporal structure of the novel remains chronological, and covers a one-year period, starting in the summer days just before the outbreak of the war in 1939. Smart's modernist experimentalism rests mostly on a practice of writing that enhances linguistic texture at the expense of the overtly linear plot typical of the realist narrative. In this respect, her text shares with modernist works such as *Ulysses* (1922) and *Mrs. Dalloway* (1925) the project of a reconfiguration of time in terms of duration that derives from linguistic experimentation.

With its succession of short paragraphs, metaphors, and similes, Smart's text yields a complex texture that borrows from the Surrealist reinterpretation of collage to effect a rapprochement of incongruous elements. Among visual Surrealists, Max Ernst remained a major practitioner of collage, a technique he borrowed from Cubism and revamped. As Gerard Durozoi explains, collage was for Cubists a means of referring to the materiality of the represented object. For Surrealists like Ernst, the role of the glued element in collage was not so much to foreground the materiality of the object as to unsettle and transform the meaning conventionally associated with the object. From a writerly viewpoint, André Breton saw the linguistic potential of this technique and created texts out of the collage of fragmented lines from newspapers (Durozoi 71). In 1918, Pierre Reverdy provided a poetics of linguistic collage when he defined the poetic image as the "rapprochement of two relatively distinct elements. The greater and more just the distance between the two approaching realities, the stronger the image" (qtd. in Durozoi 68).[11] This definition can help us grasp the significance of Smart's Surrealist style which is exemplified in a passage where the narrator expresses her complex sense of guilt towards the wife of her lover: "I am blind, but blood, not love, blinded my eye. Love lifted the weapon and guided my crime, locked my limbs when, like a drowning man with the last lifeboat in sight, her anguish rose out of the sea to cry Help, and now over that piercing face superimposes the cloudy mask of my desire" (*By Grand* 32). The passage is based on a series of tensions resulting from the rapprochement between love and murder, betrayed wife and drowning man, sacrifice and desire. The texture of the passage is reinforced by the alliteration of "blind," "blood," and "blinded." The incongruous elements, the metaphors, and the simile are incorporated in the narrative flow signalled by the pivotal "when" and "and now." In developing this style, Smart succeeds in wedding her penchant for a rhetoric of the sublime with a linguistic practice of Surrealist collage to produce jolts of novelty and defeat the lurking cliché.

Buller's experimental art in the *Song* prints does not indicate any Surrealist influence, but as in Smart's experimental writing, the innovative character of her designs derives from a rapprochement of two distinct elements: figurative art and abstract wood engraving. Her experimental practice not only allows her to create bodies that incorporate a visual code of abstraction, but also enhances the sense of texture while remaining indebted to the figurative representation of anatomy. All the major modernists who were obsessed with representations of the body—Cézanne, Picasso, Lewis, Frida Kalho, Fernando Botero—never abandoned figurative art. In Buller's case, we can ascribe her figurative approach in part to her training; as Patricia Ainslie states, Buller was trained at the Art Association of Montreal and possibly at Julian's in Paris where emphasis was laid on the study and representation of human anatomy (12). However, her prints are not concerned with realistic representation: the technique of wood engraving allows for effects of shading, chiaroscuro, and spatial ambivalence that can yield a highly abstract play with texture. With the exception of her lithographic art, which tends to create purer effects of lines and surfaces, Buller's wood prints are profuse with details and textural effects that became even more conspicuous in her prints of the 1950s. She achieves this texture by drawing upon the traditional technique of wood engraving, which includes the basic elements of the furrow, white and dark areas, shading, and the steeple effect. It is the combination of textural surfaces and three-dimensional representation that creates the tension between the abstract and the figurative in her modernist art.

In her experimentation with line and texture, Buller establishes a dialogical relation to the modernist theory of pure and abstract form. At the turn of the twentieth century Eric Gill and Herbert Furst were advocating a practice of wood engraving or xylography that would illustrate the principles of purity and abstraction in reaction to what they saw as the cheapening commercialization of a traditional art.[12] Furst's and Gill's modernist definitions of wood engraving have to be understood in the context of the evolution from woodcut to wood-engraving prints. Sander's brief history of block printing shows that woodcut printing preceding the eighteenth century relied on the black-line method whereby the black outlines emerged against a white background in order to produce a realistic, three-dimensional picture. In the history of block printing, British artist Thomas Bewick (1753–1828) revolutionized the art by reversing the method so as to allow the white outline to emerge against a black background. In the former case, the artist creates a sculptural relief corresponding to the black design against a white background; in the latter case, the artist uses furrows as a means of creating white outlines and white areas.[13] It is with reference to this technical evolution that Furst defines his search for pure plasticity: "The white line ... is the natural method of the creative artist, and as such, used by the truly modern woodcutter, whether as light or as colour value, whether for its plastic or its decorative worth" (10). Similarly, Gill in England advanced a conception of wood engraving that privileges its formal and aesthetic features:

> The graver and the wood both make their own demands and make mere imitation of nature almost impossible. The workman is compelled to consider his work primarily as an engraving and only secondarily as representation. This is a good thing, for a work of art is primarily a thing of beauty in itself and not a representation of something else however beautiful that other thing may be. (Gill n. pag.)

In addition, Furst organized the narrative of his book so as to represent a historical development towards abstract woodcutting. Although Buller was influenced by the aestheticist discourse common to Furst and Gill, the evolution of her work does not fit Furst's teleological narrative. I suggest that the discrepancy between her practice and the formalist dictates of artists such as Furst and Gill has its origins in a gendered vision that led her to draw upon the lessons of the wood-engraving revival, but also to transform the significance of its formal experimentation.

Her own gendered practice of visual experimentation in wood engraving can be brought out by a comparison to American John J.A. Murphy who, besides religious representations and literary illustrations, produced prints of bodies engaged in athletic activities. Murphy's representation of athletic bodies is heavily influenced by modernist techniques of geometric abstraction while remaining indebted to figurative representation. In this respect, he stands very close to visual representation of the Vorticist type, as exemplified by Wyndham Lewis's plates on Shakespeare's *Timon of Athens* (Farrington 61–62). But what is most relevant here is the visual effect that his technique produces: the bodies are angular and the energy that is created is one of sculptural and strenuous tension. By contrast, Buller's bodies are both tense and lush with desire. Denis Martin identifies the visual difference in terms of traditional gender binaries and associates Murphy's approach with the intellect and Buller's with sensuality (36). I suggest, instead, that we are faced with two kinds of intellect and two kinds of sensuality. Murphy produced his prints of athletic bodies in 1924, that is, five years before Buller's series on the *Song*. Both his and her prints explore the body in tension, but interestingly enough, the tensions of the bodies do not share the same origin. In Murphy's case, the bodies as represented in *Shadow Boxing* or *Sprinters* are taut with the tension of athletic effort and physical affirmation; in Buller's case, the origin of physical tension is erotic and is redoubled in the relation established between the male and female bodies. Murphy's bodies are either isolated or in situations of combat, whereas Buller's speak of bodies in touch with other bodies as well as with the broader world of nature. It would be simplistic to conclude with a binary and essentialist opposition between man's aggressive world of representation and woman's harmonious world of representation. However, it could be argued that the conspicuous contrast between Murphy's and Buller's approaches has its origin in a cultural script whereby Murphy's representation of bodies fulfills a desire for self-assertion and Buller's presents a narrative of gift and exchange.

We can further locate Smart's and Buller's works in the modernist field by interpreting the spiritual significance of their artistic experiments. Smart's and Buller's selection of *The Song of Songs* has also to be analyzed in the context of the spirituality that characterized the earlier decades of modernism and that, according to Tuchman, tended to be overlooked later in the 1930s.[14] The relationship between spirituality and modernist art is illustrated by Wassily Kandinsky's *Concerning the Spiritual in Art* (1911), in which he states: "The spiritual life, to which art belongs, and of which she is one of the mightiest elements, is a complicated but definite and easily definable movement forwards and upwards. This movement is the movement of experience, which can be translated into simplicity. It may take different forms, but it holds at bottom to the same inner thought and purpose" (4). In "Concerning the Spiritual in Contemporary Art," Donald Kuspit brings out the extent to which, for a number of modernist visual artists, abstraction did not amount to a pure exercise in formalism; instead, it functioned as a means of access to and expression of the spiritual that could result in the visual equivalent of silence—as in Kasimir Malevich's case. Mircea Eliade makes a similar interpretation of the spiritual in modernist art in the following terms:

> From cubism to tachism, we are witnessing a desperate effort on the part of the artist to free himself of the "surface" of things and to penetrate into matter in order to lay bare its ultimate struc-

tures. To abolish form and volume, to descend into the interior of substance while revealing its secret or larval modalities—these are not, according to the artist, operations undertaken for the purpose of some sort of objective knowledge; they are ventures provoked by his desire to grasp the deepest meaning of his plastic universe. (181)

In this context, Smart's and Buller's intertextual and experimental reinterpretation of the *Song* becomes spiritually significant, and their exploration of the erotic body can be further interpreted as a means of access to a transcendental state of ecstasy. If this is the case, then their experiments in linguistic and visual texture cannot be abstracted from a spiritual quest that leads them to revisit biblical tradition and to position themselves in dialogical reaction to the modernist discourse of streamlined abstraction that came to dominate the 1930s.

We can gain insight into the spiritual significance of Buller's and Smart's intertextual and experimental approaches to *The Song of Songs* by taking into account Francis Landy's interpretation of the biblical text, in which he establishes the link between the physical and metaphysical levels of meaning of the poem. "The germinal paradox of the Song," he writes, "is the union of two people through love. The lovers search for each other through the world and through language that separates them and enfolds them. The body is the medium for this search and is the boundary between the world and the self. Thus the body comes to represent the self to the world, and the world to the self. It becomes the focus of metaphor, the conjunction of differentiated terms" (305). Although our secular eyes might focus only on the erotic significance of Smart's and Buller's representations of the body and the relationship between man and woman, it is also possible to demonstrate that the transition from the physical to the metaphysical is at work in both approaches. Smart's and Buller's works both display an idealized relation between self and world that requires as its first realization the erotic relation between bodies.[15]

Smart's mysticism takes on a mythopoeic form that recalls the type of empathy with nature that the English poet Mary Butts expresses in poems such as "Corfe" (1932). While Butts relies on magic and incantation to convey a sense of unity with nature, Smart refers to the motif of metamorphosis, as in the following passage: "But I have become a part of the earth: I am one of its waves flooding and leaping. I am the same tune now as the trees, hummingbirds, sky, fruits, vegetables in rows. I am all or any of these. I can metamorphose at will" (*By Grand* 42). The key to Smart's text is the theme of passion and its hyperbolic expression. Passion is what allows the transition from the sexual love between the narrator and her lover to empathy with nature and the mysteries of creation, which can also be related to the creative passion that the narrator identifies as the power to "metamorphose at will."[16] In all cases, the attempt to create identity among these disparate levels is sustained through the rhetoric of hyperbole that transports both the narrator and the reader towards higher levels of meaning. By the end of the narrative, the narrator identifies the language of love as a means of conveying the ineffable or unsayable: "O the tumult, the unavailing ineffectual uproar of the damned, O the language of love. The uninterpreted. The inarticulate" (*By Grand* 110). While Smart establishes a mystical relationship with nature through empathic passion, Buller's mysticism rests on a belief in correspondences between the organic world and the transcendental. In "Hidden Meanings in Abstract Art," Maurice Tuchman comments on these relations of analogy and correspondence between the material world and the spiritual: "The universe is a single, living substance; mind and matter also are one; all things evolve in dialectical opposition, thus the universe comprises pairs of opposites (male-female, light-dark, vertical-horizontal, positive-negative); everything corresponds in a universal analogy, with things above as they are below" (19). This mystical sense of dialectical relationship is at the centre of Buller's representation of the *Song* and is most conspicuous in the relation established by the male and the female bodies in the different prints. Buller was also able to exploit the tension between dark and light, which the technique of wood engraving affords to the artist. Thus Smart's and Buller's representations of mysticism are in part determined by the specificity of their respective artistic media. While Smart's rhetoric of mysticism thrives on the temporal fluidity of narration, Buller's vision of mysticism draws on the stasis as well as the dynamic contrasts that engraving techniques can generate.

That the formal and geometric character of visual representation by artists such as Buller is not the sign of a purely autotelic approach to art can be demonstrated in an analysis of the triangular shape that recurrently frames the central themes of her prints. From a spiritualist standpoint, the triangle has a particular significance and contributes to the symbolic language of sacred geometry that thinkers from Hermes Trisgemistus to Helena Petrovna Blavatsky have developed (Tuchman 19–31; Welsh 66). As Kandinsky stated in 1911, "Every man who steeps himself in the spiritual possibilities of his art is a valuable helper in the building of the spiritual pyramid which will some day reach to heaven" (20). As a young artist, Buller went to study with the Symbolist Maurice Denis, and it can be surmised that she would have been exposed to the esoteric interest in sacred signs and geometry that he shared with painters such as Paul Sérusier and Odilon Redon. In later prints such as the 1953 *Memory Fragments*, Buller overtly uses the geometry of the triangle, but in the prints of the *Song* and other separate representations such as *Women Bathing* (c. 1920) or *Repose* (c. 1920), either the triangular shape is subtly incorporated in the compositional lines that delineate the setting of the picture, or it results from the interplay between areas of dark and areas of light. Its recurrence in Buller's prints is no coincidence and I ascribe to it a mystical significance.[17] The first instance is illustrated by the print entitled *Man* (1929–31; see fig. 4) from *The Song of Songs*, in which the head and the shoulders of the figure are framed by a triangular design of leafy vegetation. The second instance is illustrated by *Kneeling* (1929–31; see fig. 3) from the same series, representing a man and a woman locked in a tight embrace. The man is sitting, his legs open, while the woman is seen from the back kneeling between the man's legs. Their two bodies are enclosed by a triangular shape that begins on the left-hand side of the print as the edge of a rock, represented in white and shaded areas, and ends with the outline of the man's shoulder on the right-hand side of the print.

Critics have also been puzzled by the insertion of the final print in Buller's representation of the *Song*, which illustrates the following biblical passage: "*I will get up now and go about the city, in the streets and broad ways, I will seek him whom my soul loveth*" (1929–31; *Song* 3:2; see fig. 2). By referring to an urban setting, the print creates a dissonance with the first ten plates and their focus on the natural world. I suggest that the link between these two types of setting is the recurrence of this sacred geometry of the triangle. The principle of composition in this last print is verticality, and at first sight it looks as though Buller relies on the verticality of American skyscrapers to convey a sense of elevation. However, the chief device is the triangle: the lovers stand in the foreground in the right-hand corner of the print, and their embracing bodies are enshrined by a halo of light itself surmounted by an area of darkness rising in a triangular shape. In addition, the central piece of urban architecture in the middle ground of the print is shaped like a pyramid. Finally, as in the case of Georgia O'Keeffe's representation of *The Shelton with Sunspots* (1926), the skyscrapers of Buller's design are distorted by the effect of parallax error, which usually characterizes close-up photographs of tall buildings (Benke 44–48).[18] This effect allows Buller to reiterate another version of the triangular shape throughout the surface of her print. The recurrence of the triangle in Buller's prints demonstrates the extent to which geometric figures in modernist art exceed formalist abstraction in a search for what Eliade refers to as "the deepest meaning of [the] plastic universe" (181). In her search for this meaning, Buller uses the triangle as a means of signifying the transition from the plane of gendered and bodily existence to the plane of sacred and mystical existence.

To bring into focus the complexity and originality of Smart's and Buller's works, I have proposed to regard gender as the key to our understanding of their dialogical relationship to the international modernist movement. In their works, gender functions as a means of accounting for the genesis of their experimental art and its mystical significance. It is because of their gender-inflected approach to the world, the body, and systems of signs that both were led to question the poetics of impersonality and the aesthetics of purity of their respective arts as well as to create practices of writing and visual representation that today we recognize as both innovative and experimental. Their gendered and experimental exploration of the body, sexuality, and the phenomenal world offers a mystical vision of life that takes matter as the point of origin in a quest for spiritual meaning. It is this gender inflection that in part defines Smart's and Buller's contribution to the historical development of Canadian modernism.

In 1984 Barbara Godard argued that the deleting of women writers from the history of Canadian literature had led to the erasure of modernism in Canadian literature ("Ex-centriques" 64). Today, by reappraising artists such as Smart and Buller, one is able to do some archaeological work in Canadian modernism and its international ramifications. Buller and Smart were gifted and active participants in the international development of modernism. Like Emily Carr and Sara Jeanette Duncan, they were privileged to shuttle between the American and European continents as well as Britain, and this enabled them to acquire an informed and wide knowledge of modernist developments. To some extent, and perhaps ironically, their unusual and difficult artistic progress illustrates what in his essay "Eclectic Detachment: Aspects of Identity in Canadian Poetry" A.J.M. Smith calls the "eclectic" poet who is able to draw on diverse cultures and traditions (23). Smart and Buller achieved this eclecticism while engaging dialogically with some of the fundamental tenets of modernism. Their ability to have access to the multiplicity and complexity of modernism is something that is singular and specific to Canadian modernism. On account of its historical links with Britain and Europe and of an identity irretrievably shaped by the presence of the United States, Canadian culture has functioned like an international linchpin. This international awareness, which should be regarded as the counterpart to the nationalist and regionalist characteristics of Canadian art, functions as a constitutive and defining criterion of Canadian modernism.

Figure 1. Cecil Buller, *Song of Solomon: I am my beloved's and my beloved is mine; he browses among the lilies* (1929–31).[19]

Figure 2. Cecil Buller, *Song of Solomon: I will get up now and go about the city, in the streets and broad ways, I will seek him whom my soul loveth* (1929–31).

Figure 3. Cecil Buller, *Song of Solomon: Kneeling* (1929–31).

Figure 4. Cecil Buller, *Song of Solomon*: *Man* (1929–31).

NOTES

[1] Some of the major articles and essays include Oliver; Godard, "Transgressions"; Sand; Van Wart, "*By Grand*" and "Life"; Lobdell; Horne; Heaps; Podnieks; Sullivan; and Walton.

[2] See Ainslie; Martin.

[3] Ellmann argues that the "difficulty is that Eliot and Pound both advocate impersonality (though Eliot more tenaciously than Pound), yet both resist its implications, too. Their theory diverges from their practice, but the theory also contradicts itself: and they often smuggle personality back into their poetics in the very terms that they use to cast it out" (2–3).

[4] Benstock argues that "female Modernism challenged the white, male, heterosexual ethic underlying the Modernist aesthetic of 'impersonality' (e.g., the transformation of the textual 'I' from the personal to the cultural)" (21). Referring to American modernism, Suzanne Clark states that "modernist women worked to change gendered identity within writing; we should not risk missing the extent to which *women* were the modernist revolutionaries" (8).

[5] See Quéma; see also Heaps.

[6] In her edition of Smart's journals, Alice Van Wart notes the evolution of the style of Smart's writing. As early as March 1937, Smart wrote an entry in a style that heralds what was to become her signature: "Red whips of the willow. Soft earthy red—against live green. O that I were a poet—such conglomerating, life form surfeit, running richly waste. I begin to see life—however little I know. Knowledge now—wisdom distilled—sudden understanding. But ah! Inarticulate—urgent sympathy unsaid—lame uttered, in vain. Never conveyed. Write, speak, search. The Word—in the beginning was the Word" (*Necessary Secrets* 165).

[7] Heather Walton compares Smart's vision to H.D.'s and Virginia Woolf's and argues that "these women were well known for their radical vision and innovative writing styles. They also found the female body to be a possible alternative location from which to contemplate the conflict and imagine a future very different from the bloody regeneration of masculinist values assumed to take place after the slaughter of the sons" (47).

[8] According to Herbert Furst, the earliest known woodcut is to be found in the frontispiece of a Chinese text of a Sanskrit book (11). Other non-biblical narratives illustrated in block print include Aesop's fables, Bocaccio's stories, Petrarch's poems, Dante's *Inferno*, and the Danse Macabre.

[9] In *By Heart*, Rosemary Sullivan comments on Smart's departure from Canada in the following terms: "Certainly she wanted to protect her parents from her infamy

and she dreaded the consequences [of her mother's] discovery of her 'illegitimate' children. But she may have also wanted to get George [Barker] to England, away from Jessica" (197). In "Tantalus Love," Sullivan states, "At a time when civilian travel was severely restricted, Elizabeth managed to book passage to England. She was fleeing Barker and family. But he soon followed" (111).

[10] In "The Newly Born Woman," Cixous shares with Smart a dithyrambic conception of gendered writing, as exemplified in the following passage: "Writing is working; being worked; questioning (in) the between (letting oneself be questioned) of same *and of* other without which nothing lives; undoing death's work by willing the togetherness of one-another, infinitely charged with a ceaseless exchange of one with another—not knowing one another and beginning again only from what is most distant, from self, from other, from the other within. A course that multiplies transformations by the thousands" (43).

[11] In his 1924 *Surrealist Manifesto*, Breton modified the formula in the following terms: "The two terms of the image are not deduced one from the other by the mind *with a view to* the necessary spark ... they are the simultaneous products of the activity I will call surrealist, and reason confines itself to the recognition and appreciation of this luminous phenomenon" (qtd. in Durozoi 71). In her journals, Smart records her acquaintance with Wolfgang Paalen who participated in Surrealist exhibitions in New York, London, and Paris in 1936. He also organized with César Moro an international Surrealist exhibition at the Galeria de Arte Mexicano in Mexico City in 1940, and was a cofounder of the mystical group Dynaton ("Biography" 1–2). In 1944–45, Paalen painted pictures such as *The Cosmogons* (Tuchman 48).

[12] Incidentally, Sander sheds a different light on the relation between commercialization and the techniques of woodcuts that allowed the printing media to produce high-quality and visually precise reproductions of commodities in newspapers and magazines (20–21).

[13] Sander describes Bewick's revolutionary approach in the following terms: "Instead of thinking of the surface of the block as white on which black lines were to be drawn, Bewick thought of the block as black and the lines as white, used to lighten the areas that were not meant to be black. His tones were composed of white lines, his textures were white lines, all in a kind of short-hand to get his ideas onto the block as rapidly as possible" (16).

[14] Tuchman indicates that "few abstract artists in either Europe or America during the 1930s were involved with spiritual issues.... A strong international trend toward streamlined design and various forms of utilitarianism ... helped to make something as apparently useless as the occult seem trivial or counterproductive" (47).

[15] Walton establishes a parallel between Smart's approach to "sensual mysticism" and Luce Irigaray who states in *Marine Lover of Friedrich Nietzsche* that love "is

the vehicle which permits a passage between the sensible and the transcendent, sensible and intelligible, mortal and immortal, above and below, immanent and transcendent" (qtd. in Walton 48).

[16] In this she reinforces the original meaning of the *Song* in which, as Landy argues, "the union of lovers is … a means for the discovery of a common identity between discrete terms; it is a metaphor for the poetic process" (306).

[17] Martin proposes another interpretation: "The compositions' triangular architecture, their format and layout, the rendering of solid space, seem to issue from a search reminiscent of Cézanne's lessons on the solidity and density of natural forms in space—notably the cone" (41).

[18] Eisenstaedt defines parallax error in the following terms: "the difference between the image as seen by the picture-taking lens and by the photographer looking through the camera's viewing system. This slight difference is most apparent when the camera-to-subject distance is short. The only viewing systems completely free of parallax error are those in which you view directly through the picture-taking lens" (175).

[19] Buller's *Song of Solomon* prints reproduced by permission of Dr. Sean B. Murphy.

WORKS CITED

Ainslie, Patricia. *Cecil Buller: Modernist Printmaker*. Calgary: Glenbow Museum, 1989.

Benke, Britta. *Georgia O'Keeffe*. Köln: Taschen, 2000.

Benstock, Shari, ed. *The Private Self: Theory and Practice of Women's Autobiographical Writings*. Chapel Hill: U of North Carolina P, 1988.

"Biography." *Paalen-Archiv*. 16 January 2004. <http://www.paalen-archiv.com/en/literatur/Biographical-Chronology-WP.pdf >.

Buller, Cecil. *Song of Solomon: I am my beloved's and my beloved is mine; he browses among the lilies*.1929–31. Musée National des Beaux-Arts du Québec, Québec.

———. *Song of Solomon: I will get up now and go about the city, in the streets and broad ways, I will seek him whom my soul loveth*. 1929–31. Musée National des Beaux-Arts du Québec, Québec.

———. *Song of Solomon: Kneeling*. 1929–31. Musée National des Beaux-Arts du Québec, Québec.

———. *Song of Solomon: Man*. 1929–31. Musée National des Beaux-Arts du Québec, Québec.

Chamberlain, Walter. *Manual of Wood Engraving*. London: Thames and Hudson, 1978.

Cixous, Hélène. "The Newly Born Woman." *The Hélène Cixous Reader*. Ed. Susan Sellers. London: Routledge, 1994. 35–45.

Clark, Suzanne. *Sentimental Modernism: Women Writers and the Revolution of the Word*. Bloomington: Indiana UP, 1991.

Dudek, Louis, and Michael Gnarowski, eds. *The Making of Modern Poetry in Canada: Essential Articles on Contemporary Canadian Poetry in English*. Toronto: Ryerson, 1967.

Durozoi, Gérard. *History of the Surrealist Movement*. Trans. Alison Anderson. Chicago and London: U of Chicago P, 2002.

Eisenstaedt, Alfred. *Einsenstaedt's Guide to Photography*. New York: Viking, 1978.

Eliade, Mircea. "The Sacred and the Modern Artist." *Art, Creativity, and the Sacred: An Anthology in Religion and Art*. Ed. Diane Apostolos-Cappadona. New York: Crossroad, 1984. 179–83.

Eliot, T.S. "Tradition and the Individual Talent." 1919. *The Sacred Wood: Essays on Poetry and Criticism*. London: Methuen, 1934. 47–59.

Ellmann, Maud. *The Poetics of Impersonality: T.S. Eliot and Ezra Pound*. Cambridge: Harvard UP, 1987.

Farrington, Jane. *Wyndham Lewis*. London: Lund Humphries, 1980.

Furst, Herbert. *The Modern Woodcut*. New York: Dodd, Mead, 1924.

Gill, Eric. Introduction. *Wood Engraving*. By R.J. Beedham. London: Ditchling, 1921. <http://www.woodblock.com/encyclopedia/entries/011_11/intro.html>.

Godard, Barbara. "Ex-centriques, Eccentric, Avant-Garde: Women and Modernism in the Literatures of Canada." *Room of One's Own* 8.4 (Jan. 1984): 57–75.

———. "Transgressions." *Fireweed* 5.6 (1979–80): 120–29.

Heaps, Denise A. "The Inscription of 'Feminine Jouissance' in Elizabeth Smart's *By Grand Central Station I Sat Down and Wept*." *Studies in Canadian Literature* 19.1 (1994): 142–55.

Hind, Arthur M. *An Introduction to a History of Woodcut*. 2 vols. New York: Dover, 1963.

Horne, Dee. "Elizabeth Smart's Novel-Journal." *Studies in Canadian Literature* 16.2 (1991): 128–46.

Kandinsky, Wassily. *Concerning the Spiritual in Art*. 1911. Trans. M.T.H. Sadler. New York: Dover, 1977.

Kenner, Hugh. *The Pound Era: The Age of Ezra Pound, T.S. Eliot, James Joyce and Wyndham Lewis*. London: Faber and Faber, 1975.

Kristeva, Julia. *La révolution du langage poétique*. Paris: Seuil, 1974.

Kuspit, Donald. "Concerning the Spiritual in Contemporary Art." *The Spiritual in Art* 313–25.

Landy, Francis. "The Song of Songs." *The Literary Guide to the Bible*. Ed. Robert Alter and Frank Kermode. Cambridge: The Belknap P of Harvard UP, 1987. 305–19.

Lobdell, David. "Eros in the Age of Anxiety: Elizabeth Smart and Louise Maheux-Forcier." *Essays on Canadian Writing* 40 (spring 1990): 57–79.

Martin, Denis. *Husband and Wife: The Wood Engravings of John J.A. Murphy and Cecil Buller*. Quebec City: Musée du Québec, 1997.

Oliver, Michael B. "Elizabeth Smart: Recognition." *Essays on Canadian Writing* 12 (1978): 106–33.

Podnieks, Elizabeth. "'Keep Out/Keep Out/Your Snooting Snout…' The Irresistible Journals of Elizabeth Smart." *AB: Auto-Biography Studies* 11.1 (spring 1996): 56–81.

Quéma, Anne. "The Passionate and Sublime Modernism of Elizabeth Smart." Proceedings of "'Wider boundaries of daring': The Modernist Impulse in Canadian Women's Poetry." University of Windsor, Windsor, on, October 2001. Ed. Barbara Godard and Di Brandt. Toronto: utp, forthcoming.

Sand, Cy-Thea. "The Novels of Elizabeth Smart: Biological Imperialism and the Trap of Language." *Canadian Woman Studies* 5.1 (fall 1983): 11–14.

Sander, David M. *Wood Engraving: An Adventure in Printmaking*. New York: Viking, 1978.

Smart, Elizabeth. *Autobiographies*. Ed. Christina Burridge. Vancouver: Tanks, 1987.

———. *By Grand Central Station I Sat Down and Wept*. London: Flamingo, 1992.

———. *In the Meantime*. Ed. Alice Van Wart. Toronto: Deneau, 1984.

———. *Necessary Secrets: The Journals of Elizabeth Smart*. Ed. Alice Van Wart. Toronto: Deneau, 1988.

Smith, A.J.M. "Eclectic Detachment: Aspects of Identity in Canadian Poetry." *Towards a View of Canadian Letters*. Vancouver: ubc P, 1973. 22–30.

The Spiritual in Art: Abstract Painting 1890–1985. Los Angeles: Los Angeles County Museum of Art; New York: Abbeville, 1986.

Stone, Reynolds. *The Wood Engravings of Gwen Raverat*. London: Faber and Faber, 1959.

Sullivan, Rosemary. *By Heart. Elizabeth Smart: A Life*. Toronto: Penguin, 1992.

———. "Tantalus Love." *Labyrinth of Desire*. Toronto: Harper Flamingo, 2001. 102–13.

Tuchman, Maurice. "Hidden Meanings in Abstract Art." *The Spiritual in Art* 17–61.

Van Wart, Alice. "*By Grand Central Station I Sat Down and Wept*: The Novel as a Poem." *Studies in Canadian Literature* 11.1 (spring 1986): 38–51.

———. "'Life out of Art': Elizabeth Smart's Early Journals." *Essays on Life Writing: From Genre to Critical Practice*. Toronto: utp, 1992. 21–27.

Walton, Heather. "Extreme Faith in the Work of Elizabeth Smart and Luce Irigaray." *Literature and Theology* 16.1 (Mar. 2002): 40–50.

Welsh, Robert P. "Sacred Geometry: French Symbolism and Early Abstraction." *The Spiritual in Art* 63–87.

Willmott, Glenn. *Unreal Country: Modernity in the Canadian Novel in English*. Montreal and Kingston: McGill-Queen's UP, 2002.

The Hunger To Be Seen: *The Mountain and the Valley*'s Modernist New Eyes

MEDRIE PURDHAM

It was as if you'd been given eyes for the first time; your first sight was met by the teeming insatiable hunger to be seen, of everything there was.

—Ernest Buckler, *The Mountain and the Valley* (285)

IN THE LAST pages of Ernest Buckler's 1952 novel, *The Mountain and the Valley*, the protagonist is accosted by the spectacle of his world made marvelously, simultaneously, explicit. As he draws near to the summit of the mountain he has been attempting to climb since boyhood, David Canaan approaches the omniscient point of view and the panoramic vision "towards which his entire being has been tending" (Bhojwani 108). At thirty, David has exhausted his own life in the valley, and lost the shape and form of his experience. He has cherished every detail of his Annapolis Valley childhood, bringing his unflagging attention to everything: the texture of squaw-blossoms, the interstices of the window-screen, the minute expressive shifts on the faces of others. But he has also jealously collected his perceptions in the spirit of an "inviolab[le]" secrecy that has progressively alienated him from his family and dissolved his sense of his own integrity (146). *The Mountain and the Valley* portrays in David an artistic imagination that is obsessed with evoking a vision that is (impossibly) *both* particular and essential, illuminating *everything there was*, and, in the novel's frequent formulation, *how it was with everything*.[1] The epigraph above presents David's vision of a landscape that meets his "first sight" rushingly and overwhelms him with its infinite demand for representation. Of course, it also reveals, with a disingenuous objectivity, the artist's own "hunger to be seen," as David senses himself becoming increasingly invisible against the morass of everything that lies outside him; moments later, he lies dead beneath a heap of snow.[2]

In Buckler's handling of the "hunger to be seen, of everything," two connected issues emerge that confirm *The Mountain and the Valley*'s importance in the canon of Canadian modernism. First, the novel expresses the struggle of the artist-protagonist to rise to a sense of real presence. David Canaan's own bid for visibility against a world that teems with particularity produces a "crisis of the subject" in which the protagonist's desperation to assert himself makes him "selfish" (Eysteinsson 27; Barbour 72) without ever being self-possessed. Second, the conflicting demand to be seen that appears to emanate directly from the object-world itself suggests the modernist imperative to "reflect the character of phenomena with fidelity" (Ortega y Gasset 13). Damagingly, Buckler's artist *identifies* the infinite presence of the object-world with a kind of distended self-concept, perhaps because he has always sought in himself a "condition for universality" that mimics modernist impersonality (223). At stake in the "awful challenge" of seeing everything precisely and without omission is nothing less than the integrity of the self: "it was as if, in having neglected to perceive *every*-thing exactly, he had been guilty of making the object, as well as himself, incomplete" (273; original emphasis). And nothing can accommodate the breadth of this objectively faithful and infinitely self-creating vision except the collapse of time.

If, as Henri Bergson lectured a century ago, "time is what prevents everything from being given all at once" (qtd. in Cohen iii–iv), then David's temporal sense is suppressed in his impression of the world's total *givenness,* the final vision that expressively extends his lifelong patterns of perception. Buckler shows that David's overdetermined seeing is crippling to his sense of self, especially as it bars him from a natural time-conception. Identity depends upon the sense of temporal persistence, which is each person's intuition that he or she changes but remains identical with past selves. Buckler's novel illustrates, crucially for Canadian modernism, a recurrent and often provocatively absolute contest between space and time, between the aesthetic experience and the temporally-constituted sense of self. Buckler explores, on one hand, the modern novelist's obligation *to look at everything* accurately, and, on the other hand, the personalist impulse to obey the intuitive device of sense-making that Bergson identifies as the blind, subjective feeling of *duration.* Glenn Willmott proposes a similar binary when he suggests that the modernist English-Canadian novel in general and the *Bildungsroman* in particular seeks out an expression of "the authority of experience" (29) that inevitably pits the impetus towards abstraction against the urge towards empathy (52).[3] These terms, borrowed from expressionist theorist Wilhelm Worringer, oppose perception and intuition. Worringer suggests that modern art's prizing of perception and *form* redresses a primitive dread of extended space. For Worringer and his followers (notably Joseph Frank), modernist art aspires to "timelessness" in its high evaluation of the "instantaneous aesthetic experience" (Tate viii–ix). A certain strain of Buckler criticism, offering epiphanic and transcendental readings of the novel's close and avowals of impersonality in the novel's style, supports the idea of the novel's deliberate movement towards timelessness.

This essay, on the other hand, seeks to restore temporal being and representation as the real issues of *The Mountain and the Valley*. The novel's teeming world and effusive style abstract time in such a way that the self is conspicuously distended. The motor of David Canaan's overactive perception is a fear of change and death; his emphatic seeing reflects his mistaken belief that time can be controlled through attention and that he can circumvent loss. It appears that David is trapped by the "cold physics of time" itself, as Bruce Macdonald argues (205), but the greater threat to David's identity is his determinedly inauthentic experience of time. Intense visual experience becomes a consolation and eventually a device to David as he loses that which, to a point, defines and circumscribes his life: his family bonds. Over the years, the family naturally disperses: David's twin sister Anna moves away and marries; his brother Chris falls into the rhythms of valley life; his parents Martha and Joseph die; his grandmother Ellen grows forgetful and remote. In light of his growing isolation, David's deliberate and increasingly self-conscious attempts to make the moment "brim over" with unreflective sensation preserve, artificially, the "texture of youth" (227). David's perceptual thirst is not for long an innocent mode of seeing that embraces "new" experience. It represents, rather, his insulation of himself against a fear, precociously manifested, of the possible exhaustion of *all* experience. David staves off some future moment of reflection or performance by overwhelming himself with perception. Over the course of the novel his visual experience becomes a perverse strategy of deferring self-realization and keeping his world artificially "new." Buckler's David consciously pursues a vision of the world's totality, but also unconsciously mitigates it. Buckler offers us an original nuance on modernist impersonality and the practice of "suspending the process of individual reference temporarily until the entire pattern of internal references can be apprehended as a unity" (Frank 13). Damagingly, Buckler's protagonist *seeks out* an unintegrable, unassimilable vision of the world in order to *avoid* the consolidation and limitation of his own identity.

Marta Dvorak's meticulous study of the rhetorical strategy of accumulation in the novel suggests that Buckler's style conveys an "ontological vehemence" or an insistence on immediacy and "there-ness." Dvorak argues that Buckler's realism is held in tension with an impersonal idealism by which David finally becomes the "clear eye of the world" a sensible seer who overcomes the boundaries of his own personality to fuse his own subjectivity with the world of objects (72). But I find that Buckler's strategic presentation of David as the (unselective) "eye of the world" in every case reveals a subjectivity so persistently under-realized that it cannot properly be *overcome*. And wherever Buckler's own style is impressionistic, responding to reality as a "continuous mass of presentation" (Schwartz 32), the reader tangibly feels the lack of equilibrium between the world and the "organizing" consciousness. In a passage that goes so far as to present the day as an "unwithheld entirety" (113), Buckler's speaker is remote but straining for presence, unidentified and yet obtrusive. Buckler creates a sense, not quite of "there-ness" (as a crux of time, place, and *self*), but of the world's total *appearance*. The passage is self-consciously superficial, dwelling on the "faces" and facets of things, their spatiality, and their formal patterning:

> [...] [T]he albino light, simmering patiently in the aspic air like a sound after the ear for it is gone, lacquered [the squaw weed and the goldenrod] like the shells of the pumpkins piled before the shop. It hung clearly and expandingly between the branches of the chestnut tree before the house, bare now as a tree a child draws. The bones of the tree seemed to have a luminosity of their own. It diamonded the bits of glass on the ground, prodigally and sadly, because it would not come again. It furred a strand of the wire fence with light distilled pure and memoryless from the light of summer [...] The pasture decayed gently, lingering after sentience, and lacquered after death with the wistful fall-stain: the burning red of the hardhacks, the blood-red of

the wild-rose berries, and the age-brown of the wafered alder leaves. The mud of the mountain road flaked like a pie crust. But wherever a puddle remained in the ruts from last night's rain the yellow light sought it as a mirror. It looked for its own face but made no image but the bright reflection of its own transparency [...]. (112)

This is a perturbed omniscience. The personality of the speaker obtrudes in the passage's verbal coinages ("expandingly," "diamonded," "furred"), suggesting David's own naive relationship to language, but it is concealed again in the sheer quantity of observation and the apparently omniscient perspective. The speaker *aspires* to a visionary omniscience and non-identity in pursuit of the neutrality, "transparency," and compass of the light's own nature and reach, but neither the speaker's omniscience, nor his subjective *"there-ness"* is fully established. Buckler's use of the descriptive terms "aspic," "lacquered," and "diamonded" seems to imitate the hard, clean, impersonal perceptions of modernism. The "luminosity" of the stark bones of the tree may refer to Stephen Dedalus's requirement that the object of (modernist) attention is "luminously apprehended self-bounded and selfcontained against the expanse of space and time which is not it" (Joyce 230). The speaker is too purely an *observer* to really convey a sense of immediacy. And yet, the passage never achieves the restraint of high-modernist objectivity, either. The speaker's "eye" never comes to rest on an image in such a way to suggest that, as Pound would have it, "the natural object is always the adequate symbol" (Levenson 110). Without a sense of the sufficiency of the percept, the narrator is driven to further and further acts of attention; the passage quoted above continues at some length. Though the narrator seeks to present himself as "transparent" and "memoryless" and "albino" and "pure" as the scene, the visible non-fulfillment of this intention emphasizes the subject's more intuitive struggle to declare itself, just as the fugitive light "look[s] for its own face" (112).

In Buckler's more typical style, the narration seems to express the private movements of David's *own* consciousness, which likewise appears disconcertingly unlimited. In such instances, the narrative conveys, in almost Pater-esque fashion, David's life of "constant and eager observation" (Pater 249) and boundless free association. Now the narrative is not impersonal but radically *personal*, engulfing everything in a voracious subjectivity.[4] Any one of David's experiences will find dozens of analogies in memory, generating *lateral* associations that occur to David *"like the figures of space"* (75; emphasis added). Early in the novel, he plays a starring role in a play. He feels a sweeping pleasure in being the one to show his family and neighbours (none of whom share his artistic temperament) his ability to transform everything imaginatively. He describes the encompassing "shine" that goes "out over everything" as he creates himself onstage as the object of everyone's attention. Buckler portrays the movements of David's mind as "glimpsed" and, pointedly, "not time-taking" (75). In spatializing David's memories and moods, Buckler denaturalizes David's thought and reveals the degree of self-abstraction implicit even in what appears to be a deeply interior passage:

> A shine [...] went out over everything now.
> None of this was consecutive and time-taking like thought. It was glimpsed instantaneously, like the figures of space. And orchestrated in the subliminal key of memory: cold water reaching to the roots of his tongue when thirst in the haymow was like meal in his mouth ... the touch of the crisp dollar bill he had changed his dented pennies for at the bank in town ... the light on the water curling white over the dam when his line first came alive with the dark, secret sweep of the trout ... the cut clover breathing through his open window just before summer sleep ... the sound of his father's sleighbells the night of the day he'd sent for the fountain pen ... the date of the Battle of Flodden looked up tremblingly in the book and found to be exactly the same as the one he'd put down, uncertainly, in the examination ... the doctor coming out of the room and saying [David's sister] Anna would be alright. [...] (75; original ellipses)

What experience could be equivalent to *all* of these, and many more? The voicing of this passage in a manner closely sympathetic to David's own consciousness does nothing to secure its meaning or limit its scope, because his unselective ego is so encompassing as to eventually forbid his own individuality.

Buckler's novel puts the incoherence of personhood at stake in the incoherence of the encompassing vision and, accordingly, in the accumulative style. In this respect, Buckler seems to embody something essential to his generation. Brian Trehearne cites Buckler's artist's determination to "get it all in" as an illustration, in the fictional mode, of the desire for the *integritas*[5] (150, 261) that was the "quest object" for the poets of the Montreal forties (67). The ambivalent status of the poet as an anxious inventory-taker or accumulator of images reflects, for Trehearne, the embattled status of the *subject* in the works of the second generation of Canadian poets to respond to high-modernist impersonality (73). The organizing poetic consciousness, emergent but not explicit, is generative because it is not free to assert its own "limits." A reluctance to make subjectivity the appreciable standard for the poem's coherence produces a tension in the work whereby the subject's inability to come to the fore conspicuously mitigates both the integrity of the work and the "psychic wholeness" of the poetic persona itself (69). Buckler's novel, too, suggests a relationship between its artist-figure's inability to limit his vision and, as we will discover, his inability to operate comfortably within the bounds of a practical subjectivity.

It may be pressing Trehearne's point too far, though, to suggest that Buckler likewise writes in response to the pressures of modernist doctrine. *The Mountain and the Valley* was composed in geographical isolation and pursued secondarily to the unremitting demands of Buckler's farm; in fact, Buckler describes penning his work on days when the brindle-heifer wasn't due for "romance" (22). Buckler's essay, "My First Novel," makes it clear that he had no desire to participate actively in any literary culture, to write according to any purposive statement or manifesto, or to intentionally carve out a place for himself in any tradition, though he names a number of modernist writers whose works permeated his thought at the time: Elizabeth Bowen, E.M. Forster, Henry James, Dylan Thomas, Ernest Hemingway, William Faulkner, and Marcel Proust (24). *The Mountain and the Valley* nonetheless provocatively illuminates modernist philosophies of time and space, modernist aesthetics, and modernist experimentation with personality and impersonality. Buckler's philosophical interest in the boundaries of perception and self complements modernist aesthetic concerns. As an MPhil candidate (in metaphysics), Buckler formally considered the problem of whether there could exist an "all-encompassing absolute self" and concluded (through Hegel and Schelling) that there was a frustrating double-bind at the centre of the question. By necessity, the all-encompassing perspective must also comprehend *itself*, meaning that it must be self-conscious to be absolute. But as soon as a perspective is self-conscious, it is *excluded* from the absolute; it is, rather, concerned with discriminating the boundary of the self and distinguishing it from the not-self. Buckler remarks on the paradox in his notes: "the self-conscious being is of necessity limited, and [...] the absolute being because unlimited, may not be personal" ("Progress of Idealism").[6] This tension, finding expression in Buckler's novel, helps to produce modernist values in *The Mountain and the Valley* that that may not explicitly be modernist *commitments*.

Laurie Ricou shares my interest both in what he calls the "aesthetic of getting-it-all-in" and in David's conscious manipulation of the stretch of time in order to do so, but ultimately characterizes the novel's modernism differently. For Ricou, David figuratively remains a child for all his thirty years, and retains the sense of wonder that gives a childlike coherence to his world. Naive apprehension is a type of impersonal (unselective) encompassment, which, by Ricou's analysis, complements Buckler's. For Ricou, the "draftsmanlike precision" and "cinematic magic" of Marcel Duchamp's *Nude Descending A Staircase* (1912), a painting that crosses David Canaan's mind in the epilogue, models Buckler's own style, with its "multiple overlapping images at once static and spatial yet containing the movement of time" (695). This analogy suggests Buckler's allegiance to an impersonal high modernism: precision, stasis, image, and the abstraction and containment of time. Ricou's reading suggests that Buckler's novel treats spatiality in a way that is faithful to theorists in the tradition of Worringer and Frank, in whose view "static images simultaneously apprehended" offer a "liberation from time" (Hollington 431). But my reading asserts that David's propensity for "stretching" time illustrates not the preservation of his sense of wonder but the wilful delay of his self-realization. The value that Buckler wishes to promote is not "liberation from time" but rather the *significant experience* of time.

Buckler's mountain itself is a figure for "natural" time-conception, where the movement toward and away from the peak represents the structure of anticipation, experience, and remembrance. Eleven-year-old David awakens to the possibility of climbing the south mountain to a fishing camp with his father and brother. Buckler's third-person narrator exclaims, in David's idiom that "This was the very day!" (13). Despite conveying the sense that this day will deliver something David has long hoped for, the scene is marked everywhere with indications of his contradictory wish to defer the entire experience. Walking along the log road, he discovers that the *anticipation* of climbing the mountain is preferable to the climb itself;

he prefers to *look* at the mountain in the distance (23). "Let's wait," thinks David, "I can be near the mountain and save it at the same time" (22). A problem of personal commitment, which will become a problem of artistic commitment, is taking root. David's desire to be near, and yet to save, the mountain expresses his desire to be near, but ultimately *not to have*, his dynamic experience, his "very day." His visual perception preserves rather than delivers the sought-after experience, and he seizes upon the damaging idea that experience does not have to be unique and irrecoverable: "He thought, we could do this every day! We will! We'll come back here and eat every day!" (23). His original sense of the import of his day dissolves, as does his general impetus towards personal progress in time. Buckler, through Aristotle, once described the shape of a cone as a symbol for "the vital principle of all action" ("Aristotle's Psychology" 7). The peak signifies self-sophistication, representing that towards which one strives. The base represents unrefined soul and matter, and movement towards it suggests the energy of avoidance. One can easily see the shape of the Aristotelian cone reflected in the form of Buckler's mountain. David's arrested progress towards his self-sophistication and his tendency to balk before "the vital principle" turn the novel's major episodes into a catalogue of abortive experience and persistent self-loss.

At the end of the novel, in a contrasting episode, David's twin sister climbs the same mountain in adulthood with her husband Toby, in the full knowledge that their return to the valley will mean Toby's departure for war. Anna asserts a view, similar to David's and likewise hyperbolically asserted, that she is coming not only to "the peak of the day" but also to "the peak of her whole life" (263). But she is willing, unlike David, to *feel* the moment of arrival: "It lasted, and she couldn't speak.[...] It lasted for one long minute." As Anna descends, "the time began to go. This would be the last day; and the day before the going is shadowed with the going, so that there is no free time left" (263). Anna's experience of *duration*—the palpable change in her consciousness as she anticipates, experiences, and mourns the "peak of the day"—gives the interval its form. The curtailment of her freedom on the way down is the cost of the genuine emotion she experiences. David, in generating the idea over the course of his lifetime that "nothing behind you is sealed, you can live it again. You can begin again…" (283), preserves his ostensible freedom. But in doing so, he cuts himself off from the possibility of authentic emotion and leaves his true freedom unrealized.

A lifelong immersion in visual experience insulates David, or so he believes, against time. As an adolescent, he tends a graveyard with his family and shudders at the sight of the tombstones of young family members. He wonders how death could have overtaken them, and significantly observes that "They couldn't have been *watching*" (86; original emphasis). Under the implicit belief that time can be suspended and death deferred through attention, David becomes a consummate observer. Bergson claims that determined visual attention (unnaturally) maintains the present tense and that dropping the gaze is what relegates each percept ipso facto into the past ("Perception of Change" 173). Of course, Bergson is most strenuous in his belief that our intuition of change and death is fundamental to our sense of vitality. It is one of *The Mountain and the Valley*'s cruel ironies that David is vigilant and accumulates perceptions in order to stave off death, but that vigorous attention is, in itself, an anti-vital attitude. David, fascinated, is also fixated and perfectly still. Standing before a window on the last day of his life, he perceives an intractable world: "Detail came clearly enough to David's sight; but it was as if another glass, beyond the glass of the window pane, covered everything, made touch between any two things impossible" (8). The objects of his sight are autonomous and individual: apple trees and bushes are "locked and separate," ice is "honeycomb[ed]," even movements themselves are spatialized as "line drawings of movements" (8). In marshalling these particulars, he loses his own impetus to act: "any impulse to movement receded before the compulsion of the emptiness" (8). The perception of objects as bounded and self-contained—modernist aesthetic perception—produces in David a sense of momentary personal incoherence and lack of motivation. He lifts the objects of his perception out of time, but loses himself in the act, his personality dissolved and his will paralyzed in the exaggerated drive to see with objective clarity.

Enthusiastic visual perception, sometimes expressed in the novel as a drive to see objectively and sometimes expressed as a desire to see quantitatively, is a strategy by which David avoids "real" temporality. Likewise, he embraces the *mediating* property of language as it guards him against a too-direct contact with his world. His pleasure in words is one derived from the power of language to abstract himself from experience, rather than from the power of language to *represent* it. Even as a child, David cannot immerse himself directly in the onslaught of sensory experience that Buckler gives us in eager catalogues. David regulates the time in which he experiences these things through the ritual recitation of lines to the upcoming town play, individuating the "brimming" moments:

> [He thought of the words when] Joseph thrust his fork slowly into the great cock of hay, lifting the whole thing except for a few scatterings that clung to the ground, above his head: settling it carefully into place on the side of the load and then walking patiently alongside the snail-slow oxen on the sun-parched stubble[....] He thought of them when Chris was dropping seed potatoes, aligning the odd one that tumbled out of place, with his foot; pressing it into the soft brooch-coils of manure automatically. He'd say, "It'll soon be time for swimmin, Chris"—so that Chris could break away a second from the steadiness of the furrow; so that he could think of his naked body in the water and have somewhere outside the moment to go, too. [...] And to think of them, with Anna, was best of all. For Anna was like a second safety: a place he would still have—to go to, if his secret thoughts ever failed. (50)

In reciting the lines, David uses language not *referentially* to represent his experience, but as a pacing device to help him *watch* (notably, this passage figures David's sister as a "place"). Language distracts David from each source of his joy, thereby sharpening his perception of it. This sharpened perception, however, awakens in turn his need to preserve and contain such moments, to represent them properly. David's exaggerated self-consciousness perpetuates the need to be inside and outside the moment all at once, seeking out a way to possess yet prolong his entire experience. Through attention, he marks (and stretches) moments, but each small act of acute recognition makes him prematurely—and neurotically—self-conscious.

David comes to recognize and fear his rapid exhaustion of "new" experience as the novel delivers several episodes of easy fulfilment. Buckler develops the Christmas scene similarly to the "very day" of the climb, suggesting that each special day of David's life takes on qualities of the original abortive event, the incident repeated with diminishing sincerity. "[T]his was the morning itself," writes Buckler (61), echoing "This was the very day!" but without the same degree of complicity in David's excitement. On Christmas Eve, David dreams about climbing the mountain, and imagines that "all the trees along the road are Christmas trees" (60).

The proliferation of Christmas trees suggests David's hope for the inexhaustibility of Christmas, recalling his original resolution that the trip to the fishing camp need not be singular ("He thought, we'll do this every day!" [23]). The resurgence of the memory of the climb also reflects the intensity of his time-conception around a special event, and the sensation of coming to the "peak" of an experience through anticipation and then regret: "There were the three days: the day before Christmas, the day of Christmas, and the day after" (54); the episode pervasively expresses his anxiety about the "spending" of Christmas. The difference between this day and the day of the climb up the mountain is that David must confront a devastating eventuality: the gratification of his desires. Thus Christmas gifts form part of the novel's general motif of givenness and withholding, mystery and unveiling. By "holding back" presents for each of the children Joseph and Martha delay the moment when each child's "allotment *must* be exhausted"; the parents unconsciously contribute to their younger son's fear that there are sharp limitations on the experience of the "new." David's misapprehension about "the plain having" (63) reflects his general anxiety about the moment when the novelty of his experience is exhausted and when he has figuratively "run out of gifts." In "[t]he tree, delivered now of its mysteries" (63), Buckler suggests the exhaustion of the archetypal tree of knowledge and implies, with a kind of postlapsarian regret, David's diminishing ability to enter innocently into contact with the mysteries of life.

David's gifts, particularly the kaleidoscope and the skates, suggest his "gifts" of perception. These objects reflect his potential to conceive of his world in different kinds of unity: one visual and composite, the other transcendent and epiphanic, both subject to Buckler's implicit criticism. A "mosaic," kaleidoscopic vision contributes to a sense of self-alienation: "In his lectures, Bergson argues that philosophers since Zeno have misconstrued the self because they have confused duration with extension, treating mental states in spatial terms. In their thinking, consciousness becomes a mere mosaic, rather than an interpretive movement" (Ellmann 23). The "stereoscopic immaculacy" of David's vision (Buckler, *Mountain* 96) contributes to a damaging, "mosaic" mode of consciousness. Buckler expresses skepticism about this kind of mosaic perception in that the kaleidoscope has been purchased literally at the cost of vitality; David's brother Chris has bought the kaleidoscope with money he has earned by trapping rabbits. The gift of the skates also suggests a (dubious) movement towards impersonality and self-abstraction. David wants to master the "crossover" (the footwork necessary for a smooth turn), a term that implies his urge toward self-transcendence:

> Then, just then— [...] when the dark spruces began to come in closer around the blue meadow ice and the blue ice seemed to stretch farther away toward the other side of the woods, hardening and booming with a far-off sound so it would bruise you if you fell on it and you were alone, but not now, because Anna was there with you, watching—just then, he did it. (66)

Most striking in this passage is the pronoun shift at the moment of the "crossover," when "you" becomes "he" (66). The unexpected use of the third-person looks forward to the (ironic) impersonality of David's mountaintop omniscience; in fact, David remembers the gift of the skates at the moment of his death. But irony is richly present in Buckler's depiction of the crossover, as its validity to David depends on Anna's witnessing of it. Likewise, his final epiphany disintegrates when he adopts an externalized perspective in order to anticipate the praise that Anna will give him. Therefore, the Christmas gifts that describe David's "gifts" of perception also describe two ambivalent forms of self-abstraction.

In David's first artistic enterprise—the town play—time is objectified in the rising and falling curtain that separates the scenes. David visualizes the moment in which he will have to bring himself to an audience by concentrating on the curtain that will be lifted to reveal him; as such, the curtain comes to embody the separation of moments ("The moment stopped moving. The curtain was pulled back" [71]). When "the relentless minute" arrives, he surprises himself with the joy of making himself into someone else (another wavering instant of self-transcendence):

> Oh, it was perfect now. He was creating something out of nothing. [...] He'd take them with him always, in their watching[....] Oh, this was perfect. There was a bated wonder coming from their faces: to know that this was David, but a David with the shine on him (they'd never suspected!) of understanding and showing them how everything was. (75)

The moment of David's artistic performance has been rendered so significant by his anxiety and anticipation that when it arrives, it strikes him with a unity-conferring power. But the aesthetically individuated moment proves to be one of absolute self-division. The "spell" of the play is broken when David breaks from the script to kiss his sweetheart, Effie, and is (lightly, but devastatingly) taunted by a neighbour. David curses ("as if it were another person") the part of himself that imaginatively created the moment as "perfect" (77, 76). According to Bergson, "we are free when our acts spring from our whole personality, when they express it, when they have that indefinable resemblance to it which one sometimes finds between the artist and his work" (qtd. in Lacey 83). By this criterion, one would expect David's spontaneous kiss to *be* a "free act" of which his "whole self" has been the author, his scripted character momentarily identical with himself. But his sense of self-betrayal reveals his growing conviction that his spontaneous self is *not* his true self. David will resolve this dichotomy by coming to prefer the less participatory version of himself, the persona who concentrates upon and individuates moments and who stands apart to show everyone "how it was."

Though his portrait of David Canaan emphasizes pathologies of perception and character, Buckler also illustrates that David's attunement to his own life had the potential to unfold into writerly intuition and social concord. The Baptizing Pool—the swimming hole where the boys of Entremont are exuberant and ribald with one another—is where David, far from being excluded, is "in the thick of it" (97). He "seemed forever, by the twist of essentiality he gave to whatever they said or did, to be disclosing and illuminating a part of [his friends that] they'd never recognized before" (98). Not only is David able to show the boys "how it was," but he is able to do it from a participatory perspective and without contrived time-conception strategies.[7] Paul Fussell describes "boys bathing" as a literary convention, a pastoral set-piece meant to highlight the "vulnerability of the flesh" and the poignancy of "youth unscathed" (301, 306). Buckler's description is nostalgic, even romantic: "Summer impregnated their flesh like the flesh of Early Transparents" (97). Notably, Buckler does not seem to be speaking here with a diction inflected by David's style of thought at all; it is as if David's "naturalness" enables the narrator's full omniscience, a rare feature of the novel.

But David's lack of personal integrity is most evident in his treatment of his girlfriend Effie, and the scene of his sexual conquest of her is rife with indications of the collapse and distention of identity. Their premature loss of virginity—suggesting his general rapid exhaustion of the "new"—is marked by his manipulation of events in time. David boasts of his seduction of Effie ahead of the fact, and then feels pressed to render it true, his skewed version of sincerity. All the young boys of Entremont grapple with the unknown nature of sex by abstracting it, carving into trees and rails "rude diamond shapes supposed to represent that part of a girl known to them in imagination only" (97). But David's advance symbolic possession of the sexual act is so far in excess of rude diamond shapes that he scripts the entire event beforehand—his part and Effie's. The incident forms part of a general pattern where advance over-representation purports to give David his experience in its ideal form, but only really mitigates its truth. The script, including such lines as "It's hot, ain't it? […] I'm frozen stiff," is hopelessly contrived, meant to protect David against a too-personal engagement (102). He cannot bear the idea that Effie's spontaneous responses could throw off his formula, and "wishes he could do it with Effie as if somehow she wasn't there […]" (102). The extreme impersonality of this act is exacerbated later in the novel when Effie dies of leukemia but David, not knowing the cause, believes he has killed her by taking her into a damp field (even though she has a cold) to impress his friend Toby. He martyrs himself to her memory and quickly inoculates himself against any sincere sadness by over-immersing in his guilt and thereby dissolving it (Williams 167). As such, his later mourning takes the form of the seduction itself and, indeed, the form of most of David's experience: over-represented and under-realized.

David's vulnerability to the opinions of others (to which Effie is a sacrifice) arises from the coherence of character he perceives in them. Other people, like objective things, "accuse" David with an integrity he feels lacking in himself. His first written self-representation in the novel is a letter to his prospective friend (and future brother-in-law), Toby Richmond. David notices, daunted, that Toby's letter is perfectly contained and defined by the length of the page: "The message ended where the page ended. Not as if it had exhausted itself; but as if, what was the sense of digging out more paper, to prolong it?"(109). Buckler (transmitting David's neurosis) remarks obsessively on Toby's impermeable "limit of trespass" (137), his "demarcat[ion]" (245), and his "fulfilled" face beside David's "inconsummate" one (204). It is under the compulsion of Toby's solidity, his capacity for adventure, and his cosmopolitanism that David is driven to betray himself by dissociating from everything that is important to him.

Tragically, David cannot identify with his father's inner "tune" (150); melody to Bergson is the very symbol of inner continuity (*Duration* 44). David strives instead to identify with Toby, a boy who conspicuously possesses a wristwatch, time abstracted. When the two boys are drifting off to sleep one night, David sits up in bed and asks Toby if he has remembered to wind his watch. The possible allusion to *Tristram Shandy*[8] suggests a link between David's desire to possess his whole experience and Tristram's attempt to write the Tristrapoedia. Just as Tristram's story—one that aims at total self-possession—is one of deferred engenderment, so David's is also full of paradoxical relationships to time, where he cannot both inhabit and possess his experience, and where he loses his sense of personality in the struggle to do both. David's crises of personal significance, such as a fight with his father, are marked by a Bergsonian rupture of *duration*, an abrupt conversion of time into space: "[David] felt as if time had turned into space and was crushing against him" (164). David asserts, against his own inner conviction, that time exists in "rooms" and "waits for you to straighten things out before you move on" (282). Similarly, when he thinks of having betrayed Effie, he imagines that "by sheer will" he can "reach back through the [...] partition of time" (142). His constant reconceptualization of time in order to create himself in his own best light has become an outright denial of his own mortality and the irrevocability of his actions.

The delusion of eternal new beginnings that destroys David's sense of the shape and continuity of things also affects his literary efforts. His inability to grasp the shape of time unfolding is a problem of form that extends to his writing. David's first attempt at a story, the ill-fated "Thanks For Listening," bears out all the problems that cripple the "naturalness" of his daily perceptions. The mediate quality of his knowledge has an unacknowledged impact on the war story he is attempting to write: "He'd never seen a war, but that didn't matter..." (254). His idea expands in such a way that sheer detail stands in for the essence of an experience he knows he cannot grasp. The equation Buckler makes between mediate experience and the need for endless substantiation imitates, of course, David's attempts to grasp the meaning of his existence through intense observation. Just as this intensity in David's everyday perception leads to the fragmentation of time into "instants," the lines of the story come to him in decontextualized pieces, posing a challenge to the story's form: "A whole line came to him out of nowhere. He didn't know where it would fit, but he wrote it down" (254). And with every piece of apt description, David resolves that "he could do as much for everything in the world" (227), a vision of ultimate authorship that scatters his thinking to "the limit of what can be borne without madness" (227). Despite its pitifully confessional title, "Thanks For Listening" lacks the hallmark of the confession, which is "the integrat[ion] [of] mind on a subject" (Frye 208).

In the novel's epilogue, David's climb up the mountain finally severs him from time. Breathlessly, he is pressed toward the absolute realization of his vocation. His ascent from base to peak extrapolates him from his life in the valley, towards the omniscient position of being at the summit, and delivers percepts that kaleidoscopically splinter inwardly and outwardly into infinite facets. Every percept branches into an infinity of yet more particular seen and unseen parts: from trees to pine needles to *cells* of pine needles. And, as usual, only a sense of timelessness can accommodate the fullness of his vision: "Time was not a movement now, but a *feature* of the frozen fields" (275; original emphasis). In a rapid interplay of "inner" and "outer" vision, David finds intuition: suddenly, he apprehends the meaning behind things, the feelings behind the faces, and, for a second, he feels the desire to merge with his surroundings. Unprepared to give in to this fluidity, David brings himself back into focus by grabbing a tree or yelling "stop" and then presses on, taxing his congenitally deficient heart. At the summit, David resolves to bind the villagers' lives together in an artwork that will touch "their single core of meaning" (292). This admirable vision, merging the particular and the essential, is his would-be epiphany. But David's lack of commitment to this ideal comes through when he imagines phoning Anna to announce that his as-yet-unwritten book has won a prize. David's self-regard in this moment is objictified in expectation of the praise that others will bestow on him. His binding vision disintegrates under his habitual tendency to step out of the moment and adopt a self-gratifying external survey of it.

David's death in the snow—a "transcendence" for J.M. Kertzer (82), a "godlike vision" for Alan Young (225), a "release into the infinitude of being" for L.M. Doerksen (55)—is also an ambivalent expression of the impersonality and atemporality necessary to his total vision. David has repeatedly had to sacrifice his sense of self in order to "get it all in"; and finally he has become "absolute[ly] white, made of all the other colours but of no colour itself at all" (294). His last "release" expressively extends his lack of commitment, his lack of colour. His vitality has always been sacrificed to his vision. The mountaintop vista, the most comprehensive scope, has likewise cut him off most literally from his life. As his vision gives way to self-aggrandizement, David dies in the snow or, figuratively, under a heap of unassimilated particulars (Kertzer 82–83). Here Buckler conclusively challenges, in my view, the portrait of the artist as the "eye of the world," the one who subordinates his personality to the telling (Dvorak 72). Expressively, David fatally collapses from his constitutional inner weakness at the moment when everything is given all at once. In this total vision, which is only achievable with the total distension of David's sense of time (and, therefore, self), Buckler interrogates the "enlargement of the [modernist] poetic domain" that entails the "[weakening] hold of the organizing consciousness" (Levenson 163).

As David dies in the snow, his grandmother Ellen composes a round rug from bits of the family's old clothing, her craft an alternate mode of author-ship. The metaphorical device of the round rug demands that readers see David in light of this second artist-figure. Grandmother Ellen is a counter-point to David in many respects, seeming to have the gift of creating organic unities out of pieces. Nearly blind, she is free from the material distraction that overwhelms David's sight; her art is a synthetic art. Whereas David operates on a pretext of infinite futurity in which to realize his design, Ellen operates, at least for a time, in the realm of memory—and memory, being selective, automatically imparts form. She is a storyteller and a crafts-woman, artisanal traits that Stephen Ross associates with authenticity (59). She composes her rug of inwardly concentric circles, meaning that her task is realizable, teleological. David, as I have argued, actively *denies* teleology. The binding together of the rug and the necessity of placing a final, central ring seems, on the surface, to give Ellen's task a certain virtue. An awareness of teleology and finitude defines our subjectivity; a sense of fatality is the very system by which we constitute our vital awareness (Lingis 6). Buckler complicates the significance of Ellen's final ring, however, by colouring it white and thereby juxtaposing it with the snowfall that buries David, suggesting the ultimate blindness they share.

Although critics tend to portray Ellen as a sort of "answer" to artistic problems that Buckler raises in David, Ellen's art is fraught with an equal and opposite set of ambiguities. By the time Ellen makes the rug, from pieces of the family's clothing, her memory is failing. The concept of "family" that the rug is meant to embody is tenuous, as Ellen mistakes the various relationships of those involved. In the end, the competing forms of David's and Ellen's art collectively enact an idea that Buckler quotes twice in his MPhil papers and that evidently arrested him. This idea is Immanuel Kant's notion that "concepts without percepts are empty but percepts without concepts are blind" (Buckler, "Kant's"; "Relation of Leibniz"). In fact, David is figuratively empty ("my life brimmed and emptied so soon, and I could never fill it again" [269]) and Ellen is literally blind. The synthesis that Ellen is creating means nothing precise to her; the relationships are askew and so the arrangement of particulars lacks idea. David's absolute idea ("I could realize the whole content of everything there is…") can obviously never be substantiated (290). Out of these two negative expressions—concepts without percepts, percepts without concepts—Buckler himself nonetheless creates a formal and unified piece of work.

The pressing question in Buckler criticism—an important and unresolved one—is whether Buckler writes himself out of the pathologies of perception that are David's. In other words, are David's perceptual faults Buckler's intuitive virtues? It is clear enough that the narrator's voice is often inflected by David's idiom, and yet the ironic distance between the character and the implied author is often quite pronounced. But while David's problem of integrity is a general problem of form-giving, Buckler's own novel is conspicuously structured. It has a narrative frame, it organizes each of its sections around well-marked coordinating symbols, and it creates endless structural echoes of the "very day" in the unfolding patterns of David's life, patterns of which he is generally unaware as he incoherently inhabits "This day … this day …" before dying (273; original ellipses). Buckler's irony is often quite pronounced: David is excluded from the absolving knowledge that he has no part in Effie's death by a "big word," just as he has often alienated others with language. (Effie's mother cannot remember the word for what killed Effie: leukemia.) And, elsewhere, the irony is stark as Buckler recounts—catalogically—the scene of David's day-long unconsciousness after a fall from the barn:

He knew nothing about Chris carrying him to the house [...] or of his father's cold rage when the doctor's horse came in sight, walking. Steve went back later to pick up his cap. He slipped the tablecloth from under David, with a sort of apology in him for being exempt from the unseemliness which these actions would hold if one of the family performed them. But David didn't know that. Nor did he see Ellen put her hand not to her head or her heart, when they told her, but to her mouth, as if it were her breath that was threatened. He knew nothing, the next morning, of Anna rushing from Toby's car to Martha's arms. [...] He didn't see Anna look at Toby when Toby made reference to the record speed of their trip. [...] He knew nothing until the next afternoon. He remembered opening his eyes. They were all standing there, dressed, in his room. He had the instant feeling that he'd overslept, so long that now he'd never catch up with them. (187–88)

The irony here is not only in the conclusive separation of Buckler's consciousness from David's as David lies insensate on the table, but in the highly ordered prose, the formalization of what he does not see in the same paratactic style that has been used so often to show us what he *does* see. David is blind to the litany of evidence of his inalienable connection to his loved ones, and Buckler's revelatory catalogue is a bitterly ironic ritual of exclusion. Finally, it is evident from a look at the revisions Buckler made to his epilogue that the author worked to discredit David's vision somewhat, to render his "translation" less than total. An early draft of *The Mountain and the Valley* describes David's intention to answer the call of everything as if it were actually possible for him to internalize his total experience: "As he thought of telling these things exactly, it was as if all the voices came close about him, but not crowding and sharp now. And he went out into them until there was no inside left and he became the thing he told" ("Revised Epilogue"). But the finished version *qualifies* the same passage to a telling degree: "As he thought of telling these things exactly, all the voices came close about him. They weren't swarming now. He went out into them until there was no inside left. He saw at last how you could *become* the thing you told" (292; original emphasis). Here, David does not "become the thing [he] told" but simply sees how "you" might do so in theory, so that we are left to evaluate his idea: that he does not have to understand people "one by one" but only as an aggregate with a "single core" of meaning to be found (292). And Buckler elaborates in the finished version, "He didn't consider *how* he would find it" (293; original emphasis). We rightly remain distrustful of what David "saw."

The problem with overemphasizing an ironic distance between Buckler and David Canaan, however, is that too often critics will invoke the distinction between author and character as part of a defence of Buckler's style. In other words, the charge of overwrittenness that has been levied against the novel since its prepublication phase is excusable insofar as the novel's superfluous description expresses the mentality of a scattered young boy who, Buckler plainly shows us, does not know any better. It may make more sense to minimize a sense of difference between Buckler and David—a relationship sometimes ironic and often sympathetic—even if it means aligning the novel's style with the authorial and not just the personative voice. It may be that Buckler's style is effusive independently of his characterization of David. In a letter of 14 January 1952, Buckler expresses his happiness about the news of his novel's acceptance for publication:

> The day the news came I was sitting in my room, gazing out over the bleak indrawn winter fields, quite stopped in the writing problem I was trying to work out, and feeling that frightening loneliness you get when you think: Even if I *could* turn out something good, where's the listening—except for that awful almost-taunting listening of the objects in the room when you've struck an impasse like that. Then the news came, and suddenly the whole face of things shifted like the crowd's face at the station shifts when the one you've given up as not having come (you're just turning for home) all at once steps off the train. (Letter to William Raney)

This passage contains features of thought that could easily be David's, even at the height of his distraction. The "listening of the objects in [Buckler's] room" echoes "the listening fact of the presence outside him" of all the things David wishes to write about (290). Buckler shares with David a sense of accusation (or at least "taunting") that springs from these objects. Buckler's evocation of one experience entirely in terms of another is David's manner of thinking, and there is even some telling similarity of diction ("faces," "struck").[9] Buckler's identification with David (and even with his artistic problems) must not be undermined in an attempt to ascribe the novel's excesses exclusively to its jejune protagonist.

Fictionally, Buckler shows us the productivity of quasi-identification. One night, in the dark, with his eyes free from stimulus and his self-consciousness relaxed, David talks to Toby *"with an interplay of affinity and divergence"* (110; emphasis added) and it is arguably David's most successful self-representation. It seals the friendship between the two boys and, more to the point, it confirms David's personal "limit" with respect to the other. Perhaps the limited-omniscient perspective, with its own gestures of identification and dissociation allow for the successful expression that is *The Mountain and The Valley*. And perhaps the most absolving mode for Buckler is not in any of the novel's marked moments of irony, but simply in its retrospective stance, the use of a synthetic time-perspective that David could not adopt. The novel asserts the need to palpably feel the personal "limit." David denies all shaping forces; he subsumes his own character to his belief that he has a "condition for universality" (223) and he denies the exigency to *act* that the existential limit of his own mortality should have placed on him. He resists forms of realization to circumvent loss; consequently, death overtakes him and satisfaction eludes him. Feeling one's "limit" means performing personality-driven acts of identification *and* dissociation. By and large, David is unilateral in these decisions: he wants to absorb everything or nothing; he wants to include everyone or no one. Perhaps Buckler manages to articulate a productive "limit" for himself as author by investing his novel with the clear pursuit of *essences* that belongs to autobiographical writing but voicing it in the third person. This way, he can accept his own dividedness as a fact and not feel the need to overcome it—that is, to be *altogether* personal or impersonal in his perspective. And perhaps this consciously conditional stance enables Buckler to express "how it was" without being caught up too murkily in our greatest experiential paradox: that we experience ourselves at once as knowing subjects and, problematically, as known objects.

In Buckler's second novel, in an assaultingly self-conscious moment, one figure asks another, "How does it feel to be a character?" (*Cruelest Month* 11). Buckler has a clear fascination with the boundary of personality and with the way in which the unity of the person must maintain itself against the vastness of everything that lies outside it. *The Mountain and the Valley* poignantly explores the instability of this self when it is influenced by the artistic orientation towards perfection and the desire for an all-inclusive representation. In the end, this orientation may imply inevitable inner division; there is no artist-figure, after all, among those who are spontaneous and "natural": not Chris, who is compassionate, Toby, who is outgoing, or Joseph, whose inner life is a melody. There is no question that Buckler portrays self-consciousness as a kind of aporia, but he also casts doubt on whether the impasse requires, in a telling word, "surmounting" (189).

NOTES

[1] In foregrounding these phrases, I should like to acknowledge D.O. Spettigue's "The Way It Was," which similarly calls attention to them.

[2] The final indistinguishability of the artist from the landscape is a trope best and most profoundly expressed by A.M. Klein's "Portrait of the Poet as Landscape." Margaret Atwood's *Survival* places Klein and Buckler in a common genealogy of works in which the artist is "buried" in particularity and the figure is indistinguishable from the ground. Her poem "This is a Photograph of Me" is an extension and a revision of this paradigm.

[3] Willmott's specific discussion of *The Mountain and the Valley*, meanwhile, is slightly farther afield of my own discussion. Willmott explores the "unreal" and thus expressionist world of *The Mountain and the Valley* as a result of the largely unacknowledged imprint of urban consciousness by which David and others evaluate their own reality.

[4] Walter Pater, whose concern for the "whole scope of observation" David Canaan seems to share, would have no objection to David's cultivation of sense-impression at the expense of his manifestation of his individuality. Pater decried the "thick wall of personality" that refines and limits one's contact with the world (248). Pater's prizing of the strictly experiential response to the world (unfiltered by consciousness) anticipates early-modernist impressionism and high-modernist objectivity. Buckler's David Canaan embodies a Pater-esque attitude, but only ironically; we will find that Buckler implicitly calls for the reassertion of the personality, especially as a selective and limiting mechanism.

[5] Trehearne chooses the term *integritas* in consideration of Stephen Dedalus's extrapolations on Aquinas, and evaluation of the image in terms of its *integritas*, its *consonantia* and its *claritas*. Trehearne proposes that we take *integritas* to mean "the limits of reference and structural tension that stabilize a rich crowding of images and make submission to their density a pleasure rather than a frustration" (78).

[6] Quotations from unpublished documents in the Ernest Buckler Papers appear by permission of the author's estate.

[7] Buckler contrasts the moving waters where David is free from self-consciousness with the typically frozen landscapes where David is alienated from or ahead of himself: his paralysis before the window and its frosty winter scene; his conviction, on the frozen pond, that he will be the "best skater in the world" (67); his death in the snow. Frozenness marks his artifices (in his planned seduction of Effie, David intends to show her where he is "frozen stiff") and also suggests his idealist "glass of the mind" (Bhojwani 116).

[8] Laurence Sterne's Tristram Shandy obsessively "remembers" that at the moment of his conception, his mother sat up in bed and asked his father whether he had remembered to wind the clock. This, for Tristram, was the moment in which his own "animal spirits" were forever dispersed (Watt xiii). The fact that Tristram was conceived in a moment of ruptured spontaneity partially accounts, in his mind, for the inner division that compels him to write his life in place of living it. More to the point, his mother's question represents for Tristram the "unhappy connections" of consciousness: that is, his mother's momentary association of the monthly duties of winding the clock and fulfilling her marital duties (Watt xiii). Buckler's David Canaan, in his boundless pursuit of the "connectedness" of things, makes a mockery of E.M. Forster's modernist dictum "only connect" (a benefactor sends David a book of Forster's). For David, the *unlimited* enchaining of perceptions (and visually "glimpsed" memories) illustrates his ridiculously unlimited sense of self.

[9] Strickenness and struck faces form a central part of Buckler's idiom as well as David's (see *Mountain* 193, 205, 210, 211, 215, 228, 234, 254, 256–57, 259, 269, 270, 281). David Williams comments at length on David's original line of prose in his never-completed story, "Thanks for Listening": "His brother's face looked struck" (196). Williams explains that David's compulsion to write arises from his unwillingness to give up his own "hurting power" and make amends after fighting with Chris (163). J.A. Wainwright also remarks on this line, suggesting that the "violent twisting by Buckler of the art-catharsis image" predicts the stunting of David's creativity (81).

WORKS CITED

Atwood, Margaret. *Survival: A Thematic Guide to Canadian Literature*. Toronto: Anansi, 1989.

Barbour, Douglas. "David Canaan: The Failing Heart." *Studies in Canadian Literature* 1.1 (1976): 64–75.

Bergson, Henri. *Duration and Simultaneity with Reference to Einstein's Theory*. 1922. Trans. Leon Jacobson. Indianapolis: Bobbs-Merrill Co., 1965.

———. "The Perception of Change." *The Creative Mind*. 1946. Trans. Mabelle L. Anderson. New York: Greenwood, 1968. 153–86.

Bhojwani, Maia. "The Double Ending of *The Mountain and the Valley*: From Aristotle to Dante." *Studies in Canadian Literature* 26.2 (2001): 107–26.

Buckler, Ernest. "Aristotle's Psychology of Conduct." Ernest Buckler Papers. MS. coll. 99, box 2, file 7. Thomas Fisher Rare Book Library, University of Toronto.

———. *The Cruelest Month*. 1963. Toronto: McClelland and Stewart, 1977.

———. "Kant's Theory of Knowledge." Ernest Buckler Papers. MS. coll 99, box 2, file 1. Thomas Fisher Rare Book Library, University of Toronto.

———. Letter to William Raney. 14 January 1952. Ernest Buckler Papers. MS. coll. 99, box 13, file 45. Thomas Fisher Rare Book Library, University of Toronto.

———. *The Mountain and the Valley*. 1952. Toronto: McClelland and Stewart, 1989.

———. "My First Novel." *Ernest Buckler*. Ed. Gregory M. Cook. *Critical Views on Canadian Writers*. Toronto: McGraw-Hill Ryerson, 1972. 22–27.

———. "Progress of Idealism From Kant to Lötze." Ernest Buckler Papers. MS. coll 99, box 2, file 3. Thomas Fisher Rare Book Library, University of Toronto.

———. "Relation of Leibniz to Locke." Ernest Buckler Papers. MS. coll 99, box 2, file 5. Thomas Fisher Rare Book Library, University of Toronto.

———. "Revised Epilogue." 14 March 1950. Ernest Buckler Papers. MS. coll. 99, box 13, file 42. Thomas Fisher Rare Book Library, University of Toronto.

Cohen, Richard Alan. "Time in the Philosophy of Emmanuel Levinas." Diss. SUNY, 1979.

Doerksen, L.M. "*The Mountain and the Valley*: An Evaluation." *World Literatures Written in English* 19.1 (1980): 45–56.

Dvorak, Marta. *Ernest Buckler: Rediscovery and Reassessment*. Waterloo: Wilfrid Laurier UP, 2001.

Ellmann, Maud. *The Poetics of Impersonality: T.S. Eliot and Ezra Pound*. Brighton, Sussex: Harvester, 1987.

Eysteinsson, Astradur. *The Concept of Modernism*. Ithaca: Cornell UP, 1990.

Frank, Joseph. *The Widening Gyre: Crisis and Mastery in Modern Literature*. New Brunswick, NJ: Rutgers UP, 1963.

Frye, Northrop. "Specific Continuous Forms." *Anatomy of Criticism: Four Essays*. Princeton: Princeton UP, 1957. 303–14.

Fussell, Paul. *The Great War and Modern Memory*. New York: Oxford UP, 1975.

Gasset, José Ortega y. *The Modern Theme*. Trans. James Cleugh. London: C.W. Daniel, 1931.

Hollington, Michael. "Svevo, Joyce and Modernist Time." *Modernism 1890–1930*. 1976. Ed. Malcolm Bradbury and James McFarlane. London: Penguin, 1991. 430–39.

Joyce, James. *A Portrait of the Artist as a Young Man*. 1916. Ed. Seamus Deane. New York: Penguin, 1992.

Kertzer, J.M. "The Past Recaptured." *Canadian Literature* 65 (1975): 74–85.

Lacey, A.R. *Bergson*. London: Routledge, 1989.

Levenson, Michael H. *A Genealogy of Modernism: A Study of English Literary Doctrine 1908–1922*. Cambridge: Cambridge UP, 1984.

Lingis, Alphonso. *Deathbound Subjectivity*. Studies in Phenomenology and Existential Philosophy. Gen. ed. James M. Edie. Bloomington: Indiana UP, 1989.

Macdonald, Bruce. "Word-Shapes, Time and the Theme of Isolation in *The Mountain and the Valley*." *Studies in Canadian Literature* 1 (1976): 194–209.

Pater, Walter. "Conclusion." *The Renaissance: Studies in Art and Poetry*. 1868. London: Macmillan, 1912.

Ricou, Laurie. "David Canaan and Buckler's Style in *The Mountain and the Valley*." *Dalhousie Review* 57 (1978): 684–96.

Ross, Stephen. "Authenticity and its Discontents: *The Mountain and the Valley*." *Canadian Literature* 165 (2000): 59–75.

Schwartz, Sanford. *The Matrix of Modernism: Pound, Eliot, and Early Twentieth-Century Thought*. Princeton, NJ: Princeton UP, 1985.

Spettigue, D.O. "The Way It Was." *Ernest Buckler*. Ed. Gregory M. Cook. *Critical Views on Canadian Writers*. Toronto: McGraw-Hill Ryerson, 1972. 95–115.

Tate, Allen. Introduction. *The Widening Gyre: Crisis and Mastery in Modern Literature*. By Joseph Frank. New Brunswick, NJ: Rutgers UP, 1963.

Trehearne, Brian. *The Montreal Forties: Modernist Poetry in Transition*. Toronto: UTP, 1999.

Wainwright, J.A. "Fern Hill Revisited: Isolation and Death in *The Mountain and the Valley*." *Studies in Canadian Literature* 7.1 (1982): 63–89.

Watt, Ian. Introduction. *The Life and Opinions of Tristram Shandy, Gentleman*. By Laurence Sterne. 1759–67. Boston: Houghton-Mifflin, 1965. vii–xxxv.

Williams, David. "Looking Homeward in *The Mountain and the Valley*." *Confessional Fictions: A Portrait of the Artist in the Canadian Novel*. Toronto: UTP, 1991. 148–73.

Willmott, Glenn. *Unreal Country: Modernity in the Canadian Novel in English*. Montreal: McGill-Queen's UP, 2002.

Young, Alan R. "The Pastoral Vision of Ernest Buckler in *The Mountain and the Valley*." *Dalhousie Review* 53 (1973): 219–26.

Canadian Modernism, P.K. Page's "Arras," and the Idea of the Emotions

SHELLEY HULAN

I

T.S. ELIOT'S DECLARATION in "Tradition and the Individual Talent" that poetry "is not a turning loose of emotion, but an escape from emotion" (21) famously places the emotions under modernist suspicion, suggesting that the role they play in poetic composition ought to be carefully circumscribed. Good poets, Eliot affirms, should be able to transcend their emotional states in favour of a more distant, craftsmanly approach to their writing. Eminent mid-twentieth-century literary critics such as I.A. Richards expected the same detachment from readers, who were charged with the task of mastering the poem partly by "expel[ling]" affect from it (Armstrong 406).[1] Yet though Eliot's is one of the best-known modernist statements on the emotions, it is only one among a surprising variety, many of which assign importance to "emotion" as a term of protest. It is understandable that "emotions" would possess some power as an oppositional term useful to the movement's ongoing engagement with the grand nineteenth-century explanatory philosophies of Hegel or Marx. As Michael Bell has observed, that engagement represents more the "transformed continuity" of these philosophies, with their emphasis on transcendent reason and the Absolute, than a thorough rejection of them (19). Instead of dispensing with these thought systems altogether, modernist writers attempted to renegotiate their terms. In these earlier teleologies, "emotion" was defined as the undesirable opposite of reason, something that had to be absorbed by reason's aims or rejected altogether.

Influential as Eliot's work was to generations of twentieth-century literary critics, his implied definition of the emotions as the mere tributary to some greater aesthetic project does not epitomize modernist efforts to rethink the reason/emotion divide. Canadian modernist critical discourse provides a substantial body of work through which to explore the question, not least because of its many engagements with Eliot's arguments. Although a survey of this discourse reveals some of the same Enlightenment disparaging of the emotions that continues to shape approaches to literature like Eliot's, it also brings to light a desire to discover a liberating model of the emotions that would attribute to them an energy more disruptive than subordinate to the governorship of reason. And if few Canadian modernist critics fully shed a concept of mind that ranked emotion below reason, they also constructed binary opposites such as reason/emotion[2] positively rather than portraying emotion simply as a problem for reason to surmount. They were not concerned with synthesizing binary terms but with exploiting the tension in them. Instead of equating the pair with higher/lower or dominant/subordinate categories, these modernists sought alternatives to the view that reason transcends emotion. They treated "reason" and the cluster of ideas associated with it (the conscious mind, order, detachment) as separate from but not greater than "emotion" and the cluster of ideas attached to it (the unconscious mind, passion, particular feelings). They used "emotion" as a term of resistance, if not always an adequate or clear one, which designated a part of the mind that could not be co-opted by the order-making activity identified with reason.

On international modernism's aesthetic front, imagism provided a means of protecting the integrity of binary opposites by insisting, as Graham Hough explains in *Image and Experience*, on the "clear presentation of the object" (12) via the "naked and unexplained" image (11). One of its fundamental principles, "direct treatment of the 'thing,' whether subjective or objective" (Zach 230),[3] could be understood to promote the refusal to view the object in the residually idealist way that Hough argues much nineteenth-century poetry did—as the mere extension of the subject, existing only through his or her understanding and desires (13–14). In *The Montreal Forties: Modernist Poetry in Transition*, Brian Trehearne detects imagist influences in the work of Canadian poets such as P.K. Page and Louis Dudek. Because imagism's "concentration on the image may be interpreted in terms of the desire for a resistant hardness" that only the object can supply (Zach 238), the movement arguably encouraged the rejection of dialectical, progressivist pressures to transform the world into a property of the conscious mind. But did Canadian modernist poets value binary concepts in the same way that Canadian modernist critics did?

Page's well-known poem "Arras" outlines one answer to this question. A poem that foregrounds the activity of the speaker's mind, it also bears a debt to imagism perceptible enough to advance the idea that Page uses the possibilities that the movement had opened up in order to radicalize the emotions as the independent mediator of a new vision. Oppositional pairs—the imagist partnering of subject and object, and a more psychologically oriented one of emotion and reason—are both central to the poem. Through them, "Arras" introduces a focus on mind into an aesthetics of the "object itself." The feat involves transforming the subject into *both* subject and object, a move that simultaneously questions and maintains the binary opposition between the two. It also entails portraying emotion as a legitimate register of experience that is not assimilated into a rational explanation of the speaker's vision. In doing both these things, "Arras" makes available a non-transcendental model of emotion that rebuffs pressure to integrate the phenomenon into some other, "greater" faculty of the mind.

II

At its most general, "reason" means the "human capacity for truth-seeking and problem-solving" ("Reason"). When invoked as emotion's opposite, the concept of reason takes on detachment as a key characteristic essential to decision-making. As Jon Elster adds in *Alchemies of the Mind*, "reason" as it is commonly used refers to "any kind of impartial motivation or concern for the common good," a motivation that is "disinterested as well as dispassionate" (102). In order to reason well, subjects have to be free of the self-interest of desire and the possible excesses of emotion. As reason's other, the emotions are portrayed as threatening to this impartiality.

Implicit in this notion of emotion as inimical to reason's competency is the idea of the mind-body split, which is usually attributed to René Descartes. Its corollary—that reason is divorced from and superior to the physical faculties that generate emotion—is often understood as part of a blameworthy Enlightenment tendency to represent the world in terms of antithetical concepts. The concept of a mind-body split remained influential even though, as Robert C. Solomon explains in "The Philosophy of Emotions," its model of a hierarchical division of mental faculties succumbed almost at once to the contrary view that the emotions link the mind and the body together.[4] Descartes himself eventually suggests not only that "the mind and body 'meet' in a small gland at the base of the brain," but that the body affects the mind "by means of the agitation of 'animal spirits'…, which bring about the emotions and their physical effects in various parts of the body" (Solomon 6). In spite of this nearly immediate challenge to reason/emotion, the concept of two major but hierarchically arranged faculties has proven much more tenacious than the claims that originally supported it (Solomon 3).

Freud's early twentieth-century characterizations of the unconscious maintained that the mind consisted of two major but separate components. "Everything conscious has an unconscious preliminary stage," he declared in *The Interpretation of Dreams*; the unconscious was a much more powerful part of the mind than anyone had suspected—the very foundation, in fact, of all "psychical life" (612). Still, the contents of the unconscious were detectable only as traces in consciousness, and although Freud's ideas accorded a new power to the former, they also encouraged ways of thinking about the mind that subordinated its every element to the latter. As Barbara Rosenwein points out in "Worrying About the Emotions in History," Freud also subscribed to the "'hydraulic' model" of the mind (7), a model that arguably translated his conscious/unconscious distinction into the stereotyped opposition between "reason" and "emotion." In the "hydraulic" view, the emotions consist of an intense energy, alien to reason, always accumulating and potentially out of control, an energy that must be released in some way (Rosenwein 7). Ironically, this conception of emotion as a turbulent and inexplicable energy might also have made more plausible the idea that emotion may disrupt reason rather than integrate peacefully with it.

In keeping with their general rejection of the progressivist, meliorist teleologies centred on an understanding of "reason," modernist critics tried to treat reason and emotion as concepts freed from the higher/lower relationship that they inherited from the Enlightenment. They were not always successful; hierarchies between the two and their associated pairings (mind/body, order/disorder) never completely disappeared from the critical conversation, for few critics managed consistently to avoid relegating the emotions to a primitive position in relation to the more sophisticated mental capabilities called "reason."

In Canada, much of the critical commentary on Page's work appears to provide a case in point. John Sutherland declares in "The Poetry of P.K. Page" (1947) that Page's work is characterized by "emotional simplicity," implying both that it is "independent of conscious ideas or beliefs" and that this independence sometimes betrays an immature poetic talent (107–08).[5] In his essay of the same title (1971), A.J.M. Smith seems to argue the reverse of Sutherland by praising what he calls the "feeling and perceiving Mind" in Page's poetry. However, his use of the term "emotion" still appears to dissociate emotion from rational thought. The "overflowing of powerful emotion" in her "most moving poems" presents paired opposites—"innocence and experience, illusion and disillusionment"—that are recollected from a distance with a distinctly Eliotian "craftsmanly excitement" (150). But emotions remain too overwhelming, excessive, or immediate to be directly involved in the "craftsmanly" act of writing poetry. The emotions as they appear in Page's book of poems *The Metal and the Flower* (1954) are mentioned in a favourable review by Northrop Frye (1954), though favourable because he can sort what he sees as the "lower level of emotion and instinct" in the poems from the "upper level of intelligence symbolized by angels and abstract patterns in white" ("Letters in Canada: Poetry" 131).

But apparent critical dismissals like these obscure the more complex consideration to which Canadian critics, as well as those beyond Canadian borders, submitted the term in their writing. Modernist attempts to revise the grand teleologies of previous generations often involved revaluing emotion significantly, as Raymond Williams does in *Marxism and Literature* (1977). In this essay of his later career, Williams attempts to intervene in Marxist historical materialism by arguing that the traditional Marxist emphasis on the historical dialectic between dominant and counter-hegemonic forces in a given culture fails to recognize that "*no mode of production and therefore no dominant social order and therefore no dominant culture ever in reality includes or exhausts all human practice, human energy, and human intention*" (125; original emphasis). As part of what he calls a new "cultural materialist" approach (5), Williams attacks what he regards as the false stability of the reason/emotion binary, which denies the richness, contingency, and particularity of human experience in time. He uses the term "feeling" in his argument to describe a concept of the emotions as part of a larger idea of reason, advancing it as an appropriate name for the ever-present remainder of human life that the dominant social order can never explain. An additional term, "structure of feeling," encompasses a "kind of feeling and thinking which is ... social and material" (131) that emerges "in the true social present" as individuals live it in a given moment (132).

Emergent phenomena of this kind may "be seen as the personal or the private," the "natural or ... the metaphysical," aspects of the world and of daily life that constitute a critical remnant of things that the historical dialectic "excludes, represses, or simply fails to recognize" (125), though they are more often detectable as changes to a collective mentality. Williams believes that "specifically affective elements of consciousness and relationships" are important components of the structure of feeling; he adds carefully that he does not mean "feeling against thought" but "thought as felt and feeling as thought" (133). By introducing the idea of "feeling" as an alternative to the binary of reason/emotion and its association with dialectical history, Williams does not reinvent the usual narrative of emotion as a more primitive mental experience that ultimately leads back to reason, but he does try to weaken the antithetical pairing of the two, a pairing contaminated, he believes, by reason's always-presumed authority.

And yet, as attractive as Williams's intervention appears from a present-day perspective that is typically suspicious of binary oppositions, it really serves to emphasize the fact that the more common modernist revaluing of emotion involved *preserving* the reason/emotion binary, not replacing it. Patronizing as Sutherland sounds on the subject of Page's poetry, he supports the division that he perceives in her work between the realms of imagination and dream on one hand and the conscious mind on the other, and he does not seek their reconciliation. On the contrary, their *opposition* is the thing—the "tension" between them that may be found in "Miss Page's better poems where there is never any truce between the opposing attitudes" ("Poetry of P.K. Page" 108). Canadian modernist critics often redefined "emotion" to make it the name for mental activities that reason cannot control or perhaps even recognize. These abilities alter reason by being its permanent, powerful, and unpredictable antithesis.

Two major statements by these critics on the role of the emotions are found in the works of A.J.M. Smith and Northrop Frye, both of whom invoke and rethink the reason/emotion binary. Smith's definitions of the emotions often emerge in the various assessments that he makes of Eliot's work over several decades. In his reviews of the Anglo-American poet's treatment of emotion, Smith affirms the power of the subconscious, which he associates with the emotions, as distinct from that of reason, which dominates consciousness. In his early article "Hamlet in Modern Dress" (1926) he asserts that the most "striking" feature of Eliot's poetry is its "rejection of a conscious intellectual sequence of ideas in favour of a subconscious emotional one." A proper reading of it depends on recognizing that emotion has a "logic of its own" that is as compelling in its own right as anything that the rational mind can articulate. He sees this "subconscious" emotion as residing in Eliot's depiction of objects as opposed to a subject. Suggesting that its logic is revealed in the "splintered images and broken sequences" of *The Waste Land*, he indicates that these fragmented images alone provide the loci for the poem's emotional content. Smith devotes less attention than one might expect to the speaker's mind, though he believes that the mind portrayed in Eliot's poem is breaking apart (2). But while "[m]emory and subconscious association play their part in the introduction of intellectually unrelated motifs" (3), both emanate from the poet's mind *outside* the poem, rather than a fictional speaker's mind within it. If his frankly imagistic reading of *The Waste Land* seems at times to minimize the poem's possibilities as a psychological study, the titular reference to Hamlet in the piece and his concern with the subconscious betokens Smith's interest in relating this interpretation to a new psychology.

Smith's later response to symbolist poet Paul Valéry's disquisition on "poetic emotions," "The Poetic Process" (1964), turns more clearly to psychology.[6] But Smith maintains the same concepts of emotion and reason as two separate and equal domains that he first established in "Hamlet in Modern Dress." Valéry, writes Smith, believed that "poetic emotion" is a special kind, one engendered in the "reverberat[ing] feelings … more or less intense and more or less conscious" and inspired by great natural phenomena when the subject confronts them. The consciousness of poetic emotion is located exactly in the moment when the subject's "dawning perception" first grasps that it is perceiving a world quite different from the one in which it ordinarily functions (Valéry qtd. in Smith 221). Smith suggests that when it comes to the poet's creative act, the experience of "poetic emotion" cannot be separated from the deliberate choices of a careful mind composing poetry. However, these deliberate choices condition the poem through the poet's recollection of, *not* his or her moving beyond, the original emotional state.[7]

Smith's view of the emotions is not always clear or consistent. In the same essay, he praises the analogy between poetic creation and chemistry that Eliot makes in "Tradition and the Individual Talent" (1919) when he claims that the poet's mind is a "catalyst" (18) that transforms personal emotion into "art emotion" (20). Elsewhere, too, Smith takes up more of an Eliotian stance on the reading of poetry, accepting that the initial part that emotion plays in the reader's response to a poem soon gives way to the intellectual "exhilaration" to which "great" poetry always leads ("Refining Fire" 61–62).[8] The purpose of that exhilaration is to train the reader's mind to perceive more carefully by removing it from the immediacy of the emotion.

Still, Smith is concerned in a way that Eliot is not with validating the emotions as a disruptive force rather than as a potentially transcendent one. On their own, Eliot insists, an individual's emotions count for little; the idea that poetry is "an escape from emotion" (21) suggests that the individual experience of emotions provides the writer with a primitive working material that a "catalysis" alters into something better. It also intimates that the writer thoroughly reinvents, and thereby controls, immediate emotional responses: "The business of the poet is not to find new emotions, but to use the ordinary ones and, in working them up into poetry, to express feelings which are not in actual emotions at all" (Eliot 20). In "A Self-Review," Smith broaches a similar topic—that of the role of the artist's "personality, conscious and unconscious," in "artistic creation" (213). It is possible and indeed likely, he argues, that

> the controlling mind, the critical shaping faculty of the rational consciousness sends the tremulous instinctive and sensuous fancy packing.
>
> It is this rather bossy intelligence which chooses what is to be expressed, considers how, and judges the final outcome. *But what a lot escapes it—or cajoles it, or fools it.* It did not choose the images, the metaphors, the sensations, or the sounds that chime and clash in the consonants—though it did eventually approve them. (214; emphasis added)

In spite of the conscious mind's power over expression, its uneasy relationship with emotion is not the consecutive one to which Eliot commits himself. Rather, it is the relationship between two almost mutually exclusive faculties of mind that come into contact during the process of artistic creation. "Conscious discipline," a phrase that Smith uses while discussing F.R. Scott's poetry ("F.R. Scott" 119), is an attribute that he consistently praises in his essays. But that praise does not simply absorb emotion, or the unconscious that Smith often identifies with it, into the poet's "controlling" vision.

For his part, Northrop Frye accepts Eliot's idea of the emotions in poetry as "a presentation, as immediate experience, of a complex of images and ideas" (*T.S. Eliot* 29). However, in *T.S. Eliot* (1963) he objects to what he sees as Eliot's failure to explain clearly how the poet represents such emotions, or how readers respond to them. Like Eliot (and, indeed, Smith), Frye sometimes defines the emotions as most valuable when transformed into something else. For instance, Aristotelian catharsis—the purgation of the audience's emotions—has little to do with lived emotion, but is a necessary step in the liberation of the imagination. As the "emotional response to art," catharsis is really "the raising and casting out of actual emotion on a wave of something else" (*Anatomy of Criticism* 93). Much like Eliot's "art emotion," Frye's "imagination" transcends the particulars of lived experience.

Acutely aware, though, of the limitations of models of consciousness that split "reason" off from non-rational activities, Frye locates that split in a historical context that presents various mental faculties as not only having once been much more closely associated with one another, but as having had more power than reason/emotion allows. Frye makes the case that the "other" realm of the emotions and the unconscious has been falsely subordinated to reason at the expense of a fuller understanding of the contemporary world. The alignment of reason and science after the beginning of the modern era in the late eighteenth century constituted, he argues, the second of "two primary mythological constructions in Western culture" (*Modern Century* 60). The first mythology, which had conceived reason as the effort to understand the design of nature, emphasized that "man and nature were creatures of God, and were united by that fact" (60). Modernity brought with it a second mythology that advanced a new, narrower idea of reason that eventually came under the influence of Darwinian science. This mythology reconceived nature as "self-developing" and humanity as separate from that development (62). If nature, which was now no longer regarded as the product of a divine intelligence, had any "rational design" at all, it was only the rational design that human minds projected upon it.

In the meantime, reason attached itself to this idea of nature and the science that posited and investigated it. As Frye argues in "The Instruments of Mental Production" (1970), both this modern concept of nature and its science have promoted an attitude of "detachment" that is regarded as indispensable to clear-headed inquiry. He counters, however, that such detachment in fact constitutes only one of the "two moral attitudes which are also intellectual virtues" (17), both of which are necessary to an understanding of reality. The other, "concern," is the special property of the arts. The polar opposite of "detachment," "concern" values "many human factors relevant to [the arts] but not to science as such: emotion, value, aesthetic standards, the portrayal of objects of desire and hope and dream as realities…" (17). Emotion, then, is the first element in an ample collection of "factors" that modern science and the reason identified with it ignore. The humanities help to remedy this unfortunate turn of events by recognizing that the emotions and the other "human factors" to which the arts attend make vital contributions to human understanding. As "the two great divisions of liberal knowledge" (17), science and art embody separate mental spheres; the subject's efforts to achieve *both* "detachment" and "concern" produce a more complete view of the world.

Like Smith, Frye does not relinquish the idea of binary opposition altogether, idealizing as he does the balance between the two antithetical means by which the mind grasps the world in its full complexity. While this balance might be interpreted as compatible with the hydraulic metaphor of a reason that constrains and manages the liberated, creative, but also uncontrolled emotions, it is just as compatible with an understanding of that metaphor that emphasizes the discreteness and independence of the emotions. In Frye's view, it is the congress of emotion and reason, not the assimilation of one by the other, that brings about a fuller understanding of reality.

This sense of an irreducible distinction between emotion and reason informs other Canadian modernist critics' work as well, though that distinction is sometimes less well drawn. In "F.R. Scott and the Modern Poets" (1951), Louis Dudek echoes Smith's interests in "Hamlet in Modern Dress," uniting imagism with psychology by drawing Eliot's poetry together with that of F.R. Scott on the grounds that they share a similar "emotion situation" (13). "Successful emotion," Dudek argues, is not "cerebral," not the "baffled pain which most of us know as 'feeling'" (14). It "is in love with the objects of the world, throws bits of reality on the page; … it attaches itself to the *images* of objects" (14). Undeterred by the implicit contradiction, Dudek declares that both imagism and "modern psychology" help to rescue poetry from the "cosmic abstractions" of the previous age by insisting on a "concretize[d]" emotion that refuses to be limited by the "encroach[ments]" of "the intellect, or reason" (14). More cryptically, Eli Mandel calls in 1966 for an "irrational" criticism that would enable an escape from the detached attitude that encourages the critic to ignore the importance of the subject's immediate experience for critical inquiry (72). Such references to a tension between opposites are underwritten by earlier modernist criticism, like Smith's and Frye's, that prioritizes tension over transcendence, and that represents emotion as the name for mental events that have anything but a sequential or subordinate relationship to reason.

III

"I had read a bit of Eliot, but not much," P.K. Page has said of her first meeting in 1942 with the *Preview* group, "and I certainly didn't have any theories" (Djwa 41). But if Page prefers creative endeavours to critical ones, her archival papers demonstrate a sustained attention to the complex and unresolved relation among the different faculties of the mind. They contain more than thirty years' worth of clippings detailing psychological, neurological, and sociological research on how the mind works.[9] No single set of views dominates the collection. While several articles focus on "left hemisphere/right hemisphere" research on the idea that the brain divides its tasks between two distinct halves responsible for opposite functions,[10] others question the accuracy of representing the brain as split into two. Although "Arras" was published in *The Metal and the Flower* (1954), more than ten years before the earliest article in the collection,[11] it, too, puts readers on notice that it is a poem about the mind. The speaker's strange environment has invited interpretation as a dreamscape (Rooke 137) and as an anxious projection of the speaker's fears (Djwa 46–47). At the same time, any temptation to interpret the speaker as schizophrenically alienated from her[12] surroundings is moderated by the subjective coherence towards which her responses to her surroundings point. In "Arras," no moment of emotion-discarding transcendence is possible. Indeed, to understand how the emotions operate in this poem is to understand that reason does not transcend them at all.

The poem mounts its first challenge to reason's supremacy by not meeting a basic requirement of the detachment that Elster identifies with reason—the confidence that the subject is distinct from its object. As other readers of "Arras" have observed,[13] the speaker in this poem seems not to occupy a stable subject position. She is, somehow, both the subject and the object, the seeing and the seen, the "I" and the other in one. The point develops over the poem's opening lines:

> Consider a new habit—classical,
> and trees espaliered on the wall like candelabra.
> How still upon that lawn our sandalled feet.
>
> But a peacock rattling his rattan tail and screaming
> has found a point of entry. Through whose eye
> did it insinuate in furled disguise
> to shake its jewels and silk upon that grass?
>
> The peaches hang like lanterns. No one joins
> those figures on the arras. (63)

The speaker appears by turns to be outside the tapestry she describes and inside it as well. The word "habit" in the first line suggests both a practice of some kind and a garment. The speaker may be on the outside looking at the tapestry, or she may be on the inside, as a part of it, or she may be both. Simultaneously, the status of the "arras" as the poem's primary object of description is undermined. Although the speaker's apparent focus in the first few lines on its description initially meets the imagist criterion for the "direct treatment" of an object, *this* object almost immediately becomes part of the puzzle of the subject's location. Though the opening verse paragraph indicates that the speaker has become part of the arras, her observation in the third that "No one joins / *those* figures on the arras" (emphasis added) locates her back on the outside. This location is in turn contradicted by the subsequent statement that she is "walking here" (63), words that remind readers of her reference to the arras's lawn, on which she stands at the beginning. The speaker reveals an awareness of her strangely double status, describing herself as both "observer" and "other" as well as "Gemini," the zodiac sign of the twins.

This said, the blurring of the subject–object boundary does not represent the demise of the object, which has been reinvented rather than destroyed. The third verse paragraph's final, mystifying image of the "I" who is "starred for a green garden of cinema" (63)—is this the "observer" or the "other"?— alludes both to the possible garden setting of the arras, where the speaker's subjectivity first comes into question, and to the viewing situation of a movie, where the subject observes screen images from which he or she is distinct. Though the *initial* object recedes into the background, then, the speaker replaces it with another one—herself.

Just as the speaker's detachment is challenged and ultimately redefined, so is that of the readers, who can no more be conceived as the sense-making agents of the poem than the speaker can. A review of the fourth verse paragraph makes the point clear:

> I ask, what did they deal me in this pack?
> The cards, all suits, are royal when I look.
> My fingers slipping on a monarch's face
> twitch and grow slack.
> I want a hand to clutch, a heart to crack. (63)

While no explanation has yet been found that makes sense of every image in the poem's middle section, these particular lines have enough consistency to tempt readers to a diligent effort. The speaker's demand to know "what did they deal me in this pack?" introduces the extended metaphor of a card game to describe her confusion, a metaphor that makes possible a metaphysical answer to the question; after all, the "suits" are "royal," and as J.C. Cooper points out, the King, Queen, and Knave sometimes symbolize "the spiritual triad," while the Joker represents "the non-material world" ("Cards" 29). Even the apparently unrelated image of a "heart to crack" can be connected to card games, since "crack" is a term associated with poker.[14] Still, this explanation sheds little light on surrounding lines (particularly the "green garden of cinema"), and so the consistency of the images in these lines only gives readers the false illusion that they are beginning to solve the puzzle of the poem.

I do not mean to suggest that every interpretation of this part of the poem dissolves into unmeaning. But if readers presume that their minds can do what the mind in the poem cannot, they may become absorbed in the effort to assemble the images of the verse paragraph into a consistent pattern. The individual "pieces" here seem to promise a whole picture. However, the poem remains a riddle, and as a riddle-solver, a reader never reaches the mental place where detachment, and subsequently the determination of the whole, is possible. As a puzzle, this part of "Arras" interpellates a close reader whose task is not the "questioning" or analysis of the poem as a finally knowable object (Armstrong 405), but simply the discovery of what the object is. This act of puzzle-solving emphasizes what Eleanor Cook has called a form of creative play valued for its own sake, as opposed to being valued only because it leads to the mastery of the object.[15] Indeed, readers never fully "master" the poem—and never move beyond it to the sense-making paraphrase that subordinates the original to a "greater" understanding—because they can never be absolutely certain what that object is.

The attack on the subject–object distinction is, of course, a feature of modernist poetry that, as Louis Sass observes in *Madness and Modernism*, is often attended by a multiperspectivism so intense as to invite comparisons with schizophrenia (136–37). There are signs that the absence of this distinction in "Arras" may indeed be explained by the speaker's mental alienation. The peacock's earlier "insinuat[ion]" of itself "in furled disguise" through the speaker's eye (63) suggests that it was outside the control of that eye, or that some sort of trickery was practised upon the speaker. That entry is beyond her conscious will, perhaps part of a projection from the unconscious that expresses some of the anxieties that the subject is experiencing in these unfamiliar surroundings.

The stillness on the arras seems to support such a reading. While the peacock arrives as the speaker grows increasingly uneasy at the absence of movement on the arras, the scene is presented as a static one from the very beginning, before the peacock's arrival and even before readers learn that the "figures" on the arras are motionless. The verbs that might have indicated action in the opening verse paragraph are neutralized, one as an adjective ("espaliered") and the other as an ellipsis (the "are" or "were" needed to complete "How still upon that lawn our sandalled feet"). The poem's syntax also emphasizes the motionlessness of the "figures on the arras," who, as figures "No one joins," are not the subject of a verb but rather its object. The perception of one's environment as frozen or flat is another hallmark of the schizophrenic subject, for whom the perceived lack of dynamism in his or her surroundings marks an entry into the frightening, alienated world of psychosis.[16] Viewed from this angle, the peacock seems once more most understandable as the psychological projection of a speaker whose ability to make a coherent meaning out of her surroundings is in severe doubt.

Yet, without refuting the possibility that the speaker's fearful unease is generated from an inner psychological turmoil that impairs her ability to respond rationally to her surroundings, a decidedly *un*-paranoid coherence emerges together with these signals of unconscious projection and upset. The first word, the verb "Consider," foregrounds an act of careful deliberation. Moreover, as an imperative command it involves both the speaker and readers. Being asked to "[c]onsider a new habit" means being asked to maintain the kind of deliberative attention commonly identified with the mind that enjoys a certain control over all its own workings, a mind that, like the one Frye imagines in pursuit of modern scientific inquiry, carefully invigilates the data presented to it. As surreal as the scene seems, then, readers are steered away from automatically concluding that the speaker is alienated, or that the scene results from a fragmenting (and by implication sub-rational) mind.

On the contrary, reason and emotion coexist in the poem as distinct registers of experience. The speaker expresses her confusion with regard to the two- and three-dimensional world of the arras in the form of questions about her own identity—"Who am I / or who am I become ..." (63)— and about the game in which she appears to be involved ("what did they deal me in this pack?"). Though these questions express alarm, they also reveal a capacity for thought and judgement that emphasizes the speaker's ability to receive and deliberate on information. The speaker's imagining herself "mak[ing] a break" from the scene (63) may betray panic, but it may just as well indicate an ability to strategize, to see beyond and outside her bizarre environment. Her ability eventually to articulate her agitation as a "fear" of "the future on this arras" bespeaks a consistency of mind capable, at least sometimes, of extrapolating a single unified message from the strange scene. Following a series of increasingly apprehensive reactions to her experience as it does, the speaker's naming of her fear reflects a good deal of self-awareness. Obviously an emotional moment, it is far from a desperate or incoherent one.

Put succinctly, this speaker possesses the intentionality and deliberation usually associated only with reason even though the poem may still be
read as manifesting unconscious unease through her emotional responses.
The emotions, in other words, are not comfortably identifiable as reason's
subordinate or, indeed, as its other. The peacock, which lends itself most
readily to a reading of itself as a dream projection onto the landscape,
possesses a symbolic meaning that accommodates this idea. The bird can
be understood to symbolize the "Eye of the Heart" (Cooper, "Peacock"
129); since Page has said that she thought of the peacock as coming out of
the speaker's eye (Djwa 47), the peacock may be interpreted as the eye of
the speaker's own heart. At the same time, however, the peacock can also
be read as the figure of the speaker's hope for contact with the others on
the arras, a hope of which the speaker may be unaware until the latter half
of the poem. If the familiar trope of the heart puts readers in mind once
more of the speaker's emotions, then they must also be reminded that the
emotions, for this speaker, both include unconscious turmoil and yet are
also more than its symptoms. Once more, the poem asks readers to regard
the emotions as something other than reason's poor cousin.

The speaker's confession in the middle of the poem that "[i]t was [her]
eye" (64) that allowed the peacock to enter the arras again portrays her as
capable of forming intentions concerning her situation. With this admission, she suggests that she *chose* to enable the peacock's entry, and perhaps
had some foreknowledge of the havoc that it would wreak. People do not
usually confess to events that are thoroughly beyond their control or understanding. Confessions are for knowingly committed acts of transgression,
acts that the doer understands are wrong or disruptive. Furthermore, the
confession arrives at the poem's halfway mark, far enough along for readers
to doubt that it is just a frenzied response to the peacock's arrival, which is
described much closer to the beginning. The fact that the speaker articu-
lates her fear just before this confession reaffirms that she makes decisions
based on assessments of her experience that are reflexive and considered as
well as emotional. This said, the question of whether the subject knew for
sure what the peacock was before it entered through her eye remains unan-
swerable. It is undoubtedly also a projection of an anxiety still locked, for
all the speaker's coherence and intentionality, somewhere in her subconscious; surreal landscapes gesture toward a dream world.

The speaker's description of the peacock as "living patina, / eye-bright, maculate!" and the question that follows it, "Does no one care?" (64), return readers once more to ideas of intentionality and coherence. "Care" suggests that, in the speaker's view, the peacock's arrival on the arras ought to inspire a conjointly emotional and intellectual response. The "burdened state of mind resulting from fear, doubt, or concern" (OED), "care" points to a mind simultaneously emotional and articulately directed at a specific object, a mind "concerned" in Frye's sense of valuing an object "of desire and hope" for the beauty and promise that it embodies. But if the speaker was expecting to generate emotional change and care-ful consideration in the figures on the arras, then the mere arrival of the peacock has not had the effect on the arras that she hoped it might. "[H]ands" that, she thought, "would hold [her] if [she] spoke" will not be doing anything. The motionless figures continue motionless to the end, without so much as a glance at the peacock from their "slow eyes" (64). The peacock's arrival, then, produces no result that might impose a clear meaning on the scene.

Moreover, a firm conclusion about the rationality or the irrationality of the emotions continues to be difficult to determine. By the time the speaker asks whether no one cares, the peacock is vanishing as "another bird assumes its furled disguise." More mysteriously, the peacock is also replaced by the image of "another line" moving through the air. Though a line seems a bland (and odd) substitute for the "eye-bright" fowl, the image returns readers to the initial troubling of opposites at the poem's beginning. As it "troll[s] the *encircling* air" (64; emphasis added), the line stands for both circle and line, enclosure and endless extension. It is another enigmatic image, not only because a final interpretation again eludes readers, but because the moment of experience described in this poem has passed, even as the final lines of the poem suggest a new beginning. As her vision disappears, the speaker remains unable to say for certain what anything in her final view means, perhaps because the peacock and its moment cannot be frozen in time and thereby made into discrete objects of analysis. This mind is directed at a specific object, but it has a purchase neither on the object's meaning nor on her own responses to it.

What is missing is not the sense that this speaker grasps her object rationally—as readers see throughout the poem, she *can* do so—but that she is able to arrange her diverse reactions to the arras, the stillness, and the peacock into a single unified response. The "cautious subjectivism" that Trehearne sees affirmed in "Arras" is one that is capable, as he argues, of being ironic (95) and thus capable of attaining a certain distance from its object. Though this speaker can attain this distance, however, her ability to do so never turns into a rational control over all of her experiences. She never makes her emotional register fully supportive of her "reasonable" one. She can judge that in the "infinite" stillness there may be a chance for her to "make a break" from the scene, but she cannot avoid becoming paralyzed with fear at the very same time. No overcoming of the speaker's apprehension and desire will ever change the speaker's ironic distance into a full-fledged detachment.

Perhaps it is whimsical to suggest that these final lines bring the poem full circle to the "classical" habit of the first line. The speaker in "Arras" ends near her beginning, with a version of the "classical" attitude (habit?) that Hulme defines in "Romanticism and Classicism" as an attitude that requires its holders to be "faithful to the conception of a limit" (63) in human beings because they are always "mixed up with earth" (62).[17] Standing on a ground, the speaker has a vision of something transcendent in the bird above her. She does not occupy the transcendent position herself. The final image brings to mind the attitude that Hulme opposes to the "classical"—the "romantic," which identifies humanity with infinity and which often does so through images of flight (62). To end with an image of flight intimates that the poem is itself balanced between two oppositional concepts, with the speaker caught somewhere in the middle. Yet as long as there is some dynamic tension between the figure on (or near) the arras and the bird in the air, one suspects that the speaker is not badly off. After all, the movement between two poles, not the elimination of the difference between them, is the poem's guiding theme, whether those poles are subject and object or emotion and reason. On (or near) the arras, the speaker is not master of all she experiences but the observer and recorder of two separate and equally rich streams of responses to it. In this position, she can await with fear and hope the arrival of the next bird without shortchanging either its promise or its unknown quality. That she continues to experience phenomena both "reasonably" and "emotionally" may be understood as a modernist protest of a certain Canadian character against the real limitation that would be posed by resolving the tension between her two kinds of responses to the scene. Like Smith's and Frye's critical model, Page's aesthetic one in "Arras" inveighs not against transcendence itself but against the false flight that does not represent a legitimate moving beyond emotion so much as a denial of its many facets, and the ways that these emphasize that meaning is an ever-unfolding thing.

NOTES

I am very grateful to Dean Irvine for his insightful comments on an earlier draft of this essay.

[1] For one explanation of how modernist scholars such as Richards and William Empson removed affective responses to poetry from the poetic analysis, see Armstrong.

[2] For the sake of convenience, this binary pairing will hereafter be referred to as reason/emotion.

[3] In "Imagism and Vorticism," from which this quotation is taken, Natan Zach cites the "interview" of Ezra Pound by Frank Stewart Flint, which appeared in *Poetry*'s March 1913 issue. The interview presented three tenets of imagism, of which this is the first.

[4] The rejection of transcendent reason goes hand in hand with the rejection of the mind-body hierarchy that underpins it. Not surprisingly, modernist queries about the place of the emotions are echoed in today's neurological studies of the brain. Contemporary researchers have increasingly questioned the rigid separation of body-mind functions. Exploring how the brain's neural and cognitive processes take in, save, and interpret information, Antonio Damasio posits that an emotion is a whole series of changes signalled from and to the brain in response to a "mental image" that could come from perception, imagination, or memory (*Descartes' Error* 136). He finds that setting "emotional" and "rational" responses to the images into a chronological sequence is often impossible. Instead of continuing to treat reason as the privileged term in relation to which the emotions must be defined, Damasio advances "feeling" as a vital third term to describe the symbiosis of bodily and mental experience, arguing that "feeling is the perception of a certain state of the body along with the perception of a certain mode of thinking and of thoughts with certain themes" (*Looking for Spinoza* 86). How current mind mapping like Damasio's bears out modernist speculation is an area of inquiry still in its early stages and beyond the limits of this essay; still, one need only note the parallels between Damasio's concept of "feeling" and Raymond Williams's "structure of feeling" (to be discussed later in this essay) to recognize the potential in comparing modernist to contemporary neuroscientific discourse.

[5] Sutherland means this more positively than it sounds. Still, he views the emotional content in some of Page's poems as a sign of their weakness.

[6] Smith was doubtless inspired to discuss Eliot and Valéry together because of Eliot's well-known introduction to the translation of the other poet's *Art of Poetry*.

[7] Here and elsewhere, Smith is influenced by Wordsworth's argument that poets work with "emotion recollected in tranquillity," another idea of the emotions that he discusses in "The Poetic Process."

[8] See also Smith, "F.R. Scott" 118–19 (1967), in which he implies that the conscious mind has full access to and control over "sensuous" perception and experience.

[9] The clippings date from Isaac Asimov's "That Odd Chemical Complex, The Human Brain" in 1966, and they reflect an eclectic range of topics from the effects of advertising on the brain (Joyce Nelson, "As the brain tunes out, the TV admen tune in," *Globe and Mail* 16 April 1983: 10) to Oliver Sacks's "The Man Who Mistook His Wife for a Hat," *London Review of Books* 19 May–2 June 1983: 3+. I describe the contents of the files on "Brains-Mind" located in the P.K. Page Fonds, MG30 D311, National Archives of Canada (vol. 47, files 1 and 2, and vol. 52, file 2) with the permission of P.K. Page.

[10] For example, according to Marcel Kinsbourne in "Sad Hemisphere, Happy Hemisphere" (also in Page's collection), "the left side ... controls language and other sequential skills, and the right side, spatial relations" (92).

[11] This fact may be explained by Page's ten-year sojourn outside Canada during the 1950s and early 1960s, a time from which little in the way of clippings or other space-consuming detritus appears to have survived in her miscellaneous papers.

[12] I will use the pronoun "she" to refer to the speaker of this poem, with the caveat that this "she" is not P.K. Page.

[13] See Rooke and Young.

[14] One "cracks" a hand when one defeats another hand that may have seemed too big to defeat (see "Crack").

[15] According to Cook's *Against Coercion: Games Poets Play*, this verse paragraph would be an example of Oedipal riddling, or a riddle the answer to which is obscure or even undiscoverable—unless God supplies it (206). I am indebted to Cook for drawing my attention to the riddle and particularly to the griph as literary devices through her conference paper "How Rhetoric Helps Poetics: The Griph From Aristotle to Ashbery."

[16] Cf. Sass 43–75 for his discussion of the patient Renee.

[17] This is not the first time that an affinity has been noted between Page's work and the criticism of T.E. Hulme. See Durrant 176.

WORKS CITED

Armstrong, Isobel. "Textual Harassment: The Ideology of Close Reading, or How Close is Close?" *Textual Practice* 9.3 (1995): 401–20.

Bell, Michael. "The Metaphysics of Modernism." *The Cambridge Companion to Modernism*. Ed. Michael Levenson. New York and Cambridge: Cambridge UP, 1999. 9–33.

"Care." *Oxford English Dictionary*. Vol. 2. 1933. Oxford: Clarendon, 1961. 115–16.

Cook, Eleanor. *Against Coercion: Games Poets Play*. Stanford: Stanford UP, 1998.

———. "How Rhetoric Helps Poetics: The Griph from Aristotle to Ashbery." "Inventio: Rereading the Rhetorical Tradition." Waterloo, ON, University of Waterloo, 8–9 August 2003.

Cooper, J.C. "Cards." *Illustrated Encyclopedia of Traditional Symbols*. London: Thames and Hudson, 1978. 29–30.

———. "Peacock." *Illustrated Encyclopedia of Traditional Symbols*. London: Thames and Hudson, 1978. 127–28.

"Crack." *Get Into Poker: Poker Terms*. 2003–04. 5 March 2004. <http://www.getinto-poker.com/poker_terms.php>.

Damasio, Antonio. *Descartes' Error: Emotion, Reason, and the Human Brain*. New York: G.P. Putnam, 1994.

———. *Looking for Spinoza: Joy, Sorrow, and the Feeling Brain*. New York: Harcourt, 2003.

Djwa, Sandra. "P.K. Page: A Biographical Interview." *Malahat Review* 117 (winter 1996): 33–54.

Dudek, Louis. "F.R. Scott and the Modern Poets." *Northern Review* 4.2 (1950–51): 4–16.

Durrant, Geoffrey. "P.K. Page's 'Portrait of Marina.'" *Inside the Poem: Essays and Poems in Honour of Donald Stephens*. Ed. W.H. New. Toronto: Oxford UP, 1992. 174–77.

Eliot, T.S. "Tradition and the Individual Talent." *Selected Essays*. 3rd ed. Rpt. London: Faber and Faber, 1972. 13–23.

Elster, Jon. *Alchemies of the Mind: Rationality and the Emotions*. New York and Cambridge: Cambridge UP, 1999.

Freud, Sigmund. *The Interpretation of Dreams*. 8th rev. ed. 1930. Trans. James Strachey. New York: Basic Books, 1958.

Frye, Northrop. *Anatomy of Criticism*. Princeton: Princeton UP, 1956.

———. "The Instruments of Mental Production." *The Stubborn Structure: Essays on Criticism and Society*. Ithaca: Cornell UP, 1970. 3–22.

———. "Letters in Canada: Poetry." *Collected Works of Northrop Frye, Vol. 12: Northrop Frye on Canada*. Ed. Jean O'Grady and David Staines. Toronto: UTP, 2003. 91–230.

———. *T.S. Eliot*. Rpt. Edinburgh and London: Oliver and Boyd, 1965.

Hough, Graham. *Image and Experience: Studies in a Literary Revolution*. Lincoln: U of Nebraska P, 1960.

Hulme, T.E. "Romanticism and Classicism." *The Collected Writings of T.E. Hulme*. Ed. Karen Csengeri. Oxford: Clarendon, 1994. 59–74.

Kinsbourne, Marcel. "Sad Hemisphere, Happy Hemisphere." *Psychology Today* 15.5 (May 1981): 92.

Mandel, Eli. "The Function of Criticism at the Present Time." *Criticism: The Silent-Speaking Words. Eight Talks for CBC Radio.* Toronto: Canadian Broadcasting Corporation, 1966. 65–73.

Page, P.K. "Arras." *The Metal and the Flower.* Toronto: McClelland and Stewart, 1954. 63–4.

"Reason." *The Oxford Companion to Philosophy.* Ed. Ted Honderich. Oxford: Oxford UP, 1995. 748.

Rooke, Constance. "Approaching P.K. Page's 'Arras.'" *Fear of the Open Heart.* Toronto: Coach House, 1989. 136–44.

Rosenwein, Barbara H. "Worrying about Emotions in History." *American Historical Review* 107.3 (2002). <www.historycooperative.org/journals/ahr/107.3/ah0302000821.html>. 1–45.

Sass, Louis A. *Madness and Modernism: Insanity in the Light of Modern Art, Literature, and Thought.* New York: Basic Books, 1992.

Smith, A.J.M. "F.R. Scott and Some of His Poems." *Towards a View of Canadian Letters: Selected Critical Essays 1928–1971.* Vancouver: UBC P, 1973. 115–25.

———. "Hamlet in Modern Dress." *McGill Fortnightly Review* 2.1 (1926): 2–4.

———. "The Poetic Process: On the Making of Poems." *Towards a View of Canadian Letters: Selected Critical Essays 1928–1971.* Vancouver: UBC P, 1973. 217–30.

———. "The Poetry of P.K. Page." *Towards a View of Canadian Letters: Selected Critical Essays 1928–1971.* Vancouver: UBC P, 1972. 146–56.

———. "The Refining Fire: The Meaning and Use of Poetry." *A.J.M. Smith: On Poetry and Poets.* Toronto: McClelland and Stewart, 1977. 59–70.

———. "A Self-Review." *Towards a View of Canadian Letters: Selected Critical Essays 1928–1971.* Vancouver: UBC P, 1973. 211–17.

Solomon, Robert C. "The Philosophy of Emotions." *Handbook of Emotions.* 2nd ed. Ed. Michael Lewis and Jeannette M. Haviland-Jones. New York and London: Guilford, 2000. 3–16.

Sutherland, John. "P.K. Page and *Preview.*" *John Sutherland: Essays, Controversies and Poems.* Ed. Miriam Waddington. Toronto: McClelland and Stewart, 1972. 96–98.

———. "The Poetry of P.K. Page." *John Sutherland: Essays, Controversies and Poems.* Ed. Miriam Waddington. Toronto: McClelland and Stewart, 1972. 101–12.

Trehearne, Brian. *The Montreal Forties: Modernist Poetry in Transition.* Toronto and Buffalo: UTP, 1999.

Williams, Raymond. *Marxism and Literature.* Oxford: Oxford UP, 1977.

Young, Patricia. "A Reading of P.K. Page's 'Arras.'" *P.K. Page: Essays on Her Works.* Ed. Linda Rogers and Barbara Colebrook Peace. Toronto: Guernica, 2001. 22–32.

Zach, Natan. "Imagism and Vorticism." *Modernism: 1890–1930.* Ed. Malcolm Bradbury and James McFarlane. Harmondsworth: Penguin, 1976. 228–43.

Index

REAPPRAISALS: CANADIAN WRITERS

Reappraisals: Canadian Writers was begun in 1973 in response to a need for single volumes of essays on Canadian authors who had not received the critical attention they deserved or who warranted extensive and intensive reconsideration. It is the longest running series dedicated to the study of Canadian literary subjects. The annual symposium hosted by the Department of English at the University of Ottawa began in 1972 and the following year University of Ottawa Press published the first title in the series, *The Grove Symposium*. Since then our editorial policy has remained straightforward: each year to make permanently available in a single volume the best of the criticsim and evaluation presented at our symposia on Canadian literature, thereby creating a body of work on and a critical base for the study of Canadian writers and literary subjects.

Gerald Lynch
General Editor

Titles in the series:

THE GROVE SYMPOSIUM, edited and with an introduction by John Nause

THE A.M. KLEIN SYMPOSIUM, edited and with an introduction by Seymour Mayne

THE LAMPMAN SYMPOSIUM, edited and with an introduction by Lorraine McMullen

THE E.J. PRATT SYMPOSIUM, edited and with an introduction by Glenn Clever

THE ISABELLA VALANCY CRAWFORD SYMPOSIUM, edited and with an introduction by Frank M. Tierney

THE DUNCAN CAMPBELL SCOTT SYMPOSIUM, edited and with an introduction by K.P. Stich

THE CALLAGHAN SYMPOSIUM, edited and with an introduction by David Staines

THE ETHEL WILSON SYMPOSIUM, edited and with an introduction by Lorraine McMullen

TRANSLATION IN CANADIAN LITERATURE, edited and with an introduction by Camille R. La Bossière

THE SIR CHARLES G.D. ROBERTS SYMPOSIUM, edited and with an introduction by Glenn Clever

THE THOMAS CHANDLER HALIBURTON SYMPOSIUM, edited and with an introduction by Frank M. Tierney

STEPHEN LEACOCK: A REAPPRAISAL, edited and with an introduction by David Staines

FUTURE INDICATIVE: LITERARY THEORY AND CANADIAN LITERATURE, edited and with an introduction by John Moss

REFLECTIONS: AUTOBIOGRAPHY AND CANADIAN LITERATURE, edited and with an introduction by K.P. Stich

RE(DIS)COVERING OUR FOREMOTHERS: NINETEENTH-CENTURY CANADIAN WOMEN WRITERS, edited and with an introduction by Lorraine McMullen

BLISS CARMAN: A REAPPRAISAL, edited and with an introduction by Gerald Lynch

FROM THE HEART OF THE HEARTLAND: THE FICTION OF SINCLAIR ROSS, edited by John Moss

CONTEXT NORTH AMERICA: CANADIAN/U.S. LITERARY RELATIONS, edited by Camille R. La Bossière

HUGH MACLENNAN, edited by Frank M. Tierney

ECHOING SILENCE: ESSAYS ON ARCTIC NARRATIVE, edited and with a preface by John Moss

BOLDER FLIGHTS: ESSAYS ON THE CANADIAN LONG POEM, edited and with a preface by Frank M. Tierney and Angela Robbeson

DOMINANT IMPRESSIONS: ESSAYS ON THE CANADIAN SHORT STORY, edited by Gerald Lynch and Angela Robbeson

MARGARET LAURENCE: CRITICAL REFLECTIONS, edited and with an introduction by David Staines

ROBERTSON DAVIES: A MINGLING OF CONTRARIETIES, edited by Camille R. La Bossière and Linda M. Morra

WINDOWS AND WORDS: A LOOK AT CANADIAN CHILDREN'S LITERATURE IN ENGLISH, edited by Aïda Hudson and Susan-Ann Cooper

WORLDS OF WONDER: READINGS IN CANADIAN SCIENCE FICTION AND FANTASY LITERATURE, edited by Jean-François Leroux and Camille R. La Bossière

AT THE SPEED OF LIGHT THERE IS ONLY ILLUMINATION: A REAPPRAISAL OF MARSHALL MCLUHAN, edited by John Moss and Linda M. Morra

HOME-WORK: POSTCOLONIALISM, PEDAGOGY, AND CANADIAN LITERATURE, edited and with an introduction by Cynthia Sugars

THE CANADIAN MODERNISTS MEET, edited and with an introduction by Dean Irvine